From the original painting by J. Neagle.

ONGPATONGA.
[BIG ELK.]
CHIEF OF THE OMAWHAWS.

See page 292.

Drawn for Morton's Crania Americana by M.S. Weaver.

Lith. of T. Sinclair, N⁰ 79 S. Third St. Philᵃ

CRANIA AMERICANA;

OR,

A COMPARATIVE VIEW

OF THE

SKULLS OF VARIOUS ABORIGINAL NATIONS

OF

NORTH AND SOUTH AMERICA:

TO WHICH IS PREFIXED

AN ESSAY ON THE VARIETIES OF THE HUMAN SPECIES.

Illustrated by Seventy-eight Plates and a Colored Map.

BY

SAMUEL GEORGE MORTON, M. D.

PROFESSOR OF ANATOMY IN THE MEDICAL DEPARTMENT OF PENNSYLVANIA COLLEGE AT PHILADELPHIA; MEMBER OF THE ACADEMY OF NATURAL SCIENCES OF PHILADELPHIA; OF THE AMERICAN PHILOSOPHICAL SOCIETY; OF THE HISTORICAL SOCIETY OF PENNSYLVANIA; OF THE BOSTON SOCIETY OF NATURAL HISTORY, &c., &c.

PHILADELPHIA:
J. DOBSON, CHESTNUT STREET.
LONDON:
SIMPKIN, MARSHALL & CO.
1839.

COPY-RIGHT SECURED ACCORDING TO LAW.

T K. & P G. COLLINS, PRINTERS,
No. 1 Lodge Alley.

TO

JAMES COWLES PRICHARD, M. D., F. R. S., &c. &c. &c.,

OF BRISTOL, ENGLAND,

THE LEARNED AND INGENIOUS AUTHOR

OF

"Researches into the Physical History of Mankind,"

THE FOLLOWING WORK,

WHICH IS DESIGNED TO ILLUSTRATE A PORTION OF THE SAME INTERESTING INQUIRY,

IS MOST RESPECTFULLY

DEDICATED.

To JAMES MORTON, Esq.,

OF CLONMEL, IRELAND.

My Dear Uncle—

The paternal kindness with which you have ever regarded my course through life, and the solicitude you have expressed for the successful completion of this work, prompt me, with feelings of mingled pleasure and gratitude, to inscribe it to you.

That Providence may continue to brighten the evening of your useful life with health and tranquility, is the sincere prayer of

Your very affectionate Nephew,

SAMUEL GEORGE MORTON.

Philadelphia, *November* 1, 1839.

PREFACE.

The title of this work is perhaps sufficiently explanatory of its objects. The principal design has been to give accurate delineations of the crania of more than forty Indian nations, Peruvian, Brazilian and Mexican, together with a particularly extended series from North America, from the Pacific Ocean to the Atlantic, and from Florida to the region of the Polar tribes. Especial attention has also been given to the singular distortions of the skull caused by mechanical contrivances in use among various nations, Peruvians, Charibs, Natchez, and the tribes inhabiting the Oregon Territory. The author's materials in this department are ample, and have enabled him to give a full exposition of a subject which was long involved in doubt and controversy. Particular attention has been bestowed on the crania from the Mounds of this country, which have been compared with similar relics derived both from ancient and modern tribes, in order to examine, by the evidence of osteological facts, whether the American aborigines, of all epochs, have belonged to one Race, or to a plurality of Races.

I was, from the beginning, desirous to introduce into this work a brief chapter on Phrenology; but, conscious of my own inability to do justice to the subject, I applied to a professional friend to supply the deficiency. He engaged to do so, and commenced his task with great zeal; but ill health soon obliged him to abandon it, and to seek a distant and more genial climate. Under these circumstances I resolved to complete the Phrenological Table, and omit the proposed essay altogether. Early in the present year, however, and just as my work was ready for the press, George Combe, Esq., the distinguished phrenologist, arrived in this country; and I seized the occasion to express my wants to that gentleman, who, with great zeal and promptness, agreed to furnish the desired Essay, and actually placed the MS. in my hands before he left this city. It is with great pleasure that I also record Mr. Combe's liberality in providing this memoir without having seen a word of my manuscript, or even knowing what I had written; at the same time that I was under the necessity, owing to certain pre-arrangements, of limiting him to a given number of pages, in which he acquiesced with the most obliging frankness. By means of this Essay, which is accompanied by two illustrative plates, the reader will be able to apply Phrenological rules to every skull in the series here figured.

Neither care nor expense has been spared in the endeavor to give accuracy to the lithographed illustrations of this work, which have been chiefly executed by Mr. John Collins, one of the most successful cultivators of his art in this country. Many of the plates have been drawn the second and third time; and in several instances the entire edition was cancelled, in order to correct inaccuracies that had previously escaped observation.

I have given much more space to the INTRODUCTION than was at first intended, in the hope of inviting, throughout this country, a greater interest to this important and attractive study. It is impossible to treat of such a subject, without drawing largely on the researches of those distinguished men who have devoted their time and talent to inquiries of this nature; among whom it is especially necessary to mention Buffon, Blumenbach, Humboldt, Prichard, Lawrence, Virey and Bory de St. Vincent; while, among the writers of this country, I have derived much instruction from the writings of the late Dr. Barton, Professor Caldwell, Dr. J. C. Warren, Professor Gibson, Dr. B. H. Coates and Dr. M'Culloh. The "Researches" of the last named gentleman, embody more facts relating to the Aborigines of America than almost any other work. To these and other sources of information, I have made specific acknowledgments throughout the following pages. The great work on Mexican Antiquities by Lord Kingsborough I have never seen; and Le Noir's splendid work on the same subject, and Mr. Delafield's American Antiquities, did not reach this city until my last sheets were already in press.

It will be observed, by comparing the prospectus issued three years ago with this work as now published, that I have greatly extended the original design by the addition of eighteen plates and nearly two hundred minor illustrations, together with a corresponding enlargement of the text. This object has been chiefly attained through the liberal and unsolicited patronage of two individuals living at a remote distance from each other and from me, to whom I take this occasion to express my grateful acknowledgments. The first of these gentlemen is my venerable and much-honored uncle, James Morton, Esq., of Clonmel, Ireland; the other, my friend William Maclure, Esq., late of this city, and now resident in Mexico, well known as the distinguished President of the Academy of Natural Sciences of Philadelphia. I claim, however, some merit for having commenced publication when my subscription list bore but fifteen names; and I persisted for a long time on my own resources, although frequently apprehensive that an enterprise which never had gain for its object, would add pecuniary loss to numberless vexations.

I do not even now consider my task as wholly completed. On the contrary the illustrations of the Mexican nations are too few for satisfactory comparison owing to the extreme difficulty of obtaining authentic crania of those people. This deficiency, however, is likely to be soon obviated by the kindness of some friends of science in Mexico; and these materials, when received, together with some that came to hand too late for use, and many others that are expected, will enable me to complete my design by the publication of a small *Supplementary Volume;* in which it will further be my aim to extend and revise both the Anatomical and Phrenological Tables, and to give basal views of at least a part of the crania delineated. I shall also take occasion to measure the anterior and posterior chambers of the skull in the four exotic races of men, in order to institute a comparison between them respectively, and between them and the American Race. But in order to accomplish this object, a very extended series of crania is of course indispensable; and the author therefore respectfully solicits the further aid of gentlemen interested in the cause of science, in procuring the *skulls of all nations,* and forwarding them to his address in this city. Nor can I close this preface without recording my sincere thanks to George R. Gliddon, Esq., United States Consul at Cairo, in Egypt, for the singular zeal with which he has promoted my wishes in this respect; the series of crania he has already obtained for my use, of many nations, both ancient and modern, is perhaps without a rival in any existing collection; and will enable me, when it reaches this country, to pursue my comparisons on an extended scale.

PHILADELPHIA, *October,* 1, 1839.

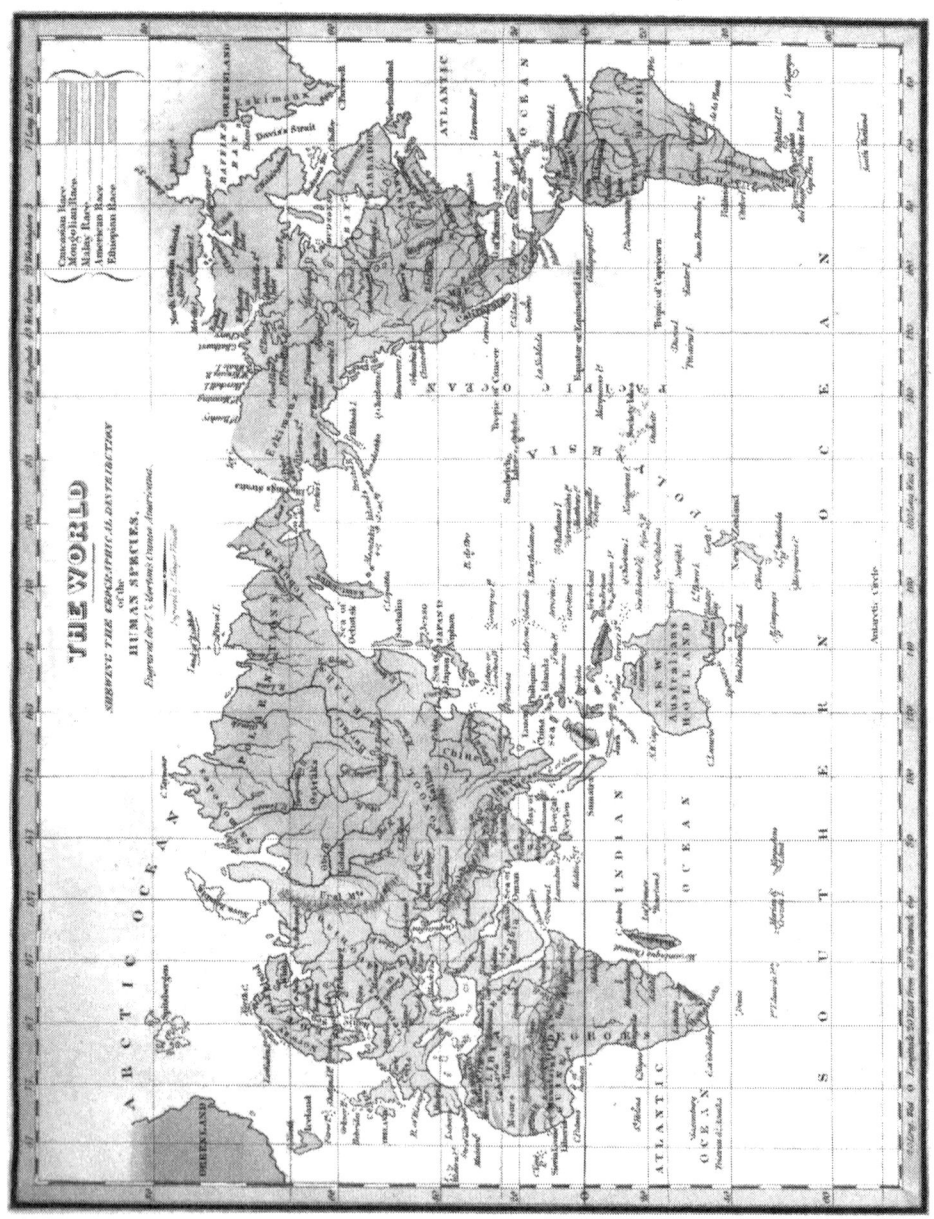

CRANIA AMERICANA.

INTRODUCTORY ESSAY

ON THE VARIETIES OF THE HUMAN SPECIES.

The geographical distribution of the human race, is one of the most interesting problems in history. The oldest records seldom allude to an uninhabited country. The extremes of heat and cold, and the intervention of seas and mountains, have presented but trifling barriers to the peopling of the earth.

The condition of man, under these infinitely varied circumstances, is less the effect of coercion than of choice. Thus the Eskimau, surrounded by an atmosphere that freezes mercury, rejoices in his snowy deserts, and has pined in unhappiness when removed to more genial climes. On the other hand, the native of the torrid regions of Africa, oppressed by a vertical sun, and often delirious with thirst, thinks no part of the world so desirable and delightful as his own. The arid province of Chaco, in Paraguay, which the Spaniards stigmatise as a desert, is crowded by forty Indian nations, who regard it as an earthly paradise. It may be further remarked, in illustration of this subject, that extensive migrations have been mostly confined to the temperate zones: it is rare, for example, to find the Polar tribes wandering to the south, or the people of the torrid zones attempting to establish themselves in a colder climate. The exceptions to this rule are chiefly to be seen in the civilised communities of modern times, in which the spirit of migratory enterprise is without a limit.

From remote ages the inhabitants of every extended locality have been marked by certain physical and moral peculiarities, common among themselves, and serving to distinguish them from all other people. The Arabians are at this time precisely what they were in the days of the patriarchs: the Hindoos have

altered in nothing since they were described by the earlies[t]
three thousand years made any difference in the skin and hai[r]
like manner the characteristic features of the Jews may b[e]
sculpture of the temples of Luxor and Karnak, in Egypt, w[here]
depicted for nearly thirty centuries.*

This identity of physical characteristics, preserved [through]
generations, and often under very dissimilar circumstances, ha[s]
speculations in respect to the origin of the human family. T[hose]
derived from the sacred writings, which, in their literal and ob[vious]
teach us that all men have originated from a single pair;†
hastily and unnecessarily inferred, that the differences now ob[served]
are owing solely to vicissitudes of climate, locality, habits
collateral circumstances.

Without attempting to pursue this intricate question
inquire, whether it is not more consistent with the known
universe to suppose, that the same Omnipotence that create[d]

---

* See Description de l'Egypte, Tome II, pl. 6, and Tome III, pl. 40.

† "That the three sons of Noah overspread and peopled the whole ear[th,]
in Scripture that, had we not to argue against those who unfortunately disb[elieve]
might here stop: let us, however, inquire how far the truth of this declar[ation]
other considerations. Enough has been said to show that there is a cur[ious]
analogy between the predictions of Noah on the future descendants of his th[ree sons]
state of those races which are generally supposed to have sprung from then[ce]
remarked, that, to render the subject more clear, we have adopted the
Professor Blumenbach; yet that Cuvier and other learned physiologists [assert]
primary varieties of the human form are more properly but *three*, viz: th[e Caucasian, Mongolian]
and Ethiopian. This number corresponds with that of Noah's sons:
Mongolian race to Japheth, and the Ethiopian to Ham, the Caucasian, the
to Shem, the third son of Noah, himself descended from Seth, the third s[on]
primary distinctions of the human varieties are but *three*, has been further m[aintained by]
Prichard, who, while he rejects the nomenclature both of Blumenbach a[nd Cuvier]
absolute divisions, arranges the leading varieties of the human skull unde[r heads differing]
from those of Cuvier only by name. That the three sons of Noah who
earth,' and on whose progeny very opposite destinies were pronounced, shou[ld be the founders of]
races, is what might reasonably be conjectured. But that the observations
those who do *not* believe the Mosaic history, should tend to confirm its [truth, and that]
what these three races do actually differ, both physically and morally, is, to [say the least, a remarkable]
coincidence. It amounts, in short, to presumptive evidence, that a myste[rious]
analogy pervades throughout, and teaches us to look beyond natural causes,
for effects apparently interwoven in the plans of Omnipotence."—MURRAY,

him at once to the physical, as well as to the moral* circumstances in which he was to dwell upon the earth? It is indeed difficult to imagine that an all-wise Providence, after having by the Deluge destroyed all mankind excepting the family of Noah, should leave these to combat, and with seemingly uncertain and inadequate means, the various external causes that tended to oppose the great object of their dispersion: and we are left to the reasonable conclusion, that each Race was adapted from the beginning to its peculiar local destination. In other words, it is assumed, that the physical characteristics which distinguish the different Races, are independent of external causes.

Such appear to have been the primitive distinctions among men: but hostile invasions, the migratory habits of some tribes, and the casual dispersion of others into remote localities, have a constant tendency to confound these peculiarities; and the proximity of two races has uniformly given rise to an intermediate variety, partaking of the characters of both, without being identical with either: these are called *mixed races*.

The grouping of mankind into Races, has occupied the ingenuity of many of the best naturalists of the past and present century; and here again we observe that diversity of opinion which is so frequent in human researches. Linnæus referred all the human family to five races, viz: the American, the European, the Asiatic, and the African, and individuals of preternatural conformation. The Count de Buffon proposed six great divisions, viz: 1, The Hyperborean or Laplander, which embraces the Polar nations.—2, The Tartar, which includes the eastern and central nations of Asia.—3, The Southern Asiatic, which embraces the South Sea Islanders.—4, The European.—5, The Ethiopian.—And 6, The American. At a subsequent period Buffon reduced the races to five, by grouping the Laplanders with the Tartars, inasmuch as he regarded the one as a degenerate branch of the other.†

More recently Professor Blumenbach, of Gottingen, to whom this department of science is under great obligations, has adopted the arrangement of Buffon; changing the names, however, of some of the divisions, and assigning, with much greater accuracy, their geographical distribution. Thus, the Laplander and Tartar of Buffon constitute the Mongolian variety of Blumenbach; the Southern Asiatic of the one corresponds to the Malay of the other; and the European and Caucasian represent the same people in both arrangements.

The system of the celebrated Cuvier is still more elementary, for it proposes

---

* GENESIS, IX, 25, 26, 27. † SONNINI'S BUFFON, XX, p. 120, &c.

three races only: the Caucasian, Mongolian, and Ethiopian; but the author hesitates to refer to either of these, the Malays, the Papuas, the Australians, and the South Sea Islanders.*

At the other extreme is Malte-Brun, the distinguished geographer, who enumerates sixteen races, of which the American nations form but one.†

Much has also been written in reference to the *unity* of the human species: the affirmative opinion is sustained by Linnæus, Blumenbach, Cuvier, and many other distinguished naturalists; yet, on the contrary, Virey has divided mankind into two species, Dumoulin into eleven, and Bory into no less than fifteen.‡ Finally, a French professor, overstepping the barriers of reason and nature, has attempted to establish several subgenera.§

Such wide differences of opinion have led some persons to reject all classification in Anthropology; but the same objections would apply with equal force to the whole range of Natural Science, which, divested of arrangement, presents an uninviting chaos. As our means of comparing the races of men become more extended, our classification will of course improve; and meanwhile we must rest content with an approximation to accuracy. It may here be remarked, that two leading features constitute the basis of most of the attempted classifications of the human species: one of these is called the *physical*, the other the *ethnographic* method. In the former, mankind are grouped in great divisions characterised by similarity of exterior conformation; while on the last mentioned plan, the arrangement is based on analogies of language. Each of these systems has its advocates to the exclusion of the other; but it is reasonable to suppose that method most natural and comprehensive which is derived from both these sources, as well as from all others which tend to establish analogies among men. In order to combine, as far as possible, all these advantages, it is proposed in this place to consider the human species as consisting of *twenty-two families*.

It is necessary, however, to premise, that these families are not assumed as identical with races, but merely as groups of nations possessing, to a greater or less extent, similarity of physical and moral character, and language. Some of these families possess, it is true, the peculiarities of the aboriginal races to which

---

* Règne Anim. I, 84.

† See BORY DE ST. VINCENT, T. I, p. 95.—I have not been able to find this classification in Malte-Brun, ed. 1832.

‡ Ibid. I, p. 83.

§ BROC, Essai sur les Races Humaines, 1836.

they belong; but others are of mixed and very diverse extraction, and of comparatively recent origin.

Believing, however, as I do, in the primitive distribution of mankind into races in the sense already explained, yet being unprepared to offer any thing new on the subject, I shall, for the present at least, adopt the arrangement of Professor Blumenbach as respects these great divisions:* for although his system is obviously imperfect, yet it is, perhaps, the most complete that has hitherto been attempted.

I. THE CAUCASIAN RACE.

The Caucasian Race is characterised by a naturally fair skin, susceptible of every tint; hair fine, long and curling, and of various colors. The skull is large and oval, and its anterior portion full and elevated. The face is small in proportion to the head, of an oval form, with well-proportioned features. The nasal bones are arched, the chin full, and the teeth vertical. This race is distinguished for the facility with which it attains the highest intellectual endowments.

1. The Caucasian Family.
2. The Germanic Family.
3. The Celtic Family.
4. The Arabian Family.
5. The Libyan Family.
6. The Nilotic Family.
7. The Indostanic Family.

II. THE MONGOLIAN RACE.

This great division of the human species is characterised by a sallow or olive colored skin, which appears to be drawn tight over the bones of the face; long, black, straight hair, and thin beard. The nose is broad, and short; the eyes are small, black, and obliquely placed, and the eye-brows arched and linear: the lips are turned, the cheek bones broad and flat, and the zygomatic arches salient. The skull is oblong-oval, somewhat flattened at the sides, with a low forehead. In their intellectual character the Mongolians are ingenious, imitative, and highly susceptible of cultivation.

* It will be observed, however, that the word *race* is substituted for *variety*, and the order in which these divisions follow each other in Blumenbach is somewhat changed. *Vide* BLUMENBACH, *De Gen. Humani Var. Nat.* p. 289.

8. The Mongol-Tartar Family.
9. The Turkish Family.
10. The Chinese Family.
11. The Indo-Chinese Family.
12. The Polar Family.

III. THE MALAY RACE.

The Malay Race is characterised by a dark complexion, varying from a tawny hue to a very dark brown. Their hair is black, coarse and lank, and their eye-lids drawn obliquely upwards at the outer angles. The mouth and lips are large, and the nose is short and broad, and apparently broken at its root. The face is flat and expanded, the upper jaw projecting, and the teeth salient. The skull is high and squared or rounded, and the forehead low and broad. This race is active and ingenious, and possesses all the habits of a migratory, predaceous and maritime people.

13. The Malay Family.
14. The Polynesian Family.

IV. THE AMERICAN RACE.

The American Race is marked by a brown complexion, long, black, lank hair, and deficient beard. The eyes are black and deep set, the brow low, the cheek-bones high, the nose large and aquiline, the mouth large, and the lips tumid and compressed. The skull is small, wide between the parietal protuberances, prominent at the vertex, and flat on the occiput. In their mental character the Americans are averse to cultivation, and slow in acquiring knowledge; restless, revengeful, and fond of war, and wholly destitute of maritime adventure.

15. The American Family.
16. The Toltecan Family.

V. THE ETHIOPIAN RACE.

Characterised by a black complexion, and black, woolly hair; the eyes are large and prominent, the nose broad and flat, the lips thick, and the mouth wide: the head is long and narrow, the forehead low, the cheek-bones prominent, the

THE CAUCASIAN FAMILY.

jaws projecting, and the chin small. In disposition the negro is joyous, flexible, and indolent; while the many nations which compose this race present a singular diversity of intellectual character, of which the far extreme is the lowest grade of humanity.

17. The Negro Family.
18. The Caffrarian Family.
19. The Hottentot Family.
20. The Oceanic-Negro Family.
21. The Australian Family.
22. The Alforian Family.

1. THE CAUCASIAN FAMILY.

This family, the type of the Caucasian Race, derives its name from the mountainous region of Caucasus, between the Black Sea and the Caspian, a spot to which history and tradition refer the primeval family of man. The spontaneous fertility of this tract has rendered it the hive of many nations, which extending their migrations in every direction, have peopled the finest portions of the earth, and given birth to its fairest inhabitants. On the present occasion we propose to notice the Caucasian family as consisting of three branches, the Caucasian proper, the Persian, and the Pelasgic.

1. The *Caucasians proper* are confined to the valleys and mountains of Caucasus. They are extremely numerous, and embrace many primitive tribes which differ in language, yet possess, in common, certain prominent physical characters. Independent of these aboriginal nations, it is said that five great immigrations of foreigners form as many epochs in the history of this country. These nations are the Lesghi, the Ghasazes, the Mongols, the Arabs, and the Tartars. The languages spoken are scarcely inferior in number to the remnants of nations. "There are villages perfectly insulated, each of which is a complete nation, whose language is not in the least comprehended by the people in the next village to them, and is spoken nowhere else."* Hence the observation of Major Rennel, that this remarkable tract, which forms an isthmus between the nations of the north and south, seems to have retained a specimen of each passing tribe from the date of the earliest migration.†

A few only of the most prominent of these nations will be noticed on the present occasion.

* Tooke's Russia, II, p. 107. † Freygan, Caucasus, p. 51.

VARIETIES OF THE HUMAN SPECIES.

The *Circassians** have long been celebrated for superior personal endowments. The men are distinguished by the elegance of their shape: their stature seldom exceeds the middle size, yet they are athletic and muscular without being corpulent. The women have attracted the attention and commanded the admiration of all travellers; nor can there be a question that in exquisite beauty of form and gracefulness of manner, they surpass all other people. They are distinguished by a fair skin, arched and narrow eyebrows, very long eyelashes, and black eyes and hair. Their profile approaches nearest the Grecian model, and falls little short of the beau-ideal of classic sculpture.

Of all the Circassians the tribe called *Nottahaizi* presents the most general diffusion of personal beauty. Mr. Spencer asserts, in his late travels among them, that every individual he saw was decidedly handsome.†

The Circassians are shepherds and agriculturists; and although indolent in field labor, they are extremely active and vigilant in war, which is their favorite pastime. They pass much of their time in hunting, and in making predatory excursions among the adjacent tribes. Like the Arabs, they affect great hospitality, but they are at the same time selfish and deceitful. Contrary to the common impression, they seldom sell their own women to the Turks; for this traffic is mainly supported by unfortunate captives from the different provinces of Georgia.‡

The *Caratski* tribe have, by a singular misnomer, been called Black Circassians; whereas their complexions, says Father Lamberti, are very fair; and he adds, "that this name was probably given them only because the atmosphere of the country is always gloomy and overcast with clouds."§

The *Georgians* are not less beautiful than the Circassians, possessing the same style of features, but a darker complexion.‖ They are extremely vain of their personal charms, and endeavor to enhance them by dying their hair, painting their faces, and making their eyebrows join in a continuous line.¶ The Georgians are less warlike than the Circassians, but much more literary and refined; they are fond of poetry, and have a national love of music.

---

* They call themselves Attighé, or Adigé. They are the Zychi of the Greeks and Latins, and the Tcherkess of the Russians.

† *Trav.* in Circassia, II, p. 245.

‡ KLAPROTH, Caucasus, p. 321.

§ Ibid., p. 286.

‖ Prof. BLUMENBACH has figured the skull of a Georgian female, to illustrate the perfect proportions of the Caucasian head.—*Decad. Cran.*, Tab. XXI.

¶ FREYGAN, Trav. in Caucasus, p. 136.

The *Abassians*, who call themselves *Absné*, "are distinguished from all the neighboring nations by their narrow faces, by the figure of their heads, which are compressed on both sides, by the shortness of the lower part of the face, by their prominent noses, and dark brown hair." They appear to be the aboriginal inhabitants of the northwest part of Caucasus, but have been reduced to a mere tribe by constant feuds with the Circassians. Their language has no resemblance to any known Asiatic or European tongue.*

The *Ossitinians*, or *Ireen*, are a mere horde of rapacious banditti, speaking a language allied to the Persian.

The *Inguches* and *Kists* are also lawless communities, who live by hunting and plunder, and rob for honor as well as from necessity. They worship one God, without either saints or idols. Similar to these are those mountaineers of Daghestan, called Tawlinzi and Lesghi: living in inaccessible retreats, they descend into the valleys for mutual depredation, and to pillage travellers.† Their language is peculiar to themselves, excepting a few words which resemble the Samoyede tongue.‡

It is difficult to form a just estimate of many of these tribes, who are, on the one hand, degraded by the Mahomedan faith, and on the other oppressed by the grasping policy of the Russians. Of their intelligence and bravery there can be no question; and their moral perceptions, under the influence of an equitable government, would no doubt assume a much more favorable aspect.

2. The *Persians*, who constitute the eastern branch of the Caucasian family, have been celebrated from remote antiquity for their high civilisation, their national pride and their successful valor. But since the seventh century of our era, this country has been successively invaded and conquered by the Saracens, Mongols and Tartars, whose amalgamation with the native inhabitants has produced, especially in the large towns, a very mixed population. It is chiefly among the mountain tribes that the indigenous Persians are at present found. They are a fine, athletic people, with good yet strong features, which travellers compare to those of the Highlanders of Scotland. Their complexion is naturally sallow, and becomes brown from constant exposure; and in the province of Mazunderan, Mr. Frazer saw some individuals who were almost black.§ Similar in exterior to the former are the many tribes of the mountains of Talesh, whose

---

* KLAPROTH, p. 247.   † FREYGAN, Caucasus, p. 58.
‡ ELLIS, Caucasian Nations, p. 43.   § Trav. in Persia, p. 50.

rapaciousness and cruelty are a proverb in Persia. The daughters of these mountaineers, especially in the province of Ghelan, are extremely beautiful.

In the towns, from causes already mentioned, the inhabitants present a very different aspect; for the long admixture of Georgian and Circassian blood has done much to improve the Tartar physiognomy of the rural tribes, and the somewhat heavy figures and sallow color of the original Persians.

"At the present time," says Chardin, "there is scarcely a man of rank in Persia whose mother is not either a Georgian or Circassian. The King himself is mostly derived, on the maternal side, from this exotic source; and as it is a long time since this mixture commenced, the women of Persia have also become much more beautiful, though they do not equal those of Georgia. As for the men, they are generally tall and erect, with a graceful manner and agreeable deportment."*

The modern Persians are polite and polished in their manners, and extravagantly addicted to flattery. They are obsequious to their superiors, but affect to despise all foreigners. They are proverbial adepts in deception, and like the Arabs, make a merit of their frauds when these have been practised with adroitness. They are lively and imaginative, fond of music and poetry, and idolise the names of Hafez and Saadi. The Persian language is a dialect of that of Fars, and is used in poetry and general literature, but the Turkish is the court language. The present rulers of Persia (who are Tartars of the Kujur race) have, of course, established Mahomedanism as the state religion; but the Ghebres and Parsees still worship fire as the emblem of the Supreme Being. The great body of this sect, however, was driven from Persia by the Arabs under the Chalif Omar in the seventh century. They established themselves in India, and especially in the province of Surat, where they are still numerous, and constitute an industrious population.

The *Iliyats*, or wandering tribes of Persia, are chiefly of exotic extraction, and form a distinct body of people. Morier compares them to foreign shoots, grafted on the original Persian stock. They date from the conquest by the Saracens, A. D. 651, and their numbers were augmented during the subsequent invasions of Genghiz and Tamerlane. They are of Mongol-Tartar extraction, but have mingled for centuries with the Persians, to whom they have imparted their roving propensities. They are by turns cultivators, shepherds, soldiers, and freebooters.†

---

* CHARDIN, Voy. II, p. 34. † MORIER, in Jour. Roy. Geog. Soc., VII, p. 230.

The inhabitants of AFGHANISTAN, on the skirts of Persia, are also of the Caucasian family. They are spare in person, strong and bony. Their noses are prominent and aquiline, their cheek bones high, their faces long. Their manner is singularly hospitable to strangers, at the same time that their lives are mostly spent in predatory violence on the neighboring provinces, or passing caravans. Their customs resemble those of the Arabs, from whom they claim descent; for, although they despise a Jew, they call themselves *Ben i Israel*—the children of Israel, whence some writers suppose them to be Jews converted to Mahomedanism.*

Koordistan, to the east of the Tigris, and proximate to Persia, is inhabited by two sorts of people, the clansmen, or military Koords, and the peasants, or cultivators, the latter being literally the bondsmen of the former. "The peasant," says Mr. Rich, "is in a moment to be distinguished, both in countenance and speech, from the true tribesman; nor would it be possible for him to pass himself for his countryman of nobler race. The difference in physiognomy between the clansman and peasant Koord is perfectly distinguishable. The latter has a much softer, and more regular countenance; the features are sometimes quite Grecian. The tribesman is more what is called a hard-featured man, with a thick, prominent forehead, abrupt lines, and eyes sunk in his head, which are usually fixed in a kind of stare. Light gray, and even blue, is a common color for the eye."† They treat their women more kindly than either the Turks or Persians, and have a better idea of domestic comfort; yet they are haughty and cruel, fond of war and pillage, and fight among themselves when they have no common enemy.‡

3. The *Pelasgic Branch* derives its name from the Pelasgi, who are first mentioned in history as the inhabitants of Thessaly. Enterprising and migratory in their habits, they spread over all Greece, and passing thence into northern Italy, gave birth to the Etruscans. For political reasons they assumed the name of Hellenes, and were the lineal progenitors of the Greeks or Acheans. It has been observed by a late writer, that the Greeks had no sooner obtained the elements of literature and the arts from the Phœnicians, than they advanced rapidly to the highest state of civilisation, until they may be said to have become, in their descendants, the masters of the world. We are taught even from our infancy to study their letters and their arts, which are justly regarded as models of perfection, seldom equalled and still more rarely surpassed.

* BARNES, Trav. in Bokhara, II, p. 32. WOLFF, Miss. Res. p. 157.
† Residence in Koordistan, p. 89, 320.
‡ Ibid. p. 150.

The unmixed Greeks are above the middle stature, of fine proportions and graceful mien. The forehead is high, expanded, and but little arched, so that it forms with the straight and pointed nose, a nearly rectilinear outline. This conformation sometimes imparts an appearance of disproportion to the upper part of the face, which, however, is in a great measure counteracted by the largeness of the eye. The Greek face is a fine oval, and small in comparison to the voluminous head. The statues of the Olympian Jupiter, and the Apollo Belvidere, convey an exact idea of the perfect Grecian countenance.*

"The women of Cyprus are handsomer than those of any other Grecian island. They have a taller and more stately figure; and the features, particularly those of the women of Nicosia, are regular and dignified, exhibiting that elevated cast of countenance so universally admired in the works of Grecian artists. At present this kind of beauty seems peculiar to the women of Cyprus: the sort of expression exhibited by one set of features, may be traced with different gradations in them all. Hence were possibly derived those celebrated models of female beauty, conspicuous in the statues, vases, medals and gems of Greece."†

Perhaps of all the population of modern Greece, that of Roumelia in moral traits most resembles the ancient. They are hardy, warlike, and brave, and have never been completely subjected by the Turks. The inhabitants of the Morea—called Moreotes, on the contrary, have been long the acknowledged vassals of the Porte. The coasts and maritime towns are inhabited by a motley people of various races, who are called by the general name of Greeks, but who have little claim to Grecian lineage or character.

The degeneration of the modern Greeks, however, is rather moral than physical; for their athletic limbs, their broad shoulders and their strong lineaments, are not inferior to those of their ancestors.‡

The Trojans, like the Etruscans, were cognate with the Greeks; and Æneas, flying from the flames of Troy, founded in Italy the kingdom of Alba. The striking difference, however, between the Roman and Greek physiognomy, is familiar to all observers, but is readily accounted for by the free intercourse of the primitive Romans with the surrounding nations, of which the Rape of the

---

* BORY DE ST. VINCENT, L'Homme, I, p. 40.   † CLARKE, Trav. II, p. 338.

‡ "It appears from numerous instances, especially from the case of the Greeks, that moral causes, infinitely more than physical circumstances, influence national character, since arts, sciences and letters, now flourish on the cold and foggy shores of the Baltic sea and the German ocean, while, during a period of several centuries, not a single poet or philosopher has arisen in the country of Homer and Plato."—BIGLAND, *Effects of Phys. and Moral Causes on the Charac. of Nations*, p. 144.

Sabines is one of many examples. The Roman head differs from the Greek in having the forehead lower and more arched, and the nose strongly aquiline, together with a marked depression of the nasal bones between the eyes.

"Look," says Dr. Wiseman, "at the sarcophagi on which the busts are carved in relief, or raised from their reclining statues on the lid, or even examine the series of imperial busts in the capitol, and you cannot fail to discover a striking type, essentially the same, from the wreathed image of Scipio's tomb, to Trajan or Vespasian, consisting in a large and flat head, a low and wide forehead, a face, in childhood, heavy and round—later, broad and square, a short and thick neck, and a stout and broad figure. Nor need we go far to find their descendants; they are to be found every day in the streets, principally among the burgesses, or middle class, the most invariable portion of every population."*

During the period of Roman greatness, the colonies of Greece and Rome extended themselves widely into Spain, where they blended with the primitive Celtiberians or Basques, and the Phenicians. The later invasions of the Vandals and the Saracens, have added their diversities to the physical and moral character of the Spaniard, which, with some redeeming qualities, has the selfishness of the Arab, the pride and cruelty of the Roman and the superstition of the Greek.

2. THE GERMANIC FAMILY.

This great family has occupied, both in ancient and modern time, a large proportion of Europe, which it gradually overspread from east to west, thus encroaching on the Celts, with whom they are often inseparably blended.

The Germans are familiar to us by their middling stature, their robust form inclining to obesity, their fair, florid complexion, and their light hair. The head is large and spheroidal, the forehead broad and arched, the face round, the eyes blue and the neck rather short.

The moral character of the Germans is marked by decided personal courage, great endurance of fatigue, firmness and perseverance, and a strong attachment to their families and their native land. Intellectually they are conspicuous for industry and success in the acquisition of knowledge: with a singular blending of taciturnity and enthusiasm, they rival all modern nations in music, poetry and the drama; nor are they less conspicuous for their critical attainments in language, and the exact sciences.

---

* WISEMAN, Lectures on the Connection between Science and Revealed Religion, p. 152. *Am. ed.*

M. Bory de St. Vincent has so happily illustrated this division of the Caucasian race, that I shall chiefly avail myself of his observations in respect to it. He separates the Germanic family into two divisions, the *Teutonic* and *Sclavonic*.

1. "The *Teutonic variety* is traced to the Hyrcinian forests, the Tyrolese Alps, and the sources of the Sâle. Following the Danube, which rises in their country, they advanced eastwardly only into Austria, nor passed the southern Alps; but they spread towards the north, disdaining the rest of the Caucasian race, and reached the sea coast, at first between the Elbe and the Rhine. These were the people who, under the name of Cimbri, occupied the peninsula of Jutland and the neighbouring islands; passing thence into Scandinavia, they became the *Sunones*, who have since been called Goths.* Coasting the Baltic to the estuary of the Niemen, they were the primitive stock of the Borussi, the ancestors of those Prussians who are now, as it were, lost in the midst of the Sclavonic tribes. Under the names of Saxons, Danes and Normans, they ravaged the Celtic coasts, established themselves at the mouth of the Seine, and passing into the British islands, drove the primitive Celts into the western parts of the country. At a still later period the Teutonic tribes, under the name of Norwegians, peopled the remote island of Iceland."

The Teutonic language, adds this author, has become the root of the English, Dutch, Danish and Swedish tongues.

To the preceding statement it may merely be added, that the Goths having issued from Scandinavia in vast numbers, passed to the south, and harassed the Roman provinces. In the second century they settled on the shores of the Palus Mæotis, and thence possessed themselves of Dacia. They were called Ostrogoths and Visigoths, the Eastern and Western Goths. Their subsequent military enterprises, and especially the conquest and sack of Rome in the fifth century, are familiar to all readers of history. The Vandals were also from the Gothic hive; they emigrated with King Edric, settled for a time on the borders of the Rhine,

---

* The late Mr. Pinkerton has written an elaborate work to prove that the Scythians, Getæ and Goths were one people, who originated in Persia, and entered Europe by a northwestern route; and that the German nations, and even the Pelasgi of Greece, were all lineal descendants of this Asiatic family. I leave these mooted points to the learned in national genealogy, and content myself with the more reasonable exposition of the ingenious French writer, which, in the main, coincides with the researches of Dr. Prichard. The latter author has established the fact that the Getæ of the ancients were not Goths, but Thracians; and that the domestic history of the Goths themselves establishes their northern origin and German descent. *See* PRICHARD, II, p. 162.—PINKERTON, *Diss. on the Goths*, p. 14, 31, &c.

and subsequently ravaged a great part of Europe, and established a monarchy in Spain. They crossed also into Africa, and took and occupied several of the Roman provinces on that continent.

Austria and Hungary, (the ancient Pannonia,) and the adjoining states, are at this time peopled by the lineal descendants of the Goths, whose harsh features contrast strongly with those of the more polished nations of southern Europe.

2. *The Sclavonic Variety.* "This second Germanic variety is composed of men issuing probably from Mount Krapack, whence, turning to the south they peopled Hungary, crossed the Danube, and pressed their migrations to the Adriatic sea. In the north they followed the marshy track of the Vistula and Niemen. Descending the Dneister towards the Black sea, they mingled with bands of Tartars from the Scythian provinces, until becoming identified with them, a mixed race was formed; the latter, assuming the name of Scythians, are celebrated in history for their incursions on Persia on the one hand, and on the Roman empire on the other."*

Under this denomination are also embraced the Russians, Poles, Lithuanians and part of the Bohemians and Hungarians. They are for the most part characterised by darker hair and complexion than the Teutonic tribes. The Tartars who conquered Russia in the twelfth century under the renowned Zenghis Khan, retained their dominion for more than two hundred years, and have left evident traces of their sojourn both in the physical character and social institutions of the Russians.† The people of this division of the Germanic family are brave and enterprising, but generally rude and uncultivated; and the Russians, perhaps the most polished branch, emerged from the deepest barbarism so lately as the reign of Peter the Great.

3. THE CELTIC FAMILY.

This branch of the great Caucasian race, occupied at one period nearly all western Europe. They extended from the Pyrenees to the Rhine, and from the base of the Alps to the western islands of Britain. They bore the general name of Celtæ, and their continental territory was the "Gallia Celtica" of the Romans.

The long continued intercourse of these people with other and dissimilar nations, has tended to obliterate their primitive characteristics, excepting in certain parts of the extreme west of Europe. Thus they are yet numerous in

---

* L'Homme, I, p. 132-136.   † KLAPROTH, Trav. in Caucasus, p. 90.

Brittany, Scotland and Ireland, where in certain districts they retain their primitive name of Gaël.

The features of these people are strongly marked. They are tall, and athletic, and little prone to obesity, while their physical strength corresponds to their muscular proportions. They have the head rather elongated, and the forehead narrow and but slightly arched: the brow is low, straight and bushy; the eyes and hair are light, the nose and mouth large, and the cheek bones high. The general contour of the face is angular, and the expression harsh.

They are slow but laborious, and endure fatigue beyond the sufferance of other men. In disposition they are frank, generous and grateful, yet quick-tempered, pugnacious and brave to a proverb.

In some localities their physical traits, their moral character and their peculiar customs, have undergone little change since the time of Cæsar. It is probable that the most unsophisticated Celts are those of the southwest of Ireland, whose wild look and manner, mud cabins and funereal howlings, recall the memory of a barbarous age.

The Celts have generally been considered the aboriginal inhabitants of western Europe; but Sir William Betham has recently undertaken to show "that ancient colonies of Phenicians settled in Spain, Ireland, Britain and Gaul, long before the Christian era; that they called themselves Gael or Celtæ; and that the Irish, the Gael of Scotland and the Manks (of the Isle of Man) are now the only descendants of that ancient people who speak their language."* The author then proceeds with an ingenious comparison between the Gaëlic and Phenician languages, and illustrates their affinity to a degree truly surprising.† Strong as the evidence is on this point, we may still hesitate to acknowledge the affiliation of the Celts and Phenicians until some remaining discrepancies are explained: for is it not singular, if the Celts were Phenicians, that they should have inherited so little of the national splendor, refinement and maritime enterprise of their progenitors? Betham brings but slender evidence of the civilisation of the ancient Irish; and Cæsar's account is any thing but complimentary to their domestic and civil relations.

The same learned author gives plausible reasons for supposing that the Picts or Caledonians of Scotland were not, as is commonly believed, of Celtic origin,

---

* Inquiry into the Origin of the Gael and Cimbri, Introd. p. 16.

† Betham shows, after Vallancey and others, that the Carthaginian speeches in the Pænulus of Plautus are absolutely Gaelic. See his work above quoted, p. 112.

but a branch of the Cymbri of Jutland; and that the Pictish Cimbri conquered Wales and Cornwall on the fall of the Roman Empire, and are the ancestors of the present Welsh population of Britain.

At the invasion of Cæsar the Belgæ, a branch of the Teutonic stock, were already numerous in the maritime parts of England. Subsequently the establishment of Roman colonies, the invasion and conquest by the Saxons, and still later by the Normans, have all contributed to form that extraordinary people whom we call the English or Anglo-Saxons. Inferior to no one of the Caucasian families in intellectual endowments, and possessed of indomitable courage and unbounded enterprise, it has spread its colonies widely over Asia, Africa and America; and, the mother of the Anglo-American family, it has already peopled the new world with a race in no respect inferior to the parent stock.

While the Celtic appears to be but partially blended with the English blood, the present French nation partakes of it much more largely. The Romans, the Germanic tribes, the Goths, the Burgundians and the Franks, who successively established themselves in France, amalgamated with the native population, thus forming a new race singularly different from that of the adjacent islands, wherein, as we have already seen, the social condition of the Celts has always been much more isolated. "It is thus," says Bory de St. Vincent, " that the Celts and Gauls have become the modern French, of whom the Franks of the middle ages are not the parent stock, as those assert who trace their genealogy to the latter barbarians. It is from their Celtic ancestors that the French derive their vivacity, their inconstancy, their impetuous courage devoid of perseverance, a vanity often puerile, and remarkable quickness of perception, together with that levity which is the jest of a neighboring country."*

We may in this place remark, that the Caucasian, Germanic and Celtic families already described, and the Hindoo family to be hereafter noticed, constitute the great chain of what are called the *Indo-European nations*. "It is now well known," observes Dr. Prichard, "that a greater or less degree of affinity exists between the dialects of some nations in the south-eastern parts of Asia, and the most extensively spread and most civilised languages of Europe. By this affinity is not meant a resemblance of some particular words in the vocabularies of several nations, such as a casual intercourse may have occasioned, but that sort of analogy in the primitive words and grammatical structure, which requires a

* L'Homme, I, p. 125.

different explanation; and is supposed plainly to indicate those languages in which it is displayed, however they may differ in some respects, to have sprung from a common original. This analogy has been remarked more especially between the Sanscrit, or the ancient language of India, and the Greek, Latin and German."*

Without undervaluing these philological analogies, I am disposed to believe, with Humboldt, that we shall never be able to trace the afiliation of nations by a mere comparison of languages; for this, after all, is but one of many clews by which that great problem is to be solved. Dr. Prichard himself admits that Europe was inhabited by "a more ancient people," before the Asiatics made their appearance; and although the language of the former was modified by this intercommunication, there is no satisfactory evidence that the physical character of these primitive people sustained any obvious change by the gradual immigration of the intruders from Asia. Dr. Prichard places the Celtic tribes among the Indo-Europeans; while Sir William Betham, as we have seen, judging also from similarity of language, pronounces the Celts to be of the Phenician branch of Arabians. With these discrepancies before us, we may inquire whether the term *Indo-European* is not more applicable to certain *languages* of Europe, than to the inhabitants themselves?

4. THE ARABIAN FAMILY.

The physical conformation of the Arabs proper is not very unlike that of their neighbors the Circassians, although, especially in the women, it possesses much less of the beautiful. Their skin is generally sallow, but is never black in the unmixed race; and in those whose rank permits them to avoid exposure to the sun, the complexion is a light and clear brunette. The Arab face is a somewhat elongated oval, with a delicately pointed chin, and a high forehead. Their eyes are large, dark and full of vivacity; their eyebrows are finely arched; the nose is narrow and gently aquiline, the lips thin, and the mouth small and expressive. Such at least is the appearance of the higher classes; but from these there is every grade of exterior feature until, in the Arab of the desert, the traveller sees all that is ferocious and repugnant in human nature. The Arabs in general are below the middle stature; their persons are spare and often meagre, and yet they possess an extraordinary vigilance and activity.

* Phys. Hist. of Man, I, p. 491.

THE ARABIAN FAMILY.

The habits of the Arab are strictly pastoral and wandering. His tent is his home, and he perpetually varies its location as his wants or caprice may prompt him.

The moral character of this race blends some very opposite elements; they are the children of impulse, at one moment raising the sword against the unresisting traveller, and the next receiving, with open hospitality, the stranger whose necessities have driven him to their tents. They are indolent excepting in their wars and pastimes, and remarkable for their covetousness and duplicity. Vanity is characteristic of all classes, from the chief of a tribe to the humblest Bedouin. Their politeness is extreme, and sobriety is a national trait.

Their intellectual character is conspicuous for a fertile imagination, and the successful cultivation of music, poetry and romance.

The migratory disposition of the Arabians has led to their dispersion over countries very remote from the parent land, so that at the present time Arabia does not contain a twentieth part of the descendants of Ishmael. Africa has always been one of their favorite retreats, and history records three principal irruptions, at distant periods from each other. The first was that of the Canaanites who were expelled by Joshua, and established themselves in northern Africa, and were the Mauri of the ancients: the second migration took place in the first century of the Christian era, and the third and last great influx was in the seventh and eighth centuries, by the Mahometan Arabs.

The *Moors* who inhabit the present kingdom of Morocco, and other parts of Africa, are in part descended from the Mauri, and partly from the Saracens who were expelled from Spain, together with the intruding Arabs of the different epochs. But the term Moor is used in Barbary to designate the inhabitant of a town or city, while Arab is the collective designation of the wandering tribes of this family. The Moors are of the middle stature, with complexions varying from black to white, owing to their intercourse with the negroes of Sudan. The women of Fez, however, are fair as Europeans, with uniformly dark eyes and hair. Those of Mequinez are even more beautiful, with remarkable grace and suavity of manner.

The men of Duquella have regular features, and are tall and well limbed: those of Temensa and Shawia, are a strong, robust race, of a copper color.* The nomadic Arab tribes live chiefly in tents; they are a restless and turbulent people, who are engaged in constant broils with each other, and with the adjacent Berbers

---

* JACKSON, Morocco, p. 128. *Am. ed.*

and Negroes. They are slightly made, and below the middle size, yet hardy and untiring in whatever they attempt. Cruelty and selfishness are their characteristic traits, and they possess also the vices which flow from ignorance and bigotry.

The Saracens, so celebrated for their conquests, first occupied the country between Mecca and the Euphrates; but they spread themselves rapidly over Africa, and soon established their kingdom in Spain, whence they were not expelled until the sixteenth century, after a dominion of seven hundred years. The Saracens, who are no longer known as a nation, surpassed the contemporary Arabians in the cultivation of literature, science and art.

The *Bedouins*, whose original country is northern Arabia, are among the most primitive and characteristic people of this family. Some of their tribes pass the spring and summer on the frontiers of Syria, seeking pasture and water: in the autumn they purchase their winter provision of wheat and barley, and return after the first rains into the interior of the desert. Tribes of this family inhabit or rather ambulate the district of Balbec, and the vicinity of Homs and Palmyra: a few pay tribute to the Pasha of Damascus, but most of them acknowledge no superior. "The Aenzes, a powerful Bedouin tribe, are easily distinguished from the Shemal Arabs by their diminutive size, few of them being above five feet two or three inches in height: their features are good, their noses often aquiline, their persons extremely well formed, and not so meagre or slight as some travellers have reported; their deep-set, dark eyes sparkle from under their bushy black eyebrows, with a fire unknown in our northern climes; their beard is short and thin, but the black hair of all abundantly thick. The females seem taller in proportion than the men; their features in general are handsome, and their deportment very graceful. In complexion these Arabs are very tawny; the children, however, at their birth are fair, but of a livid whiteness."[*] They are a nation of robber-shepherds, among whom wealth creates no influence, for the chief and the meanest Arab eat daily of the same dishes, partake of the same privations, and mingle in the same amusements. Like all Arabs they are passionately fond of music and poetry, but whole tribes of them can neither read nor write. They are highly courageous, but they fight rather for the acquisition of plunder than for the love of glory.

The *Wahabys*, so celebrated in recent times for having overrun and conquered all Arabia, were at first a mere tribe of sectarian Bedouins, who derived their name from a favorite chief. Their creed has been defined "a mussulman puritan-

---

[*] BURKHARDT, Bedouins and Wahabys, p. 28.

ism and a Bedouin government, in which the great chief is both the political and religious leader of the nation, exercising his authority in the same manner as the followers of Mohammed did over his converted countrymen."* Yet their chief sectarian distinction appears to be their hostility to the domes of the mosques, and to ornamented tombs, which they uniformly destroy with fanatical zeal. In their moral character the Wahabys are no better than the other Bedouins.

The Bedouins claim lineal descent from Ishmael. They are not only spread over nearly all Arabia to the confines of Persia, but across the entire continent of Africa to the Atlantic ocean. They skirt the Mediterranean on the north, and thence rove almost to the centre of the African continent. Even the territory of Houssa is said to derive its social character from the numerous Arabs who inhabit it. Change of locality and the lapse of time have effected no change in the habits of this people, who, in the time of Diodorus, were forbidden by their laws "to sow corn, to plant fruit trees, to make use of wine, or to inhabit houses," in order that there might be nothing to tempt the avarice of an enemy. They who plundered all nations, provided against a like calamity to themselves.

The Jews or Hebrews were in their origin a pastoral nation, but in progress of time they established themselves in the cities of Palestine. Their physiognomy is familiar in the receding forehead, the elongated face, and the large and aquiline nose. Their high attainments in literature are fully attested by the sacred writings; and their zealous attachment to their religion, and their patient endurance of adversity, are among the most striking traits of their character. Dispersed by a divine judgment, they are to be found almost every where on the habitable earth, recognised by the same features, and the same undeviating form of worship.

Travellers describe a colony of black Jews at Cochin and Cranganore, in Malabar: they, however, are not Jews by nation, but only by conversion. The date of their original apostacy is very ancient: they are, in fact, Hindoos in all respects but their religion; and Mr. Wolff informs us that "even at this time many of the Hindoos become converts to Judaism."†

The Hebrews are supposed to be derived from the Chaldeans, an elder branch of this race, whose capitol, Babylon, is among the proverbial wonders of antiquity. Belonging to the same stock, were the Idumeans, or Edomites,‡ renowned for their dwellings excavated from the solid rock, and other architectural remains in the recently revealed city of Petra.

---

* BURKHARDT, Bedouins and Wahabys, p. 274.   † Missionary Researches, p. 308.
‡ Called also the Nabathean Arabs.

VARIETIES OF THE HUMAN SPECIES.

Phenicia, one of the smallest yet most illustrious states of antiquity, was, as already hinted, an Arabian nation of the Chaldean stock. They roved upon the ocean as the cognate tribes did upon the land; their very name signifies a *wanderer by sea*, an appropriate appellation when we reflect on their fearless voyages to every part of the world then known, and their successful doubling of the Cape of Good Hope six hundred years before the Christian era. Tyre and Sidon were their principal cities in Phenicia proper. They joined the Mauri and built Carthage, and on the destruction of this city by the Romans, the two nations were blended in a common family.* This again became mixed with the Arab immigrations of various epochs, and partially with the Berbers, whom we have next to mention.†

5. THE LIBYAN FAMILY.

It is proposed in this name to include the various tribes of aboriginal Africans who have long been designated by the Arabic term of *Berbers*. I adopt the former designation from Prichard and Heeren, who consider these people to be the descendants of the ancient Libyans. They are found both to the north and south of Mount Atlas, extending their wanderings into Morocco and Barbary: on the east they inhabit as far as the Gulf of Cabes, or the Little Syrtis, while on the west they reach the Atlantic. They call themselves by the collective or national name of *Amazirgh*.

The various communities of this family are characterised by handsome Caucasian features, but in complexion they present all the shades from white to nearly black.

The *Tuariks* are perhaps the best known of all the Berber tribes. Captain Lyon describes them as the finest men he ever saw; tall, straight and handsome,

---

* CHENIER, Resch. sur les Maures, I, p. 19.

† The term *Semitic* has been applied to the Syrian nations between the Mediterranean sea and western Persia, "from Shem, the son of Noah, from whom, in the table of nations in the book of Genesis, entitled Toldoth Beni Noach, many of them are declared to have descended." The principal Semitic communities are or were the following:
1. Elam, to the northward of the Persian Gulf.
2. Ashar, or the people of Assyria.
3. The Chasdim or Chaldeans, from whom are descended the Hebrews and Arabs.
4. The Lydians.
5. Aram, or the proper Syrians.

See PRICHARD, Res. II, p. 208.

with an imposing air of pride and independence. Their features resemble those of southern Europeans; their natural complexion is nearly white, much darkened, however, by exposure to a hot sun, and their hair is long, black and glossy. They are said to be less treacherous than the Arabs, yet passionate, cruel and revengeful. They are fond of war, and plunder both their Arab and Negro neighbors, and reduce the latter to slavery. They are chiefly pastoral in their mode of life; and although they have horses, they mostly travel and fight on foot.

The *Shillooks* inhabit south of the Tuariks, are less robust and have darker complexions: they are also said to be more industrious, peaceful, civilised and humane, having some manufactures, and being more husbandmen than shepherds. They occupy the western valleys of Mount Atlas, in the province of Temsna, but are still more numerous south of the city of Morocco.

The *Adem* inhabit the oasis of Ghadamis, south of Tripoli, and are said to be divided into two hostile tribes which are at constant war with each other.

To this family also belong the *Beni-Mozab*, and other tribes of Belad-el-gerid, south of Atlas, the Zuaves of the Tunisian territory, the Kolluvians in the neighborhood of Soudan, the Tagama near Tombuctoo, who are white, and the Hagara and Matkara, who are yellowish.*

"The Kabyles," says Dr. Prichard, "who appear to be intimately connected with the Berbers, inhabit the higher part of the Algerine and Tunisian territories, living in mountain villages composed of huts, which resemble the *magalia* of the old Numidians. The Kabyles, as we learn from Dr. Shaw, are in general of a swarthy color, with dark hair; but those who inhabit the mountains of Auress, though they speak the same idiom, are of a fair and ruddy complexion, and their hair is of a deep yellow."†

It is probably a tribe of Berbers to whom M. Arago alludes when he informs us, that, "in going from Bougia to Algiers in 1808, by land, he saw women of all ages in the different villages, who were white, had blue eyes and fair hair; but that the nature of his journey did not permit him to stop and ask if they came from any particular tribe."

The GUANCHES of the Canary Islands appear to have been a colony of Berbers, as is inferred from the remains of their language, their features and their customs. The singular perfection with which they practised the art of embalm-

---

* PRICHARD, I, p. 246, &c.—The best account of the Berbers I have any where seen is contained under that article in the Penny Cyclopædia, a learned and elaborate work with a very humble title.
† Idem. p. 243.

ing, has led to the supposition that they were of Egyptian origin; but the analogy between the two nations appears not to have extended beyond this solitary rite.

The Berbers have generally been confounded with the Arabs, whom they chiefly resemble in their wandering and predatory habits. The Berber language is wholly different from the Arabic: neither do they claim to the Arabs, or the Arabs to them any national afliliation: and there is sufficient reason to believe, as already stated, that they are identical with the Libyæ of the ancients, the people who inhabited the country before the first influx of the Arabians.

I am at a loss where to class the *Gallas* of eastern Africa, yet they bear a general physical resemblance to some tribes of Berbers. They are of small stature, with long black hair, and complexions varying from brown to black. They are among the most warlike and remorseless barbarians of Africa, and their principal tribe, the Boren-galla, now governs by conquest in Abyssinia, and even occupies Gondar, the capital. They are supposed to spring from that unknown region which constitutes the southern interior of the continent.

In the immediate vicinity of Mount Atlas the distinctions of Race are often altogether confounded, owing to the proximity of the Negro tribes. Thus the *Tibboos* are nearly black, and have long wiry hair, intermediate between that of the Tuarick and the Negro; yet their features are good and their forms delicately and even beautifully moulded. The immemorial predatory habits of these various tribes amply account for this blending of physical character; for the Tibboos mix with the Negroes, the Tuaricks enslave the Tibboos, and the Moors, in their turn, make enemies and slaves of them all.

6. THE NILOTIC FAMILY.

The valley of the Nile, a narrow strip of land six hundred miles long and but ten broad—the *Nilotica tellus* of the ancients, presents at the present time at least two cognate nations, which, though dwindled and degenerate, appear to constitute a family distinct from the rest of mankind. These nations, if they now deserve that name, are the EGYPTIANS and NUBIANS.

The modern Egyptians are composed of two classes, or castes, the Copts and Fellahs.

The Copts, though now remarkably distinct from the people who surround them, derive from their remote ancestors some mixture of Greek, Arabian and perhaps even Negro blood. They present various shades of complexion, from a pale yellow to a deep bronze or brown. "The eyes of the Copt are generally large and elongated, slightly inclining from the nose upwards, and always black. The nose is straight, excepting at the end, where it is rounded and wide; the lips are rather thick, and the hair is black and curly."* Mr. Madden says that they are also marked by the great distance between the eyes. Their legs and feet are badly formed, and they are seldom graceful or pleasing in their manner. These people, now reduced to about one hundred and fifty thousand souls, are Christians, but they bear a bitter hatred to all other sects. They are said to be of sullen temper, avaricious, ignorant, dissembling and faithless.

The Coptic language is extremely ancient and very peculiar; nor can there be a question of the identity of the pure Coptic with the ancient vernacular Egyptian. It does not appear to have undergone any change of grammatical structure, and it is of greater antiquity than any Indo-European or Semitic language.† The knowledge of the Coptic language is at present known to but few of the Copts themselves. The Ptolemies first attempted to eradicate it by substituting the Greek in its place, and they even made it a capital offence to speak the Coptic in common conversation. The Turks have pursued the same policy, by requiring the Arabic to supersede both Greek and Coptic.

The Copts are supposed by Niebuhr, Denon and others, to be the descendants of the ancient Egyptians; and it has often been observed, that a strong resemblance may be traced between the Coptic visage and that presented in the ancient mummies, paintings and statues:‡ but it is in vain that we look for absolute identity in a country that has groaned in bondage for two thousand years. The Persians, the Greeks, the Romans, the Arabians and the Turks, have successively held dominion in this fated valley, and subjected it, in turn, to every species of oppression. The Copts, therefore, can be at most but the degenerate remains, both physically and intellectually, of that mighty people who have claimed the admiration of all ages.

The great mass of the present Egyptian population is composed of a mixed race of Copts and Arabs, who are called *Moslem-Egyptians*, or *Fellahs*. They are handsomer than the purer Copts. "Their heads are a fine oval, the forehead of moderate size, not high, but generally prominent; their eyes are deep sunk, black and brilliant; the nose is straight and rather thick; the mouth well formed; the lips are rather full than otherwise; the teeth particularly beautiful, and the beard is commonly black and curly, but scanty."§

---

* LANE, Mod. Egypt, II, p. 310.   † LIPSIUS, in Wiseman's Lect. p. 63.
‡ NIEBUHR, Trav. in Africa, p. 71.   § LANE, Mod. Egypt, II, p. 32.

In person they are remarkably well proportioned; the men being large and robust, and the women beautifully formed. They have a yellowish but clear complexion, and their whole exterior has derived from their Arab lineage some advantages which the genuine Copt but rarely possesses.

The NUBIANS constitute the second division of the Nilotic family. They call themselves *Nouba*, or *Kenous*, but are known in Egypt by the name of Berâbera.* "The figure of the Nubian," says Mr. Stevens, "is tall, thin, sinewy, and graceful, possessing what would be called in civilised life an uncommon degree of gentility. His face is rather dark, though far removed from African blackness; and his features are long and aquiline, decidedly resembling the Roman."†

The hair of the Nubian is thick and black, often curled either by nature or by art, and sometimes partially frizzled, but never woolly. In fact, judging from the painting and sculpture of their temples, the ancient Nubians, like the modern, were in no respect analogous to the Negroes, excepting in the occasional blackness of their skin: and it is also worthy of remark, that their most frequent scenic decorations represent their triumphs over the Negroes, who uniformly appear as menials or as captives.

"It is among the Nubians," says Mr. Madden, "we are to search for the true descendants of the Egyptians; a swarthy race, surpassing in the beauty of their slender forms, all the people of the East; living on the confines of Egypt, where, probably, their ancestors had been driven by the Persians; and possessing a dialect somewhat mixed with Arabic, but which I have observed no Arab understands."

Although the Nubians occasionally present their national characters unmixed, they generally show traces of their social intercourse with the Arabs, and even with the Negroes; and the long domination of the former has impressed on these people many of their peculiar traits, including their religious observances; for although the Nubians early embraced Christianity, they are now all Moslems, and boast that they have not a Christian among them.

The *Abyssinians*, the Axomites of the Romans, inhabit the country to the south of Nubia, and appear to have been originally affiliated with the Egyptians and Nubians. But at present they have utterly lost their identity from their intercourse with various nations of different origin and language, but especially the Arabs, Gallas and Negroes. Thus constituted, the Abyssinians present one of

---

* BURKHARDT, Trav. p. 210.
† STEVENS, Egypt, &c., I, p. 104.—BURKHARDT, Trav. p. 144.

the most motley and barbarous states in existence. Yet the Arab and Nubian lineaments predominate; and are seen in the oval face, the narrow pointed nose, the long, black hair and delicate limbs; while the immemorial amalgamation of the Abyssinians with their Negro slaves, imparts to many the thick lips, the flat nose, and even the crisped and woolly hair of the genuine African. The present inhabitants are to the last degree barbarous, cruel and licentious. Even the Christian population is said to partake of the national anarchy, for they are divided into three parties, who are so inimical to each other that they refuse to take the sacrament together. "The Abyssinians," says Gobat, in extenuation, "are liars, as well as the Arabs; but they yet have a feeling of shame which the Arabs have not."

Their written language, the Gheez, has some affinity with the Arabic, which may be attributed to the long intercourse of the two nations.

The ancient intercourse of the Abyssinians with the Egyptians, is proved by the temples and obelisks among the ruins of Axoum, the port of Abyssinia on the Red Sea; while at Meröe, in the interior, and at other places, are seen some stupendous architectural remains of high antiquity.

The Ancient Egyptians.—The physical traits of the Egyptians, as derivable from their monuments and mummies, may be embraced in the following summary.

They appear to have been spare in person, with long limbs and delicate hands and feet. Their heads were formed as in the Hindoo, thus differing from the Caucasian only in being somewhat smaller in proportion to the body, and having a narrower and less elevated forehead. Mr. Madden, who speaks of having examined a great number of heads in the Theban catacombs, says "that the old Egyptian skull is extremely narrow across the forehead, and of an oblong shape anteriorly. I never found one with a broad expanded forehead."* There is a remarkable resemblance among the innumerable heads sculptured in the temples of the Nile; and one who is accustomed to examine them becomes so familiar with the Egyptian physiognomy, that when other races are introduced, as the Jews and Negroes, the eye can mostly detect them. There is also a singular accordance in conformation between the sculptured heads, and the real ones taken from the Theban catacombs. Two prominent varieties are discernible in each: one of these has the rather low and narrow forehead above mentioned, while the other presents the full development of the Caucasian head. The

---

* Trav. in Egypt, &c., II, p. 93.

former greatly predominates in the Egyptian sculpture, and is possibly characteristic of the Egyptians as a race. The nose was rather long, and joined the head much in the Grecian manner; the eye was elongated and rather oblique; the lips were well formed, the chin rounded and moderately full, and the whole expression mild and pleasing. It may be added that the Egyptian ear is said to have been placed higher than in the Caucasian; but on this point I cannot speak from observation. It is curious, however, that the same remark has been made in reference to the Hindoos of Malabar.*

As to the complexion of these people, history is strangely silent; but judging from the paintings which have been copied by Belzoni, Champollion and others, their prevalent color appears to have been swarthy or brown, with a tinge of red. It is certain, however, that there was a difference in color in the different castes, as in the modern Hindoos, presenting every shade from nearly white to a very dark brown, or even black. Their hair was long, straight, and generally black, although in the mummies it has a brownish color, which has been attributed to the process of embalming.†

The antiquity of the Egyptian nation, and their skill in the arts and sciences, have been proverbial in all ages. "It is a remarkable fact," says Mr. Wilkinson, "that the first glimpse we obtain of the history and manners of the Egyptians, shows a nation already advanced in the arts of civilised life; and the same customs and inventions that prevailed in the Augustan era of that people, after the accession of the eighteenth dynasty, are found in the remote age of Osirtasen, the contemporary of Joseph."‡

In illustration of the antiquity and the "learning of the Egyptians," we may briefly notice a few facts in connection with the received chronology: thus, they had completed the pyramids of Memphis within three hundred years after the era assigned to the deluge;—they wrote their hieroglyphic characters on papyrus as early as the age of Cheops, two thousand years before Christ;—they discovered and constructed the arch at least three thousand four hundred years ago;—the *Greek Scroll* is common in the tombs of the Pharoahs;—and the so called Doric column and entablature ornamented the porticos of Beni-Hassan before sculpture was an art in Greece.§ Hence the observation of a late writer, that "this

---

* Virey, Dict. d'Hist. Nat. Art. L'Homme.

† The Egyptians kept their heads shaved excepting a lock on the crown, and their head-dresses were as varied as the capitals of their columns.

‡ Ancient Egypt, III, p. 260. § Ancient Egypt, II, p. 117 — III, p. 150, 261, 318.

singular people had attained a high degree of civilisation and refinement at a time when the whole western world was still involved in barbarism; when the history of Europe had not yet begun; and long before Carthage, Athens and Rome were thought of."

NOTE.—*On the Supposed Affinity between the Egyptians and Negroes.*—I trust I shall be excused for offering, in this place, a few brief remarks in reference to an opinion which, however much at variance with multiplied facts, has still some strenuous advocates: I allude to that hypothesis which classes the ancient Egyptians with the Negro race. Among the advocates of this opinion was Volney, the celebrated traveller. He looked upon the *Sphinx*, and hastily inferred from its flat features and bushy hair, that the Egyptians were real Negroes: yet these circumstances have no weight when we recur to the fact, that the Budhists of Asia (the most numerous sect in existence) represent their principal god with Negro features and hair, and often sculptured in black marble;* yet among the three hundred millions who worship Budha, there is not, perhaps, a solitary Negro nation. The Egyptians borrowed many of their mythological rites from their southern neighbors, in the same way that, in after time, the Greeks borrowed from the Egyptians, and the Romans from the Greeks: but such facts are no proofs of the affiliation of races. The ruins of Pompeii contain a temple of Isis; yet would any one thence infer that the inhabitants of that city were Egyptians? There is no absolute proof, moreover, that the Sphinx represented an Egyptian deity: it may have been a shrine of the Negro population of Egypt, who, as traffickers, servants and slaves, were a very numerous body; whence the boast of the Egyptian kings, recorded by Diodorus, that the vast structures of Karnak and Luxor were erected by the labor of foreigners, and that none of the native Egyptians were employed on them. This remark may be coupled with another statement of the same historian, that the people of Egypt followed their own fancies in religion, every one being allowed to worship that object which his ancestors had worshipped before him.† Hence the number and diversity of their gods, from a leek or a reptile to the deified Osiris.

Another point much insisted on is the following: Herodotus, speaking of the Colchians, says that the Egyptians believed them "to be descended from part of the troops of Sesostris." He then adds, "to this I myself was also inclined, because they are black, and have hair short and curling."‡ This description, however, is not sufficient to characterise a Negro, and would apply with equal truth to a large proportion of the Nubians of the present day, merely making allowance for the well known vagueness with which the Greeks applied the term *black* to all complexions darker than their own. Even if it be admitted that these Colchians were real Negroes, it does not prove the point at issue; for the remark that they were "part of the *troops* of Sesostris" leads to the reasonable inference that they were either wholly or in part derived from the servile or Negro caste in Egypt, and not of the Egyptian race. This opinion is sustained by another passage in the same historian, who tells us that in the army of Xerxes which invaded Greece, there was a legion of western Ethiopians, who, he adds, "have their hair more crisp and curling than any other men."§ Now, if the Persian army was composed in part of genuine Negroes, how much more likely were the troops of Sesostris to embrace a portion of that race, he being himself a king of Egypt? But it may be said

* HEBER, Narr. l, p. 254. *Am. ed.*   † DIOD. SIC. Hist. (Booth's Tr.) B. I, chap. 7.
‡ Μελάγχροες καὶ οὐλότριχες. *Euterpe, Cap. C.*   § HEROD. Polhym. Cap. LXX.

that Herodotus speaks of the Colchians as Egyptians: to which it may be answered, that he does so in a generic or comprehensive sense; precisely as in our own time the army of Ibrahim Pacha is said to be composed of *Negroes* and Fellahs, who, with all their motley grades, receive the collective name of Egyptians.* As Herodotus is chiefly appealed to by those who would merge the Egyptian in the Negro, I think some extracts from his work will show that he himself had no such view. He has for example the following passage: "The priests afterwards recited to me the names of three hundred and thirty sovereigns (successors of Menes‡) in this continued series, eighteen were Ethiopians, and one a female native of the country—*all the rest were men and Egyptians.*" Let us analyse this passage. It is admitted that these eighteen *Ethiopians*† were foreigners; yet in all probability Nubians, and not Negroes. If it be contended, however, that they were real Negroes, then it will follow that only one-eighteenth part of this long line of monarchs could have been of Negro origin. It is also reasonable to infer, that whatever may have been the national character of this exotic minority, they reigned in Egypt by usurpation or by conquest.‡ Moreover, this "female native of the country," was Nitocris, who is described by Manetho as "remarkably beautiful, with a fair skin and flaxen hair."§ It is unnecessary to remark that no two personal traits could be more diametrically opposite to those of the Negro than these; and as Nitocris was a native Egyptian, and of the royal line, we may reasonably infer that she possessed, in an eminent degree, the national characteristics of the high-caste Egyptians.

This question is further elucidated by the numberless pictorial and other representations in the tombs of Egypt and Nubia. Thus, in the plates to Belzoni's Researches, among the most ancient Nubian remains, we see figures of various complexions, from a light flesh-color to a dark red, and these are conjoined with strictly Caucasian or Asiatic features. Another series represents four unequivocal Negroes, marked by every characteristic trait, including, of course, a jet black skin; while, on the same picture, and as if to enforce the distinction of race by a direct contrast, several other personages are seen with fair skins and Caucasian lineaments.||

"Black people," says Mr. Wilkinson, "designated as natives of the *foreign land of Cush*, are generally represented on the Egyptian monuments either as captives, or as the bearers of tribute to the Pharaohs."¶ "I remarked," says Denon, "many decapitated figures: these were all dark, while those who had struck off their heads, and still stood over them sword in hand, were red."**

---

* This feature of the modern Egyptian army is well explained in Burkhardt, Trav. p. 341, &c.—Long after this part of my manuscript was ready for the press, I read the learned Dr. Wiseman's Lectures on the Natural History of Man, in which I find the following corroborative passage: "It is ot easy," he remarks, "to reconcile the conflicting results thus obtained from writers and from monuments, and it is no wonder that learned men should have differed widely in opinion on the subject. I should think the best solution is, that Egypt was the country where the Greeks most easily saw the inhabitants of interior Africa, many of whom doubtless flocked thither and were settled there, or served in the army as tributaries or provincials, as they have done in later times; and thus they came to be confounded by writers with the country where alone they knew them, and were considere l a part of the indigenous population." *Am. ed.* p. 97.

† The geographical meaning of the word *Ethiopian* will be explained in the chapter on the Negro Race.

‡ Herod. Euterpe, lib. c.

§ Manetho, as quoted in Wilkinson's Anc. Egypt, I, pp. 28, 91. The reader may also put his own construction on the following passage in Herodotus: "We may venture to assert," says he, "*that after the Africans*, there is no people in health and constitution to be compared to the Egyptians."—*Euterpe*, cap. LXXVI.

|| Researches, folio plates.—Dr. Wiseman also refers for further proof to Hoskins's Trav. in Ethiopia, which I have not seen.

¶ Ancient Egypt, I, p. 4.   ** Voy. II, p. 296.

At the entrance of the temple of Ipsamboul, in Nubia, Burkhardt saw the remains of several colossal statues, cut out of the solid rock; of the most perfect of them he remarks: "The head which is above the surface [of the sand] has a most expressive, youthful countenance, approaching nearer to the Grecian model of beauty than that of any ancient Egyptian figure I have seen."*

But with reference to the physical character of the Egyptians, there is a source of evidence to which some allusion has already been made, and which is more conclusive than any other: I refer to the embalmed bodies of the Theban catacombs. These vast cemeteries are crowded with genuine Egyptians, whose remains even now retain almost every feature in perfection. Here are the very people who walked the streets of Thebes, they who built Luxor and the Pyramids; and yet among the thousands whose bodies curiosity and avarice have dragged from their tombs, I am not aware that a solitary Negro has been discovered.

"It is now clearly proved," says the illustrious Cuvier—"yet it is necessary to repeat the truth, because the contrary error is still found in the newest works—that neither the Gallas, (who border on Abyssinia,) nor the Bosjesmans, nor any race of Negroes, produced the celebrated people who gave birth to the civilisation of ancient Egypt, and of whom we may say that the whole world has inherited the principles of its laws, sciences, and perhaps also religion. It is easy to prove, that *whatever may have been the hue of their skin*, they belonged to the same race with ourselves. I have examined in Paris, and in the various collections of Europe, more than fifty heads of mummies, and not one amongst them presented the characters of the Negro or Hottentot."†

It may justly be inquired, if science, art and literature, had their origin with a Negro tribe on the skirts of Africa, how does it happen that the stream of knowledge has never flowed into, but always from that country? For while it has been permanently diffused through Asia and Europe, in Africa itself it cannot be traced beyond the mountains of Nubia. Again, it is now proved almost beyond controversy, that Egypt, and not Nubia, was the mother of the arts; and that the stupendous monuments of the Upper Nile, and especially those of Meröe, were the works of the Pharaohs, and indicate the great marts of commerce between Egypt and the other nations of Africa.‡

The passages from the Greek poets which bear on this subject, have been ingeniously analysed by Dr. Prichard, to whose work on the Physical History of Mankind, the reader is referred for much valuable information on this subject. "Some of these passages," says Dr. Prichard, "are very strongly expressed as if the Egyptians were Negroes; and yet it must be confessed that if they really were such, it is singular that we do not find more frequent allusion to the fact. The Hebrews were a fair people, fairer at least than the Arabs; yet in all the intercourse they had with Egypt, we never find in the Sacred History the least intimation that the Egyptians were Negroes; not even on the memorable occasion of the marriage of Solomon with Pharaoh's daughter. Were a modern historian to record the nuptials of an European monarch with the daughter of a Negro king, such a circumstance would surely find its place. And since Egypt was so closely connected with Grecian affairs when under the Ptolemies, and afterwards with the rest of Europe when it became a Roman province, it is very singular, on the supposition that this nation was so remarkably different from the rest of mankind, that we have no allusion to it."§

* Trav. in Nubia, p. 91.   † Lawrence's Lect. on Zool. p. 347, &c.
‡ Heeren, Anc. African Nations, I, p. 426.—Wilkinson, Anc. Egypt, I, p. 4, 13.
§ Res. I, p. 319.

7. THE INDOSTANIC FAMILY.

THE HINDOOS.

There are perhaps no people on the globe who present more varied physical traits than the Hindoos. In general, however, the face is oval, the nose straight or slightly aquiline, the mouth small, the teeth vertical and well formed, and the chin rounded and generally dimpled. The eyes are black, bright and expressive, the eye lashes long, and the brow thin and arched. The hair is long, black and glossy, and the beard very thin. The head of the Hindoo is small in proportion to the body, elongated, and narrow especially across the forehead, which is only moderately elevated.

India presents every tint of complexion from an absolute black to a clear and beautiful brunette; but the different shades of olive are predominant, especially among the higher castes, while the Pariahs, and others of the lowest class, are as uniformly dark.

"The great difference in color between the different natives," says Bishop Heber, "struck me much: of the crowd by whom we were surrounded, some were black as Negroes, others merely copper-colored, and others little darker than Tunisians. It is not merely the difference of exposure, since this variety is visible in the fishermen, who are naked all alike. Nor does it depend on caste, since very high-caste Brahmins are sometimes black, while Pariahs are comparatively fair."*

The people of Cambaia are said to be nearly of an ash color; those of Guzerat and Mahratta are yellow, while olive is the prevalent tint in Goa.

The women of the Brahminical caste are celebrated for their beauty, especially those of Canara and Malabar, who are said to bear a comparison with those of Georgia and Circassia. They are often mothers at ten years of age.

The stature of the Hindoos is low, in general not exceeding five feet three or four inches; their persons are slender, their limbs long and delicate, but well moulded, and their hands and feet small and beautifully formed.

The moral character of the Hindoos varies much in the different sections of India, whence the discrepant statements of modern travellers. They appear by nature to be a mild, sober and industrious race, warm in their attachments and

---

* Narr. I, p. 45. *Am. ed.*

fond of their children. But their love of the marvellous, fostered as it is by a fantastic religion, is almost without a parallel among nations. They are of a timid disposition, and not inclined to cruelty, yet their avarice, which is extreme, leads them readily to commit murder for the most trifling acquisition. Notwithstanding the apparent mildness of their manners, says Bishop Heber, the criminal calendar is generally full of gang-robberies, incendiarism, and analogous crimes; "and the number of children who are decoyed aside, and murdered for the sake of their ornaments, is dreadful." They practise deception with infinite art, to which falsehood and perjury form no obstacles. "For all these horrors their system of religion is mainly answerable, inasmuch as whatever moral lessons their sacred books contain—and they are very few—are shut up from the mass of the people, while the direct tendency of their institutions is to evil. The national temper is decidedly good, gentle and kind. They are sober, industrious, affectionate to their relations, generally speaking faithful to their masters, easily attached by kindness and confidence, and in case of the military oath, are of admirable obedience, courage and fidelity in life and death. But their morality does not extend beyond the reach of positive obligations; and where these do not exist, they are oppressive, cruel, treacherous, and every thing that is bad."* The intellectual character of the Hindoos is distinguished among the present Asiatic nations; but their learning has been very much devoted to comments on their sacred books, which are extremely numerous. They have had many admirable writers in poetry and the drama, and excel in some branches of mathematics, and especially in algebra. Their antique architectural remains are on a stupendous scale, and consist chiefly of rock-hewn temples ornamented with elaborate sculpture. Such are the caverns and galleries at Ellora and Elephanta, which rival the similar efforts of ancient Egypt.

Among the varied population of India are some tribes and nations who differ so widely, physically and morally, from the great mass of people, as to claim at least a passing notice.

The *Tudas* of the Neilgherry Hills, in the southern peninsula, appear to have been the aboriginal inhabitants of the region they occupy. They are described as above the common height, athletic and well made; with a large, full and sparkling eye, Roman nose, and fine teeth. Their hair is long, black and curling, with a full beard. They are of grave deportment, cheerful manner, and peaceful disposition, not even carrying defensive weapons: yet on the other hand they are

* HEBER, Narr. II, p. 240. *Am. ed.*

indolent and dirty, and their moral code permits to their women a plurality of husbands. Their religion, which forbids the worship of idols, is in no respect analogous to any existing Asiatic creed, and their language has no affinity to the Sanscrit.* They are believed to be aborigines of southern India, exhibiting what their ancestors were before they received those institutions which have stamped upon the Hindoo race so peculiar a character.†

The *Rajpoots* are of light complexion, with more aquiline features than the people of the adjacent provinces.

They are, however, genuine Hindoos. They were formerly engaged in incessant wars : they have the vices of slaves added to those of robbers, with as little regard for truth as the other Hindoos, while they possess a blood-thirstiness from which the latter are very far removed.‡ In their demi-civilisation, their extravagant fondness for their bards and their romantic chivalry, they strongly resemble the Europeans of the middle ages. The *Rarejas* are a Rajpoot tribe who, owing to some singular dilemma of *caste*, cannot find a single individual with whom a daughter of theirs can be matched; whence they have adopted the horrid expedient of putting to death all their female children, so that in 1818, in a population of twelve thousand souls, there were not more than thirty women alive !§

The *Sikhs* were originally a kind of dissenters from the Hindoo faith, whose fundamental principles were "devotion to God and peace towards man." Their numbers augmented rapidly, embracing multitudes of Hindoos and many Mahometans; but being pressed beyond endurance by the tyranny of their Mussulman neighbors, they at length discarded the olive branch and took up the sword, possessed themselves of their native province of Lahor, and conquered the Punjab; and now constitute, under the sway of Runjeet Singh, the most powerful native government in India.‖

In Malabar the inhabitants are black, but have good features and the general exterior of the Hindoos; but the prejudices of caste are carried to an extent unknown in other parts of India. Thus, "if a cultivator or a fisherman presumes to touch one of the *nairs*, or military class, the nair is considered fully justified in killing him on the spot. The same fate befals the paria who ventures even to look him in the face, and does not, on seeing him at a distance, instantly take

---

* HARKNESS. On the Aborig. Race of the Neilgherry Hills, p. 7, 25.
† British India, II, p. 273.   ‡ HEBER, Narr. II, p. 56. *Am. ed.*
§ British India. By MURRAY and others, II, p. 370.
‖ MALCOLM, Sketch of the Sikhs, *passim*.

flight. This last race are all slaves, a condition not common in the rest of Hindostan. But there is another class of sufferers whom a barbarous pride has stripped beyond any other of the most common rights of humanity: the *niadis* are excluded from all human intercourse, forced to wander in unfrequented places, without any means of support except the alms of passengers. These they endeavor to attract by standing at a little distance from the public road, and howling like hungry dogs, till the charitable wayfarer lays on the ground some donation, which, after his departure, they hastily carry off."*

The inhabitants of Ceylon, who are called Singalese, are black like those of Malabar, but are less oppressed and therefore less degraded. They are represented as courteous in their manner, and despise both theft and falsehood. Their disposition is mild; yet when their anger is once roused, they are singularly violent and implacable. The dominant religion is that of Budha, the remaining sectaries being chiefly of the Brahminical persuasion. The Singalese have a tradition of their former affiliation with the people of Siam, and they certainly possess, both in their religious rites and their physical conformation, some resemblance to that people. Perhaps the latter circumstance may be accounted for by the presence of the Malays, who have long colonised their coasts.

The Hindoos are among the oldest nations of the earth. Their present civilisation, with its institution of castes—their religion, which is Brahminical—and their language, which is Sanscrit, may all be traced to an antiquity of nearly three thousand years.

The *castes* are four great divisions or classes, each designed to be isolated and exclusive in all its relations. They are, 1st, the *Brahmins*, or Priests; 2d, the *Rajahs*, (or Kishatrias,) or Soldiers; 3d, the *Vaisya*, or merchants and cultivators; and 4, the *Sudras*, or subordinate cultivators, who are, in fact, the slave population of Hindostan. Each of these tribes is subdivided into several more, of which the number is uncertain.† This singular thraldom prohibits all intermixture or association of castes: yet notwithstanding the severest social and bodily penalties, the impure or mixed castes are very numerous; for of these the Pariahs alone are said to constitute one fifth of all the people of India. Inferior, if possible, to these are the Pallis of Madura, and the Puliahs of Malabar, whose touch is defilement even to a Sudra.

The Brahminical religion of the Hindoos is essentially idolatrous. The

---

* Murray, Encyc. of Geog. p. 997.   † Dubois, People of India, p. 54.

Trimurti, or trinity, is composed of Brahma, Vishnu and Siva, with an infinite ramification of minor deities. Budhism, which is a persecuted schism of the Brahminical creed, has still some followers in India, among whom are the *Jains* of western India, Benares and Ceylon.* What is much more remarkable is the fact, that on the Malabar coast is a colony of Christians, whose traditions extend back to the time of St. Thomas. Another, and still more unsophisticated body of them occupies the interior of Travancore. They inhabited their present localities centuries before the modern discovery of the passage to India by the Cape of Good Hope.

Hindostan was among the countries which were overrun and conquered by Jenghis Khan and Timur. But in the year 1525, Sultan Baber, king of Persia, seized upon India, subduing the native inhabitants, and driving out the Mongol-Tartars of the then existing dynasty. He established his court at Delhi, and India from that epoch was called the *Mogul Empire*, the sovereign himself assuming the title of the Great Mogul; but this once powerful dominion sunk into comparative insignificance during the early part of the past century. The northern Hindoos having mingled for centuries with the Mongol-Tartars, received in common with those people the conventional name of *Moguls*, which embraces Persians, Greeks of Bactriana, and Arabs, who are called Moors; but the latter appellation is more strictly applied to the Mahomedans only.

The people of India have only been called Hindoos since the Tartar conquest: previous to that event all the inhabitants who professed the Brahminical faith were called Gentoos.

We may add that the gipseys of Europe, whose origin has been so long a paradox to the learned, are now ascertained to be of Hindoo extraction.

The original country of the Hindoos has been a question among historians. Their reverence for the north, added to the traditions of the Brahmins, and various collateral circumstances, have led Bory de St. Vincent and Malte-Brun to suppose the cradle of these people to have been the lofty table-land about the sources of the Indus, and the elevated valleys of Serinagur; while Heeren and others are of the opinion that "the Brahmins, and perhaps the Kishatriya and Vaisya castes

---

* HEBER, Narr. I, p. 154.—II, p. 19, 74, 290. *Am. ed.*—Budhism, though of much more recent date than the primitive Brahminical religion, is supposed to have arisen in India a thousand years before Christ, and to have had many followers: but in the sixth century of our era a persecution arose, which expelled nearly all the Budhists from Hindostan, whence they took refuge in the central and eastern provinces of Asia.

were originally a race of northern conquerors of fair complexion; while the Sudras and other inferior tribes were an aboriginal and darker race."*

NOTE.—*On the Resemblances between the Hindoos and Egyptians.*—History and the arts discover many remarkable analogies between the Hindoos and Egyptians, whence they have been supposed by some able writers to be affiliated nations. That there was extensive and long-continued intercourse between them is sufficiently obvious, and history speaks vaguely of conquest and migration. Which was the dominant power? The Egyptians very naturally decided this point in their own favor; for they assert that Osiris crossed Arabia to the utmost inhabited parts of India, and that he built many cities there. "He left likewise," says Diodorus, "many other marks of his being in these parts, which have induced the inhabitants to believe and affirm that this god (Osiris) was born in India."† Thus it appears that in the age of Diodorus, the Hindoos not only worshipped, but claimed as original to themselves, the principal divinity of the Egyptians.

These resemblances may be traced throughout the mythology and usages of the two nations. Apis, the Egyptian Bull, was the symbol of Osiris; and the White Bull is the animal on which Siva is represented on the Indian pagodas. Worship was bestowed alike on the Ganges and the Nile. Both nations worshipped the sun and the serpent; and even at the present time the objects held in the greatest veneration by the Hindoos of the Vishnu sect, are the ape, the monkey, the bird called Garuda, and the serpent Capella.‡ Among the symbols of superstition in each are seen the sphinx, the lotus, the lingam and the cross. "The *crux ansata* which is constantly observed in the hands of the Nilotic statues, is nothing but the yoni-lingam of the Hindoos; and it is a curious fact that in the *terra cotta* images of Isis, dug up near her temple at Pæstum, she holds in her right hand an exact representation of the Hindoo lingam and yoni combined."§

Their affinity is also recognised in their almost exclusive vegetable diet, their use of a sacerdotal language, their numerous ablutions, and by the institution of *castes*, which the Egyptians enforced with as much rigidness as the Hindoos do now. Among them no mechanic or artificer could exercise any other vocation than that which his parents had followed before him;‖ and this system gave rise to the same exclusiveness in their domestic arrangements which is so remarkable among the modern Hindoos, who will not permit their viands or their vessels to be touched by a stranger; for Herodotus observes that the Egyptians would not use a knife belonging to a Greek, "nor will they even eat of the flesh of such beasts as by their law are pure, if it has been cut with a Grecian knife."¶

Similar analogies are discernible in the architecture of the two nations, whether it relates to their monolithic temples, or their subterranean sanctuaries, or the statuary and minor decorations of their stupendous edifices. Even the obelisk is seen in the excavated temple of Kylas, in India; and the antique pagodas of Tanjore and Chalambroom, are but slight modifications of the Egyptian pyramid.**
Dr. Russell mentions the interesting fact, that "the Sepoys who joined the British army in Egypt

---

* Lib. of Entertaining Knowl. Art. Hindoos, p. 103.
† BOOTH's Diodorus, B. I, chap. 2.   ‡ DUBOIS. On the People of India, p. 54.
§ Library of Entertaining Knowl. Art. Hindoos, I, p. 167.   ‖ BOOTH's Diodorus, B. I, chap. 6.
¶ EUTERPE, cap. XLI.—This fact is also recorded in Genesis, wherein it is stated that "the Egyptians might not eat bread with the Hebrews; for that is an abomination unto the Egyptians." Chap. xliii, v. 39.
** MAURICE, Indian Antiq. vols. 2 and 3, *passim.*—Sir William Jones derives the name of the river of Egypt from the Sanscrit word *nila*, blue; and the Indus is called *Nilab* in the early part of its course from the blue color of its waters.

VARIETIES OF THE HUMAN SPECIES.

under Lord Hutchinson, imagined that they found their own temples in the ruins of Dendera, and were greatly exasperated at the natives for their neglect of the ancient deities whose images are still preserved; and they proceeded to perform their devotions with all the ceremonies practised in their own land."*

8. THE MONGOL-TARTAR FAMILY.

This vast family, which is called by the various names of Tartar, Mongol and Scythian, now occupies nearly half of Asia and part of Europe, and is composed of several branches speaking different languages, yet possessing a general resemblance in their manners and personal appearance. In order to avoid repetition we shall proceed at once to give some account of these several divisions.†

1. *The Finnish Branch*, or *Tchudes*. Of these the *Finns* inhabit the north of Europe between the 60th and 65th degree of north latitude. Though a colony from Asia, they have for many ages occupied their present seats, and are now subject to Sweden. They are of middling stature, with broad faces, dark eyes and sallow complexion. They have schools and academies, are slow but shrewd, and have made considerable progress in the arts and sciences.

The *Ingrians* resemble the Finns in exterior, but they are stupid, suspicious and thievish, whence their poverty and vagabond habits.

The *Cheremish* inhabit the province of Kasan. They were originally a pastoral and wandering tribe, and even now never dwell in towns; but they have assumed agricultural habits, though without industry or enterprise.

The *Mordvines* are settled on the rivers Oka and Volga in the government of Kasan. They are of a brown complexion, with harsh hair, and lean face, of inactive habits yet honest and hospitable.

The *Votiaks*, who also inhabit the province of Kasan, are of meagre person and middling stature, and resemble the Finns more than any nation that derives its origin from them.

The *Vogouls*, who dwell in the forests north of Mount Ural, are of a gay disposition, honest, shrewd, and laborious, yet fickle and slovenly to excess. They are a pastoral tribe, and the northern horde domesticates the reindeer. Other communities of the Finnish stock inhabit the Russian province of Permia, where they are called Permians.

---

* Anc. and Mod. Egypt, Introd. p. 20.—See also London Quart. Rev. XVI, p. 18. *Am. ed.*

† The materials of this chapter are derived almost exclusively from Tooke's Russia, *passim*, and ABUL GHAZE, History of the Tartars.—In distributing the Mongol-Tartar family into branches, I have been chiefly governed by the difference in language, and have followed the first named author.

2. The *Mongols proper* embrace several subordinate divisions, of which the *Calmucks*, who are the most prominent, occupy the western section of the great Mongol region. "They are characterised by obliquity of the eyes, which are depressed towards the nose, and by the rounded internal angle of the eyelids; by their black and scarcely curved eyebrows; by the nose, which is altogether small and flat, being particularly broad towards the forehead; by high cheek-bones, and round head and face. A black-brown iris, large and thick lips, short chin, white teeth, remaining firm and sound even in advanced age, and large ears standing off from the head, are universal. They are of middling size, and we see very few tall people amongst them: the women are particularly small, and very delicately formed."* They have a good understanding and quick comprehension; are lively and tractable, yet extremely improvident, and thievish, but not disposed to cruelty even in their predatory excursions. They are divided into four principal tribes, the Koschots, Derbets, Soongars and Torgots, which for a long time constituted an independent and powerful nation; but their hordes, which are now subject to Russia, at present inhabit the deserts between the rivers Don and Volga, and the Ural river from Igris to the Caspian sea. They are part idolaters, part Christians, and their religious rites are characterised by superstition and inconstancy.

The Burats. In the middle of the past century the Burats inhabited the government of Irkutsk, almost from the Yenisei, along the Mongolian and Chinese borders, to the Angara and Tunguska, and thence to the lake Baikal, which latter place appears to have been their primitive home. In personal appearance the Burats much resemble the Kalmucks, yet they are less inclined to corpulency. "Their flesh seems sodden, and their countenance is pale and yellow. Their bodies have very little solidity and strength. A Russian of the same size weighs much more; and either in play or earnest, overcomes several Burats with ease."† They are indolent, dishonest, and spiritless, and have scarcely any possessions but their flocks. Allied to the Burats are the *Kalkas*, who inhabit the country between Siberia and the great desert of Cobi; a superstitious and uncivilised people, who are said to present, in their domestic customs, a humiliating picture of human degradation.

3. *The Tartar Branch.* The Tartar hordes were originally derived from Great Tartary, in other words from the vast territory between Siberia and the mountains of India, from the river Oural to Mongolia, one part of which is now comprehended in Soongaria. Yet at this time they have ceased to maintain their

---

* PALLAS, in Lawrence's Lectures, p. 556. † TOOKE, Russia, IV, p. 132.

sovereignty in this region excepting in Bokhara and some other eastern provinces, at the same time that they have established themselves in countries yet further east, and possess a corner of Europe.

The *Tartars* of *Kasan* and *Orenburg* have acquired much of the Russian mien and exterior. They are thin in person, have a fresh complexion, with small eyes and nose, and light hair. They are well made, have a sprightly, agreeable address, and are said to excel in the mechanic arts.

The *Touralinzes* differ from the former in their large heads, and robust forms inclined to obesity, yet they speak the Tartar language.

The *Nogay Tartars* occupy Little Tartary, embracing the provinces of Krimea, Kuban and part of Circassia, between Russia and the Black Sea. They have much the exterior of the proper Mongols, as seen in their small eyes, their large ears and their clumsy persons; and the resemblance is further sustained by their rude and deceitful manner, and their proneness to rapine. They constitute many hordes, which are for the most part nomadic.

During the expeditions of the Tartars to the west of Asia, the *Usbecks* fixed themselves in the province of Bokhara, on the frontier of Persia, where, more provident than the other hordes, they formed a permanent settlement, changing their pastoral and nomadic life for that of agriculture, and their movable tents into settled habitations.* Their language is one of the sweetest dialects of the Tartar language; and the people of Bokhara are themselves among the handsomest of this family, owing to their proximity to Persia, and their intermarriages with the native inhabitants, and with captives from Georgia and Circassia. It is even asserted that no less than three-fourths of the Bokharians are of slave extraction, and that their features no longer identify them with the Tartar race.†

The *Baschkirs* dwell on the rivers Oural, Volga and Kama. They have the large ears and small eyes of the Mongols, and their hair is often red or chestnut color. Among them are individuals of the most repulsive physiognomy, while the manners of the horde are gross and brutal in the extreme. "They have natural good sense, but not the least inclination to cultivate their intellectual faculties: they are courageous, suspicious, obstinate, severe and consequently dangerous. If they were not well looked after, they would none of them follow any other trade than that of pilfering and plunder."‡

The *Barabainzes* rove over the deserts between the Ob and the Irtisch, in

---

* TOOKE, Russia, II, p. 130.   † BARNES, Trav. in Bokhara, II, p. 103. *Am. ed.*
‡ TOOKE, Russia, II, p. 182.

Siberia. Their features partake most of the Kalmouk character, although their language is a Tartar dialect. They have few wants, are dull, indifferent, inoffensive and honest. Unlike the neighboring hordes, they were never known to combine for predatory purposes.

The *Kirgusians*, although their language is Tartar, have the strong Mongol features, with a sharp and fierce look, indicative of their real character. They are proverbially fickle, undertaking the rashest and most contradictory measures, one moment revolting, the next returning to obedience. In spite of treaties and largesses, they cannot forego their characteristic love of plunder on every occasion that offers; and after having oppressed all the barbarous nations around them, they have in turn become the tributary vassals of Russia.*

Beside the Mongul and Tartar hordes already enumerated, there are many others that are so evidently a mixture of both, that they cannot justly be classed with either. Such are the *Tchoulmins*, between the upper parts of the Ob and Yenisei; a people, fickle and ambulatory in their habits, yet docile and readily instructed.

The *Yakuts*, persecuted by the Burats, fled to the north from the Sayan mountains, and now dwell on the shores of the Lena, in the government of Irkutsk. It is rare to see either short or tall persons among them, and in feature, as in language, they are both Mongols and Tartars. They are slow, kind and honest, and derive their chief subsistence from their herds. The Yakuts have been placed by some writers as a horde of the Polar race.

To the north of China, in the province of Kin, live the *Maudshurs*, one of the most brave and politic of the Tartar nations. Although they do not speak the Tartar language, they are in all other respects, in manners, customs and personal appearance, a cognate branch of that people. They invaded China in the 17th century, effected a complete conquest and placed on the throne a king of their own nation. They have, however, rather adopted than subverted the Chinese government and institutions, and the two nations appear to be now blended in singular harmony.

To the north and east the Mongol-Tartars gradually mingle with the tribes of the Polar race, until their characters become blended in the Kamstchatkans, the Tungusians, and the inhabitants of the isle of Jezo.

We may here add a few words respecting the HUNS. These people were genuine Mongol-Tartars, whose original seats were west and north of China; and

---

* TOOKE, Russia, II, p. 244, 254.

it would appear that the great Chinese wall, which was erected three centuries before Christ, was designed to prevent the inroads of the Huns. Their migrations, like those of the other hordes of their race, were unlimited, and they at length appeared in two divisions on the skirts of Europe, one near the Caspian sea, the other on the Volga. These at length invaded Europe itself, and drove the Goths, A. D. 375, beyond the Danube into the Roman territory. They then took possession of all the country between the Danube and the Tanais, and established their empire in Pannonia. They repeatedly ravaged Greece and Asia Minor, until at length their ferocity, and habitual predatory inroads on the neighboring provinces, led the princes of eastern Europe to combine for their destruction, which was effected in the eighth century, when they were all destroyed or driven out of the country; for the present Hungarians are not the descendants of the Huns, but of the Goths who succeeded them in the possession of the country.

The preceding details illustrate the fact, that no absolute line of demarcation, geographical or physical, can be drawn between the several branches of the Mongul family. However they differ in language, and occasionally in exterior, and whatever may have been their original characteristics, they are now so blended that every horde possesses some of the lineaments of all the others.

The name *Tartar* was originally confined to a single horde, being derived from a distinguished khan or chief; and in progress of time this designation embraced all the tribes from the Oxus to the country of the Mongols, between whom and Europe the Tartars were interposed as a sort of barrier. The Mongols themselves occupied all the territory east of the Tartars as far as China, and to the north of that kingdom. Genghiz Khan, though a Mongol, began his career at the head of a Tartar horde, but his singular success soon combined both nations under his sway, the Mongols taking precedence : whence it happens that from the time the Tartar history begins to excite attention, it ceases to be that of a particular nation. "Distributed under the banners and commanders of the Mongols, these enjoy with posterity the glory of their conquests, while the Tartars are constrained to lend their name to the devastations with which both nations everywhere marked the bloody progress of their armies."

The rapidity of the conquests of the Mongol-Tartars, and the cruelty and rapine that marked their course, are without a parallel in history; for at the death of Genghiz, nearly all Asia, excepting China and the Indo-Chinese nations, united in vassalage to form that mighty dominion since called the Mogul empire.

The latter name was more recently restricted to the Mahomedan possessions in India, of which Delhi was the capitol. The Mogul empire was invaded by the Persians in 1738, and has since declined into total insignificance; the nominal Great Mogul being at this time a mere stipendiary of the British East India Company.*

9. THE TURKISH FAMILY.

The primitive Turks appear to have been a Mongol nation; but their rapid conquest of some of the fairest portions of the Caucasian region, and their early amalgamation with the Circassians, Georgians, Greeks, and Arabs, has totally changed their physical character, and rendered them a handsome people.†

The modern Turks are of a middling stature, with an athletic form and well proportioned limbs: the head is round, the eyes dark and animated, and the whole face expressive and intelligent; while the short nose and open nostrils are indicative of Mongol extraction. In manner they are proverbially courteous and taciturn; but their true character is marked by violence of passion, cruelty and vindictiveness. Intelligent, and ready in the acquisition of every species of knowledge, they would soon assume an elevated literary rank were it not for the trammels of superstition and fatalism.

According to Ritter, the Turks, under the name of Hiong-nu, had their primitive seats in the north of China, where they formed two kingdoms in the first century, disappeared from history in the fourth, recovered their power in the fifth, and were subsequently merged (together with the Tartars, who, as we have seen, were also Mongols,) in the armies of Genghiz Khan. The Turks, at a later period, separated from their Mongol masters, and established themselves in Persia, whence passing into Asia Minor they made repeated attacks on the Greek empire, which they finally subverted in the middle of the fifteenth century. The powerful

---

* In India there remain some traces of the ancient Mongols, who have probably occupied their present seats from immemorial time. Such are the Bheels and Gooand tribes of Guzerat and other parts of western India, who appear to be branches of the same great family " which pervades all the mountainous centre of India, the Gaëls of the east, who have probably at some period been driven from all these wildernesses by the tribes possessing the Brahminical faith." In the same group may be placed the Puharrees, also of central India, the Cohatars in the southern peninsula, and the Jauts in the west. The latter retain the warlike and pastoral habits of the ancient Scythians. HEBER, Narrative, &c., I, p. 194. *Am. ed.*

† This fact has led some writers to class the Turks with the Caucasians, and to doubt the Mongol origin of the parent stock; an objection that may be met by a fact from Professor Pallas, who says that even the mixed blood of the repulsive-looking Calmucks and Russians produces beautiful children.

and jealous Mongols followed on the footsteps of their former allies, and entering Asia Minor, defeated them in a pitched battle. But the Turks recovered themselves after a desperate struggle, drove the Mongols out of Asiatic Turkey, regained the ascendancy, and have kept it from that time to the present.

We now find them in possession of Asia Minor, Syria, European Turkey, Egypt, and various strong holds on the Barbary coast.

Osman, the Turkish chief who vanquished the Mongols in Asia Minor, transmitted his name to his nation, whence they call themselves *Osmanlies*, which in Europe has been perverted to Ottomans.*

10. THE CHINESE FAMILY.

These people are rather below the middle stature, stout limbed and inclined to flesh. The head is large, rounded and somewhat conical, owing to a high, retreating forehead. The face is flat, and the cheek bones expanded; the eye is small, half closed, and drawn obliquely upwards towards the temple, at the same time that the upper lid is a little projecting beyond the lower: the eyebrows are black, highly arched and linear: the nose is small, flattened towards the nostril, broad at its root, and separated from the forehead by a strongly marked depression. The mouth is large, and the lips rather fleshy. They have uniformly black hair; and the complexion of young persons of the higher classes is fresh and fair, but that of the multitude is pallid or sallow, and has been compared to a dried leaf.

"People in Europe have been strangely misled in their notions of Chinese physiognomy and appearance, by the figures represented on those specimens of manufacture which proceed from Canton, and which are commonly in a style of broad caricature. A Chinese of Peking might as well form an idea of us from some of the performances of Cruikshank. The consequence is, that a character of silly levity and farce has been associated, in the minds of many persons, with the most steady, considerate and matter of fact people in the world. Their features have, perhaps, less of the harsh angularity of the Tartar countenance in the south than in Peking. Among those who are not exposed to the climate, the complexion is fully as fair as that of the Spaniards and Portuguese. Up to the age of twenty they are often very good looking; soon after that period the prominent cheek bones generally give a harshness to the features, as the roundness

---

* For a brief and graphic view of the connections between the Turks, Tartars and Mongols, in relation to language, history and physical character, see WISEMAN's Lectures, p. 110.

of youth wears off."* The old people of both sexes are for the most part much wrinkled and very ugly; and the women are proverbially celebrated for the artificial smallness and deformity of their feet.

The Chinese skull, so far as I can judge from the specimens that have come under my inspection, is oblong-oval in its general form; the os frontis is narrow in proportion to the width of the face, and the vertex is prominent: the occiput is moderately flattened; the face projects more than in the Caucasian, giving an angle of about seventy-five degrees; the teeth are nearly vertical, in which respect they differ essentially from those of the Malay; and the orbits are of moderate dimensions, and rounded.

The moral character of the Chinese is thus summed up by Dr. Morrison, whose opinion is derived from long and intimate acquaintance with these people. "The good traits of the Chinese character, amongst themselves, are mildness and urbanity; a wish to show that their conduct is reasonable, and, generally, a willingness to yield to what appears so: docility, industry, subordination of juniors; respect for the aged and for parents; acknowledging the claims of poor kindred. These are virtues of public opinion, which, of course, are in particular cases often more show than reality; for, on the other hand, the Chinese are specious, but insincere; jealous, envious, and distrustful to a high degree. Conscience has few checks but the laws of the land; and a little frigid ratiocination on the fitness of things, which is not generally found effectual to restrain, when the selfish and vicious propensities of our nature may be indulged with present impunity. The Chinese are generally selfish, cold-blooded and inhumane."† "He might with great propriety have added," says Mr. Ellis, "that in the punishment of criminals, in the infliction of torture, they are barbarously cruel; that human suffering, or human life, are but rarely regarded by those in authority, when the infliction of the one, or the destruction of the other, can be made subservient to the acquisition of wealth or power."

The intellectual character of the Chinese is deserving of especial attention, although in letters, in science and in art, they are the same now what they were many centuries ago. They have their national music and their national poetry, but of sculpture, painting and architecture, they have no just conceptions, and their national pride prevents their adopting the arts of other countries. Their faculty of imitation is a proverb; and their mechanical ingenuity is universally known. "That nation cannot be viewed with indifference which possessed an

---

* Davies, Descrip. of the Emp. of China, I, p. 253. † Morrison, in Gutzlaff, Introd. p. 28.

organised government, an army, a written language, historians and other literati, in a period so remote as to be coeval with the immediate successors of the inspired historian of Creation, and the lawgiver of the ancient people of God."* They have a copious literature, both ancient and modern; they have possessed the art of printing for eight hundred years; and their written language, with the same characters that they use at the present day, is of extreme antiquity, not less, according to Remusat and others, than four thousand years. A solitary fact will prove this position. Vessels of porcelain, of Chinese manufacture, have of late been repeatedly found in the catacombs of Thebes, in Egypt. Some of these are as old as the Pharaonic period; or, in other words, they must have been made at least fifteen hundred years before the Christian era. The inscriptions on these vessels have been read with ease by Chinese scholars, and in three instances record the following legend :—The flower opens, and lo! another year.†

The civilisation of China is nearly as old as that of Egypt, and has probably remained stationary for thirty centuries; and, although it is based on a heartless religion, no doubt embraces as many both of the comforts and luxuries of life as the social institutions of Europe; at the same time that similar wants and indulgences, in these widely separated communities, are often gratified by very different yet equally adequate means. European civilisation has borrowed largely from China, the Chinese nothing from Europe. When the king of France introduced the luxury of silk stockings, says Mr. Barrow, the peasantry of the middle provinces of China were clothed in silks from head to foot; and when the nobility of England were sleeping on straw, a peasant of China had his mat and his pillow, and the man in office enjoyed his silken mattress.

These were equally the luxuries of their ancestors, and they have not chosen to improve upon them. To prevent innovations, the laws prescribe for every thing, and a man must dress, and build, and regulate all his actions according to a certain form. Hence it has been observed that unmovableness is the characteristic of the nation; every implement retains its original shape; every invention has stopped at the first step. The plough is still drawn by men; the written characters of their monosyllabic language stand for ideas, not for simple sounds; and the laborious task of merely learning to read, occupies the time that might be employed in the acquisition of many branches of useful knowledge.‡

The religions of China are three—that of Confucius, Laou-tse and Budha.

---

* ELLIS, Introd. to Gutzlaff's Voy. p. 13. † WILKINSON, Anc. Egypt, III, p. 108.
‡ Outlines of Univ. Hist. p. 17.

It appears that the great philosopher of China is actually worshipped by his countrymen, that no less than fifteen hundred and sixty temples are dedicated to him, and that upwards of sixty thousand animals of different kinds are sacrificed to his manes every year.* The Laou-tse doctrine appears to be a mere tissue of moral subtleties; while the Budhism of the Chinese is essentially the same with that of the neighboring nations—a gross and enervating idolatry.

The Japanese bear a striking resemblance to the people of China, whose features the former possess in an exaggerated degree. According to Thunberg "the eyelids form in the great angle of the eye a deep furrow, which makes the Japanese look as if they were sharpsighted, and discriminates them from the other nations."† In general they are of short stature, with heavy limbs, large heads, and sunken eyes. Like the Chinese they are laborious artificers, but less ingenious than that nation, nor have they equalled them in the art of navigation. They have two religious sects, but the dominant creed is that of Budha, mixed up with some peculiar superstitions. Their vernacular tongue is said to have no resemblance to that of the Chinese, but they derive their classical or learned language from that people. Their alphabet, instead of whole words, designs single letters only.‡

The peninsula of Corea is inhabited by a branch of this family, rougher, however, in their exterior, and less advanced in the arts than the Chinese proper, whose vassals they are. Their vernacular language and alphabet are altogether peculiar, but they are required to use the Chinese characters.

11. THE INDO-CHINESE FAMILY.

The Indo-Chinese nations have been so called more on account of their geographical position between Hindostan and China than for their resemblance to the Hindoos, from whom they differ widely. The Indo-Chinese are real Mongolians, yet their proximity to India has undoubtedly given rise to some intermixture with the Hindoos, and in some instances the partial adoption of the letters and religion of that people.

The nations embraced in this family are those of Ava, Pegu, Aracan, Siam, Cochin-China, Cambodia, Tsiompa, Laos, and Tonquin.

The states of Ava, Pegu and Aracan, constitute the Burmese empire. The

---

* MEDHURST, China, p. 193.   † MALTE-BRUN, II, p. 537
‡ TUCKEY, Mar. Geog. III, p. 300.

complexion of the inhabitants varies from brown to nearly black. Their figure is short and robust, and in physiognomy they resemble the Chinese, yet are much uglier. They profess the religion of Budha. Their literature is, for the most part, metrical, consisting of songs and romances; a fact which corresponds with their moral character, for they are represented to be a lively, inquisitive race, volatile, impatient and irascible. They are greatly inferior to the Chinese, and have made but little progress in the useful arts.* Besides the Burmese, the kingdom of Ava contains, especially towards the north, many wild tribes of people who have no seeming affinity with the dominant population, and who are said not even to be Budhists, and to speak dialects and perhaps languages of their own.†

The *Aracanese* are much the most uncultivated and barbarous people of this family. They are accustomed to flatten the heads of their children by means of a plate of lead, applied soon after birth, and they slit and distend their ears to a frightful degree.

The Siamese present strong analogies to the Burmans. The following graphic description, from the pen of my friend Dr. Ruschenberger, will convey an accurate idea of these people. "Their average height, according to the measure of Mr. Crawford, is five feet two inches, which I suspect to be near the truth, from the few to whom I have applied the rule. The lower limbs are stout and well formed; the body is long, and hence the figure is not graceful. The shoulders are broad, and the muscles of the chest are well developed. The neck is short and the head is in fair proportion. The hands are large, and the complexion of a dark olive, but not jetty. Among females of the higher classes, who pass their time mostly within the harem of their lords, the skin is of a very much lighter hue; in some instances it might be described as a very dark brunette. The forehead is narrow at the superior part, the face, between the cheek bones broad, and the chin is, again, narrow, so that the whole contour is rather lozenge-shaped than oval. The eyes are remarkable, for the upper lid being extended below the under one, at the corner next to the nose, but it is not elongated like that organ in the Chinese or Tartar races. The eyes are dark, or black, and the white is dirty, or of a yellowish tint. The nostrils are broad, but the nose is not flattened, like that of the African. The mouth is not well formed, the lips projecting slightly; and it is always disfigured, according to our notions of beauty, by the universal and disgusting habit of chewing arecanut. The hair is jet black, renitent, and coarse, almost bristly, and is worn in a tuft on the top of the head,

---

* CRAWFORD, Ava, &c., p. 372.   † Ibid, p. 470.

about four inches in diameter, the rest being shaved, or clipped very close. A few scattering hairs, which scarcely merit the name of beard, grow upon the chin and upper lip, and these they customarily pluck out.

"The occipital portion of the head is nearly vertical, and, compared with the anterior and sincipital divisions, very small; and I remarked, what I have not seen in any other than in some ancient Peruvian skulls from Pachacamac, that the lateral halves of the head are not symmetrical. In the region of firmness, the skull is very prominent; this is remarkably true of the talapoins."* Mr. Finlayson's observations are to the same purpose. "The head," says he, "is peculiar: the diameter from the front backwards is uncommonly short, and hence the general form is somewhat cylindrical. The occipital foramen in a great number of instances is placed so far back, that from the crown to the nape of the neck is nearly a straight line."†

The moral character of the Siamese appears to be at a very low ebb. The intelligent voyager first quoted, describes them as suspicious, vacillating and cruel. Cringing and servile to their superiors in the extreme, they are arrogant and tyrannical in regard to those who are below them in rank.‡ Their virtues and their vices are venal; and the services of the judge and the assassin have each their price. "I regret," says Mr. Gutzlaff, "not to have found one honest man: sordid oppression, priestcraft, allied with wretchedness and filth, are everywhere to be met with." They are remarkable, nevertheless, for filial respect, and regard for their rulers.

The inhabitants of *Cochin-China*, or *Annam*, are smaller in stature than the Siamese, and they are also less clumsily formed. The general form of the face is round, so that the two diameters are nearly equal. The forehead is short and broad, but the occipital portion of the head is more elongated than in the people of Siam. The chin is large and broad; the beard grisly and thin, the hair copious, coarse and black; the nose small, but well formed, and the lips moderately thick. Obesity is rare. The color of the Cochin-Chinese is usually as fair as that of the inhabitants of southern Europe, yet the dark Malay hue is not unfrequently met with. They are, nevertheless, a coarse featured people, and render themselves repulsive by the constant use of areca and betel, which reddens the lips and blackens the teeth.

---

* Voy. Round the World, p. 299.—In the same work, p. 300, the reader will find some detailed measurements of Siamese heads.
† Siam and Cochin-China, p. 229.   ‡ Voy. p. 301.

They are said to be the gayest of the oriental nations; good-natured and polite, but extravagantly fond of etiquette. So versatile are their feelings and actions, that they have been compared to the monkey race, whose attention is perpetually changing from one object to another. Hence while they are more active and warlike than the Chinese, they want the industry and perseverance of that nation.* Their language is a dialect of the Chinese, though considerably altered, and their written characters are the same.

The *Laos*, or Chaus, to the north of Siam, are wretchedly poor, dirty in their habits, sportful in their temper, careless in their actions, and great lovers of music and dancing. Their language is soft and melodious, and very similar to that of the Siamese.

The *Kamehs*, or inhabitants of Cambogia, to the southeast of Siam, are of higher antiquity and more literary character than any of the surrounding states. They must be a very imaginative people; for Mr. Gutzlaff states that nearly all their books, with the exception of their national laws and history, are in poetry. They are, nevertheless, a coarse people, cringing or insolent according to circumstances.†

The natives of the Nicobar islands appear to be of Indo-Chinese extraction. Their color is a deep copper, and they have thick lips and wide mouths. It is asserted that they compress the heads of newly born infants in such manner as to flatten the occiput and cause the teeth to project outwards. They live in a very uncivilised state, compel their women to cultivate the ground, and have hitherto resisted all measures for the melioration of their condition.‡

12. THE POLAR FAMILY.

This singular race is exclusively seen on the northern skirts of the continents of Europe, Asia, and America. They are of short stature, of clumsy proportions, with large heads and short necks. They have the flat faces and small noses of the Mongol-Tartars, with some obliquity in the position of the eyes. Their color is brown, lighter or darker, but often disguised by accumulated filth.

The concurrent testimony of all voyagers shows these people to be, both in

---

* FINLAYSON, Siam and Cochin-China, p. 299.—RUSCHENBERGER, Voy. p. 354.—BARROW, Cochin-China, p. 308.
† GUTZLAFF, Three Voy. to the Coasts of China, p. 47.
‡ TUCKEY, Mar. Geog. III, p. 328.

THE POLAR FAMILY.

appearance and manner, among the most repulsive of the human species: yet they possess considerable differences, which will be best considered geographically.

At the northwestern extremity of Europe are the *Laplanders*, who, by pretty general consent, have been enumerated with the Polar family, although their dialect is more closely allied to the Finnish than to any other. They have the flat face and diminutive stature of the Samoyedes; but their hair is brown, their cheeks hollow and their eyes gray. Their complexion varies from yellowish to dark brown. "Their manner of life renders them hardy, agile and supple, but at the same time much inclined to laziness. They have plain common sense, are peaceable, and obedient to their superiors."* In their dealings, however, they are described as mistrustful and given to cheating.

The *Ostiaks* present a remarkable example of a nation composed of three great communities, each of which differs in customs and language from the others: of these the northern horde is of Samoyede extraction, while the southern is allied to the Finns. They are of the middle stature, with a pale, yellowish complexion, harsh, dark hair, together with the ordinary exterior of the Polar race. They are of the phlegmatic temperament, timid, indolent and uncleanly in their habits, yet of docile disposition, and possessed of much natural kindness. In common with most of the cognate tribes, they have reduced their women to the condition of slaves.†

The *Samoyedes* call themselves *Chosova*, which merely means *men*. They inhabit the frozen margin of Asia from the 65th degree of north latitude to the sea shore, and extend also into Europe. These people are seldom more than five feet high. "They seem all of a heap; have short legs, small neck, a large head, flat nose and face, with the lower part of the face projecting outwards: they have large mouths and ears, little black eyes, but wide eyelids, small lips and little feet."‡ The women reach maturity early, and are often mothers at twelve years of age. They are more savage than the Ostiaks, and extremely indifferent on all those subjects that excite the feelings of other people.

The *Tungusians* rove the deserts which extend from the Yenisei eastward to the ocean. Their features resemble those of the other families of this race; but their complexion is fresh, and their women are said to be of agreeable appearance and manner. The men have a hoarse voice, and possess sight and hearing in perfection, with a singular obtuseness of the organs of touch and smell.§ They

---

* Tooke, Russia, I, p. 5.   † Tooke, Russia, &c., I, p. 178.—Pallas, Voy. IV, p. 52.
‡ Ibid. III, p. 12.   § Ibid. III, p. 77.

are frank and sanguine in their manner, averse to theft, fraud and falsehood, improvident and insensible in their social relations.

The *Yakaguires* traverse the icy region between the Yakouts and the Frozen ocean, and avoid all other people.

The *Kamschatkans* have the physical traits of the adjacent Polar tribes, excepting that their women are handsomer; but their moral and intellectual character is different. They are said to possess a strong memory, and a remarkable tact at mimicry; despise labor, which they resume only from the necessities of the passing hour, and are cowardly in the extreme. It must be admitted that the southern Kamschatkans, in common with the southern tribes of Tungusians and Ostiaks, have so long mixed with the proximate Mongol-Tartar hordes, that it is in some measure arbitrary to class them definitively with either family, for their characters are obviously derived from both.

The *Koriaks*, who inhabit north of the Kamschatkans, are dull of comprehension, obstinate and revengeful, yet industrious and susceptible of friendship. Their language, though in many respects peculiar, has a near affinity to that of their neighbors the Tchukchi.

The *Tchukches* resemble the Koriaks in person, manners and language, and form the intermediate link between the latter nation and the Polar tribes of America. They are barbarous and cruel, and repugnant to every form of civilisation. "In short," says Mr. Tooke, "they are naturally as wicked and as dangerous as the Tungusians are mild and gentle."* In person they are small and spare, yet have the round, flat face of the other people of this race. Their chief riches consist in herds of reindeer, of which animals it is not uncommon for individuals to possess ten thousand.†

The *Kurilians* inhabit the Kurile islands, which stretch from the peninsula of Kamschatka almost to Japan. These people have good complexions and a copious beard, but in other particulars resemble the adjacent hordes.

Crossing to the American continent we find the Polar race composed of the Eskimaux and Greenlanders, who are both generally included in the former name, an Algonkin word signifying "eaters of raw flesh;" but their own national designation is *Keralit*. They are the sole inhabitants of the shores of all the seas, bays, inlets and islands of America, north of the 60th degree of north latitude, from the eastern coast of Greenland in longitude 21°, to the straits of Behring in longitude 127° west. On the Atlantic they also skirt the coast of Labrador, and are even

---

* Russia, III, p. 177.   † Ibid. III, p. 187.

seen as far south as the Straits of Belle-Isle and the Gulf of St. Lawrence. In the west they extend along the shores of the Pacific Ocean southwards as far as Mount St. Elias and Behring's Bay, embracing the Konaji and some other tribes, including the islanders of Kadjack.* They seldom wander more than a hundred miles from the sea, and subsist in a great measure by fishing.

The western Eskimaux, or those living to the west of Mackenzie's river, are said by Captain Beechey to be taller in stature than the eastern tribes, their average height being about five feet seven and a half inches. They are also better looking, more industrious, and more irascible and warlike. Their countenances, however, are represented as much deformed by habitual sore eyes, and teeth worn down by the constant mastication of hard substances; and above all by the barbarous custom of slitting the lower lip, and wearing in the aperture an elliptical piece of wood or bone.†

Captain Lyon, in his account of the Eskimaux seen by him at Igloolik and Winter Island, on the northeast coast, has given a detailed and graphic description of the American division of this race. "They may," says he, "more properly be termed a small than even a middle sized race: for though in some few instances, and in particular families, the men are tall and stout, yet the greater portion are beneath the standard of what, in Europe, would be called small men. The tallest I saw was five feet nine inches and three quarters in height; the shortest only four feet ten inches; and the highest woman was five feet six inches, while the smallest was four feet eight inches only. Even in the young and strong men the muscles are not clearly defined, but are smoothly covered, as in the limbs of women. However prominent and well shaped the chest may be, the neck is small, weak, and often shrivelled. They all stand well on their feet, walking erect and freely, with the toes rather turned inwards, and the legs slightly bowed. The neck and shoulders of the young women are generally in good, though large proportion; and the arm and wrists are sometimes handsome. The feet of both sexes are small and neat, well joined at the ankle, and free from blemishes. The complexion of the Eskimaux, when clearly shown by a previous washing, is not darker than that of a Portuguese; and such parts of the body as are constantly covered, do not fall short in fairness to the generality of the natives of the Mediterranean. A very fine healthy blush tinges the cheek of females and young children, but the men are more inclined to a sallow complexion.

"The inner corner of the eye points downwards, like that of a Chinese; and

---

* GALLATIN, in Archæolog. Amer. II, p. 10.   † BEECHEY, Voy. II, p. 570.

the caruncula lachrymalis, which in Europeans is exposed, is covered by a membrane which passes over it vertically. The eyes are small and black, expressive and sparkling when animated. Another peculiarity is the prominence of the cheek bones; and it is in consequence of this form that the noses of such as are full-faced are literally buried between the projections; and one of our chief belles was so remarkable in this way that a ruler, when placed from cheek to cheek, would not touch the nose. The mouth is generally kept open with a kind of idiotic expression, so that the teeth of either jaw are generally shown. The mouths are large. The teeth are strong, and deeply fixed in the gums; they are formed like rounded ivory pegs, and are flat on the upper end as if filed down. The chin is small and peaked; and what we call a double chin is rare."*

The Eskimaux of Prince Regent's Bay,† to the northeast of Baffin's Bay, and about 76° north, are of a dirty copper color, and very corpulent; while those on the west side of Baffin's Bay have clear complexions, which only become darker by old age and exposure.‡

On the icy shores of the great island of Greenland, are seen the easternmost tribes of this singular race. Their features do dot materially differ from those already described, but their complexion is decidedly darker, varying from brown to olive, while at Oppernivick they are as dark as mulattoes. It is needless to add that many are much lighter, and others quite fair. In the moral scale they rank extremely low. Crantz, the missionary, who lived many years among them, reluctantly declares that "it is no injustice to allow them no true virtue, and only the absence of certain vices."§ They are crafty, sensual, ungrateful, obstinate and unfeeling, and much of their affection for their children may be traced to purely selfish motives. They devour the most disgusting aliments uncooked and uncleaned, and seem to have no ideas beyond providing for the present moment.

With respect to the moral and intellectual character of this widely distributed family, little need be added to what has already been said. Their mental faculties, from infancy to old age, present a continued childhood: they reach a certain limit and expand no farther. What Crantz says of the Greenlanders may be applied to other tribes, viz: that they possess simplicity without silliness, and good sense without the art of reasoning.‖ They are fickle and facetious, and their connubial

---

* Private Journal, *Boston ed.* p. 222.
† Called also the *Arctic Highlands*, Ross. Voy. 1819, p. 115.
‡ PARRY, First Voy. p. 282.   § CRANTZ, Hist. of Greenland, I, p. 188.
‖ Hist. of Greenland, I, p. 135.

infidelity is a proverb among voyagers.* In gluttony, selfishness and ingratitude, they are perhaps unequalled by any other nation of people; and they are habitually unfeeling without designing to be cruel.† On the other hand they are mild in their tempers, and tractable in their manners; but their chief redeeming virtue is their fondness for their children, which knows no bounds. They are devoid of warlike propensities; and even the resistance made by the Samoïedes to the yoke of the Russians, has been two or three local and abortive attempts at insurrection. Buffon states that Gustavus Adolphus, King of Sweden, attempted to discipline a regiment of Laplanders, but they could never be brought to action.‡ Finally, though grossly puerile in their superstitions, they have no combination of sentiments that deserves the name of religion.

Most readers are aware that colonies of Scandinavians and Icelanders peopled Greenland in the middle ages. Since the fourteenth century, however, nothing has been heard of them, and they were supposed to have been blocked up and destroyed by the accumulating ice, whence the name of *Lost Greenland.* In 1829 the Danish government sent Captain Graah to explore these icy solitudes, and to ascertain at least the locality of the lost colony. This enterprising voyager discovered a community of which he gives the following account: "They have little analogy with the Eskimaux, and resemble, on the contrary, the Scandinavians of Europe. They have neither the flat heads, short broad persons nor flabby features of the Eskimaux; but are for the most part above the middle stature, having the European form of head and expression of countenance. Their persons are rather meagre, but nervous and finely formed, without any appearance of weakness, and they are more active and robust than the inhabitants of the western coast. The color of the skin of the women and children is quite clear and pure as that of Europeans, and they have often brown hair, which is never seen in the other inhabitants of Greenland."§ The moral character of these people is said to be characterised by great honesty, simplicity and truth: yet they are pagans, have their sorcerers like the Eskimaux, and speak probably a dialect of their language, for Captain Graah could not understand it. It will be readily surmised from the preceding facts, that these people constitute the real remains of the Scandinavian

---

* Parry, Second Voy. p. 529.

† They sometimes destroy children who have lost their parents, and bury alive or otherwise destroy such old persons as have by their infirmities become a burthen on the community.—*See* Crantz, *loco cital.,* and Ellis, *Voy. to Hudson's Bay,* p. 191.

‡ Sonnini's Buffon, XX, p. 67.   § Jour. Roy. Geog. Soc. of London, VII, p. 240.

colony which, to Europeans, have been lost for ages; and their long intercourse with the Greenland tribes has led them to adopt the superstitions of that people and more or less their language and mode of life.

13. THE MALAY FAMILY.

The head of the Malay is large, and the nose short, depressed, and flattened towards the nostrils: the eyes are small, black, oblique and expressive; the face is broad, compressed, and very prominent, and the mouth and lips are large. Their limbs are thick and they are below the middle stature. The color of the Malay is a decided brown, often with a bronze tint. Their hair is long, black and lank; but they have little beard, and this they for the most part eradicate.

The skull of the Malay presents the following characters: the forehead is low, moderately prominent and arched: the occiput is much compressed, and often projecting at its upper and lateral parts: the orbits are oblique, oblong and remarkably quadrangular, the upper and lower margins being almost straight and parallel: the nasal bones are broad, and flattened, or even concave: the cheek bones are high and expanded: the jaws are greatly projected; and the upper jaw, together with the teeth, is much inclined outwards, and often nearly horizontal. The teeth are by nature remarkably fine, but are almost uniformly filed away in front to enable them to imbibe the color of the betel nut, which renders them black and unsightly.

The facial angle is less than in the Mongol and Chinese; for the average, derived from a measurement of thirteen perfect skulls in my possession, gives about seventy-three degrees.

Among a considerable number of Malays whom I have seen in this country as mariners, there has been a remarkable uniformity of appearance; as much so, indeed, as if they had belonged to the same social family. Even their complexion seems little altered by the diversified latitudes they inhabit; and Mr. Crawford has remarked that they are a very distinct people, strikingly alike among themselves, but unlike all other nations.*

The Malays are a strictly maritime nation, making considerable voyages in their light vessels, and for the most part establishing themselves on the rivers and along the sea coasts of the islands they invade. They possess an active and

---

* Indian Archipel. v. I, p. 25.—M. Lesson (Voy. du Coquille, Zool. p. 43,) supposes the Malays to be a mixed race of Indo-Caucasians and Mongols.

enterprising spirit, but in their temper are ferocious and vindictive. Caprice and treachery are among their characteristic vices; and their habitual piracies on the vessels of all nations, are often conducted under the mask of peace and friendship.

The Malays are said, by the annals of their nation, not to be natives of Malacca, as their name imports, and as strangers have generally supposed, but to have originated in the district of Menangkabao, in the island of Sumatra. They date their first migrations from the parent hive in the year 1160, first fixing themselves in the peninsula of Malacca, where they built the city of Singapore; and it was from this colony, and not from the parent stock, that the Malayan name and nation were so widely disseminated over the Archipelago.* The Malays are now proverbially scattered throughout the Indian islands, and have especially established themselves in Sumatra, Java, Borneo, Amboyna, Formosa, Celebes, the Philippines, the Moluccas, and parts of Ceylon and Madagascar.

The Malay inhabitants of Sumatra correspond, in their exterior, to the characters already given of this race, excepting that their complexion is yellower, and they are said to flatten the heads and noses of their children.† In the interior of the island live the Battas, a people of still fairer complexion, but the most habitual and remorseless cannibals on the face of the earth. According to Sir Stamford Raffles "they have a regular government and deliberative assemblies; they possess a peculiar language and written character, can generally write, and have a talent for eloquence: they acknowledge a God, are fair and honorable in their dealings, crimes amongst them are few, and their country is highly cultivated; and yet these people, so far advanced in civilisation, are cannibals upon principle and system." Nay more, they not only eat their victims, but eat them alive; in other words they do not previously put them to death; and these victims are their own people, and not unfrequently their own relations. Such is the penalty for adultery, midnight robbery, for intermarrying in the same tribe, and for treacherous attacks on a house, village or person. Prisoners taken in war are eaten at once; and the slain are devoured in like manner.‡

The inhabitants of JAVA are of a yellowish complexion, and remarkably well formed. Their wrists and ankles are very small, although they are otherwise of a robust make, and resemble the Chinese, between whom and the other Malays they are a connecting link. The Javanese are more tractable and less sanguinary

---

* CRAWFORD, Indian Archipel. II, p. 376.   † MARSDEN's Sumatra, p. 38.
‡ Life and Public Services of Sir S. Raffles, p. 425. Quoted in the Library of Entertaining Knowledge, article New Zealanders, p. 107.

than the other islanders; and in their domestic relations they approach nearer to the usages of civilised society.* The *Sunda* people, however, who inhabit the mountainous districts of the island, are in all respects a much ruder people. The *Chacrelas*, with fair complexion, white hair and feeble eyes, are obviously Albinoes, although their number was formerly very considerable.

In the great island of BORNEO the Malays have possession of the entire sea coast, and the shores of all the navigable rivers. They form, however, but a fractional part of the inhabitants of Borneo; for the mountainous region of the interior is peopled by the savage Dayacks, and Eidahans, who belong perhaps to another race; yet they are represented as being fairer than the Malays, and more sanguinary and ferocious. CELEBES has long been in possession of two Malay nations, the Bugis and Macassars, who divide the island between them: the latter are reputed for their bravery, which appears to be rather a temporary desperation than cool courage.

The Malays of the PHILIPPINE ARCHIPELAGO are said to resemble the Sumatrans and Macassars in person, as well as in language and manners. They are described by Zuniga as possessing a good stature, an olive complexion, flat noses, large eyes, and long hair. They call themselves *Tagels*, or *Tagelos*, in the island of Luzon, and *Bisayas* in the central islands. The interior and mountainous parts of the larger islands of this group, especially Luzon, Mindanao and Mindoro, are peopled by a very different race, who possess all the characters of Negroes, and are regarded as the aboriginal inhabitants.

The Malay inhabitants of the MOLUCCA ISLANDS occupy all parts of them excepting the mountainous interior, which is possessed by the Alfoers, a Negro tribe. The women of Amboyna are remarkably handsome, and have more resemblance to the natives of New Zealand than to the neighboring Malay islands.

FORMOSA, although but twenty leagues distant from the coast of China, is inhabited by Malays of rude and intractable character.

The island of Ceylon has a numerous Malay population on its coast, and they are represented as a singularly lawless and desperate people. The same remark is applicable to such of this nation as have established themselves on the eastern coasts of Madagascar.

Besides the Malay and Negro races, the Indian Archipelago is peopled by great numbers of Chinese and Arabs, among whom the latter enjoyed the almost exclusive privilege of these seas between the ninth and fourteenth centuries, since

---

* RAFFLES, Java, I, p. 57.

which period they have been superseded by the Malays. The Hindoos and Indo-Chinese have also contributed largely to people these islands.

14. THE POLYNESIAN FAMILY.

The name POLYNESIA has been given by geographers to all the islands in the Pacific Ocean from the Ladrones to Easter Island, embracing also the Pelew group, the Carolinas, the Sandwich, Friendly, Society, Navigators', Harvey's and the Marquesas islands.

The Polynesians are of the middle stature, and athletic, with small hands, heavy limbs and large feet. Their faces are round, or delicately oval, and somewhat compressed. The nose is well formed, straight or aquiline, yet sometimes spread, without, however, presenting the peculiar flatness that distinguishes the Negro.* The forehead is low, but not receding; the eyes black, bright and expressive: the lips are full, and the teeth remarkably fine. Their complexion varies from nearly white to olive, and from dark brown to nearly black; but the latter color is said to result chiefly from elaborate tattooing, and is particularly observed in persons advanced in years.† Their hair is long, black and curling, and not unfrequently more or less frizzled.

All voyagers, however, have noticed the great disparity that exists between the plebeians and the aristocratic class, as respects stature, features and complexion. The privileged order is much fairer and much taller than the other; their heads are better developed, and their profile shows more regular features, including the arched and aquiline nose. The indolent habits of this caste tend also to obesity, which often becomes extreme after middle life.‡

The eastern groups of the Polynesian islands present the most pleasing examples of this race. Thus, in the Sandwich Islands the inhabitants, who call themselves Kanakas, are the most docile and imitative, and perhaps also the most easy of instruction, of all the Polynesians.

The Archipelago, called the TONGA, or FRIENDLY ISLANDS, is composed of three groups, the Tonga, the Hapai, and the Hafaloo Islands, one hundred and fifty in number, containing a vast population of the Polynesian race. "Their features are very various, insomuch that it is scarcely possible to fix on any general likeness by means of which to characterise them, unless it be a fulness at

---

* RUSCHENBERGER, Voy. Round the World, p. 454. † PORTER, Voy. II, p. 14
‡ WILLIAMS, Missionary Enterprises in the South Sea Islands, p. 460.

the point of the nose, which is very common. But on the other hand we met with hundreds of truly European faces, and many genuine Roman noses, amongst them. Their eyes and teeth are good; but the last neither so remarkably white, nor so well set, as is often found amongst Indian nations."* The general complexion is "a cast deeper than the copper-brown," although many have a true olive tint, and others, especially among the women, are comparatively fair.

The inhabitants of Tongataboo and the adjacent islands, are warlike, vindictive and superstitious, and even indulge in occasional cannibalism, which they are said to have learned from the Fegee islanders. They maintain the institution of castes to a degree not surpassed by the Hindoos; for they extend it even to their gods, whom they divide into six different classes.†

The people of the SOCIETY ISLANDS, together with those of the groups called the Georgian, Austral, and Harvey's Islands, are generally less muscular than the Sandwich islanders, whom, in other respects, they closely resemble. They are well formed, and often beautifully proportioned, and possess an uncommon share both of activity and gracefulness. Their countenance is open, and the facial angle is often as good as in the European. The eyes are black, bright and full; the lips rather tumid, the teeth remarkably good, and the nose rectilinear or aquiline. The whole face is round or oval, "*without any resemblance to the angular form of the Tartar visage.*"‡ Their hair is long and black, generally straight, but often curly, and sometimes frizzled. "The prevailing color of the natives is an olive, a bronze or a reddish-brown—equally removed from the jet black of the African and the Asiatic, the yellow of the Malay, and the red or copper color of the aboriginal American." Yet the color of the people of some of these islands, and especially in the Harvey and Austral islands, is as fair as that of the inhabitants of some parts of southern Europe.

Forster has given a graphic description of the people of Tahiti. Their complexion is white tinctured with brownish yellow, from which there is every tint to a swarthy hue. The shape of the face is more round than oval, and the features very symmetrical and often beautiful. Their hands and fingers are delicately formed, but their feet are disproportionately large. Like the other

---

* COOK's Last Voyage, I, p. 380.

† MARRINER, Tonga Islands, p. 330.—It is worthy of remark that among the Tonga people, children acquire their rank *by inheritance from the mother's side.* MARRINER, p. 325. Such also was the custom of the Natchez of Florida.

‡ ELLIS, Polynes. Res. II, p. 17.

islanders of this race, they are fickle, indolent and sensual, yet when engaged in war they fight with great intrepidity.*

The MARQUESAS ISLANDS present a population very similar to that of the Society Isles; in youth sprightly and beautiful, somewhat darker than the Tahitians, and less inclined to flesh.

In EASTER ISLAND (which is fifteen hundred miles from the nearest inhabited islands) the natives possess a tawny skin, a slender frame, and well proportioned limbs, but with features less prepossessing than those of the islanders already noticed. Some remains of cyclopean architecture and sculpture, indicate the present population to be, in comparison, an ignorant and degenerate race.

Of all the Polynesians the NEW ZEALANDERS are the most sanguinary and intractable. Their combined treachery, cruelty and cannibalism, have made them proverbial ever since the discovery of their island by Tasman. Captain Crozet, whose crew they attempted to destroy, illustrates their character in very few words: "They treated us," says he, "with every show of friendship for thirty-three days, with the intention of eating us on the thirty-fourth." These islanders are tall, athletic, and admirably well shaped. Their complexion is varied between white, brown and black; but in the majority of the common people it is of a deep bronze color. The better classes have the olive and yellowish brown tint of the Malays, with hair long and black, and generally more or less frizzled. The New Zealanders practise the operation of tattooing with an elaborateness and perfection elsewhere unknown. It is a principal means of distinction between the chiefs and common people, and may, according to its pattern, "be regarded as the crest or coat of arms of the New Zealand aristocracy."†

The Fegee islanders vie with the New Zealanders in treachery and cannibalism. Captain Dillon gives a melancholy narrative of the murder of fourteen of his men, most of whom were subsequently baked in ovens and devoured in his presence.‡

The Tikopians are robust in form, and inoffensive and hospitable in their manners. They live almost exclusively on vegetable food, which has been suggested as the cause of their singular docility.§ They are of a bright copper color, and use the betel nut like the Malays.

All the Polynesian islanders are characterised by a volatile disposition and fugitive habits. They act from the impulse of the moment, without reflection

---

* FORSTER, Voy. Round the World, p. 229. † ELLIS, Polynes. Res. I, p. 31.
‡ Voyage to Discover the Fate of La Perouse, I, p. 19, &c. § Ibid. II, p. 135.

and almost without motive. Thus they are kind or cruel, loquacious or taciturn, active or indolent, according to the promptings of caprice or passion; and they have been truly said to possess the foibles of children, with the vices of men. The more their character has been studied, the more evident it becomes that their good qualities were greatly overrated by the first voyagers and missionaries who visited them. The correctness of these remarks is sustained by the laxity of moral feeling throughout these islands; by their absurd superstitions and human sacrifices; by their remorseless cruelty to prisoners taken in war, and their general recklessness of life; and last, not least, by the Arreois society, (now happily obsolete,) which enjoined the murder of the offspring of its members.

The Polynesians, nevertheless, are intelligent, imitative, and amenable to instruction, as is manifest in their rapid progress in elementary literature and the more useful arts: and if we except the New Zealanders, the Fegee islanders, and a few other groups, perhaps no people on the globe have been more readily amenable to the usages of civilised life, and the doctrines of Christianity. Their intellectual capacities have by some authors been considered equal in all respects to those of the Caucasian race; which, however, is by no means certain; for although they rapidly acquire ideas by means of active perceptive powers, their reflective faculties have not hitherto expanded in proportion.

In their uncivilised state they are singularly devoted to the pastimes of boxing, wrestling, archery and boat racing; but their most striking predilection is for maritime amusement and adventure. Their canoes are large, and constructed with great ingenuity, and will in many instances accommodate fifty men. In these vessels they prosecute their wars upon the neighboring islanders, and undertake considerable voyages for profit and pleasure.* Their fondness for the sea is in fact a national and dominant feature in their character, and shows itself in the eagerness with which they enter as sailors in the ships of all nations; and their ingenuity is in nothing so conspicuous as in the construction of their vessels.†

15 THE AMERICAN FAMILY.

The concurrent testimony of all travellers goes to prove that the native Americans are possessed of certain physical traits that serve to identify them in

---

* For an instructive account of the protracted and successful voyages of the Polynesians, see ELLIS, I, p. 126, and II, p. 51.—WILLIAMS' South Sea Islands, p. 422.—BEECHEY, Voy. I, p. 172.

† FORSTER, Obs. p. 457.

localities the most remote from each other; nor do they, as a general rule, assimilate less in their moral character and usages. It is not to be denied that different tribes occasionally present very dissimilar features; but these differences are more obvious in small communities than in collective nations. There are also, in their multitudinous languages, the traces of a common origin; and it may be assumed as a fact that no other race of men maintains such a striking analogy through all its subdivisions, and amidst all its variety of physical circumstances.

By what rule of Anthropology, then, are we to group the American nations into families, or, as some writers have attempted, into species? The ingenious Bory de St. Vincent has endeavored to show that the American race embraces four *species* exclusive of the Eskimaux;* but he has certainly failed to point out any differences that have a claim to specific character.

It appears to me, as heretofore indicated, that the most natural division of the American race is into two families, one of which, the Toltecan family, bears evidence of centuries of demi-civilisation, while the other, under the collective title of the American family, embraces all the barbarous nations of the new world excepting the Polar tribes or Mongol-Americans. Some writers, however, suppose even the Eskimaux to be a part of the same original stock, partly because there is some resemblance in features, partly from partial analogy of language, and partly again from a determination to merge the American in the Mongolian. It is obvious, nevertheless, that the continent of America was originally peopled, as it yet is, by a very distinct race, and that the Eskimaux arriving in small and straggling parties from Asia, necessarily adopted more or less of the language and customs of the people among whom they settled: hence the Eskimaux, and especially the Greenlanders, are to be regarded as a partially mixed race, among whom the physical character of the Mongolian predominates, while their language presents obvious analogies to that of the Chippewyans who border them to the south.† In the American family itself we observe several subordinate groups or branches which may be designated under the following heads:

---

* For example, the Mexicans and Peruvians are considered cognate with the Malays, and are by this author referred to his *Neptunian species*, (Homo neptunianus.) His *Columbian species*, (Homo columbicus,) he supposes to have had their original seats among the Alleghany mountains, and to have spread themselves from the basin of the St. Lawrence to Florida, the West Indies, Honduras, Terra Firma, and Guyana. The *American species*, (Homo americanus,) includes the tribes of the Orinoco and the Amazon, and those of Brazil, Paraguay, &c. The fourth or *Patagonian species*, includes the nations of the far south.—*L'Homme, Espèces* 8, 9, 10 *et* 11.

† Archæolog. Amer. II, p. 118.

64   VARIETIES OF THE HUMAN SPECIES.

1. The *Appalachian Branch* may include all the nations of North America excepting the Mexicans, together with the tribes north of the river of Amazons and east of the Andes. The head is rounded, the nose large, salient and aquiline; the eyes dark brown, and with little or no obliquity of position; the mouth is large and straight, the teeth nearly vertical, and the whole face triangular. The neck is long, the chest broad but rarely deep, the body and limbs muscular, and seldom disposed to obesity. In character these nations are warlike, cruel and unforgiving. They turn with aversion from the restraints of civilised life, and have made but trifling progress in mental culture or the useful arts.*

2. The *Brazilian Branch* is spread over a great part of South America east of the Andes: its geographical position may be indicated in general terms as embraced between the rivers Amazon and La Plata, and between the Andes and the Atlantic; thus including the whole of Brazil and Paraguay north of the 35th degree of south latitude. The physical traits of these people differ but little from those of the Appalachian branch; they possess, perhaps, a larger and more expanded nose, and larger mouths and lips. The eyes are small, more or less oblique and set far apart: the neck is short and thick, and the body and limbs stout and full even to clumsiness.† In character the Brazilian nations scarcely differ from the Appalachian: none of the American tribes are less susceptible of cultivation than these; and what they are taught by compulsion in the missions seldom exceeds the humblest elements of knowledge.‡

3. *The Patagonian Branch.* This group includes the nations south of the La Plata to the Straits of Magellan, and the mountain tribes of Chili. They are for the most part distinguished for their tall stature, their fine forms and their indomitable courage, of all which traits the Araucanians possess a conspicuous share.

4. *The Fuegian Branch.* These people, who inhabit the island of Terra del Fuego, are often called *Patagonians;* but this name is objectionable because it is also applied to numerous tribes of common Indians who inhabit the plains from the Rio de la Plata to the Straits of Magellan; wherefore, as a more local

---

* This division is nearly identical with the *Columbian species* (Homo columbicus) of Bory de St. Vincent.

† I derive these characters chiefly from an inspection of the beautiful plates in the folio Atlas of Spix and Martius's Travels in Brazil.

‡ This division is almost the same with the *American species* of M. Bory, and is embraced in the group bearing that name in the classification of M. Dumoulins.

designation, it is proposed to adopt the name of Fuegians. Their own national appellation is *Yacannacunnee*. They rove over a sterile waste which is computed to be as large as the half of Ireland, and yet their whole number has been computed by Forster at two thousand souls.* The physical aspect of these people is altogether repulsive, and their domestic usages tend to heighten the defects of nature. They are of low stature, seldom exceeding five feet four or five inches. They have large heads, broad faces, and small eyes. Their chests are large, their bodies clumsy, with large knees and ill-shaped legs. Their hair is lank, black and coarse, and their complexion a decided brown, like that of the more northern tribes. The expression of face is vacant, and their mental operations are to the last degree slow and stupid; they are almost destitute of the usual curiosity of savages, caring little for any thing that does not minister to their present wants. The difference between the Fuegians and the other Americans is no doubt attributable to the effects of climate and locality, and the consequent habits of life, which tend, in this instance, to depress and brutalise the mind, and to impair the physical man.

General Observations on the Barbarous Nations composing the American Family.—After examining a great number of skulls, I find that the nations east of the Alleghany mountains, together with the cognate tribes, have the head more elongated than any other Americans. This remark applies especially to the great Lenapé stock, the Iroquois, and the Cherokees. To the west of the Mississippi we again meet with the elongated head in the Mandans, Ricaras, Assinaboins and some other tribes. Yet even in these instances the characteristic truncation of the occiput is more or less obvious, while many nations east of the Rocky Mountains have the rounded head so characteristic of the race, as the Osages, Ottoes, Missouris, Dacotas, and numerous others. The same conformation is common in Florida; but some of these nations are evidently of the Toltecan family, as both their characters and traditions testify. The head of the Charibs, as well of the Antilles as of Terra Firma, are also naturally rounded; and we trace this character, so far as we have had opportunity for examination, through the nations east of the Andes, the Patagonians and the tribes of Chili. In fact, the flatness of the occipital portion of the cranium will probably be found to characterise a greater or less number of individuals in every existing tribe, from Terra del Fuego to the Canadas. If these skulls be viewed from behind, we observe the occipital outline

---

* Obs. During a Voy. Round the World, p. 225.

to be moderately curved outwards, wide at the occipital protuberances, and full from those points to the opening of the ear. From the parietal protuberances there is a slightly curved slope to the vertex, producing a conical, or rather a wedge-shaped outline.

Humboldt has remarked that "there is no race on the globe in which the frontal bone is so much pressed backwards, and in which the forehead is so small."* It must be observed, however, that the lowness of the forehead is in some measure compensated by its breadth, which is generally considerable. The flat forehead was esteemed beautiful among a vast number of tribes; and this fancy has been the principal incentive to the moulding of the head by art.

Although the orbital cavities are large, the eyes themselves are smaller than in Europeans; and Fresier asserts that the Puelché women he saw in Chili were absolutely hideous from the smallness of the eyes.† The latter are also deeply set or sunk in the head; an appearance which is much increased by the low and prominent frontal ridges.

Among the North American Indians there is rarely any decided obliquity in the position of the eyes which is so universal among the Malays and Mongols; but Spix and Martius have observed it in some Brazilian tribes, and Humboldt in those of the Orinoco: and among the Pourys, the Prince de Wied describes a man who bore, in this and other respects, a marked resemblance to a Calmuck.

What has been said of the bony orbits obtains with surprising uniformity: thus the superior margin is but slightly curved, while the inferior may be compared to an inverted arch. The lateral margins form curves rather mediate between the other two. This fact is the more interesting on account of the contrast it presents to the oblong orbit and parallel margins observable in the Malay. The latter conformation, however, is sometimes seen in the American, but chiefly in those skulls which have been altered by pressure to the frontal bone.

The nose constitutes one of the strongest and most uniform features of the Indian countenance: it mostly presents the decidedly arched form, without being strictly aquiline, and still more rarely flat.

The nasal cavities correspond to the size of the nose itself; and the remarkable acuteness of smell possessed by the American Indian has been attributed to the great expansion of the olfactory membrane.‡ But the perfection of this sense,

---

* Monuments, T. I, p. 158.   † Voy. p. 64.
‡ BLUMENBACH, Dec. Cran. p. 25.

like that of hearing among the same people, is perhaps chiefly to be attributed to its constant and assiduous cultivation. The cheek bones are large and prominent, and incline rapidly towards the lower jaw, giving the face an angular conformation. The upper jaw is often elongated and much inclined outwards, but the teeth are for the most part vertical. The lower jaw is broad and ponderous, and truncated in front. The teeth are also very large, and seldom decayed; for among the many that remain in the skulls in my possession, very few present any marks of disease, although they are often much worn down by attrition in the mastication of hard substances. The long, black, lank hair, is common to all the American tribes, among whom no trace of the frizzled locks of the Polynesian, or the woolly texture of the Negro, has ever been observed. The beard is very deficient among the Americans generally, and the little that nature gives them they assiduously eradicate from early manhood. It is perhaps in this respect that we observe the nearest analogy between the Americans and Mongols, although it is far from being peculiar to them alone. It is not, however, as De Pauw asserts, that the beard is wholly wanting,* for travellers have occasionally noticed it long and full where it has been allowed its natural growth. Examples of this kind have been particularly observed among the Chippewyans, and the Slave and Dog-ribbed Indians of the far north.† Lewis and Clarke remark that the beard, among the Chopunnish west of the Rocky Mountains, "is very often suffered to grow, nor does there appear to be any natural deficiency in that respect; for we observed several men who, if they had adopted the practice of shaving, would have been as well supplied as ourselves."‡ La Perouse observed good beards in about one half of the Indians of New California, and the rest had probably eradicated theirs by art: and Molina says that the Chilians occasionally have as thick beards as the Spaniards.§ "The mustaches, which modern travellers have found among the inhabitants of the northwest coast of America," says Humboldt, "are so much the more curious, as celebrated naturalists have left the question undetermined, whether the Americans have naturally no beard, and no hairs on the rest of their bodies, or whether they pluck them carefully out. Without entering here into physiological details, I can affirm that the Indians who inhabit the torrid zone of South America have generally some beard; and that this beard increases when

---

* "Les Americains étaient surtout remarquables en ce que les sourcils manquaient à un grand nombre, *et la barbe à tous.*"

† MACKENZIE, Trav. in N. Amer. p. 36.   ‡ Exped. II, p. 292.
§ Hist. of Chili, I, p. 275.

they shave themselves, of which we have seen examples in the missions of the Capuchins of Caripe, where the Indian sextons wish to resemble the monks their masters. But many individuals are born entirely without beard, or have no hair on their bodies. M. de Galeano, in his last expedition to the Straits of Magellan, informs us that there are many old men among the Patagonians with beards, though they are short and by no means bushy. On comparing this assertion with the facts collected by Marchaud, Mears, and especially by Volney in the northern temperate zone, we are tempted to believe that the Indians have more and more beard in proportion to their distance from the equator."* Mr. Schoolcraft mentions beards as common among the Potowatomies, and alludes to a very old man of that tribe " whose long, descending gray beard would not disgrace a Nazarite."†

A copper-colored skin has been assumed by most writers as a characteristic distinction of the Americans, who have hence been called the *copper-colored race*. The investigations of Dr. M'Culloh satisfactorily prove that this designation is wholly inapplicable to the Americans as a race, and that it is more characteristic of some other and very remote nations.‡ The error has obviously arisen from the habitual use, among many tribes, of red paint to a brown skin, which occasions a coppery hue. Humboldt declares that the denomination of copper-colored men could never have originated in the equinoctial regions to designate the Americans: and I can further testify that among the individuals of many different tribes that have come under my observation, I have never seen a copper-colored man. "We consider, therefore," says Dr. M'Culloh, " that the color of the American Indians in general is brown, differing in intensity with various tribes, according to various localities; but that it is almost impossible to say what that brown color principally resembles. The *cinnamon* is, in my apprehension, the nearest approach to it, though still too inaccurate for general comparison."§ I fully coincide in opinion with Dr. M'Culloh; and believe, with him, that no epithet derivable from the color of the skin, so correctly designates the Americans collectively as that of the *Brown Race*. Although the Americans thus possess a pervading and characteristic complexion, there are occasional and very remarkable deviations, including all the tints from a decided white to an unequivocally black skin. This fact may be sufficiently illustrated by the following examples. Among the fair tribes of the Upper Orinoco, Humboldt makes especial mention of the Guariboes, the

* Polit. Essay, B. II, chap. 6. † Trav. in Valley of the Miss. p. 317.
‡ Researches, p. 16, &c. § Ibid. p. 18.

THE AMERICAN FAMILY.

Guanares, the Guayacas and the Maquiritares. "The individuals of the fair tribes whom we examined," says that traveller, "have the features, the stature, and the smooth, straight, black hair which characterise other Indians. It would be impossible to take them for a mixed race, like the descendants of natives and Europeans, and they are neither feeble, nor albinoes."* Among the Botocudys of Brazil, the Prince de Wied saw some who were almost entirely white, with a tint of red upon their cheeks, although the usual color is a reddish brown.† Molina states that the Boroanes, who inhabit the Araucanian provinces of Chili, in the thirty-ninth degree of south latitude, "are white, and as well featured as the northern Europeans."‡ Bouguer found some Peruvian Indians at the base and on the west side of the Cordilleras who were almost as white as Europeans. Bartram saw among the Cherokees some young women, whom he describes as fair and blooming; and among the nations of the island of St. Catharine, on the coast of California, young persons of both sexes have a fine mixture of red and white in their complexions.

That climate exerts a subordinate agency in producing these diversified hues, must be inferred, I think, from the facts mentioned by Humboldt, that the tribes which wander along the burning plains of the equinoctial region, have no darker skins than the mountaineers of the temperate zone. Again, the Puelchés and other inhabitants of the Magellanic region, beyond the fifty-fifth degree of south latitude, are absolutely darker than the Abipones, Macobios and Tobas, who are many degrees nearer the equator. While the Botocudys are of a clear brown color, and sometimes nearly white, at no great distance from the tropic, and moreover, while the Guyacas under the line are characterised, as we have seen, by a fair complexion, the Charruas, who are almost black, inhabit the fiftieth degree

---

* It is well known, however, that Albinoes are not unfrequent among the American Indians. Those of Darien were minutely described by Wafer about a hundred and fifty years ago. "They are quite white," says he, "but their whiteness is like that of a horse, quite different from the fair or pale European, as they have not the least tincture of a blush or sanguine complexion. * * * Their eyebrows are milk-white, as is likewise the hair of their heads, which is very fine, inclining to a curl, and growing to the length of six or eight inches. * * * They seldom go abroad in the day time, the sun being disagreeable to them, and causing their eyes, which are weak and poring, to water, especially if it shines towards them: yet they see very well by moonlight, from which we called them moon-eyed."—WAFER, *in Drake's Coll. of Voy. Fol.* p. 310.

† Voy. au Bresil, II, 212.—I, 335.
‡ History of Chili, I, p. 274.

of south latitude, and the yet blacker Californians are twenty-five degrees north of the equator.*

"The nations of New Spain are darker colored than the Indians of Quito and New Grenada, who inhabit a precisely analogous climate. We even find that the nations dispersed to the north of the Rio Gila, are browner than those that border on the kingdom of Guatimala. The people of the Rio Negro are darker than those of the Lower Orinoco, yet the banks of the former of these two rivers enjoy a cooler climate. In the forests of Guiana, especially near the sources of the Orinoco, there exist several tribes of a whitish complexion, [to whom allusion has already been made,] who are surrounded by other nations of a darker brown. The Indians who, in the torrid zone, inhabit the most elevated table land of the Andes, and those who, under forty-five degrees of south latitude, live upon fish in the Archipelago of Chonos, have a complexion as much copper-colored as they who cultivate, under a burning sun, the banana in the narrowest and deepest valleys of the equinoctial regions. To this it must be added, that the Indians who inhabit the mountains are clothed, and were so long before the conquest; while the aborigines that wander on the plains are perfectly naked, and consequently are always exposed to the perpendicular rays of the sun. Every where, in short, it is found that the color of the American depends very little on the local situation which he actually occupies; and never, in the same individual, are those parts of the body that are constantly covered, of a fairer color than those that are in contact with a hot and humid air. Their infants are never white when they are born; and the Indian caziques who enjoy a considerable degree of luxury, and who keep themselves constantly dressed in the interior of their habitations, have all the parts of their body, with the exception of the palms of their hands and the soles of their feet, of the same brownish red or copper color."†

After all, these differences in complexion are extremely partial, forming mere exceptions to the primitive and national tint that characterises these people from Cape Horn to the Canadas. The cause of these anomalies is not readily explained:

---

* " Si le climat seul était la cause de la couleur brune des Americains, les Portugais auraient dû, après plusieurs générations, prendre aussi cette couleur; et cependent il est certain qu'ils ont la même que leurs ancêtres toutes les fois que leur sang n'est pas mêlé avec celui des Nègres ou des Indians."— PRINCE DE WIED, *Voy. au Bresil*, II, p. 310.—See also, HUMBOLDT, *Monuments*, T. I, p. 23.— DOBRIZHOFFER, II, p. 9.—BORY DE ST. VINCENT, *L'Homme*, II, p. 20.

† MALTE-BRUN, Geog. *Am. ed.* 5, p. 14.

that it is not climate is sufficiently obvious; and whether it arises from partial immigrations from other countries, remains yet to be decided.

Nothing can be more variable than the stature of these people, which presents some remarkable contrasts, of which a few only need be noticed at present, as I shall revert to this subject on a future occasion. The Patagonians of the main land, after rejecting the absurd fables of the early voyagers, are the tallest nation on the American continent. Commodore Byron states that among five hundred men he saw together, the shortest were at least four inches taller than his own men.* Captain Wallace, however, took the pains to measure many of them, among whom one was six feet seven, and several were six feet five; but the greater part of them were from five feet ten to six feet.† On the other hand Humboldt found the Chaymas and some other tribes of the Upper Orinoco to be remarkably short, while in the adjacent Charib nation the men were not less conspicuous for their great stature. The Pourys and Coroados‡ of Brazil are diminutive races, while the Abipones of Paraguay are, to a man, of gigantic proportions. The late Mr. Bartram, who passed much time among the Florida nations, describes the Creek (Muscógee) Indians as strikingly tall and athletic, "a full size larger than Europeans; many of them above six feet, and few under that, or five feet eight or ten inches." Yet what is very singular, he assures us that the women of that nation are seldom above five feet high, and that the greater number of them never attain to that stature; an observation that has also been made respecting the Indians of Paraguay.§

Although the Americans are generally of good stature, they are not so generally of strictly athletic proportions. Their chests are often less expanded and their shoulders narrower than one would expect; defects which are usually ascribed to habitual indolence; for the men make little exertion with their arms beyond bending the bow. On the other hand, many nations both of North and South America, are remarkable for their perfect symmetry: among numerous examples we may instance the Patagonians of the main land, the Charruas of Brazil, and the Creeks and Seminoles of Florida. In fact there is ample evidence to disprove the hypothesis of some closet naturalists, that the physical man of the new world is of a defective and degenerate organisation.

---

* Hawks. Voy. I, p. 26.

† Ibid. I, p. 124.—The reader will find an interesting examination of this question in the Introduction to Hawksworth's Voyages, and also in De Pauw, Resch. sur les Amer. T. I, p. 283, &c.

‡ Spix and Mart. Trav. II, 239. § Pernetty, Voy. I, 299.

Among some mountain tribes of South America, and especially in Chili, the natives are remarkable for the size of their limbs, which are so large as to appear out of proportion to the body; yet it is remarkable that the Americans seldom attain a state of obesity.

Notwithstanding the general custom of going barefoot, the American Indians possess remarkably small feet, and their hands have the same delicate conformation. Most travellers have noticed this fact, which is a characteristic of the race;[*] yet the Indian is generally stiff and awkward in his gait, owing to the prevalent habit of walking with the feet turned inwards.

The unsophisticated Americans might be divided into three great classes, derived from the pursuits on which they depend for subsistence, viz: *Hunting*, *Fishing*, and *Agriculture*. The first and largest class is devoted to *hunting;* and it embraces most of the strictly nomadic tribes, and of course a great proportion of the entire race. The several Dacota nations west of the Mississippi, together with the Upsarookas, the Assinaboins, the Black Feet, and many other nations both east and west of the Rocky Mountains, cultivate nothing whatever. They live upon the flesh of the buffalo, the deer, the bear, and various other animals; and when these fail, they suffer all the privations resulting from famine and disease. In the southern continent, vast hordes now derive a ready and unfailing subsistence from the wild cattle which overrun the extensive plains or pampas of Brazil and Patagonia;[†] and a few tribes now domesticate these animals, and thus avoid the labor of the chase and the lasso. Such are the Pehuenches of the Chilian Andes, between the thirty-fourth and thirty-seventh degree of south latitude. They dwell, says Molina, in the manner of the Bedouin Arabs, in tents made of skins, disposed in a circular form, leaving in the centre a spacious field, where the cattle feed during the continuance of the herbage. When that begins to fail, they transport their habitations to another situation, and in this manner continually changing place, they traverse the valleys of the Cordilleras.[‡]

In comparison with the hunting tribes, those which subsist exclusively by *fishing* are not numerous; for among the many nations who inhabited the Atlantic

---

[*] DE AZARA, Voy. T. II, p. 32, 58, 269.—PR. DE WIED, Voy. au Bresil, art. Botocudy.—MOLINA, Hist. of Chili, I, p. 276.—HUMBOLDT, Voy. aux Reg. Equinox, III, p. 282.

[†] The domestic breed of cattle was first introduced into South America by the Spaniards, and it continues to increase beyond all calculation, notwithstanding the annual havoc made among these animals for the purposes of food and commerce.

[‡] Hist of Chili, II, p. 224.

coast of America, the greater number made their means of support a secondary consideration, some alternating it with agriculture, others with the chase. Among the proper piscatory tribes, however, may be adduced the natives of Terra del Fuego, and the Flathead nations of the Columbia river. Numerous tribes unacquainted with agriculture, are sustained for a great part of the year by fishing in the rivers and lakes; and in the interim between the ending and the recommencement of the fishing season, are driven to the greatest extremities for food sufficient for the purposes of life. Thus the Shoshones west of the Rocky Mountains, live more than half the year on roots alone; and the Ottomacs of the Orinoco are compelled for months together to assuage the cravings of nature by mixing with their food a large proportion of unctuous clay.*

In connection with this subject it may be remarked, that even the piscatory tribes are wholly destitute of the spirit of maritime adventure, or even fondness for the sea. Their boats are of the simplest construction, and in their fishing and other aquatic excursions, they seldom intentionally lose sight of land.

A few tribes were strictly agricultural before the arrival of the Europeans, but a much greater number have become so since. Among the former are the nations who inhabit the plains and open land between the Orinoco and the Amazon, a region to which even the missionaries have hitherto been denied admission.† In North America, the cultivation of the soil has been chiefly restricted to the nations inhabiting the country between the great lakes and the Gulf of Mexico, and between the Mississippi and the ocean. But even among the most industrious of these tribes agriculture was pursued in a very elementary manner, having been confined chiefly to the cultivation of maize or Indian corn, the sweet potatoe, melons and tobacco.‡ Among the Catholic missions in South

---

* "The Ottomacs during some months eat daily three quarters of a pound of clay, slightly hardened by the fire, without their health being sensibly affected by it. They moisten the earth afresh when they are going to swallow it. It has not been possible to verify hitherto with precision how much nutritious vegetable or animal matter the Indians take in a week at the same time; but it is certain that they attribute the sensation of satiety which they feel to the clay, and not to the wretched aliments which they occasionally take with it."—*Humb. Pers. Nar.* V, p. 643.

† HUMBOLDT, Pers. Nar. III, p. 312.

‡ GALLATIN, in Archæolog. Amer. II, p. 151, 152.—It is remarked by this author that "the four millions of industrious inhabitants who, within less than forty years, have peopled our western states, and derive more than ample means of subsistence from the soil, offer the most striking contrast when compared with perhaps one hundred thousand Indians whose place they occupy."—*Loco citat.* p. 154.

America, agriculture has become by coercion the business of the Indians; and among many of the independent hordes of both continents it is conjoined with hunting as a means of subsistence. Again, in the West India Islands where there was no game, the wants of an immense population were supplied in part by agricultural labor, but perhaps in a still greater degree by cultivating the indigenous fruits. Many tribes resort with regularity to all these modes of subsistence, according to the return of the seasons; thus employing the spring of the year in fishing, the summer in agriculture, the autumn and winter in hunting.

The Cherokees, as we shall hereafter see, have become an agricultural nation by the force of example; but in Mexico there are tribes which have inhabited the same localities which their ancestors possessed some centuries ago, and who lead the peaceable life of cultivators of the soil, exempt from the contingencies to which the hunting tribes are always exposed.*

Although the Americans have derived their horses from the Europeans, they have managed them from the first with surprising dexterity. Among many tribes in both Americas the fondness for these animals amounts to a passion: whole tribes have assumed the equestrian character, so that they hunt and fight exclusively on horseback; and the single province of Chaco, in Paraguay, contains no less than twenty of these nations. They are also numerous throughout Brazil and Patagonia, and in the region between the Mississippi river and the Rocky Mountains. Yet strange as it may appear, there is scarcely an example among the free Indians, of a horse being used for agricultural purposes.†

The bold physical development of the American savage is accompanied by a corresponding acuteness in the organs of sense. Although nature has done much, education has contributed more to the perfection of these faculties. The constant state of suspicion and alarm in which the Indian lives, compels him to observe a sleepless vigilance. His senses are incessantly employed to preserve himself from surprise and destruction, and to foil the stratagems of his enemy. It is said that the Charibs of the Antilles could, by the scent alone, follow a man through the woods with the same precision that a northern Indian traces another by his foot-

---

* HUMBOLDT, Polit. Essay on New Spain, B. II, chap. 6.

† Among other modes of revenging themselves on the Spaniards, the Indians committed an incessant pillage of their horses. Thus in the space of fifty years, says Dobrizhoffer, an hundred thousand of these animals were driven from the estates of the Spaniards by the Abipones of Chaco alone; and the same author adds, that no less than four thousand horses were frequently carried off by the Paraguayan Indians in a single assault.—*Hist. of the Abipones*, III, p. 8.

steps; and that they could even detect the nation to which their enemy belonged.*
"I observed," says Dobrizhoffer, "that almost all the Abipones (of Paraguay) had black but rather small eyes; yet they see more acutely with them than we do with our large ones, being able clearly to distinguish such minute and distant objects as would escape the eye of the most quicksighted European."† The singular absence of physical deformity has been noticed by all travellers. Such defects as arise in childhood are, for obvious reasons, less likely to happen in savage than in civilised life. But on the other hand, the various congenital defects probably occur in an equal ratio in both conditions; but it is well known that the Indians destroy such of their children as labor under these misfortunes, on the plea that they would be helpless, and of course dependent members of the community. This kind of infanticide is an almost universal usage among the barbarous tribes, who attribute physical deformity to the workings of an evil spirit, and children of delicate and unpromising constitutions often suffer the same fate.

How idle is that theory which attributes to these people less hardiness of constitution than belongs to the European! What, in truth, can exceed their endurance of fatigue, of hunger, of thirst and of cold? By day and by night, in summer and winter, over mountains, and through rivers and forests, they pursue their determined course, whether the object be revenge on an enemy, or food for their families at home. It has been assumed in evidence of their weakness that they sunk under the labor of the mines much sooner than either Europeans or Negroes: but it must be borne in mind that the Indian is incapable of servitude, and that his spirit sunk at once in captivity, and with it his physical energy; while, on the other hand, the more pliant Negro, yielding to his fate, and accommodating himself to his condition, bore his heavy burthen with comparative ease. Thus it was that a moral influence destroyed thousands of Indians in Hispaniola, until the race of islanders became extinct, while their fellow laborers lived and multiplied in defiance of oppression.

Dr. Robertson has been at some pains to prove the physical inferiority of the American Indians; and yet, in a note, he quotes from Godin ample evidence that the seeming weakness of these people is not a natural defect, but the mere result of an inactive life. "The Indians in warm climates," says Godin, "such as those on the coasts of the South Sea, on the River of Amazons, and the river

---

* SELDEN, Archæolog. Amer. I, p. 426.   † Hist. of the Abipones, II, p. 13.

Orinoco, are not to be compared for strength with those in cold countries; and yet boats daily set out from Para, a Portuguese settlement on the River of Amazons, to ascend that river against the rapidity of the stream, and with the same crew they proceed to San Pablo, which is eight hundred leagues distant. No crew of white people, or even of Negroes, would be found equal to such a task of persevering fatigue, and yet the Indians, being accustomed to this labor from their infancy, perform it."* From these and other facts, it is evident that where the Indian can be stimulated by ambition or the hope of reward, his bodily strength is equal to great and protracted exertion.

Cautiousness and cunning are among the most prominent features in the character of these people. A studied vigilance marks every action. If an Indian speaks, it is in a slow and studied manner, and to avoid committing himself he often resorts to metaphorical phrases which have no precise meaning. If he seeks an enemy, it is through unfrequented paths, in the dead of night, and with every device for concealment and surprise. When he meets his victim, the same instinctive feeling governs all his movements. His motive is to destroy without being destroyed, and he avails himself of every subterfuge that can protect his own person while he seeks the life of his antagonist. It is by a refinement of cautious cunning that they have so often circumvented Europeans, and they pride themselves on this faculty more than on any other. Thus also when provoked they can mask their resentment under an unruffled exterior; but the mind which thus conceals its emotions, devises at the same moment a sleepless and bloody revenge. Their very politeness is a part of their cautiousness; for in conversation they seldom contradict or deny the remarks that are made to them, so that a stranger is unable to decide whether they are pleased or displeased, convinced or the contrary. "The missionaries who have attempted to convert them to Christianity, all complain of this as one of the great difficulties of their mission. The Indians hear with patience the truths of the gospel explained to them, and give their usual tokens of assent and approbation; but this by no means implies conviction—it is mere civility."† For the same reason an Indian seldom expresses himself with surprise. If an object interests him on account of its novelty, he shows his gratification in a few subdued remarks, or by a significant gesture; but it is difficult to betray him into enthusiasm. That taciturnity which is also linked with their cautiousness, is fostered by all their usages. It is seen

---

* ROBERTSON, Hist. of Amer. Note XLVI.   † Hist. of Amer. (Anon.) p. 77.

even in the marriage ceremony, which is often joyless and even melancholy, as if it were rather the harbinger of sorrow than of happiness. It is indeed seldom that their pastimes excite enthusiasm or hilarity, unless the performers are stimulated by intoxicating drinks; in which case, as among more civilised men, a temporary madness unmasks the darkest passions, and the natural reserve of the Indian gives place to extravagant mirth and brutal ferocity.

This perpetual vigilance has led some authors to charge the Indian with cowardice; but he is taught from childhood to consider a successful stratagem more honorable than open victory; and it has been observed by an intelligent writer, that among the North American Indians generally, flight in battle is not considered disgraceful where the number or the resistance of an enemy is greater than had been anticipated. Retreat under these circumstances is a principle of their tactics; and they renew the combat without humiliation when fortune promises better chances of success. The courage of the Indian is evident in his desperate resistance to superior force; by his choice of death to capitulation, even when he has every guaranty of personal safety; and by that unshrinking firmness with which he sees and feels the approach of death under the most cruel torments. To be whole days and nights fastened to a stake and subjected to incessant but gradual mutilation—to sustain this load of misery with fortitude and even with cheerfulness, and finally to sink into death without losing for a moment this indomitable self-possession, are surely sufficient proofs of the courage of the Indian. The stoicism with which he bears every variety of bodily suffering is so extraordinary, that Ulloa and others have attempted to explain it on the ground that the Americans have a coarser, stronger and less sensitive organisation than any other race. This, however, is a mere postulate which has no foundation in fact, and might be applied with equal plausibility to the primitive martyrs: nor need we look beyond the influence of a ruling passion for a full explanation of the phenomenon. All an Indian's hope of glory, all his chance of distinction, depend on his ability to endure privation. He goes half clothed to the chase in the depth of winter, not because he is insensible to cold, but because he chooses to appear indifferent to it. In like manner he sustains himself amidst the severest agonies that can be inflicted on human nature, because to shrink from them would stamp him with cowardice and infamy. With many tribes this principle is carried so far that parents torture their children to test their self-possession; nor are they enrolled on the list of warriors until they can sustain the ordeal without complaint. Let it not be thought, however, that the Indian courts privation; on the contrary no one can dislike it more. His natural indolence is opposed to it, and he has moreover the same love of existence as other men. He will resort to every possible contrivance to avoid the ills of life, but when they fall upon him he bears them with a heroism that has become a proverb.

As a result of habitual indolence, the Indians are remarkably improvident. What a missionary writer says of a few nations, is applicable to many, and indeed to most. "They live reckless of the past, little curious about the present, and very seldom anxious about the future."[*] When the cold pinches him he commences building a hut; but should the weather soften and invite to repose, he abandons his task until again stimulated by necessity. And so it is with his other domestic concerns. He will often suffer with want before he engages in the chase; and a successful hunting expedition is followed by a protracted season of indolence and gluttony.

It is usual to charge the Indians with treachery: but in most instances it will be found that they have only retorted the perfidiousness that has been heaped upon them by others. The annals of Indian history are ample evidence of this fact. A system of encroachment and oppression has been practised upon them since the first landing of Europeans on the shores of America: their lands have been seized upon the most frivolous pretences, and they have had no redress at the hand of the white man: wars have been fomented among them to procure their mutual destruction; and when they have been weakened by the conflict, the common enemy has stepped in and seized upon their possessions. They have been taken in their villages, or inveigled on ship-board, to be sold into slavery; and in fact every art that cupidity could devise has been put in practice to deprive them of liberty and life. Is it surprising that a people thus oppressed should retaliate on their oppressors? Or shall we stigmatise them as treacherous when they have received so much treachery at our hands?

A strong feeling of gratitude is proverbially an Indian trait. General Harrison, who has had ample occasion to see and know the Indians, observes that one of the brightest parts of their character is their high regard for the obligations of friendship. "A pledge of this kind once given by an Indian of any character, becomes the ruling passion of his soul, to which every other is made to yield." It is not, however, to be denied that they are unfeeling by nature and cruel by education. To spill the blood of an enemy, to torture him to death by slow degrees, is the supreme pleasure of the American savage. He wreaks his vengeance with equal fury on all the kindred of his adversary. Old age, the helplessness of infancy or

---

[*] DOBRIZHOFFER, Abipones, II, p. 55.

the charms of youth, have no power to check his destroying spirit. His is, in truth, a demoniac love of slaughter which delights in the shriek of the wounded and the groan of the dying. Revenge is his ruling passion, and it is the first lesson a father inculcates in his child. To gratify it he cheerfully meets every difficulty, and encounters every danger; for to the eye of the Indian no treasure is equal to the scalp of an enemy. He constantly reflects on the impression which his conduct will make on a friend or an enemy: he studies to surprise the one and confound the other; and when neither is before him, he imagines the presence of departed spirits, who watch his actions and recount them in the other world.

Travellers differ on the question of Indian hospitality. They certainly possess this trait in a limited degree, and qualify it with reserve if not with reluctance. Lewis and Clark aver that after crossing and recrossing the continent of America, and meeting of course with many nations of Indians, they were never sensible of having received a really hospitable reception from more than one tribe, and that was the Chopunnish, or Nez-percés.* It should be recollected, however, that they found some of these nations in want of food; while in other instances the proverbial rapacity of the white man, and a suspicion of the motives of Captain Lewis's party, shut out the kindlier feelings which, for the most part, characterise the unsophisticated Indian.

Covetousness forms but a minor element in the character of the Indian: we have observed that he is singularly content with the supply of present need, and that his mind is seldom harassed with the idea of future want. He craves not the house nor the land of his neighbor, and shows an entire apathy to those possessions which are most prized in civilised communities. Hence it is that the tumuli of Mexico and Peru, though often immensely rich in the precious metals, were never disturbed by the native inhabitants. It remained for strangers to commit this act of sacrilege. Much of this indifference to property, however, may be ascribed to its uncertain tenure. Among most tribes their daily wants are supplied by mutual exertion, and the fruits of the chase are divided among the many. If a man dies, every one seizes what he wants from among the property of the deceased; and his wife and children receive nothing, and are left to begin the world anew for themselves, with the certainty that whatever their industry or good fortune may acquire, will be subject to the same predacious violence at their death.

It must in truth be confessed that the Indian is least to be admired at home;

* Exped. II, p. 279.

for in him the domestic virtues are but partially expanded. War and the chase, on the other hand, call forth all his energies. Hunger, fatigue and toil, are encountered without a murmur, and the mind, goaded on by the powerful impulse of ambition or revenge, becomes untiring and indomitable. The firmness of purpose, its attendant privations, and the final contest with a courageous adversary, give a seductive exaltation to the character of the American savage. He returns to his home, he is greeted by the applauding shouts of his countrymen, and the bloody deeds of a crafty and destroying spirit are recounted, even in civilised communities, as acts of heroism and greatness. How transient is this seeming glory! The excitement of the moment has passed away, and where is the warrior now? For him domestic life has no charms, and tranquillity resolves itself into the most grovelling pastimes. Behold him lounging under the shade of a tree, the victim of apathy and sloth, too vain to cultivate his fields, or to raise a hand for his own support, while he looks with complacency on the toils of a mother, a wife, or a daughter, whom the barbarous usages of Indian thraldom have condemned to perpetual slavery. To such an extent is this servitude carried, that mothers not unfrequently destroy their female children, alleging as a reason that it is better they should die than live to lead a life so miserable as that to which they are doomed;* while among some tribes grief and jealousy drive the women to suicide.† The Indian is habitually cold in his manner to the gentler sex, and stern to his children, considering it unmanly to show much tenderness to either. This exterior reserve, however, is by no means indicative of their real character; for after all that has been said to the contrary, these people are not remarkable for the purity of their morals. The very reverse, indeed, is true; for when they throw off the mask of reserve which they habitually assume in the presence of strangers, they are observed to be as much depraved by vice and sensuality as most other barbarous nations.‡

The Americans are, perhaps, less swayed by superstitious fears than most other savages; and their religion, if it merits the name, is more remarkable for its poverty than its grossness. It is chiefly a simple theism which acknowledges a good and an evil spirit; the former of course exerting a benign influence on the

---

* Bradbury, Trav. in Amer. p. 89.—Depons. Voy. à la Terre Ferme, I, p. 302.

† Keating, Exped. to the St. Peters, I, p. 227, 395.

‡ See Bradbury, Trav. in Amer. p. 37, 149, 154. *Am. ed.*—Keating, Exped. I, p. 224.—De Azara, II, p. 115.—Lewis and Clark, Exped. I, p. 105, 421; II, p. 134.—Muratori, Missions of Paraguay, p. 29.

destinies of men, while the latter is looked upon as the author of all their misfortunes. Yet there is, for the most part, no regularity in the time or manner of their worship, which appears to be the mere result of occasion or impulse. The Indian hears God in the winds, and in the cataract, and acknowledges his presence in all the phenomena of the elements; yet these are always attributed to the same spirit, and not, as with most barbarous people, to a multiplicity of spiritual agents. Again, the Americans are little prone to idolatry; for it is rare to find any community among them paying homage to an image of their own making. So far as inquiry has been extended to this subject, it appears that all the American nations believe in the immortality of the soul, which is to enjoy in a future state the most exciting temporal pleasures without fatigue or alloy: of these pastimes hunting and fishing are the most esteemed, and hence the implements used in both are buried with the dead.

The Indians have an extraordinary veneration for their dead, which sometimes induces them, on removing from one section of the country to another, to disinter the remains of their deceased relatives, and bear them to the new home of the tribe. Heckewelder says, that when at Bethlehem, in Pennsylvania, about the middle of the last century, he saw a removing party of the Nanticokes pass through that town, loaded with the bones of their dead friends, some of which were in so recent a state as to taint the air as they passed.*

The intellectual faculties of this great family appear to be of a decidedly inferior cast when compared with those of the Caucasian or Mongolian races. They are not only averse to the restraints of education, but for the most part incapable of a continued process of reasoning on abstract subjects. Their minds seize with avidity on simple truths, while they at once reject whatever requires investigation and analysis. Their proximity, for more than two centuries, to European institutions, has made scarcely any appreciable change in their mode of thinking or their manner of life; and as to their own social condition, they are probably in most respects what they were at the primitive epoch of their existence. They have made few or no improvements in building their houses or their boats; their inventive and imitative faculties appear to be of a very humble grade, nor have they the smallest predilection for the arts or sciences. The long annals of missionary labor and private benefaction bestowed upon them, offer but very few exceptions to the preceding statement, which, on the contrary, is sustained by the combined testimony of almost all practical observers. Even in cases where they

* Narr. p. 76.

have received an ample education, and have remained for many years in civilised society, they lose none of their innate love of their own national usages, which they have almost invariably resumed when chance has left them to choose for themselves. Such has been the experience of the Spanish and Portuguese missionaries in South America, and of the English and their descendants in the northern portion of the continent.*

However much the benevolent mind may regret the inaptitude of the Indian for civilisation, the affirmative of this question seems to be established beyond a doubt. His moral and physical nature are alike adapted to his position among the races of men, and it is as reasonable to expect the one to be changed as the other. The structure of his mind appears to be different from that of the white man, nor can the two harmonise in their social relations except on the most limited scale. Every one knows, however, that the mind expands by culture; nor can we yet tell how near the Indian would approach the Caucasian after education had been bestowed on a single family through several successive generations.†

---

* Those distinguished travellers, Spix and Von Martius, mention that an Indian of the Coroados tribe of Brazil, was brought up in the adjacent European colony, and so far educated that he was ordained priest, and read mass; "but all at once he renounced his new profession, threw aside his habit, and fled naked into the woods to his old way of life."—*Trav. in Brazil*, II, p. 242.

My friend Dr. Casanova, who has resided several years in Chili, informs me that instances like the preceding are not unfrequent in that country, even when the Indians have been taken at a very tender age, and every inducement has been held out to enlist their feelings in favor of civilised life.

"At an early period of the existence of Harvard University," says Dr. Warren, "our pious ancestors placed there a number of young Indians. These, after a short term of study, uniformly disappeared, and I believe the name of Caleb Chees-chaumuck stands on the college catalogue, a solitary instance of a native regularly graduated.—A recent example of the difficulty of reducing the young savage to the habits of civilised life, is well known in this vicinity. The government of the United States, after the late Indian war, placed the son of the Prophet Tecumseh at the West Point establishment of cadets. The young man conformed at first with apparent ease to the strict discipline of the institution; but on their visit to this place in 1821, he availed himself of an opportunity to quit them, and has not, I believe, since rejoined the corps."*

The Mohawk warrior *Thayendanegea*, more familiar by the name of Brant, received a Christian education, and even joined in the Christian communion; yet he was readily induced by the British government to resume his savage propensities against the American colonies, and became one of the most bloody and remorseless destroyers in the annals of Indian warfare.

† "Variety of powers in the various races," observes Mr. Laurence, "corresponds to the differ-

---

* Comparative View of the Sensorial Systems in Men and Animals, p. 95.—I may add, that Dr. Warren does not suppose the Indians incapable of attaining the sciences and arts; but that the reason of their having made so little progress, is to be traced to injudicious and inadequate means of instruction.

One of the most remarkable intellectual defects of the Indians is "a great difficulty in comprehending any thing that belongs to numerical relations. I never saw a single man who might not be made to say that he was eighteen or sixty years of age."* Wafer made the same remark in reference to the Indians of Darien; and Mr. Schoolcraft, the United States Indian Agent, assures me that this deficiency is a cause of most of the misunderstandings in respect to treaties entered into between our government and the native tribes. The latter sell their lands for a sum of money without having any conception of the amount, so that if it be a thousand dollars or a million few of them comprehend the difference until the treaty is signed and the money comes to be divided. Each man is then for the first time acquainted with his own interest in the transaction, and disappointment and murmurs invariably ensue.

15. THE TOLTECAN FAMILY.

In this group are embraced the civilised nations of Mexico, Peru and Bogota, extending from the Rio Gila in the thirty-third degree of north latitude, along the western margin of the continent to the frontiers of Chili. In North America, however, the people of this family were spread from ocean to ocean, through the present intendencies of Mexico, Vera Cruz, Puebla, Oaxaca, Guatimala, Yucatan, Nicaragua, &c. In South America, on the contrary, this family chiefly occupied a narrow strip of land between the Andes and the Pacific Ocean, and were limited on the south by the great desert of Atacama. Further north, however, in the present republic of New Grenada, lived the Bogotese, a people whose civilisation, like their geographical position, was intermediate between that of the Peruvians and Mexicans. This division of the Toltecan family had long held their mountain empire at the epoch of the Spanish invasion and conquest, and were surrounded on all sides by barbarous and uncongenial tribes.

---

ences both in kind and degree, which characterise the individuals of each race; indeed, to the general character of all nature, in which uniformity is most carefully avoided. To expect that the Americans can be raised by any culture to an equal height in moral sentiments and intellectual energy with Europeans, appears to me quite as unreasonable as it would be to hope that the bull-dog may equal the greyhound in speed; that the latter may be taught to hunt by scent like the hound; or that the mastiff may rival in talents and acquirements the sagacious and docile poodle."—*Lectures on Zoology*, p. 501.—See also a graphic view of this question in Dr. Caldwell's Thoughts on the Unity of the Human Species, p. 142.

* HUMBOLDT, in Lawrence's Lect. p. 569.

In assigning the geographical limits of the Toltecan family, it is not to be supposed that they alone inhabited this extended region; for while successive nations of that family held dominion over it for thousands of years, other and barbarous tribes were every where dispersed through the country, and, whether of aboriginal or exotic origin, may have at all times constituted a large part of the population. During these periods of power and greatness, an organised feudal system divided the nation into two great classes of nobles and plebeians; and there appears to have been as much objection to the amalgamation of these classes as ever existed in an aristocratic state of Europe. The advent of the Spaniards destroyed all distinctions by reducing both classes to equal vassalage; and three centuries of slavery and oppression on the part of the Spaniards, have left few traces of Mexican and Peruvian civilisation, excepting what we glean from their history and antiquities. These nations can no longer be identified in existing communities; and the mixed and motley people who now bear those names, are as unlike their ancestors in moral and intellectual character, as the degraded Copts of Egypt are unlike their progenitors of the age of Pharaoh.

As it will be a principal object in the sequel of this work to consider the character of these nations in reference to their cranial remains, we shall in this place merely remark that it is in the intellectual faculties that we discover the great difference between the Toltecan and American families. In the arts and sciences of the former we see the evidences of an advanced civilisation. From the Rio Gila in Calafornia, to the southern extremity of Peru, their architectural remains are every where encountered to surprise the traveller and confound the antiquary: among these are pyramids, temples, grottoes, bas-reliefs and arabesques; while their roads, aqueducts and fortifications, and the sites of their mining operations, sufficiently attest their attainments in the practical arts of life.*

---

* It will be observed that this family is identical with the Neptunian species (Homo neptunianus) of M. Bory de St. Vincent. I cannot adopt that designation, because the classification to which it belongs refers these people to the Malay race. That they are not Malays is sufficiently obvious from the difference in their character throughout; at the same time that some analogies between the skulls of the two races will be recognised from the description already given. It must moreover be granted, that there are some resemblances in language which are very interesting; but while these prove a communication and even protracted intercourse between the Americans and Asiatics, they by no means establish an affiliation of nations. But the most striking discrepancy between the Malays and Americans is seen in the extraordinary nautical habits of the one people, and the utter destitution of all maritime enterprise in the other.

It is curious to observe that in M. Dumoulin's classification, his eleventh, or *American species*, which embraces most of the barbarous tribes of South America east of the Andes, is said to possess

THE TOLTECAN FAMILY.

With respect to the American languages, it may be sufficient in this place to observe that they present resemblances not less remarkable than those we have noticed in the physical and moral traits of these people. All the nations from Cape Horn to the Arctic sea, have languages which possess "a distinct character common to all, and apparently differing from those of the other continent with which we are acquainted."* This analogy, adds Dr. Wiseman, is not of an indefinite kind, but consists for the most part in peculiar conjugational modes of modifying the verbs by the insertion of syllables; whence the remark of Vater that this wonderful uniformity observed from one extremity of America to the other, "favors in a singular manner the supposition of a primitive people, which formed the common stock of the American indigenous nations."†

Note.—*On Certain Mixed Races in America.*—The various grades of amalgamation between the white and Negro population of America, are too well known to require specification in this place; but there are two other mixed races which, from being much more partial, are much less familiar: viz, those which have resulted from intermarriages between the Europeans and Indians, and between the Indians and Negroes. Of the first class the frontier settlements every where present isolated examples; but at San Paulo, in Paraguay, there is an entire community of these people who are known by the name of *Mamelukes*. They are the offspring of Indian women by men of the Portuguese, Dutch, French, Italian, German and Spanish nations. The fathers were often outlaws, the mothers the very refuse of the Indian tribes. It is not surprising, therefore, that the children of such parents should have surpassed the indigenous savages in barbarity and devastation. Their habitual custom was to attack the missionary stations of the Jesuits, and either destroy or carry into hopeless slavery all the Indians who fell into their hands. Whole districts were thus depopulated, and even the Spanish cities were repeatedly attacked and pillaged, and the inhabitants reduced to slavery. "It is asserted that in one hundred and thirty years, two millions of Indians were slain, or carried into captivity by the Mamelukes of Brazil; and that more than one thousand leagues of country, as far as the river Amazon, were stripped of inhabitants. Pedro de Avilla, Governor of Buenos Ayres, declared that Indians were openly sold, in his sight, by the inhabitants of San Paulo at Rio Janeiro; and that six hundred thousand Indians were sold in this town alone from the year 1628 to 1630."‡ These atrocious practices were at last done away by the severest measures on the part of the parent governments of Spain and Portugal, but first by a victory gained over these lawless banditti by the combined tribes of the Guarany nation.

Allied in origin to these are the *Confusos* of Brazil, a numerous community with long and curled

for the most part a spherical head, (tête généralement sphérique,) while the *Columbian species* of the same author, embracing the Peruvians and Mexicans, is described with an elongated head, (tête allongée.) It is only necessary to compare the plates of the present work to be satisfied of the inaccuracy of the latter observation.—*Vide Bulletin des Sciences Univ.* VI, p. 245.

* GALLATIN, in Archæolog. Amer. II, p. 5, 118. † WISEMAN, Lectures, p. 80.
‡ DOBRIZHOFFER, Abipones, I, p. 161.—MURATORI, Paraguay Missions, p. 56.

hair, especially towards the end, "a mean between the wool of the Negro and the long stiff hair of the American." This bushy mass is combed out from the head so as to be between two and three feet in diameter, like that of the Papuas of New Guinea.*

The most remarkable mixture of the Indian and Negro races, is perhaps that described by Mr. Stevenson as seen by him in the republic of Colombia. "The natives of Esmeraldas, Rio Verde and Atacames," says he, "are all Zambos, apparently a mixture of Negroes and Indians; indeed the oral tradition of their origin is, that a ship having Negroes on board arrived on the coast, and having murdered a great number of the male Indians, kept their widows and daughters and laid the foundation of the present race." He describes these Esmeraldenos as "tall and rather slender, of a lightish black color, different from that called copper color; have soft curly hair, large eyes, nose rather flat, and thick lips, possessing more of the Negro than the Indian."† Dr. M'Culloh does not admit the asserted Negro origin of these people; but it so much resembles that of the black Charibs of St. Vincent, as to leave little doubt on the subject. Mr. T. R. Peale, who was some time among the Esmeraldenos, has assured me that so far as his personal observation goes they are a decided mixture of Negro and Indian blood. It has been thought by some that these are the very "blackamoors" described by Peter Martyr as having been seen by Balboa;‡ a point which, at this distance of time, is not readily decided.

17. THE NEGRO FAMILY.

The term Ethiopian is in common use to designate the Negro, yet very improperly, inasmuch as the name Ethiopia was applied by the ancients not only to certain parts of eastern Africa, including Nubia and Abyssinia, but also to southern India; and it was moreover applied to any country whose inhabitants were of a very dark complexion.§ "The Greeks," says Sir William Jones, "called all the southern nations of the world by the common appellation of Ethiopians, thus using Ethiop and Indian as convertible terms."‖ It is obvious, therefore, that the term Ethiopian, as applied by Blumenbach and others to the Negro nations collectively, is vague if not inadmissible.

The *Negro Family*, in the present instance, embraces all the proper Negro nations near and south of Mount Atlas and Abyssinia to the country inhabited by the Caffers and Hottentots. The more northern tribes, as we have already intimated, present various mixed features derived from their proximity to the Caucasian nations in their vicinity. "The people of El-wah," says Browne, "are

---

* Spix and Martius, Trav. in Brazil, I, p. 324.
† Trav. in South Amer. II, p. 387.   ‡ M'Culloh, Researches, p. 26.
§ Russell, Nubia and Abyssinia, Introd. p. 19.—Heeren, Anc. Nations of Africa, I, p. 295.— "Ethiopia, though a vague name, was applied to that country lying beyond the Cataracts, which in the Scriptures and in the Egyptian language, is called *Cush*."
‖ Leon. Jour. in Egypt, p. 89.

quite of Egyptian or Arab complexion and feature, and none of them black; so that I scarcely conceived myself to have arrived at the confines of the blacks till we reached the first inhabited parts of Darfour."* In like manner the Foulahs, who inhabit the Atlantic coast in the same parallel of latitude, are of a brown complexion, with long hair and European features; but these tribes are obviously in part of Moorish descent, and are supposed by some to be the Leucæthiopes of Ptolemy. Many nations to the north of the Mountains of the Moon, however, together with nearly all those south of them, present the peculiar features which render the people of this race more readily identified than those of any other. These characteristics, which have been already adverted to, are so uniformly bestowed, that among the thousands of Negroes of many different nations whom I saw in the West Indies, not one could have been mistaken for an individual of any other race.

The moral and intellectual character of the Africans is widely different in different nations. Thus the Makouas and Ashantees have continued to be the uncompromising enemies of the European colonists, and remain to this day unsubdued. The fiery and revengeful Eboe contrasts strongly with the docile native of Benguela. The Kroomen of the western coast are an intelligent and industrious people, while many of the tribes of the Niger are remarkably stupid and slothful. The Mandingoes are tractable and honest; but the Lucumi, who also inhabit the western coast, are a brave and independent people, who in captivity will even resort to suicide to avoid punishment or disgrace. The Caravalli tribe is remarkable for combining industry and avarice; and it is observed in the West Indies that they constitute the greater proportion of the free Negroes who become rich. On the other hand, all the tribes of Congo, and they are very numerous, are noted for indolence, deception and falsehood. The Negroes are proverbially fond of their amusements, in which they engage with great exuberance of spirit; and a day of toil is with them no bar to a night of revelry.†

Like most other barbarous nations their institutions are not unfrequently characterised by superstition and cruelty. They appear to be fond of warlike enterprises, and are not deficient in personal courage; but, once overcome, they yield to their destiny, and accommodate themselves with amazing facility to every change of circumstance.

* Trav. in Africa, p. 165.
† Lander, Trav. to Source of the Niger.—Prichard, Researches, Vol. I.—Murray, Trav. in U. States.

The Negroes have little invention, but strong powers of imitation, so that they readily acquire the mechanic arts. They have a great talent for music, and all their external senses are remarkably acute.

With respect to their intellectual character there is much diversity of opinion; some authors estimate it at a very low scale, whilst others insist that the germ of mind is as susceptible of cultivation in the Negro as in the Caucasian. That there is considerable difference in this respect in the different tribes is pretty generally admitted; but, up to the present time, the advantages of education have been inadequately bestowed on them, and instances of superior mental powers have been of extremely rare occurrence.

Note.—The great antiquity of the Negro race admits of no question, and has even led some philosophers to surmise that it was the primitive stock of mankind, and that all the other varieties may have been derived from this one by the action of physical causes. A few facts are sometimes of more weight than a host of hypotheses; and it may not be irrelevant to put this question, as well as the converse of it, to a chronological test, in the words of a distinguished author. "According to accredited dates," says he, "it is four thousand one hundred and seventy-nine years since Noah and his family came out of the ark. They are believed to have been of the Caucasian race; and the correctness of the belief there is no ground to question. We shall assume it, therefore, as a truth, without adducing the reasons which seem to sustain it. Three thousand four hundred and forty-five years ago a nation of Ethiopians is known to have existed. Their skins, of course, were dark, and they differed widely from Caucasians in many other particulars. They migrated from a remote country and took up their residence in the neighborhood of Egypt. Supposing that people to have been of the stock of Noah, the change must have been completed, and a new race formed, in seven hundred and thirty-three years, and probably in a much shorter period."*

The recent discoveries in Egypt give additional force to the preceding statement, inasmuch as they show beyond all question, that the Caucasian and Negro races were as perfectly distinct in that country upwards of three thousand years ago as they are now: whence it is evident that if the Caucasian was derived from the Negro, or the Negro from the Caucasian, by the action of external causes, the change must have been effected in at most a thousand years; a theory which the subsequent evidence of thirty centuries proves to be a physical impossibility; and we have already ventured to insist that such a commutation could be effected by nothing short of a miracle.

18. THE CAFFRO-AFRICAN FAMILY.

The country of the Caffers, now called Caffraria, is of indeterminate extent. On the eastern coast it extends from the Keiskamna river (which separates it from the Cape colony) to the south of Delagoa bay. On the west it touches Orange

---

* CALDWELL, Thoughts on the Unity of the Human Species, p. 79. *Philad.* 1830.

river; but its inland or northern limit is unknown, but is probably not less than two hundred leagues.* Thus the Caffers are interposed between the Hottentots on the south and the common Negroes on the north. Caffer, though now generally adopted among Europeans as the national designation of these people, is an Arabic word signifying infidel. Their true name appears to be *Amakosa*.

They are divided into many tribes, of which the principal are the Amakosa, Amatimba, Amaponda and the Zoulah.† The difference of physical appearances among these tribes is inconsiderable. They are tall, athletic and extremely well proportioned, and possess much natural grace of manner. Their physiognomy is remarkable for its combination of European and Negro character. The head, for example, is large, the forehead full and vaulted, the nose salient and aquiline, and the face a well formed oval: but on the other hand the mouth projects, the lips are large and fleshy, the hair black and more or less woolly, and the skin mostly black, though occasionally a dark brown. The Caffer women are much smaller than the men, seldom exceeding five feet in height, with a sleek, soft skin, and features which are strongly expressive of cheerfulness and content.

Lichtenstein, who was long among the Caffers, declares that he never saw one of these people "sneeze, yawn, cough or hawk;"‡ a fact which he found supported by the observations of his fellow travellers and others. This is truly a physiological anomaly.

If we may judge from the statements of some travellers, the Caffers are as much above the genuine Negro in morals and intelligence as in physical appearance. The tribes resident near the English colony are less cruel and superstitious than some others; but their appeals to pretended sorcery in punishing crimes and in settling disputes, and the despotic sway of their chiefs, are evidences of a great degree of barbarism.

It is very remarkable that the Caffers should have nations of genuine Negroes on both sides of them, and yet themselves possess so few Negro characteristics. Among other speculations is that of Mr. Barrow, who believes them to be of Arabic origin. "Their pastoral habits and manners," says he, "their kind and friendly reception to strangers, their tent-shaped houses, the remains of Islamism discoverable in one of its strongest features, the circumcision of male children, universally practised among the Caffer hordes, all denote their affinity to the Bedouin tribes. Their countenance also is Arabic; the color only differs, which

---

* Wolf. Trans. Roy. Geog. Soc. III, p. 200.   † Steedman, in same Journal, V, p. 322.
‡ Trav. in Africa, I, p. 252.

in some tribes varies from deep bronze to jet black, but most generally the latter is the prevailing color."* I give this hypothesis as I find it.

19. THE AUSTRO-AFRICAN FAMILY.

South of the Caffers to the extremity of Africa, live the Hottentots, one of the most singular varieties of the human species, and the nearest approximation to the lower animals. Their stature is of the mediate class, their persons large and clumsy, while their limbs are generally better moulded than in the northern Negroes. They have remarkably small hands and feet, which Sparrman considers a characteristic mark of this nation. Their complexion is a yellowish brown, compared by travellers to the peculiar hue of Europeans in the last stage of jaundice. Others call it a bright olive. Their hair, which is black and woolly, is attached to the scalp in small twisted tufts, but they are nearly destitute of beard. The head is large, the forehead low and broad, and the face extremely wide between the cheek bones, whence it retreats rapidly to a small, contracted chin. The eyes are small and far apart, the nose very broad and flat, and the mouth large; and the women are represented as even more repulsive in appearance than the men. Notwithstanding these personal disadvantages, Kolben† asserts that among many thousand Hottentots who had come under his observation, he never saw a bandy leg or a crooked limb, nor any other deformities, excepting two cripples only.

The Hottentots have but very vague ideas of religious obligations, although they are extremely superstitious. "The faults of which they are accused are, an inveterate indolence and gluttony, devouring every kind of animal garbage that falls in their way, without preparation, and when thus gorged they throw themselves down and sleep off the effects. That they are, however, capable of improvement, is evident from the conduct of those formed into an armed corps by the English, and who not only showed a sufficient degree of energy, but also grew cleanly in their persons."‡

The preceding remarks, however, apply chiefly to the Korans and the adjacent tribes, some of whom are naturally docile and inoffensive, while others have lost a part of their native rudeness by their proximity to the better sort of European colonists. But the Bosjesmans are far more savage and degraded than any other Hottentot tribes: Lichtenstein, indeed, maintains that they are a

---

* Trav. in Southern Africa, II, p. 117.   † Present State of the Cape of Good Hope, p. 53.
‡ TUCKEY, Maritime Geog. III, p. 10.

distinct people, speaking a language different from the Hottentots, and constituting the ultimate link in the scale of humanity. They are robbers by profession, cruel by nature, and have such a passion for destroying, that when they attack any of the herds belonging to the colonists, they will kill every animal they cannot drive away, rather than leave any for the owner.* These Bosjesmans, moreover, have the Hottentot features in their utmost ugliness, although their predatory life gives more activity and animation to their appearance. Like the New Hollanders, their eyelids become so much closed after middle life as to conceal the whole of the eyeball, leaving an aperture just sufficient to admit the light.†

Their dwellings are mud hovels, bushes, caves and clefts in the rock, which last often serve them in place of houses.—Many go naked, but others cover themselves in the simplest manner with the skins of animals killed in the chase. They feed on flesh when they can get it, eating it either raw or cooked indifferently; but their chief food consists of roots, berries and plants, whence their emaciated forms and shrivelled skin.‡ They have but little better idea of cleanliness than the brute creation; and a curious fact is mentioned by Lichtenstein, who says that many of the Hottentot tribes have a way of crouching down to the water, and throwing it into their mouths with the forefingers of both hands.§

20. THE OCEANIC-NEGRO FAMILY.

The Oceanic-Negro‖ family is dispersed extensively through the Indian Archipelago, and is also found in many islands of the Pacific. In the texture of the hair, in the color of the skin, and in fact in every physical relation these people are at once recognised as members of the great Negro race. M. Bory de St. Vincent describes them from personal observation in the following terms: Their physical characters consist in the color of the skin, which is even blacker than that of the darkest Ethiopians; the head is rounded, yet compressed in front and at the sides, at the same time that the facial angle is not more acute than in other Negroes: the hair is short and woolly, and more compact upon the head than in any other people; the superciliary ridges and the cheek bones are extremely

---

* LICHTENSTEIN, Trav. in S. Africa, II, p. 50.   † BURCHELL, Trav. in S. Africa, I, p. 459.
‡ SPARRMAN, Trav. in Africa, I, p. 201.   § Trav. in Africa, II, p. 48.
‖ Called *Melaniens* (Homo melanicus) by Bory de St. Vincent. They have generally borne the collective name of *Papuas*. See next section.

prominent: the eye is smaller than in the Australians, and the pupil is of a mixed greenish and brownish tint: the nose is excessively flat, the alæ being thin and depressed above, but below disgustingly open, thus corresponding in lateral extent with the wide mouth; the latter projects like a snout, with thick lips of a bright red color; and the chin is almost square, with a very scanty beard. Their lower extremities are thin, long and disproportioned, in which respect they resemble the Australians.

The more remarkable communities of this family are the following. The people of Van Diemen's Land have the preceding characteristics in the extreme. although their country is as cold as Ireland. So also the natives of the Great Andaman Island, who are of small stature, with slender limbs, protuberant abdomen, high shoulders, and large heads, exhibiting, in the language of Colonel Symes, a horrid mixture of famine and ferocity.* Forster compares the people of Mallicolo to monkeys, and asserts that he had seen no Negroes in whom the forehead was so depressed. This family is also found in the numerous islands adjacent to New Guinea, as New Britain, Admiralty Island, the Hermit Islands, &c. In Santa Cruz they are said to be less intensely black, and to have large foreheads. They also inhabit Tanna and Erromanga, Vanikoro, Viti, New Caledonia and many other islands; and there is every reason to believe that they are the aboriginal inhabitants of these various localities.

The PAPUAS. It has already been remarked, that the term *Papua* has been generally applied to all the black races of the Indian Archipelago; but Quoi and Gaimard have recently established the fact that the true Papuas are a hybrid family of Malays and Oceanic Negroes. These Papuas are of the middle stature, and generally pretty well formed, yet they occasionally have attenuated limbs. Their skin is not black, but a dark brown; and their hair is very black, neither lank nor crisped, but woolly, rather fine, and so much frizzled as to give the appearance of enormous magnitude to the head; and they comb out these wiry locks in such manner as to make the mass three feet in diameter. They have but little beard: the nose is sensibly flattened, the lips thick, and the cheek bones large; but there is nothing disgusting in their physiognomy.† The Papua skulls figured in Freycinct's Voyage, have the broad face of the Malay, and the whole head is somewhat rounded, with large parietal protuberances.‡

* Embassy to Ava, p. 130. † BORY, L'Homme, I, p. 305.
‡ Voy. de l'Uranie, Atlas, Pl. 1 and 2.

The moral and intellectual character of these people appears to differ in nothing from that of the genuine Negroes by whom they are surrounded.

The views of the French naturalists as to the origin of the Papuas are strongly confirmed by the physical characters of the *Confusos* of Brazil, who have been described in a former part of this work.* The true Papuas are for the most part confined to the northern coast of New Guinea, and the islands of Waigou, Sallawatty, Gammen and Battenta.† The people of Bougainville's island, who are darker and of more repulsive physiognomy, appear to belong to the same family. With them may also be classed the inhabitants of Solomon's isles, and those of Taomaco and Australia del Espiritu Santo.‡

21. THE AUSTRALIAN FAMILY.

The natives of New Holland are of the full stature, with broad chests, thin bodies, and long, slender limbs. Their usual color is either black or very dark brown, yet many of the women are as light colored as mulattoes. The face, which is ugly in the extreme, projects greatly from the head, and the mouth is particularly prominent owing to its width, and the great size of the lips. The nose is flat and broad, and the nostrils expanded. A deep sinus separates the nose from the forehead; the frontal ridges often overhang the eyes, while the forehead itself is low, and slopes rapidly to the top of the head. Dampier remarks of them that they hold up their heads and half close their eyes, as if looking at the sun; which he supposes is done to keep off the multitudes of insects by which they are surrounded. Their hair is longer than in the Negro, coarse and often much frizzled, yet rarely woolly.§ They are passionately fond of war; and as their fierce and vindictive tempers seldom allow them to pardon an enemy, there is a perpetual provocation to feud and bloodshed. Even their courtship, if it merits that name, consists in a violent abduction of the object of desire, and their women are treated throughout life with a brutality perhaps unparallelled in any other country. They are to the last degree filthy in their persons and gluttonous in their eating; and their dances betray the licentiousness of their morals.‖

It is not probable that these people, as a body, are capable of any other than

---

* Page 85. † Lesson, Voy. de la Coquille. Zool. I, p. 87.
‡ Prichard, Phys. Hist. of Man, I, p. 377–380.
§ Breton, N. South Wales, p. 157.—Barrington, Botany Bay, p. 63.
‖ Breton, p. 202.

a very slight degree of civilisation. "Forty years have elapsed since the country was colonised," says Mr. Breton, "and I have not yet heard of a single native having been reclaimed from barbarism."* Yet by their contact with the Europeans who have of latter years settled the country, they have lost much of the natural ferocity of their manners, and they have in many instances become industrious laborers. This is the more remarkable when we reflect on their primitive roving habits, which prevented their tilling the earth, or domesticating the indigenous animals; for they obtained from day to day a casual subsistence almost solely by fishing and the chase.†

The languages of the Australians are peculiar to themselves, and as yet but little understood; but it is now established that they borrow little or nothing from the Sanscrit.‡

The Australians are wholly deficient in maritime skill and enterprise. They paddle along their coasts seated cross-legged on a log, nor is there any evidence that they have ever crossed the straits which separate them from Van Diemen's Land.§

The western coast of New Holland, and some of the adjacent islands, are inhabited by people who have the general character of the Australians with some traits of the Oceanic-Negro: thus at Melleville Island (fifteen miles from the north coast) their feet are large, "their heads flat and broad, with low foreheads, and the back of the head projects very much: their hair is strong like horse-hair, thick, curly, and frizzled, and very black: their eyebrows and cheek bones are extremely prominent, and their eyes small, sunk, and very keen and bright: nose flat and short, the upper lip thick and projecting, mouth remarkably large, with regular, fine, white teeth: chin small, and face much contracted at bottom."‖ They have long bushy beards, and, like the Australians, scarify the skin in place of tattooing.

22. THE ALFORIAN FAMILY.

Of all the families of mankind, the Alfoers, or Horaforas, are perhaps least

---

* N. South Wales, p. 240.

† This gloomy picture is derived from the great majority of observers of Australian life. The reader may consult *Dawson's Australia* for some very different views, which, however, appear to be biassed by a genuine and active spirit of benevolence. See also Lang's Polynesian Nation.

‡ FIELD. N. S. Wales, p. 210.   § CAMPBELL, in Trans. Roy. Geog. Soc. III, p. 158.

‖ CAMPBELL, in Trans. Roy. Geog. Soc. of London, III, p. 153.

known. From the accounts of voyagers they appear to be more nearly allied to the Australians than to any other people. They have the flat nose, projecting cheek bones, large eyes, and salient teeth, of the Negro, with straight, coarse, long hair. Their limbs are long and thin, and their whole exterior repulsive in the extreme. To this it is added that they are sulky, stupid and ferocious.*

The Alfoers are considered aboriginal to many islands of the Indian Archipelago. They are most numerous in New Guinea, the Moluccas, and Magindano: in Celebes they are said to be sometimes as fair as the Malays, and the savage Dyaks of Borneo appear to belong to the same family. It is not improbable, as Dr. Prichard suggests, that the Alfoers are but a branch of the Australian stock.†

NOTE.—The map which precedes this work is designed to show, though on a small scale, the geographical distribution of the five races of men; and the lines of demarcation are those indicated by Professor Blumenbach, as separating the different varieties or races in the primitive epochs of the world. In every such attempt some anachronisms are unavoidable, and we necessarily judge of antiquity from the observation of modern times. The ancients, for example, knew little of Africa, and nothing of America and the islands of the Pacific Ocean, not to mention a multitude of subordinate details; but we assume that the inhabitants of those countries were essentially the same at the Christian era that they are now. The boundary between the Caucasian and Mongolian races is extremely vague, but Professor Blumenbach's line (which is an approximation to accuracy) runs from the Ganges in a northwestern direction to the Caspian sea, and thence to the river Obi, in Russia. At a comparatively recent period, however, several Mongolian nations have established themselves in Europe, as the Samoyedes, Laplanders, &c.

The Ethiopian line is drawn north of the Senegal river obliquely east and south to the southern frontier of Abyssinia, and thence to Cape Guardafui, thus embracing the Atlas mountains. Of the latter little is known; but many Negro nations inhabit to the north of them, at the same time that the Arab tribes have penetrated far beyond them to the south, and in some places have formed a mixed race with the native tribes.

* LESSON, Voy. de la Coquille. Zool. I, p. 103.   † Researches, I, p. 393.

CRANIA AMERICANA.

THE ANCIENT PERUVIANS.

PERU is a narrow strip of land between the Andes and the sea, bounded on the south by a desert. Its fine climate, its productive soil, and its proximity to the ocean, render it one of the most interesting divisions of the southern continent; and its advantages appear to have been fully appreciated by the aborigines themselves, for there is evidence that several populous nations held successive dominion in the country.

History, even before the advent of the Spaniards, throws much light on one of these nations; that, for instance, which was governed by the Incas: yet, with respect to the others, we know little else than what can be gleaned from their monuments and cemeteries; and however meagre these facts may appear, they possess considerable interest, and the more so because so few others are available to us.

The arid region of Atacama* was the favorite sepulchre of the Peruvian nations for successive ages; for, while the climate tends rather to the desiccation than to the decay of the dead, the mixed sand and salt of the desert have contributed to the same end; and the lifeless bodies of whole generations of the former inhabitants of Peru may now be examined, like those from the Theban catacombs, after the lapse of hundreds, perhaps of thousands of years. The great number of the dead thus remaining in Peru, has been a subject of surprise to all travellers, and serves to convey an idea of the vast population that has at different

---

* The desert of Atacama divides the kingdom of Peru from that of Chilé, and is nearly an hundred leagues in length. "In the midst of it is the River of Salt, the water whereof is so brackish that it presently grows thick in the hand, or any vessel, and the banks are covered with salt."—HERRERA, Dec. IV. Lib. IV. Cap. I.

periods derived its subsistence from that country. For example, we are told by an intelligent voyager, that having landed at Vermejo, in Peru, in the year 1687, he found the vicinity of that town so strewed with desiccated bodies, that, in his own language, a man might have walked a mile and a half, and trod on them at every step.* These circumstances long since made me desirous to obtain a series of crania from the Peruvian sepulchres, in order to ascertain, if possible, whether they present indications of more than one great family; or, in other words, to inquire whether among them I could trace such departures from the well known type of the American race, as would lead to the supposition that this continent was formerly inhabited by a plurality of races. In pursuing this inquiry I have been so fortunate as to have the examination, in my own and other collections, of nearly one hundred Peruvian crania: and the result is, that Peru appears to have been at different times peopled by two nations of differently formed crania, one of which is perhaps extinct, or at least exists only as blended by adventitious circumstances, in various remote and scattered tribes of the present Indian race. Of these two families, that which was antecedent to the appearance of the Incas is designated as the *Ancient Peruvian*, of which the remains have hitherto been found only in Peru, and especially in that division of it now called Bolivia. Their tombs, according to Mr. Pentland, abound on the shores and islands of the great Lake Titicaca, in the inter-alpine valley of the Desaguadera, and in the elevated valleys of the Peruvian Andes, between the latitudes of 14° and 19° 30′ south. The country around this inland sea was called Collao, and the site of what appears to have been their chief city, bears the name of Tiaguanaco.

Let us now glean from the few sources that are open to us, what can be discovered of the physical and intellectual character of these people, their history and tradition.

Our knowledge of their physical appearance is derived solely from their tombs. In stature they appear not to have been in any respect remarkable, nor to have differed from the cognate nations except in the conformation of the head, which is small, greatly elongated, narrow its whole length, with a very retreating forehead, and possessing more symmetry than is usual in skulls of the American race. The face projects, the upper jaw is thrust forward, and the teeth are inclined outward. The orbits of the eyes are large and rounded, the nasal bones salient, the zygomatic arches expanded; and there is a remarkable simplicity in the sutures that connect the bones of the cranium.

* WAFER, Voy. p. 165.

The first idea that occurs to every one on looking at a series of these skulls is, that their peculiarities are in a great measure artificial. If, however, we carefully examine the cranium figured on the fourth plate, together with the accompanying smaller outlines, we find no evidence of mechanical compression. This head, on the contrary, appears to be of the natural form, unaltered by art; and it is figured as an illustrative type of the cranial peculiarities of the people now under consideration.

It must almost invariably happen, that when the forehead of a naturally rounded head has been much compressed by art, the back and lateral parts of the cranium become proportionally expanded, in order to make room for the brain that has been displaced from the anterior chamber. Thus, among all the specimens I have seen of this deformity, from the tribes on the Columbia river, the ancient inhabitants of Venezuela, the Charibs of the Antilles and some tribes of Peruvians, I have met with no exceptions to the preceding rule. All these nations have, naturally, spheroidal heads, and the result of mechanical compression is such as above described; a point on which the reader can judge for himself by comparing the illustrations in various parts of this work. Now the heads of these ancient Peruvians seldom present such lateral expansion; but on the contrary are as remarkable for their narrowness as for their length. In fact their low facial angle, their sloping forehead, and their protruding face, might lead to a suspicion of a Negro origin, were it not for the unanswerable evidence derived from the texture of the hair. This is uniformly long and lank, and appears to have been worn at full length by both sexes, and its natural blackness is preserved notwithstanding centuries of inhumation. I am free to admit that the naturally elongated heads of these people were often rendered more so by the intervention of art, but such examples are for the most part readily detected. It is a feature both of civilised and savage communities to admire their own national characteristics above all others, and hence where nature has denied an imaginary grace, art is called in to supply the deficiency; and even where there has been no such deficiency, human vanity prompts to extravagance. Thus I have seen some skulls of this race which must have been naturally very low and long; yet in order to exaggerate a feature that was considered beautiful, compression has been applied until the whole head has assumed more the character of the monkey than the man. An example of this kind will be seen in the fifth plate, wherein the evidence of artificial flattening of the forehead is undeniable: but the congenital lowness of this region and great length of the head, have made very little compression necessary to effect the desired object; whence there has resulted but a trifling expansion of the posterior and lateral parts of the skull. On the other hand, had this cranium been of the rounded form common to the American Indians, and especially to the existing Peruvians, it is difficult to imagine by what complex contrivances the present shape could have been produced.

It would be natural to suppose, that a people with heads so small and badly formed would occupy the lowest place in the scale of human intelligence. Such, however, was not the case; and it remains to show, that civilisation existed in Peru anterior to the advent of the Incas, and that those anciently civilised people constituted the identical nation whose extraordinary skulls are the subject of our present inquiry.

Among the first travellers in Peru, and perhaps the very first who recorded what he saw, was Pedro de Cieca, an officer in the army of Pizarro. Although an unlettered man, he describes with simplicity and clearness whatever came under his observation; and the following passage from his work, although of some length, is so interesting and so connected with the present inquiry, that I shall venture to give it entire.

"Tiaguanico," says he, "is not a very large town, but it is deserving of notice on account of the great edifices which are still to be seen in it; near the principal of these is an artificial hill raised on a groundwork of stone. Beyond this hill are two stone idols, resembling the human figure, and apparently formed by skilful artificers. They are of somewhat gigantic size, and appear clothed in long vestments differing from those now worn by the natives of these provinces; and their heads are also ornamented. Near these statues is an edifice which, on account of its antiquity and the absence of letters, leaves us in ignorance of the people who constructed it: and such indeed has been the lapse of time since its erection, that little remains but a well built wall, which must have been there for ages, for the stones are very much worn and crumbled. In this place, also, there are stones so large and so overgrown that our wonder is excited to comprehend how the power of man could have placed them where we see them. Many of these stones are variously wrought, and some having the form of men, must have been their idols. Near the wall are many caves and excavations under the earth; but in another place more to the west are other and greater monuments, consisting of large gateways and their hinges, platforms and porches, each of a single stone.

"What most surprised me while engaged in examining and recording these things, was that the above enormous gateways were formed on other great masses of stone, some of which were thirty feet long, fifteen feet wide, and six feet thick. Nor can I conceive with what tools or instruments these stones were hewn out; for it is obvious that before they were wrought and brought to perfection, they must have been vastly larger than we now see them. Before I proceed to a further account of Tiaguanico, I must remark that this monument is the most ancient in Peru: for it is supposed that some of these structures *were built long before the dominion of the Incas*, and I have heard the Indians affirm that these sovereigns constructed their great buildings in Cuzco after the plan of the walls of Tiaguanico, and they add that the first Incas were accustomed to hold their court in this place. Another very curious fact is, that in the greater part of this territory there are no quarries nor rocks whence the materials for these structures could have been derived. I asked the natives, in the presence of Juan de Varagas, (who commands here,) if these edifices were built in the time of the Incas? But they laughed at the question, repeating what I have already stated, adding that they did not know who built them, but that they had a tradition of their ancestors that these structures appeared in a single night as we now see them."*

These statements, and many others to the same purpose, are confirmed by the Vicar-general, Diego de Alcobaza, who also visited Tiaguanico, and has left an account of the architectural wonders he saw there.†

It will be observed by the preceding narrative, that tradition among the Peruvians attributed these cyclopean structures to an era long antecedent to the appearance of the Incas, and this tradition is sustained by history; for the city of Tiaguanico did not fall into the hands of the Incas until the reign of Mayta Yupanque, the fourth king, at which period the edifices in question must have been in existence for centuries, and were already in a state of ruin and decay. Garcilaso de la Vega, himself of the royal Peruvian family, admits that these ruins existed at the time the country was conquered by his ancestors;‡ and a Peruvian author, two centuries and a half nearer our own time, states that Tiaguanico is indisputably anterior to the monarchy of the Incas, and speaks, as if from personal observation, of a gigantic pyramid and colossal human figures cut from solid rock, indicative of the power and genius of a great nation.§ The first invasion of the Incas was followed by the erection of some temples to enforce the new religion, but their only great architectural monument in these parts, the Temple of the Sun on the island in Titicaca, was not built until the reign of Tapac Yupanque, the tenth Inca, early in the fifteenth century. Herrera also alludes to a tradition

---

* PEDRO DE CIECA, Chronica del Peru, Cap. 105. 18mo. Anvers, 1554.—See also ACOSTA, Hist. de las Indias, Lib. VI, Cap. XIV.

† GARCILASO DE LA VEGA, Commentarios, Lib. III, Cap. 1.

‡ Idem. Loco citato. § MERCURIO PERUANO, Lima, 1791.

of the Indians that these edifices had been built by Amazons at a remote era, nor are the Incas mentioned as having had any part in their construction.*

"It is probable," says Humboldt, "that the edifices which are called in Peru by the name of *Inga-pilca*, or Buildings of the Inca, do not date further back than the thirteenth century. Those at Vinaque and Tiaguanico were constructed at a more remote period: so also were the walls of unbaked brick, which were made by the ancient inhabitants of Quito. It is to be desired that some intelligent traveller would visit the banks of the great lake Titicaca, the province of Collao, and more especially the elevated plain of Tiaguanico, which is the centre of an ancient civilisation in this region."†

It will now be asked what evidence can be adduced to prove that the people, whose remains we are considering, were the same with those who have left the architectural monuments of Tiaguanico and Titicaca? The fact is established by the observations of Mr. Pentland, an intelligent English traveller, who has recently visited the upper provinces of Peru. This gentleman states that in the vicinity of Titicaca he has "discovered innumerable tombs, hundreds of which he entered and examined. These monuments are of a grand species of design and architecture, resembling Cyclopean remains, and not unworthy of the arts of ancient Greece or Rome. They therefore betokened a high condition of civilisation; but the most extraordinary fact belonging to them is their invariably containing the mortal remains of a race of men, of all ages, from the earliest infancy to maturity and old age, the formation of whose crania seems to prove that they are an extinct race of natives who inhabited upper Peru above a thousand years ago, and differing from any mortals now inhabiting our globe. The site is between the fourteenth and nineteenth degrees of south latitude, and the skulls found (of which specimens are both in London and Paris) are remarkable for their extreme extent behind the occipital foramen; for two-thirds of the weight of the cerebral mass must have been deposited in this wonderfully elongated posterior chamber: and as the bones of the face were also much elongated, the general appearance must have been rather that of some of the ape family than of human beings. In the tombs, as in those of Egypt, parcels of grain were left beside the dead; and it was another

---

* Hist. Dec. III, Lib. IX, Cap. 1.

† Monuments, I, p. 5.—See also Dr. M'Culloh, (Researches, p. 406,) who remarks, in confirmation, "that a certain degree of demi-civilisation prevailed in the nations adjoining the Peruvian empire, which was not derived from their communication with the latter."

singular circumstance that the maize, or Indian corn, so left, was different from any that now existed in the country."

Mr. Pentland expresses his decided opinion "that the extraordinary forms thus brought to the light of day after their long sojourn, could not be attributed to pressure, or any external force, similar to that still employed by many American tribes; and adduced, in confirmation of this view, the opinions of Cuvier, of Gall, and of many other naturalists and anatomists. On these grounds he was of opinion that they constituted the population of these elevated regions before the arrival of the present Indian population, which in its physical characters, customs, &c., offers many analogies with the Asiatic population of the old world."*

The preceding facts appear to establish two important propositions; first, that the primitive Peruvians had attained to a considerable degree of civilisation and refinement, so far at least as architecture and sculpture may be adduced in evidence, long before the Incas appeared in their country; and secondly, that these primitive Peruvians were the same people whose elongated and seemingly brutalised crania now arrest our attention; and it remains to inquire, whether these are the same people whom the Incas found in possession of Peru, or whether their nation and power were already extinct at that epoch?

The modern Peruvian empire had existed upwards of four hundred years at the time of the Spanish conquest, so that its origin may be dated somewhere about the year 1100 of our era. Now it appears that among the first military enterprises of this new family was the conquest of Collao, which possessed a productive soil and a warlike population, and embraced within its confines the Lake Titicaca, from which the Incas pretended to have derived a supernatural origin. Every effort was therefore made to subdue and to destroy the Collas. The Inca Yupanque waged against them a war of extermination; and we are told by Herrera that in some of the towns he left so few persons alive, that inhabitants were afterwards sent from other parts of Peru to colonise the wasted districts.† The same historian adds, that in order further to depopulate the country, the inhabitants were banished from it in large bodies, and dispersed through other provinces of the empire; and yet such was the dread in which the new dynasty held these warlike people, that they forbade more than a thousand of them to

---

* Report of the Fourth Meeting of the British Association for the Advancement of Science, p. 624; and Additional Reports, which were republished in Waldie's Journal of Belles-Lettres, 1834.

† Historia de las Indias, Dec. III, Lib. IX, c. 4.

be within the walls of Cuzco at a time, lest they should attempt some revolutionary enterprise. It therefore appears that no means were left untried to subdue and exterminate the people of Colla;* yet how far such a system, persisted in at intervals for more than two centuries, could have annihilated a whole nation, I shall not attempt to decide.

When the Spaniards took possession of these provinces, they found them inhabited by barbarous tribes, and the islands in the lake Titicaca, which had once been highly cultivated, were then waste and vacant. Upon the lake were seen rafts made of the reed called by the natives *totora*, and on these rafts whole families made their home, tossed here and there upon the waters by every change of wind. They were in so brutalised a state that when asked to what nation of people they belonged, they replied, "We are not men, but Uros," as if they did not consider themselves as belonging to the human species.† Were these Uros (for so they named their tribe) the remains of the savage colonies sent from other parts of Peru to supplant the Collas? This inference bears at least the stamp of probability, but it still does not aid us in ascertaining whether the Collas themselves were the remains of the primitive civilised Peruvians.‡

It may be added, that Garcilaso describes the Peruvian tribes near the sea coasts, to whom he applies the collective name of Yuncas, as living in the utmost barbarism at the advent of the Incas. In proof of this statement he adduces their mythology, which accorded divine attributes to every thing in which they observed any dominant excellence. Thus, says he, they worshipped the fox for his cunning, the deer for his swiftness, and the eagle for the perfection of his sight. These superstitions, however, are not more surprising than those of the primitive ages of civilisation in the old world; and there appears throughout the Spanish historian an evident disposition to depreciate the character of the ancient tribes of Peru, in order to palliate the cruel measures which were resorted to by the Incas for their subjugation. Garcilaso himself describes a remarkable temple at Pachacamac, which was erected by the Yuncas; and the Chimuyans, who were something farther to the south, appear to have possessed extensive and regular edifices, together with some other attributes of civilisation. The inhabitants of Chimù resisted the Incas with great valor, and appear to have been very superior to most

* GARCILASO DE LA VEGA, Comment. Lib. III, cap. 3.

† ACOSTA, Hist. de las Indias, Lib. III, cap. 6.—DE LAET, Novus Orbis, Lib. XI.

‡ Indian tradition relates that the Collas were *all* destroyed at once, but attributes this catastrophe to an inundation. See HERRERA, Dec. III, Lib. IX, c. 1.

of the adjacent tribes at that early epoch. Nevertheless, they could not compare with the primitive nation of Collao; and when we find the remains of the latter mingled, as it were, among those of the barbarous hordes on the sea coast, their presence may be accounted for in the casualties of war or commerce, or by that forced system of colonisation to which we have already alluded.

I have followed up the researches of Baron Humboldt and Dr. M'Culloh with the more zeal, because so little notice has been taken of the subject by other writers; and especially because we are now able to take one step more in the inquiry, by studying the arts of these people in connection with their cranial remains.*

* Mr. Stevenson has described some very interesting ruins near the village of Langunilla in the province of Caxamarca, which he supposes to be anterior to the Inca dominion in Peru. He represents these remains to be those of a town, of which the houses are all built of stone, surrounding a rock or hill in a valley. "The bottom tier or range of rooms has walls of an amazing thickness, in which I have measured stones twelve feet long and seven feet high, forming the whole side of a room, with one or more large stones laid across, which serve as a roof. Above these houses another tier was built in the same manner, on the back of which are the entrances or doorways, and a second row had their backs to the mountain. The roofs of the second tier in front had been covered with stone, and probably formed a promenade; a second tier of rooms thus rested on the roofs of the first tier, which were on a level with the second front tier. In this manner one double tier of dwelling rooms was built above another to the height of seven tiers." The author adds that this series of buildings was capable of containing five thousand families, and he gives his reasons for supposing it to be, not a granary of the Incas, as some travellers have imagined, but the residence of the lord of Chicama, "when he resided in the interior of his territory before it became subject to the Inca Pachacutec." These ruins present no remains of delicate sculpture, although some of the stones are carved in arabesques. Similar to these are the remains of the fortified palace of Paramonga. *Trav. in S. Amer.* II, p. 22, 170, 173.

PLATE I.

EMBALMED HEAD, FROM THE PERUVIAN CEMETERY AT ARICA.

This head, though obviously a relic of antiquity, has not all the characters of the Ancient Peruvian, nor is it introduced as an unequivocal example of that race. The forehead is extremely retreating, and at least partially moulded by artificial means; but the whole cranium is broader, both in its frontal and parietal diameters, than is usual in the people now under consideration. It is carefully and effectually embalmed: the flesh of the neck and face has been removed and its place supplied by Lama wool, and the whole head appears to have subsequently undergone the process of tanning and drying. The skin is almost black, the sockets filled, the external appendages of the eye admirably preserved, and the hair, which is long, is elaborately plaited, and disposed with great apparent care. The sharpness of the superciliary ridges indicates the effect of a board or bandage, which has compressed the os frontis and widened the whole head. This is the most perfect instance of embalming, among the American nations, that has come under my notice. The head was found separate from the body, and enveloped in a sack of corresponding size, made of coarse thread or twine. It was disinterred in the vicinity of Arica, and politely lent me for insertion among the illustrations of this work, by Mr. James Blake, of Boston, Massachusetts.

The inhabitants of Port Mulgrave, on the northwest coast, and some other tribes, decapitate their dead chiefs, and place the head in a box by itself;[*] from which and other circumstances it is probable that the present relic was not that of an enemy, but a person of distinction.

---

[*] DIXON, Voy. p. 176, 181.—This singular custom also prevails in some of the South Sea Islands, as the Ladrone and Society Islands, and the Gambier Group.—HAWKSWORTH, Voy. II, p. 236.—BEECHEY, Voy. I. p. 121.

PLATE II.

ANCIENT PERUVIAN.

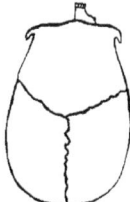 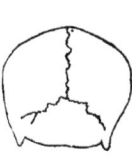

This extraordinary relic was exhumed from that part of the sandy tract of Atacama which is nearest to Arica. I received it in fragments from Mr. T. R. Peale of this city, and have been so fortunate as to recompose all the parts. The observer is struck with the greatly inclined forehead, the extreme elongation of the whole head, and more particularly by the length of the occiput behind the ear; yet there is but little lateral expansion of the head, which, with the face, is narrow in proportion throughout.

This cranium belongs to a child not more than five years of age, and presents the following measurements.

Longitudinal diameter,	6.9 inches.
Parietal diameter,	4.6 inches.
Frontal diameter,	3.7 inches.
Vertical diameter,	4.3 inches.
Extreme length of head and face,	7.5 inches.
Internal capacity,	64. cubic inches.
Capacity of the anterior chamber,	17. cubic inches.
Capacity of the posterior chamber,	47. cubic inches.

PLATE III.

ANCIENT PERUVIAN.

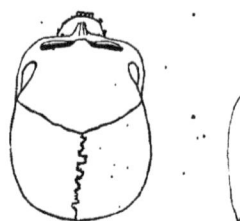 

A skull with a singularly flat and retreating forehead, and projecting face. The narrowness of the head, however, is not remarkable, and very slight pressure, if any, has been applied to the frontal bone. The latter presents a rounded ridge extending from the nasal bones backwards to the sagittal suture, which elevation would probably have been obliterated if much compression had been resorted to. On the other hand, a friend has suggested that this ridge may be the result of compression itself, from ligatures which have pressed up the bones proximate to the frontal suture of infancy; yet such a result could hardly have followed unless the compression was ingeniously withheld from that part of the forehead. Again, on plates XVII and LV of this work, two skulls are figured in which this frontal ridge is as strongly developed as in any others in my possession, and yet are obviously devoid of mechanical agency. Of the few skulls of ancient Peruvians that have come under my notice, the larger number possesses this ridge in a striking degree, and it is least obvious in those instances where the flattening process is most evident, for example in plate V.

MEASUREMENTS.

Longitudinal diameter,	6.5 inches.
Parietal diameter,	5.2 inches.
Vertical diameter,	5.1 inches.
Frontal diameter,	4.3 inches.
Extreme length of head and face,	8.3 inches.
Inter-mastoid arch,	14.5 inches.
Inter-mastoid line,	4. inches.

108   CRANIA AMERICANA.

    Occipito-frontal arch, ... 13.8 inches.
    Horizontal periphery, ... 18.5 inches.
    Internal capacity, ... 72.5 cubic inches.
    Capacity of the anterior chamber, . . . 26. cubic inches.
    Capacity of the posterior chamber, . . . 46.5 cubic inches.
    Capacity of the coronal region, . . . 14.75 cubic inches.
    Facial angle,. . . . . . . 68 degrees.

This skull belongs to the Philadelphia Museum, and was lent me by Mr. T. R. Peale. The entire desiccated body was obtained from the borders of the desert of Atacama, not far from Arica. The remains were those of a woman who may have reached her thirtieth year. The hair was very long, and had lost none of its natural black color. With the body was found a small bag, not unlike a modern reticule, in which were contained some copper fish-hooks and small instruments of bone which were probably used in forming the meshes of their nets or other fabrics. Among the envelopes were also observed small pieces of an aromatic gum.

Through the kindness of Alexander Naysmith, Esq., of London, I possess casts of the six skulls brought by Mr. Pentland from the vicinity of the lake Titicaca, and five of them are strikingly like the specimen here figured, both as respects their general form, their narrow face, their small size, and their several diameters; yet they present more obvious marks of artificial modification.

PLATE IV.

ANCIENT PERUVIAN.

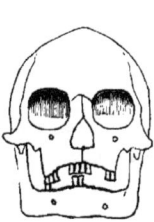  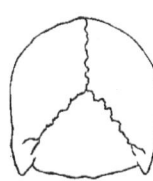

I have already alluded to this relic as furnishing an example of the head of the primitive Peruvians unaltered by art; and it may therefore stand as a type of the cranial conformation of these people. Though the forehead retreats rapidly, there is but little expansion at the sides, and from the face to the occiput inclusive there is a narrowness that seems characteristic of the race. The posterior view represents the skull elevated in that region without any unnatural width at the sides, and the vertical view sufficiently confirms the latter fact.

MEASUREMENTS.

Longitudinal diameter,	7.3 inches.
Parietal diameter,	5.3 inches.
Frontal diameter,	4.3 inches.
Vertical diameter,	5.3 inches.
Inter-mastoid arch,	14. inches.
Inter-mastoid line,	4.3 inches.
Occipito-frontal arch,	15. inches.
Horizontal periphery,	19.8 inches.
Extreme length of head and face,	8.2 inches.
Internal capacity,	81.5 cubic inches.
Capacity of the anterior chamber,	31.5 cubic inches.
Capacity of the posterior chamber,	50. cubic inches.
Capacity of the coronal region,	16.25 cubic inches.
Facial angle,	73 degrees.

My friend Dr. Ruschenberger, from whom I received this skull, has preserved the following memorandum of the circumstances under which it was found.

"About a mile from the town, (Arica,) on the south side of the *morro*, is a cemetery of the ancient Peruvians. There is one path to it over the hill, which is somewhat laborious, and another round the base of Arica Head, which is only practicable when the tide is low. On one side of the hill are found the graves of this injured people, indicated by hillocks of upturned sand, and the numbers of human bones bleaching in the sun, and portions of bodies, as legs and arms, or a hand and foot, scattered over the surface. The surface is covered with sand an inch or two deep, which being removed discovers a stratum of salt, three or four inches in thickness, that spreads all over the hill. Immediately beneath are found the bodies, in graves or holes, not more than three feet in depth. The body [to which this head belonged] was placed in a squatting posture with the knees drawn up, and the hands applied to the sides of the head. The whole was

110   CRANIA AMERICANA.

enveloped in a coarse but close fabric, with stripes of red, which has withstood wonderfully the destroying effects of ages, for these interments were made before the conquest, though at what period is not known."*

PLATE V.

ANCIENT PERUVIAN.

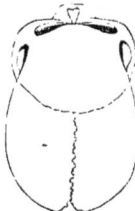 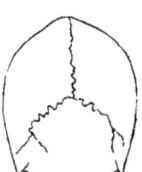

I have not ascertained from what particular part of Peru this skull was obtained, but it is strikingly analogous to the three preceding specimens. The intervention of art in flattening the skull is very manifest, yet it has been effected on a forehead extremely low by nature; for the lateral swell is not remarkable, and the parietal protuberances, in particular, are not much more inflated than was natural to these people. The depth of the cranium behind the coronal suture is remarkable; and the very narrow face in this instance proves that the head could not have been originally spheroidal, like that of the later inhabitants of Peru.

This specimen was politely lent me by Dr. J. Kearney Rodgers, of New York, of whose collection it forms a part.

MEASUREMENTS.

Longitudinal diameter,	6.7 inches.
Parietal diameter,	4.5 inches.
Frontal diameter,	4.1 inches.
Vertical diameter,	4.1 inches.
Inter-mastoid arch,	11.5 inches.
Inter-mastoid line,	3.6 inches.
Occipito-frontal arch,	14.2 inches.

* Three Years in the Pacific, p. 341.

THE ANCIENT PERUVIANS.

Horizontal periphery,	18. inches.
Extreme length of head and face,	8.8 inches.
Internal capacity,	65.5 cubic inches.
Capacity of the anterior chamber,	19.75 cubic inches.
Capacity of the posterior chamber,	45.75 cubic inches.
Capacity of the coronal region,	12.75 cubic inches.
Facial angle,	61 degrees.

It will be shown in the sequel that the average internal capacity of the Caucasian or European head is at least ninety cubic inches; and it will be observed that the three adult skulls in the preceding series of ancient Peruvians, give an aggregate of two hundred and nineteen cubic inches, or a mean of seventy-three. It will also be observed, that the mean capacity of the anterior is about one half of that of the posterior chamber, or twenty-five to forty-seven; while the mean of the facial angle is but sixty-seven degrees.

THE CHIMUYANS.

This name, Chimù, was applied rather to a chief than a territory. The province of the "Great Chimù" was very near the present site of Truxillo, in Peru, and its inhabitants had attained a certain degree of civilisation before they were conquered by the tenth Inca. My friend Dr. M. Burrough, (now United States Consul at Vera Cruz,) examined the ruins of the Chimuyan city with great care, and traced the remains of dwellings, walls and terraces, over an extensive plot of ground.*

---

* For some additional particulars respecting the remains of the ancient demi-civilisation in South America, the reader is referred to the learned *Researches* of Dr. M'Culloh, Chap IX.

112   CRANIA AMERICANA.

PLATE VI.

CHIMUYAN.

 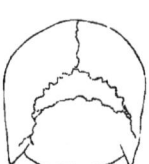

In the course of some excavations among the ruins of the Chimuyan city. Dr. Burrough found a skull in admirable preservation. It differs from both the Ancient and Inca Peruvian heads in being of a more oval form, although there is still an obvious inequality between the two sides; the forehead also is low and retreating, and the width is large between the parietal bones, and the whole head remarkably small.

MEASUREMENTS.

Longitudinal diameter,	6.5 inches.
Parietal diameter,	5.4 inches.
Frontal diameter,	4.4 inches.
Vertical diameter,	5.2 inches.
Inter-mastoid arch,	14.6 inches.
Inter-mastoid line,	4. inches.
Occipito-frontal arch,	14.4 inches.
Horizontal periphery,	19.5 inches.
Internal capacity,	67.5 cubic inches.
Capacity of the anterior chamber,	28.5 cubic inches.
Capacity of the posterior chamber,	39. cubic inches.
Capacity of the coronal region,	10.25 cubic inches.
Facial angle,	76 degrees.

THE INCA OR MODERN PERUVIANS.

The origin of the Incas of Peru is shrouded in fable. They are represented in their traditions as two celestial personages, a son and daughter of the sun himself, who were sent from heaven to instruct and civilise a favored people. These persons, says the tradition, were Manco Capac, the first Inca, and Coya Mama, who was both his sister and his wife. They appeared first on an island in the lake Titicaca, and taking the people under their jurisdiction, began at once a reform of all the institutions of the country.

Thus a fabulous tradition of the Peruvians refers the rise of their monarchy to two personages only; but this preference for a small number was calculated to render the account more marvellous, and the descendants of the individuals more respected. What goes, however, to prove that Peru was not conquered by the artful inventions of a few strangers, is the fact that the first Inca planted numerous colonies, and subdued many nations; always appearing in arms, and always victorious.* Force was appealed to from the first appearance of these new people; the laws were altered, a new language and a new religion imposed, and all the customs and rights of many populous and warlike communities, were abrogated in a very short period of time, and this by force of arms or the dread of punishment. All that absolute power could do was done in a single reign. Is it to be believed that all these changes were brought about by two strangers, who spoke a foreign language? Can it be credited that this total revolution in social and civil government was the result of moral causes, operating on nations who were as strongly devoted to their own institutions as any other people? Certainly not. On the contrary we are compelled to attribute this change to an influx of foreigners, whose number and intelligence enabled them to overcome every obstacle that arose in their path. Who could these strangers be?

The Toltecas, the most civilised nation of ancient Mexico, after governing that country for four centuries, suddenly abandoned it about the year 1050 of our era. The reasons for this step are given at some detail by the Mexican annalists. They state that during the reign of their last prince, a series of calamities gave a fatal blow to their prosperity and power. "For several years heaven denied them the necessary showers to their fields, and the earth the fruits that supported them. The air, infected by mortal contagion, filled daily the graves with the dead, and

* Garcilaso, Comment. Lib. I, passim.

the minds of those surviving with consternation, at the destruction of their countrymen. A great part of the nation died by famine and sickness; and the wretched remains of this people, willing to save themselves from the common calamity, sought timely relief to their misfortunes in other countries."* The historian then adds, that the Toltecas migrated in large bodies to various parts of the continent, and extended themselves as far south as Yucatan; and so complete was the dispersion of these people, that the land of Anahuac (the ancient name of Mexico) remained solitary and depopulated for nearly a century. Now it has been mentioned in the preceding chapter, that the Inca race date their possession of Peru from about the eleventh century of our era; and as this period corresponds with the epoch of the migration of the Toltecas, we may reasonably conjecture that both were of a common origin. This supposition gains strength when we inquire into the character of the Toltecas.

Of all the nations of the new world they had attained to the highest degree of civilisation; they lived in society, collecting themselves into cities, under the government of kings and regular laws. They were not remarkably warlike, and preferred the cultivation of the arts to the exercise of arms; they also devoted themselves to architecture, and cultivated with care various useful plants and fruits. Nor did they practise those arts only which are considered as necessary to human comfort, but those also which minister to luxury; and it is added, that although their religion was idolatrous, it does not appear that they practised those barbarous and bloody sacrifices, which became so common in Mexico after the Toltecan emigration.† Now, as we shall hereafter see, these are the leading features in the character of the modern or Inca Peruvians; and when we take into consideration that the disappearance of the Toltecas from their own country, was simultaneous with the advent of the new dynasty in Peru, may we not look upon the two as cognate nations? There is, besides, a coincidence in the squared and conical form of the head in the Toltecas and Peruvians that is very striking, and which will be more particularly adverted to in a future part of this work.

Whether the preceding inference, which is by no means new, be correct or not, there can be little doubt that the Inca family was an *intruding nation*, led perhaps by a few individuals of the sacerdotal class; and having conquered Peru, much the same political relations appear to have subsisted between them and the pre-existing inhabitants, as we at present observe between the modern Greeks and the Turks.

* CLAVIGERO, Hist. of Mexico, I, p. 118. *Cullen's Tr.* † Ibid. I, p. 114, 116.

We next proceed to examine into the physical character of the Modern Peruvians. They differ little in person from the Indians around them, being of the middling stature, well limbed, and with small feet and hands. Their faces are round, their eyes small, black, and rather distant from each other; their noses are small, the mouth somewhat large, and the teeth remarkably fine.* Their complexion is a dark brown, and their hair long, black, and rather coarse.

The skull in these people is remarkable for its small size, and also, as just observed, for its quadrangular form. The occiput is greatly compressed, sometimes absolutely vertical; the sides are swelled out, and the forehead is somewhat elevated but very retreating. The capacity of the cavity of the cranium, derived from the measurement of many specimens of the pure Inca race, shows, as we shall hereafter see, a singularly small cerebral mass for an intelligent and civilised people. These heads are remarkable not only for their smallness, but also for their irregularity; for in the whole series in my possession, there is but one that can be called symmetrical. This irregularity chiefly consists in the greater projection of the occiput to one side than the other, showing, in some instances, a surprising degree of deformity. As this condition is as often observed on one side as the other, it is not to be attributed to the intentional application of mechanical force; on the contrary it is to a certain degree common to the whole American race, and is sometimes no doubt increased by the manner in which the child is placed in the cradle.

I am in fact convinced, that among the collection of Peruvian skulls alluded to above, there is not one that has been designedly moulded by art; and hence it may be reasonably inferred, that individuals of the royal race, or those forming the higher classes among the Peruvians, seldom or never flattened their heads. What to them was natural was imitated by the inferior orders, and especially, it may be conjectured, by the inhabitants of conquered provinces, and others whose heads may not have been originally formed on the aristocratic model. While the early Spanish travellers frequently speak of the flattened heads of the people, they never mention this condition as applicable to the princes and other dignitaries who abounded in Peru at the conquest. Let it not be supposed, however, that these deformities were confined to a single model: on the contrary there were two

---

* STEVENSON, South Amer. I, p. 376.—RUSCHENBERGER, Three Years in the Pacific, p. 380.— ULLOA, Voy. to S. Amer. I, p. 267.—The latter author asserts that more natural defects are observed among the Indians of Quito than in any other race of men. If this be the fact, it must be attributed to the proximity of civilisation, which is well known to enervate and debase the Indian.

principally admired forms; but that which tended to widen and elevate the head appears to have greatly prevailed over the opposite extreme, which flattened and elongated it in the horizontal direction. I have been at some pains to inquire into the facts connected with this singular custom, as contained in the early Spanish travellers and historians, and have gleaned the following particulars.

Cieça, one of the oldest authorities, states that "in the province of Anzerma, and in that of Quinbaya, as well as in some other parts of this continent, when a child is born they fix its head in the shape they wish it to retain; thus some have no occiput, others have the forehead depressed, and a third set have the whole head elongated. This conformation is, in the first place, produced by the application of small boards, and is subsequently continued by means of ligatures."*

The same traveller adds the following notice of the Indians called Caraques, near the Spanish settlement of Puerto Viejo. "At the birth of a child," says he, "they mould its head, and then bind it between two boards, in such manner that at the age of four or five years it remains either broad or long, or destitute of the occipital prominence. They assert that this custom contributes to health, and enables them to carry greater burthens."†

Torquemada, also writing of the Peruvians, has the following passage. "As to the custom of appearing fierce in war, it was in some provinces ordered that the mothers or their attendants should make the faces of their children long and rough, and the foreheads broad, as Hippocrates and Galen relate of the Macrocephali, who had them moulded by art into the elevated and conical form. This custom is more prevalent in the province of Chicuito, than in any other part of Peru."‡

The preceding quotations are satisfactory evidence, that the custom of distorting the skull, was common in many provinces of Peru at the period of the Spanish invasion; that it was resorted to for the purpose of increasing the ferocity of the countenance in war,—augmenting an imaginary grace,—and adding to the health and strength of the body. It is also obvious that there were two principal modes of effecting this end, and that these were the opposites of each other.

The following passage from Garcilaso de la Vega, proves that this fashion was not introduced by the Incas, but was in use before they conquered the country. He states that the Inca Huyna Capac, having invaded the province of Manta with a view to its subjugation, found there a people who were living in the

---

* Chronica del Peru, Cap. XXVI.   † Loco citat. Cap. L.
‡ Monarquia Indiana, T. II, p. 581. *Fol. Madrid*, 1723.

THE INCA PERUVIANS.   117

most barbarous and demoralised condition. "Both the men and the women cut their cheeks with pointed flints; they also deform the heads of their children by placing, at birth, a small board on the forehead and another on the occiput, and drawing them tighter day by day until the child has attained the age of four or five years. By this process the head becomes broad from side to side, and narrow from back to front. Not satisfied with this deformity they shave the hair from the top of the head, and the nape of the neck, letting it grow on the sides only; and this not being combed or otherwise arranged, but rude and entangled, adds to the hideousness of their physiognomy."* The historian then gives the names of six nations or tribes to whom the above description is applicable.

It thus appears that the custom of moulding the cranium into artificial forms is of great antiquity and prevalence in Peru. We have seen that it existed among what we have termed the civilised primitive Peruvians, that it was common among many barbarous tribes at the invasion of the Incas, and that it continued to be a popular fantasy when the Spaniards took possession of the country. Professor Blumenbach quotes from Aguirre, part of a decree of the Ecclesiastical Court of Lima in the year 1585, forbidding parents, under certain specified penalties, to compress or distort the heads of their children in the various modes which were in vogue even at that late period;† and that the custom was not extinct a very few years ago, is evident from the statement of Mr. Skinner, an English traveller. Speaking of the *Connivos* of Peru, he remarks, "that all their attention is bestowed on preserving a firm texture of the body, and on flattening the forehead and hinder part of the head [in the upward direction] with a view of resembling, as they say, the full moon, and of becoming the strongest and most valiant people in the world. To attain the former of these aims, they bind the waist, and all the joints, of their male offspring, from their tender infancy, with hempen bands. With a view to the latter, they wrap the forehead in cotton, and lay on it a small square board, applying another similar board to the occiput, and adjusting them with cords until the intention has been answered. Thus the head is elongated above, and flattened both before and behind."‡

The Omaguas, who, towards the middle of the last century, inhabited the

---

* Comment. Reales, Lib. IX, Cap. VIII.

† "Cupientes penitus extirpare abusum, et superstitionem, quibus Indi passim infantum capita formis exprimunt, quos ipsi vocant Caito, Oma, Opalla," &c. Vide BLUMENBACH, *De Gen. Humani Var. Nat.* p. 220.—LAURENCE, *Lect. on Zool.* p. 377.

‡ Present State of Peru, p. 269.

shores of the Maragnon for several hundred leagues, and extended themselves quite to the Atlantic, appear to have been a Peruvian colony, both from analogy of language and customs; for they were in the practice of moulding the heads of their children so as to give them the high and lunated shape in use among the Connivos.*

I presume De Pauw alludes to the Omaguas when he tells us, that "certain Indians on the borders of the Maragnon, have square or cubic heads: in other words they are flattened on the face, on the crown, on the occiput, and on the temples, thus presenting the acme of human extravagance."†

Peru, like the co-existent feudal states of Europe, contained two classes of people wholly unlike each other, viz: the exotic Inca family, with its numberless ramifications, which held all the honor and advantage in their own hands; and the native plebeian multitude, who were in as low a state of degradation as the selfish policy of their superiors could devise and establish.

To the former of these classes was confined whatever was known of science, art or refinement. The members of the royal family prided themselves on their skill in architecture, astronomy and the national literature; and it will be observed that whenever an individual was named as pre-eminent in any of these departments of knowledge, he belonged to the dominant caste. In fact, the plebeian class was excluded from any participation in literature and science, except only when they could be employed as musicians and artisans. The Incas thus held alike the power and the knowledge in their own hands.

Their principal intellectual attainments were in geometry, music, poetry and architecture; but a people having no written language, and transmitting only by tradition their attainments in these branches of knowledge, cannot at this late period be fully appreciated, and much less can they be fairly compared in these respects with Europeans.

Architecture is one of the earliest attributes of civilisation, and in this the Peruvians had made surprising progress. Their temples, palaces and tombs bear

---

* LA CONDAMINE, Mem. de l'Acad. Roy. des Sc. Tome 62, p. 427.—ULLOA, Hist. del Viage, T. I, p. 505.—Does the following fragment of history refer to these Omaguas? "When Francisco Pizarro, Diego Almagro, and others, conquered the said empire of Peru, and had put to death Atabalipa, one of the younger sons of Guaynacapa fled out of Peru, and took with him many thousands of those soldiers of the empire called Orejones, and with those and many others that followed him, he vanquished all that tract and valley of America which is situate between the great rivers of the Amazons and Baraquan, otherwise called Orinoco and Maragnon."—SIR W. RALEIGH, Voy. to Guiana, p. 25.

† Rescherches sur les Americaines, I, p. 146.

ample evidence of this fact; and while the design is for the most part simple, the execution cannot but excite our admiration. Their great object appears to have been to erect cyclopean structures, which should at once attest their skill in art, and the power of their mechanical contrivances. They separated from the quarries enormous masses of stone, they shaped them into exact proportions, and they then conveyed them to such distances that we are at a loss to conjecture by what means the object was accomplished. Acosta, after stating that he had measured a single block of stone at Tiaguanico (the city, as we have seen, of the primitive Peruvians) which was thirty feet long, eighteen feet broad and six feet thick, declares that there were stones in the walls of the fortress of Cuzco *of far greater size*, and which were placed there by hand. Yet these masses, says Acosta, were not shaped by rule, but of unequal proportion, the irregularities of the one being exactly fitted by extreme toil and ingenuity to those of the other, without mortar or cement; and yet the place of junction was scarcely discernible.* What is equally remarkable is the fact, that these gigantic fragments of rock were brought from Muyna, which is five leagues distant from the city of Cuzco; and some of them from a much greater distance.†

Thus the seemingly superhuman efforts of the Egyptians are at least equalled by those of the Peruvians; and what most excites our admiration in the one, must be also conceded to the other. We see in the Peruvians a people destitute of horses, oxen, or any beast of burthen except the feeble lama; and yet they have left monuments which sufficiently attest their great ingenuity and indomitable perseverance. We are ignorant of the means by which they transported these cyclopean fragments of rock, and the mechanical contrivances that were used in excavating and adapting them to their destined situation. The arts of the present day, with all the refinements of successive generations of ingenious minds, would perhaps be inadequate to achieve those remarkable ends which are common in the monuments of Peru.

The Peruvians, like the primitive Egyptians, were not acquainted with the use of iron.‡ Such of their implements as in other countries are made of that

---

* Hist de las Indias, Lib. VI, Cap. XIV.—ULLOA, Voy. II, p. 130.

† GARCILASO, Comment. Lib. VII, Cap. XXVII, XXVIII, XXIX.

‡ Yet according to the best information we possess on this subject, "iron was known (in the old world) 184 years before the Trojan war, about 1370 years before Christ;" and there is sufficient proof that the Egyptians used iron instruments and utensils so early as the Pharaonic era.—WILKINSON, *Anc. Egypt*, III, p. 247.

metal, were composed of copper alloyed with a very small proportion of tin, which gave it great additional tenacity. It was with chisels of this kind that they shaped those enormous blocks of stone which have already been mentioned.

"Yet all we have said," observes Ulloa, "is surpassed by the ingenuity with which they wrought emeralds; these gems being found cut into various shapes, some spherical, others cylindrical, conical, and various other shapes, made with perfect accuracy, and drilled through with all the delicacy of our European artists. It is an almost insurmountable difficulty to explain how they could work a stone of such hardness."*

The constructive talent of the Incas was also conspicuous in their roads. One of these is eminently deserving of notice, and is thus described by Humboldt, in his journey across the plains of Assuay. "We were surprised to find in this place, and at heights which greatly surpass the top of the peak of Teneriffe, the magnificent remains of a road constructed by the Incas of Peru. This causeway, lined with freestone, may be compared to the finest Roman roads I have seen in Italy, France or Spain. It is perfectly straight, and keeps the same direction for six or eight thousand metres. We observed the continuation of this road near Caxamarca, one hundred and twenty leagues to the south of Assuay; and it is believed in the country that it led as far as the city of Cuzco."†

After a review of the preceding facts, how idle is the assertion of Dr. Robertson, that America contained no monuments older than the conquest! How replete with ignorance are also the aspersions of Pinkerton and De Pauw! Two of these authors, who wrote expressly on American history, are unpardonable for such gross misrepresentation. They appear to have veiled the truth in order to support an hypothesis.‡ It is in vain longer to contend against facts; for however difficult it may be to explain them, they are nevertheless incontrovertible. Whence the Peruvians derived their civilisation, may long remain a mooted question; that they possessed it, cannot be denied. "At a time when a public highway was either a relic of Roman greatness, or a sort of nonentity in England, there were roads fifteen hundred miles in length in the empire of Peru. The feudal system was as firmly established in these transatlantic kingdoms as in France. The Peruvians were ignorant of the art of forming an arch, but they

---

* Quoted in M'Culloh's Researches, p. 366.   † Monuments, I, p. 241.

‡ ROBERTSON, Hist. Amer. II, p. 110. *Am. ed.*—PINKERTON, Essay on the Goths, p. 68.—DE PAUW, *passim*.

had constructed suspension bridges over frightful ravines: they had no implements of iron, but their forefathers could move blocks of stone as huge as the Sphinxes and Memnons of Egypt."*

It is remarked by Dr. M'Culloh that in astronomy the Peruvians appear to have been far behind the Mexicans. "As the Peruvians," says he, "made, by means of towers, constant azimuth observations on the sun's rising and setting, and also upon the shadows cast by pillars at the times of the equinoxes and solstices, I cannot easily perceive a reason for the great inaccuracy of their year as it has been represented to us; and I am therefore inclined to think that only some grosser part of their calendar has been preserved. In this opinion I am further seemingly strengthened by not finding the Spanish writers to describe any cycle of years to have been used by them, which the nature of their observations would hardly have permitted them to dispense with."†

"Their year," says Herrera, "was divided into twelve months, distinguished by their several names; and particular festivals appointed in each of them. The year began in January, till one of the Incas ordered it should begin in December, at which time they celebrated their great festival."

"The Peruvians," adds Dr. M'Culloh, "unlike the Mexicans, were ignorant of the causes of eclipses, for they supposed the planets at such times to be sick. They particularly distinguished the planet Venus, some of the brighter fixed stars, the Pleiades, the Milky Way, &c., to all of which they gave certain names, and imagined them for the most part to be, or to represent, various animals which they were accustomed to meet with in Peru."‡

We often hear the government of the Incas characterised as one of peculiar mildness; but it was, on the contrary, an absolute rule, in which they held despotic sway over their subjects, "governing them according to their own views and pleasure, or as the exigencies of the times may have required: hence the proceedings of the government were necessarily fluctuating, and, according to the capacity and temper of the Inca, were either just or unjust, capricious or benevolent."§ All the lands of the empire were divided into three portions, of which one only fell to the share of the people; and even this they could not sell or otherwise dispose of, the title being vested in the Inca himself; and to prevent

---

* Long, Polynesian Nation, p. 87.
† Researches Concerning the Aboriginal Hist. of Amer. p. 373.
‡ Idem, p. 361. § Idem, p. 374.

any possible dispute or misunderstanding in this matter, the plebeian lands were newly distributed every year.

The monarchy appears to have had its due portion of insurrections and disturbances of various kinds, some of which reached the palace itself. One Inca, at least, was deposed and put to death; and when Atahualpa contested the empire with Guascar, he had that prince murdered, together with no less than thirty of his brothers, and a vast number of their dependants. We have already alluded to the destruction of the Collas in the early times of the monarchy; and as another example of unsparing cruelty, Huyna Capac, after a revolt of the Caranques, ordered two thousand of them to be put to death in cold blood, on a single occasion.* These facts sufficiently show, that the civilisation and comparative refinement of the Incas, were blended with some remains of the ferocity of the savage.

In their social relations, however, they appear to have been characterised by gentleness and affection; and although by a remarkable law, all crimes were alike punished with death, such was the natural docility of the temper of the Peruvians, that executions are said to have been unfrequent among them.

Matrimonial engagements were entered into with very little ceremony or forethought, and they were as readily set aside at the option of the parties. Polygamy was lawful, but not prevalent. Among the common people, incontinence among unmarried persons was scarcely regarded as a crime, and sensuality was a prevailing vice, in some degree countenanced by the royal authority. As a natural consequence, child-murder became so common, that foundling-hospitals were established by the government, in which children were received and provided for at the public expense. In truth, the morals of the Peruvians in these respects have nothing to commend them.†

Their diet was chiefly vegetables, maize entering largely into their aliments. Exhilarating drinks were in common use among the men; the principal preparation of this kind was called chica, which was fermented from the maize. So fond were the natives of this beverage, that it was even placed beside the dead in their tombs;‡ and Ulloa asserts, that among the Peruvians of the present day, spirituous liquors destroy more men in one year than the mines do in fifty.

---

* GARCILASO, Lib. IX, p. 367. *Frycaut's Tr.*—COREAL, Voy. II, p. 54.
† M'CULLOH, Researches, p. 379.—CARLI, Lettres Americaines, I. p. 138.
‡ STEVENSON, S. Amer. II, p. 371.

The great mass of people was indolent from two causes, the enervating warmth of the climate, and the humiliating nature of their political institutions, of which we have already spoken.

The apathy of the common people rendered them filthy and negligent in their persons; and in my examinations of several mummies of this class, taken from old cemeteries near the coast, I have noticed the hair in many instances to be charged with desiccated vermin, which, though buried for centuries in the sand, could not possibly be mistaken for any thing else.

The religious system of the Peruvians was marked by a great simplicity, and was divested, as we have observed, of those bloody rites which were common with the Aztecs of Mexico. They believed in one God, whom they called Viracocha, in the immortality of the soul, and in rewards and punishments in the next life. They worshipped both the sun and moon, in whose honor they erected temples and formed idols. Even the stars received their share of homage, because, as it has been happily expressed, they were esteemed the servants and handmaids of the greater luminaries. To these they sacrificed both beasts and birds, but never human beings.*

But one of the most remarkable features of the Peruvian religion was, the consecration of virgins, in the same manner as practised in modern convents.

Each temple was provided with a body of these recluses dedicated to the Sun, whose office was not to assist in religious exercises, but to weave certain fabrics for the use of the royal family. The Peruvians, moreover, enjoined vocal confession on all classes of people, and there were specified penalties for all crimes. To conceal any thing in these confessions was in itself held criminal.†

We are forcibly struck with the superstitious and barbarous funeral rites of these people. When their chief men died they mourned them many days, and buried them with great solemnity. In the grave or tomb they deposited the most valuable possessions of the deceased, his weapons, utensils, meats and drinks; and with these were also buried a number of human victims, women, boys and servants, to attend on the departed in the next world. Besides these sacrifices, which custom rendered compulsory on certain individuals, others committed suicide for

---

* Acosta charges the Peruvians with sacrificing their own children, which is denied by Garcilaso, and has, in fact, no proof. On the contrary, the Inca Roca, having conquered the ferocious tribe called Canches, forbid them, under pain of death, to sacrifice their children.—CARLI, *Lettres Americaines*, I, p. 115.

† HERRERA, Dec. III, Lib. x, Cap. 2.

the same purpose; and thus when Huayna Capac died, early in the fifteenth century, no less than four hundred persons expired by their own hands, in the ambitious delusion of accompanying their dead monarch in his new existence.*

The Peruvians were as shrewd and politic as the other Americans, and habitual victory over the nations that surrounded them, gave them both confidence and supremacy. When, however, they were opposed to a people better armed yet infinitely inferior in number to themselves, their courage in a great measure forsook them; and we are astonished at the spectacle of a powerful empire laid in ruins by a handful of brigands.† It must be granted that the latter were better armed, defended by coats of mail, and in part mounted on horseback; yet when it is recollected that after the first shock of Pizarro's treachery, the natives could have opposed a thousand men to one of their invaders, it seems at first view incredible that the Peruvians should have yielded to so contemptible a force.‡ Some redeeming circumstances, however, mark this seeming pusillanimity of the Peruvians. The Spaniards had possession of the person of their king, who was kept as a hostage for the forbearance of his subjects; and the successors of the former having excited the avarice of their countrymen, they flocked to Peru in such numbers that the disparity of force became every day less. When at last this injured people was goaded to resistance, their courage was such as better became their cause, but it was too late to be effectual. Had they possessed but a fourth part of the valor of the Araucanians, fifty years would not have sufficed for their subjugation.

* Herrera, Dec. III, Lib. VIII, Cap. 1.

† The empire of Peru ceased in 1533, by the murder of Atahualpa. There is a consolation in knowing that *all* the leaders in the atrocities which were perpetrated in this conquest, died violent deaths; from Pizarro, who fell by the hands of his countrymen, to the infamous Valverde, who was sacrificed to the vengeance of the Indians.

‡ Pizarro's invading force consisted of sixty-two horsemen, and one hundred and two foot soldiers, of whom twenty were armed with cross-bows, and three with muskets.—Robertson, *Hist. Am.* II, p. 52. *Am. Ed.*

PLATE VII.

PERUVIAN CHILD FROM SANTA.

This juvenile skull was obtained by Dr. Ruschenberger at Santa, which was once a great cemetery of the Peruvians. Of the many crania observed there, Dr. R. observes that the occiput "is almost vertical, and rises quite abruptly from the great hole at the base. The left side is generally much more prominent than the right, and the forehead is narrow and retreating."* This head is figured merely to show the characters of the genuine Peruvian as developed in infancy, and a few only of the more important measurements are subjoined.

Longitudinal diameter,	5.4 inches.
Parietal diameter,	5.4 inches.
Frontal diameter,	4. inches.
Vertical diameter,	4.6 inches.
Internal capacity,	61 cubic inches.

PLATES VIII AND IX.

PERUVIAN FROM THE TEMPLE OF THE SUN.

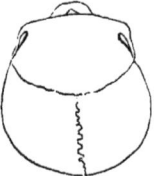 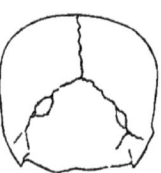

This head is remarkable alike for its squared form and its small size, and yet it is of adult age, and probably belonged to a female. It is very thin and delicate throughout; the breadth between the parietal protuberances is nearly the same with the longitudinal diameter, and there is a symmetry of parts rarely observed in Peruvian heads. The peculiarities of this relic are represented with great

* Three Years in the Pacific, p. 374.

126 CRANIA AMERICANA.

accuracy on the two annexed plates, to which it is only necessary to add the usual

MEASUREMENTS.

Longitudinal diameter,	5.8 inches.
Parietal diameter,	5.7 inches.
Frontal diameter,	4.4 inches.
Vertical diameter,	5.1 inches.
Inter-mastoid arch,	14.5 inches.
Inter-mastoid line,	4.1 inches.
Occipito-frontal arch,	12.7 inches.
Horizontal periphery,	18.4 inches.
Internal capacity,	71.75 cubic inches.
Capacity of the anterior chamber,	28.75 cubic inches.
Capacity of the posterior chamber,	43. cubic inches.
Capacity of the coronal region,	11.4 cubic inches.
Facial angle,	75 degrees.

I am indebted for this skull to my friend Dr. Ruschenberger, who obtained it from Pachacamac, the celebrated Temple of the Sun, near Lima.

PLATE X.

PERUVIAN CHILD FROM THE TEMPLE OF THE SUN.

This head is figured chiefly with a view to show the extraordinary inequality of the skull so common in the Peruvians, and especially in those from Pachacamac, which, with few exceptions, present more or less of this conformation. Dr. Ruschenberger's remark on the heads observed by him at Santa, that the left side was the most prominent, does not obtain in this instance, and among the many skulls in my possession the deformity of one side is as common as the other. Was this shape the result of accident or design? If it were intentional we might suppose there would have been some regard paid to symmetry, which was not the case. While, as we have seen, the common people distorted their heads in various ways, there is no evidence that the higher classes ever adopted the custom; and perhaps the irregularity observed in the skulls of the latter, merely resulted from a total disregard to plebeian usage by strapping the child's head loosely to the cradle-board, so that the occiput assumed any accidental form whatsoever.

This head was brought from Pachacamac and presented to me by my friend Dr. Ruschenberger.

PLATE XI.

PERUVIAN FROM THE TEMPLE OF THE SUN.

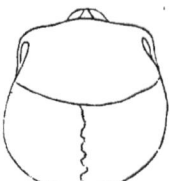 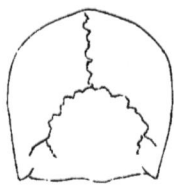

A strikingly characteristic Peruvian head, for which I am also indebted to Dr. Ruschenberger. As is common in this series of skulls, the parietal and longitudinal diameters are nearly the same.

MEASUREMENTS.

Longitudinal diameter,	6.1 inches.
Parietal diameter,	6. inches.
Frontal diameter,	4.7 inches.
Vertical diameter,	5.5 inches.
Inter-mastoid arch,	16. inches.
Inter-mastoid line,	4.5 inches.
Occipito-frontal arch,	14.1 inches.
Horizontal periphery,	19.5 inches.
Internal capacity,	83. cubic inches.
Capacity of the anterior chamber,	33.5 cubic inches.
Capacity of the posterior chamber,	49.5 cubic inches.
Capacity of the coronal region,	15.75 cubic inches.
Facial angle,	81 degrees.

PLATE XI.—A.

PERUVIAN FROM THE TEMPLE OF THE SUN.

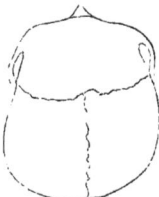 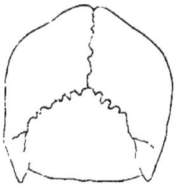

Another head from the cemetery at Pachacamac. A skull of unusual thickness, prominent vertex, great fulness of the whole parietal region, and large capacity.

MEASUREMENTS.

Longitudinal diameter,	6.7 inches.
Parietal diameter,	6. inches.
Frontal diameter,	4.5 inches.
Vertical diameter,	5.6 inches.
Inter-mastoid arch,	16.2 inches.
Inter-mastoid line,	4.5 inches.
Occipito-frontal arch,	14.5 inches.
Horizontal periphery,	20.2 inches.
Internal capacity,	89. cubic inches.
Capacity of the anterior chamber,	34. cubic inches.
Capacity of the posterior chamber,	55.5 cubic inches.
Capacity of the coronal region,	20.5 cubic inches.
Facial angle,	80 degrees.

For this relic I am also indebted to the kindness of my friend Dr. Ruschenberger.

PLATE XI.—B.

PERUVIAN FROM THE TEMPLE OF THE SUN

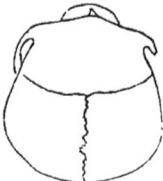 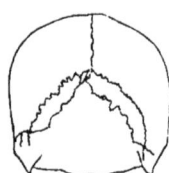

Another skull from the same sepulchral locality, and from the same intelligent voyager. It is characterised by small dimensions, a very retreating forehead, and a very prominent vertex.

MEASUREMENTS.

Longitudinal diameter,	6.3 inches.
Parietal diameter,	5.8 inches.
Frontal diameter,	4.5 inches.
Vertical diameter,	5.3 inches.
Inter-mastoid arch,	15. inches.
Inter-mastoid line,	4. inches.
Occipito-frontal arch,	13.2 inches.
Horizontal periphery,	19. inches.
Internal capacity,	76.5 cubic inches.
Capacity of the anterior chamber,	30. cubic inches.
Capacity of the posterior chamber,	46.5 cubic inches.
Capacity of the coronal region,	12.25 cubic inches.
Facial angle,	80 degrees.

PLATE XI.—C.

PERUVIAN FROM THE TEMPLE OF THE SUN.

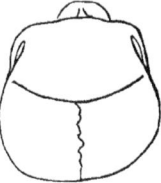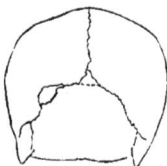

Also from Pachacamac, through the zeal and friendship of Dr. Ruschenberger. Here again the parietal and longitudinal diameters are nearly equal. The posterior and lateral swell of this cranium are very remarkable, and the vertex has the characteristic prominence. The cheek bones, though high, are not heavy, and there is a pleasing symmetry in the various parts of the face. The beauty and accuracy of the drawing require nothing to be added excepting the

MEASUREMENTS.

Longitudinal diameter,	6. inches.
Parietal diameter,	5.9 inches.
Frontal diameter,	4.4 inches.
Vertical diameter,	5. inches.
Inter-mastoid arch,	15.5 inches.
Inter-mastoid line,	4. inches.
Occipito-frontal arch,	13.2 inches.
Horizontal periphery,	19. inches.
Internal capacity,	77. cubic inches.
Capacity of the anterior chamber,	28. cubic inches.
Capacity of the posterior chamber,	49. cubic inches.
Capacity of the coronal region,	11.3 cubic inches.
Facial angle,	80 degrees.

THE INCA PERUVIANS.

PLATE XI.—D.

PERUVIAN FROM THE TEMPLE OF THE SUN.

 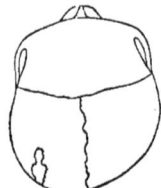

This skull, also from the Inca cemetery, presents several wounds of the occipital bone, which must have been inflicted by some blunt weapon, probably the back of a war-axe; and as the head is that of a middle aged man, we may presume he fell in battle. The occipital view has been represented merely to show the prevalent configuration of this part of the head in the Americans generally; the general conical outline,—the prominent vertex,—the full parietal protuberances, and the proportional width between the mastoid processes.

MEASUREMENTS.

Longitudinal diameter,	6.5 inches.
Parietal diameter,	5.5 inches.
Frontal diameter,	4.6 inches.
Vertical diameter,	5.6 inches.
Inter-mastoid arch,	14.8 inches.
Inter-mastoid line,	4.5 inches.
Occipito-frontal arch,	13.6 inches.
Horizontal periphery,	19.5 inches.
Internal capacity,	68.5 cubic inches.
Capacity of the anterior chamber,	33. cubic inches.
Capacity of the posterior chamber,	35.5 cubic inches.
Facial angle,	75 degrees.

This skull forms part of the fine collection from Pachacamac, presented to me by Dr. Ruschenberger.

CRANIA AMERICANA.

Result of the measurement of twenty-three adult skulls of the pure Inca Race.—Through the kindness of Dr. Ruschenberger, I possess twenty-three adult heads from the cemetery, called Pachacamac, or the Temple of the Sun, near Lima.* As this sepulchre was reserved for the exclusive use of the higher class of Peruvians, it is reasonable to infer that the skulls obtained there belonged to persons of intelligence and distinction; especially as learning among the Peruvians was an aristocratic prerogative. Six of these skulls are figured on the annexed plates, and by submitting them, together with the remainder of the series, to the measurements used in this work, the following results are obtained.

The largest cranium gives an internal capacity of 89.5 cubic inches, which is a fraction short of the Caucasian mean; while the smallest head measures but 60 cubic inches. The mean of the whole series gives but 73 cubic inches, which is probably lower than that of any other people now existing, not excepting the Hindoos.†

---

* "Four leagues from the city of Los Reyes (Lima) on the same coast, is the valley of Pachacamac, delightful and fruitful, and among the Indians very famed for the famous TEMPLE OF THE SUN, which is in it; the greatest and richest of all the Indies, which they held in the highest devotion; it was built on a small hill, (made by hand), of adobes (sun-dried bricks) and earth, and ornamented with many doors with various paintings of wild animals. In the same temple there were apartments for the priests, who professed great sanctity; for when they went to make a public sacrifice, they walked backwards, with their faces to the people and their backs to the idol. Thus with downcast eyes, and much apparent perturbation, they sacrificed human blood, and animals, and birds, and the idol gave replies. The priests were held in great veneration. Many people went in pilgrimage to this great temple with rich offerings; *no one was permitted to be buried near it except priests, nobles, and distinguished persons,* from whose interments great sums of gold were derived; and at the appointed feasts, great numbers of people assembled, and after the sacrifices they danced to the sound of instruments."—HERRERA, *Hist. de las Indias.* Lib. VI, Dec. V, p. 148.

The statement of Herrera that this Cemetery was consecrated to persons of distinction is confirmed by Gomara. "In esto templo se mandaban enterar los señores i principales, con intento que sus cuerpos se dedicasen à su Dios, i las animas purgadas in de sus delitos i pecados, tengam el descanso, goço, i placer deseado en su vida de ellos."—*Origen de los Indios, &c.,* p. 334. Madrid, 1729.

Ulloa describes the Temple of Pachacamac as a complete ruin. "It is divided into three parts; namely, a palace, a fortress and a place of prayer. Rude as this edifice appears, we may yet perceive an air of grandeur and magnificence that attests that of the princes who built it." And Garcilaso adds that it was built by the Yuncas, a Peruvian nation, before the times of the Incas. The latter, however, are supposed to have embellished the original temple, for their own use; and it even appears that the worship of the Yuncas and the Inca Peruvians was alike directed to *Pachacamac,* The Supreme God.—See M'CULLOH, *Researches, &c.,* p. 405.

† See Appendix.

THE ATURES.

The Anterior chamber gives a mean of 32 cubic inches; the highest measure being 36.5, the smallest 23 cubic inches.

The Posterior chamber gives a mean of 42 cubic inches; the highest measure being 55.5, the smallest 30 cubic inches.

The Coronal region gives 12 cubic inches as a mean; the highest measure being 20.5, the smallest 9.25 cubic inches.

The mean of the Facial angle is 75 degrees; the largest angle being 80, the smallest 72 degrees.

If to this series we add the measurements of twelve other genuine Peruvians from various localities, the mean internal capacity is increased but a single cubic inch, with but a fractional difference in the Facial angle. It will, therefore, appear in the sequel, that the internal capacity of the cranium in the demi-civilised Peruvians, is much less than that of the barbarous nations.

It may, morever, be remarked, that the heads of nine Peruvian children in my possession, appear to be nearly if not quite as large as those of children of other nations at the same age: which is the more remarkable as no specimen among the entire series of thirty-five adult skulls, reaches the European average of ninety cubic inches of internal capacity.

THE ATURES.

At the sources of the Orinoco,* among the forest solitudes of one of the remotest European missions, Baron Humboldt discovered the cavern-sepulchre of an extinct, but once powerful tribe, called *Atures*. As the annexed drawing was made from one of the identical skulls brought by that distinguished traveller, I shall describe this remarkable cemetery in his own words.

"The most remote part of the valley is covered by a thick forest. In this shady and solitary spot, on the declivity of a steep mountain, the cavern of Ataruipé opens itself. It is less a cavern than a jutting rock, in which the waters have scooped a vast hollow, when, in the ancient revolutions of our planet, they attained that height. We soon reckoned in this tomb of a whole extinct tribe

* Lat. 5° 39' north.

near six hundred skeletons, well preserved, and so regularly placed, that it would have been difficult to make an error in their number. Every skeleton reposes in a sort of basket made of the petioles of the palm-tree. These baskets, which the natives call *mapires*, have the form of a square bag. Their sizes are proportioned to the age of the dead; there are some for infants cut off the moment of their birth. We saw them from ten inches to three feet four inches long, the skeletons in them being bent together. They are all ranged near each other, and are so entire, that not a rib, or a phalanx is wanting.

The bones have been prepared in three different manners, either whitened in the air and the sun; dyed red with onoto, a coloring matter extracted from the bixa orellana; or, like real mummies, varnished with odoriferous resins, and enveloped in leaves of the heliconea or the plantain tree. The Indians related to us, that the fresh corpse is placed in damp ground, in order that the flesh may be consumed by degrees; some months after, it is taken out, and the flesh remaining on the bones is scraped off with sharp stones. Several hordes in Guyana still observe this custom. Earthen vases, half baked, are found near the *mapires*, or baskets. They appear to contain the bones of the same family. The largest of these vases, or funeral urns are three feet high, and five feet and a half long. Their color is greenish gray, and their oval form is sufficiently pleasing to the eye. The handles are made in the shape of crocodiles, or serpents, the edge is bordered with meanders, labyrinths, and real *grecques*, in straight lines variously combined. Such paintings are found in every zone, among nations the most remote from each other either with respect to the spot which they occupy on the globe, or to the degree of civilisation which they have attained. The inhabitants of the little mission of Maypures still execute them on their commonest pottery; they decorate the bucklers of the Otaheiteans, the fishing implements of the Eskimoes, the walls of the Mexican palace of Mitla, and the vases of ancient Greece. Every where a rhythmic repetition of the same forms flatters the eye, as the cadenced repetition of sounds soothes the ear. Analogies founded on the internal nature of our feelings, on the natural dispositions of our intellect, are not calculated to throw light on the affiliation and the ancient connection of nations. We could not acquire any precise idea of the period to which the origin of the *mapires* and the painted vases, contained in the ossuary cavern of Ataruipé, can be traced. The greater part seemed not to be more than a century old, but it may be supposed, that, sheltered from all humidity, under the influence of an uniform temperature, the preservation of these articles would be no less perfect, if it dated from a period far more remote. A tradition circulates among the Guahiboes, that the warlike

Atures, pursued by the Caribbees, escaped to the rocks that rise in the middle of the Great Cataracts; and there that nation, heretofore so numerous, became gradually extinct, as well as its language. The last families of the Atures still existed, in 1767, in the time of the missionary Gili. At the period of our voyage an old parrot was shown at Maypures, of which the inhabitants related, and the fact is worthy of observation, that, " they did not understand what it said, because it spoke the language of the Atures."*

PLATE XII.

ATURIAN OF THE ORINOCO.

This cranium presents the large face and ponderous jaw so common in the American race, together with the retreating forehead, prominent cheek bones and large orbits of that people. The head is more elongated than usual, and less flattened in the occipital region. This skull never came under my personal inspection, for which reason I am unable to add any measurements, or other precise observations. The original is preserved in the Museum of the Jardin du Roi, in Paris: Professor Flourens kindly permitted a drawing to be made from it, which was taken by M. Werner, an excellent artist, under the supervision of my friend Dr. Edmund C. Evans, of this city.

Baron Humboldt procured several of these skulls, but the vessel in which several of them were shipped, was lost at sea, and I believe but two reached Europe. One of these is figured by Professor Blumenbach†, and presents a much higher head and flatter occiput than the one represented above.

THE PUELCHÉS.

The Puelchés, whose name implies Eastern People, wander over the extensive plains between the 36° and 39° of south latitude. They are divided into many tribes, which extend from the Straits of Magellan to the Rio de la Plata, and

---

* Personal Narr. 5, p. 617. † Decad. Cran. Tab. XLVI.

from the Atlantic Ocean to the country of the Araucanians. In stature they much resemble the Spaniards, but they have stronger limbs than the adjacent Indians, a larger and rounder head, and a heavier and harsher person. They are also not so dark complexioned.

It is remarkable that although all the Puelché tribes are of wandering habits, none of them are strictly pastoral, neither keeping sheep nor sowing grain: but they depend entirely on hunting, for which purpose they keep a great number of dogs. They are divided into four tribes, one of which is the *Tehuelets*, who are celebrated by the name of Patagonians. They are remarkably tall, athletic men, and according to Falkner and others, average more than six feet in height. Much, however, that the early voyagers have written respecting them must be received with caution. We propose to advert to this subject again; and will now merely add, that when European voyagers visited the Patagonians, the latter showed their policy by selecting their tallest men to confer with the strangers; thus leaving the impression that they were a nation of giants.

The Puelchés are proverbially brave and skilful in war, as their protracted and bloody contests with the Spaniards bear ample testimony. They at first compelled the latter to abandon the foundation of the city of Buenos Ayres; nor did they yield in the contest until their enemies overpowered them with cavalry. In proof of their invincible courage, De Azara gives the following remarkable example. "In the heat of battle five Pampas* were made prisoners: they were put on board a seventy-four gun ship, with a complement of six hundred and fifty men, for the purpose of conveying them to Spain. When the vessel had been five days at sea, the captain allowed them the privilege of walking about without restraint, when they immediately resolved to seize the ship and murder all on board. To effect this object, one of them approached a corporal of marines, who appeared to be off his guard, seized his sabre, and in a moment of time killed two pilots and fourteen sailors and soldiers. The four other Indians also flew to arms, but finding themselves overcome by the guard, they sprang into the sea and drowned themselves, an example that was at once followed by their ringleader."†

---

* The Spaniards call them Pampas, but their own national appellation is Puelché.
† DE AZARA, Voy. T. II, p. 39.

PLATE XIII.

PUELCHÉ OF PATAGONIA.

The original of this drawing was made in Paris with the preceding one, under the inspection of Dr. E. C. Evans. I have to regret that I possess no measurements; but the accuracy and beauty of the delineation convey as perfect an idea of the cranium of the Puelchés as can be attained by a drawing. We are at once struck with the broad face, the projecting upper jaw, the arching of the zygoma, the low os frontis, the flattened occiput, and the fulness of development above the opening of the ear. The size of the lower jaw and the perfection of the teeth are also characteristic.

THE CHARRUAS.

This powerful nation originally inhabited the northern shore of the Rio de la Plata, and extended their possessions to a distance of thirty leagues parallel with that river. They are of the middle stature, well proportioned, erect and active; and according to De Azara, on whom I chiefly depend for these details, the whole nation would scarcely produce a man too fat, too meagre, or deformed. They hold the head erect, with a bold physiognomy and fierce countenance, indicative of their ferocity and haughtiness. Their color is nearer a black than a white, with very little mixture of red. Their nose is straight, their eyes rather small, bright and always black, and are never observed entirely open, at the same time that they can see better and twice as far as Europeans. Their teeth are well arranged, very white, and rarely fall out spontaneously. Their hands and feet are small and admirably proportioned.

All the energies, mental and physical, of these people are devoted to war alone. They have no diversions, nor dances, nor songs, nor instruments of music, nor social assemblages. Their habitual gravity conceals the passions; they never laugh aloud, and always address each other in a subdued tone of voice. They have no religion, no forms of politeness, no laws, no rewards and no punishments;

and their equality is so perfect that they do not even acknowledge the authority of a chief.

Yet such is the courage, the ferocity, the indomitable spirit of this warlike nation, that De Azara asserts that they have spilt more Spanish blood than ever flowed in all the contests with Montezuma and the Incas.* In fact the Charruas, with their confederate tribes, have been called the "doorkeepers of Paraguay," on account of their pertinacious and successful resistance to the encroachments of the Spaniards. To the last degree cruel, revengeful and exterminating in their wars with the native tribes, and with the Europeans, they present, in strong relief, all the prominent characteristics of the race.

PLATE XIV.

CHARRUA OF BRAZIL.

This skull possesses the characteristics of the American Indian in very strong relief. The points which we have noticed in the Puelché, are exaggerated here, together with a more retreating forehead and more flattened occipital region. This head is preserved, with the two preceding ones, in the Royal Museum in Paris; and the drawing was taken under the same circumstances as those of the Puelché and Aturian, so that I am unable to give any particulars which cannot be derived from the drawing itself.

THE BOTOCUDOS.

These people call themselves *Engerecmoung;* but they are more familiarly known by the names Aymores and Botocudos, the latter being given them by the Portuguese. They inhabit the dense forests of Brazil between the Rio Doce and the Rio Prado, or in other words within the 13th and 19th degrees of south latitude.

Nature, says the Prince de Wied, has given the Botocudos an admirable exterior conformation, for they are handsomer and better proportioned than the

---

* DE AZARA, Voy. dans l'Amer. Merid. T. 2, p. 6—28.

other Tapouyas. They are mostly of the middle stature, with broad shoulders, large chests, and delicate hands and feet. Their eyes are mostly small, black and piercing; the nose is short, straight and expanded at the nostrils. The whole face is large, and occasionally somewhat flattened. Their color is a reddish brown, much darker in some instances than others, and in some examples almost white. In other respects these people resemble the other nations of the American continent. But they have, in common with several tribes of Paraguay, the horrible custom of slitting the lower lip, and wearing in the opening thus made a round or oval piece of wood, which gives their physiognomy a frightful expression, which is heightened by the almost constant flow of saliva from the aperture.

With respect to the moral character of the Botocudos, there is little, perhaps nothing, to admire. "Being in no degree guided by the moral principle, and uncontrolled by the laws which restrict civilised man within the limits of social order, these barbarians follow the impulses of sense and instinct like the jaguars of the forest. The outbreakings of their demoniac passions, and especially their revenge and jealousy, are as terrible as they are sudden and unexpected." The most trifling incident is sufficient to excite their anger, which can never be appeased except by the death of the offender.

It will be of course inferred that their wars are constant and sanguinary. They contend with all the surrounding nations, whether of the European or Indian race, and their hatred to some adjacent tribes is so implacable, that they never spare man, woman or child. Though now nearly exterminated, they remain, as a nation, unconquered and unconquerable.

Nevertheless, unlike their neighbors, the Charruas, the Botocudos have their hours of mirth, and enliven their indolence with songs and dances: and with all their savage attributes it is due to them to state, that they have in some instances shown lasting gratitude to those who have befriended them.*

PLATE XV.

BOTOCUDO OF BRAZIL.

Being extremely desirous to obtain a drawing of one of the skulls of these singular people, I wrote for that purpose to his Highness, Maximilian Prince de Wied-Nieuwied, celebrated for his scientific researches in both Americas. My

* See Voyage au Bresil, par S. A. S. Maximilien, Prince de Wied-Nieuwied, T. II, p. 207, &c.

application was promptly responded to by that distinguished traveller, who sent me a beautiful drawing of which the annexed lithograph is an exact copy. The original is preserved in the collection of the illustrious Professor Blumenbach, and is the identical specimen brought by the Prince de Wied, and figured in the Decades Craniorum. Not having had access to the skull itself, I cannot give all its measurements according to my adopted plan; but the following description from the above work of Professor Blumenbach, will in a great degree supply the deficiency.

"The age of this man," says he, "was about five and twenty. During the war between the Botocudos and the Portuguese, he was accustomed to join his countrymen in their hostile incursions; but after hostilities ceased, he frequently visited the garrison on the Rio Doce, where he not long after fell sick and died.

"The cranium, which is large, is also very ponderous from the thickness of the bones, and their dense and hard texture: and as a whole, if you disregard for a moment the under jaw, the figure and interval of the orbits, the elevated nasal spine, and other particulars peculiar to man, the general aspect approaches nearer to that of the Orang Outang than any other skull from a barbarous nation to be seen in my collection. I have indeed one or two specimens of the Negro, in which the upper jaw is more projecting; but this skull differs from them in other respects, besides having the cheek bones more prominent, and a greater swell of the parietal bones.

"But what deserves particular notice is an indentation, shaped like the point of the finger on wax, which remains after the loss of the front teeth, the sockets of which are compressed, or rather completely absorbed. So universally, the Prince de Wied assures me, does this happen to the youth of this nation from wearing the wooden lip-ornament, already mentioned, that you will scarcely find one of them arrived at the age of thirty who retains these teeth."*

I have only to add the following measurements, which are derived from the drawing.

    Longitudinal diameter 6.5 inches.
    Vertical diameter about 5.6 inches.
    Facial angle.

---

* Decas Cran. Sexta, p. 16, et Tab. LVIII.

THE MEXICANS.

The valleys of Mexico, the ancient Anahuac, have been compared, in their political vicissitudes, to those of Italy. Beautiful and productive in a remarkable degree, and possessing a delightful climate, Mexico has excited the cupidity of many different nations, who have successfully established their dominion over it. Let us for a moment enumerate these various people, and at the same time inquire into their peculiar characteristics.

1. Mexican tradition states that the country was originally inhabited by barbarous hordes, who were no doubt analogous, in their physical appearance and social institutions, to the present population of the more northern regions of the continent. They have left no monuments; but it is probable their descendants yet exist among the uncultivated tribes which are still scattered over the country.

2. Of the civilised nations of Anahuac, those which claim the greatest antiquity are the Olmecas, who extended their migrations to Nicaragua and the Gulf of Nicoya;—the Miztecas and the Zapotecas. These people are said to have been as highly cultivated as any of the nations who succeeded them: and it seems more than probable that some of the architectural monuments of Mexico, will yet be traced to a period long antecedent to the arrival of the Toltecas.* Among the nations who inhabited the country at this early epoch, are also to be mentioned the Tarascas, and the Otomies, the latter being the least civilised of them all.

3. The first recorded invasion of Mexico was that of the Toltecas, which is dated by most historians about the year 600 of our era.† Their original seats are stated in their traditions to have been to the northwest of Mexico, in a country called Huehuetapallan. Their monarchy commenced in the year 607, and terminated, as we have already stated, A. D. 1031; at which period a series of calamities caused their partial destruction, and dispersion into other countries. Of all the nations of Anahuac, the Toltecas were the most refined in their social relations, and most skilful in the arts and sciences. They introduced the cultivation of Indian corn and cotton: they made roads, lived in towns and cities, and erected as we have seen,‡ the most surprising monuments of the new world.

---

* HUMBOLDT, Monuments, II, p. 249.

† Boturini, with much plausibility, dates the Toltecan monarchy before the Christian era. It is indeed difficult to imagine that the monuments of Palneque are but 1200 years old.

‡ See page 84, and sequel.

4. On the decline of the Toltecan monarchy, the Chechemecas appeared in Mexico. These people were also from a northern country, which their annals call Amaquemecan. They were a nation of hunters, clothed in the skins of beasts, and unacquainted with agriculture or the arts of civilised life. Their religion embraced the simple worship of the sun, to which they made offerings of fruits and flowers, unattended by human sacrifices. Although the Chechemecas were a rude people, they were not averse to civilisation: they mixed with the Toltecas who still remained in the country, adopted their agriculture, and many of those ornamental arts to which we have already adverted.*

5. It was during the Chechemecan monarchy that the *seven tribes* took up their abode in Anahuac. These tribes bore the following names: Zochimilcas, Calchese, Tapanecas, Colhuas, Tlahuicas, Tlascalans, and Aztecs or Mexicans. These nations bore the collective name of Nahautlacas; they came also from a northern country which they called Aztlan, which was contiguous to Aquemecan, the hive of the Chechemecas.† This immigration took place in the year 1178. These several tribes established themselves independently in Anahuac, the Mexicans being the last in order of arrival, A. D. 1245.

6. Subsequent to the seven tribes there arrived another great family, bearing the name of Alcohuans, whose native seats were nearly identical with those of the Chechemecas. A confederacy was early established between the Alcohuans, the Chechemecas and the Toltecas, and the national appellation was derived from the first of these tribes, which is represented to have been further advanced in civilisation than any people of Anahuac, excepting the Toltecas. These nations, together with the Naulacas, appear all to have spoken dialects of the same language, a fact which is accounted for in their cognate origin.‡

The Aztecs or Mexicans were at first tributary to the Alcohuans, but they early shook off the yoke, and became in their turn the rulers of Mexico, which they governed until the capital fell into the hands of the Spaniards under Cortez, in the year 1521.

---

* CLAVIGERO, Hist. of Mexico, B. II.

† These northern seats of civilisation, however, have been sought for in vain; and it is worthy of remark, that the learned Cabrera has attempted to show that the native seats of the nations above enumerated, were not to the north, but in the south of Mexico. After an enumeration of various plausible facts, he adds, "all these circumstances united tend to demonstrate, by evidence as clear as evidence can prove, that the kingdom of Amaquemecan was situated in the present province of Chiapa."—See *Solution of the grand Historical problem of the population of America*, p. 58.

‡ HUMBOLDT, Monuments, I, p. 81.

THE MEXICANS.

Having thus traced, in as few words as possible, the affiliation of the various tribes which intruded themselves into Mexico, we proceed in the next place to inquire into the distinguishing traits of these communities, all which are now registered in history by the collective name of MEXICANS.

All these nations were characterised, as we have observed, by similarity of language, and they possessed also similar manners, institutions, and physical traits; and Humboldt has compared their affinity to that which is known to exist between the Germans, the Norwegians, the Goths and the Danes, who are all embraced in a single race.*

The moral and physical qualities of the Mexicans, says Clavigero, their tempers and dispositions, were the same with those of the Alcohuans, the Tepanecas, the Tlascalans and other nations, with no other difference than what arose from their different mode of education, so that what is said of one may be considered applicable to all the others.† "The Mexicans are of good stature, generally rather exceeding than falling short of the middling size, and well proportioned in all their limbs: they have good complexions, narrow foreheads, black eyes, clean, firm, regular white teeth; thick, black, coarse, glossy hair, thin beards, and generally no hair upon their legs and arms. There is scarcely a nation, perhaps, upon earth in which there are fewer deformed persons, and it would be more difficult to find a single hump-backed, lame or squint-eyed man among a thousand Mexicans, than among a hundred of any other nation. The unpleasantness of their color, the smallness of their forehead, the thinness of their beard and the coarseness of their hair, are so far compensated by the regularity and fine proportion of their limbs, that they can neither be called very beautiful, nor the contrary, but seem to hold a middle place between the extremes.

"Their appearance neither engages nor disgusts; but among the young women of Mexico, there are many very beautiful and fair; whose beauty is at the same time rendered more winning by the sweetness of their manner of speaking, and by the pleasantness and natural modesty of their whole behaviour."‡

Their senses are very acute, especially that of sight, which they retain unimpaired to old age. They are moderate in eating, but like all the American nation they delight in intoxicating drinks, which have already caused a frightful waste of life. To these observations of Clavigero may be added a few others from Humboldt, who describes them as possessing "a swarthy and copper color, flat and smooth hair, squat body, long eye with the corner directed upwards

---

* Monuments, I, p. 214. † Hist. of Mexico, I, p. 103.
‡ CLAVIGERO, 1, p. 104. *Am. ed.*

towards the temples, prominent cheek-bones, thick lips, and an expression of gentleness in the mouth strongly contrasted with a gloomy and severe look."* The same author adds, that the Mexicans, especially of the Aztec and Ottomite races, have more beard than any other American nation. "Almost all the Indians in the neighborhood of the capital, (Mexico)," says he, "wear small mustaches, and it is even a mark of the tributary cast."†

This account of the physical character of the Mexicans is chiefly derived from Clavigero, who well knew the people of whom he wrote, not only from having studied all the works that have been written respecting them, but especially from having resided thirty-six years among them. This author, however, states that the Mexicans have narrow foreheads; which may be in general true of the existing tribes, but the remark does not apply to the ancient nations, as is proved both by their sculpture and their crania.

On the Heads of the Ancient Mexicans.—I have not succeeded in obtaining an adequate series of Mexican skulls, and of those in my possession but eight are older than the conquest. No one of them is altered by art, and they present a striking resemblance, both in size and configuration, to the heads of the Ancient Peruvians. In examining the delineations in Del Rio's‡ account of Palenque, I observed in the corner of his fifth plate, a small, inverted skull, which is so completely characteristic of these nations that I have had it drawn on a larger scale, preserving, however, the exact proportions of the original. On comparing this skull with those of the Peruvians§ already figured, a striking resemblance is manifest in the great lateral swell of the head, the rather expanded forehead, and the prominent aspect of the vertex or crown.

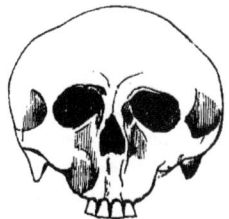

* Political Essay on New Spain, p. 105.—*N. York ed.* † Loco citat.
‡ Description of the Ruins of an Ancient City in Guatemala.
§ See more particularly the skull from the Temple of the Sun, plate XI.—C, and compare this again with the Natchez heads. The Palenquian relic is a medium between the two.

In fact, these features are so decided that they appear to result in part from the application of mechanical pressure. This drawing has great interest from the circumstance of its being an authentic copy from an antique Toltecan bas-relief, and probably represents the configuration of the head in that nation; for it is obvious from the symmetry and accuracy of the figure, that the artist accomplished his task with a skull before him.

With respect to the many heads figured by Del Rio, they present a striking resemblance to each other. They have a conical form, very narrow from front to back, and consequently very broad from side to side. The forehead retreats, the brow is low, the nose large and aquiline, the mouth wide and the lips somewhat tumid. There can be no question that some of these features are exaggerated; but they no doubt preserve the leading traits in the physiognomy of the people they represent. The two following illustrations are faithfully transcribed from the work of Del Rio, merely omitting such parts of the elaborate head-dresses as are unnecessary to the present purpose.

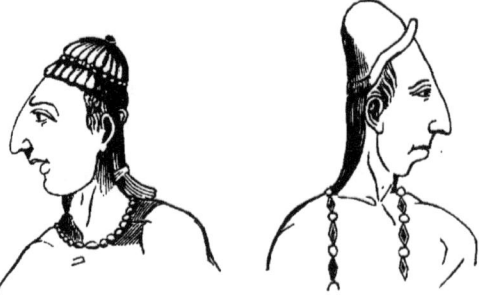

Were it not for the evidence of undeniable facts, such configuration of the head would be pronounced altogether ideal. But when the reader has examined the real skulls figured in this work, and especially those of the Natchez tribe (who appear to have been of the Toltecan stock,) he will perceive in them a distortion similar in kind to that represented in the bas-reliefs of Palenque, but in a much more exaggerated degree. With respect to the extravagantly disproportioned noses of the Toltecan sculpture, Humboldt observes that they might at first sight appear to indicate a race very different from that which now inhabits these countries; but, he adds, "it is possible that the Mexican people might have believed, with the philosopher Plato, that there was something majestic and royal in a large nose, and hence may have used it, in their paintings and reliefs, as the symbol of power and moral worth."*

With respect to the form and expression of the Toltecan face, we possess other remains of antiquity that no doubt approach very near to nature, and at least express what those people considered the beau-ideal of the human physiognomy. I allude to the heads moulded in terra-cotta, which have been so abundantly found among the Toltecan ruins of Anahuac. Hundreds, perhaps thousands, of these effigies have been obtained from the vicinity of the pyramid of Teotihuacan alone: they are mostly about an inch in length, and the features are admirably proportioned. They have high and broad foreheads, oval faces, prominent cheek bones, and rather tumid lips. They are all very much compressed from back to front, and appear to have been ornamental appendages of clay vessels in common use. A late traveller has observed, that the arts could not have been very deficient with a people "who, with such coarse materials, and for such common purposes, could fashion heads on so small a scale, and exhibiting so much character and expression."†

Dr. Frederick Edmonds, an English gentleman who passed several years in the Mexican republic, has presented me with a number of these relics, which were obtained by him from the ruins of the Temples of the Sun and Moon, at Teotihuacan. Two of these, which are similar to those described and figured by Captain Vetch,‡ are represented in the subjoined wood-cuts.

It is thus that we trace the same style of features in the sculpture of the nations of Anahuac, from the northern provinces of that country to Nicaragua§ in

---

* Monuments, I, p. 131.

† VETCH, in Trans. Roy. Geog. Soc. of London, VIII, p. 9.   ‡ Ibid, plate II.

§ From Herrera's account, the people of Nicaragua appear to have continued the custom of moulding the head up to the time of the Spanish invasion of the country. His words are as follow:

the south, a distance of twelve hundred miles; while over this vast tract was at the same time diffused a language, institutions and monuments, which all bespoke a common origin. Humboldt has somewhere remarked that it is not unlikely that the figures with enormous aquiline noses, observed in the Mexican hieroglyphic paintings, may point to a race of men already extinct. For this surmise, however, there appears to be no foundation; for this peculiarity of Toltecan sculpture is to be regarded as a conventional rule of art, like others in the bas-reliefs and statues of the Nile.

The practice of artificially moulding the head, varied, it is true, according to fancy, has been traced from Peru into Venezuela,* and thence into Nicaragua as matter of fact; and as we also find the Natchez and other tribes originally from Mexico addicted to the same usage, we may reasonably infer that the Toltecas and Aztecs, who give evidence of the same custom in their bas-reliefs, and hieroglyphics, did really practise it as a national usage; and skulls will no doubt be hereafter found that will place this question beyond controversy.†

We now turn from the physical to the moral and intellectual character of the Mexican nations. "The religion, government and economy of a state," observes Clavigero, "are three things which chiefly form the character of a nation; and without being acquainted with these it is impossible to have a perfect idea of the genius, disposition and knowledge of any people whatever."‡ The historian then adds that the religion of the Mexicans was a heap of errors, superstitions and cruel rites. Their gods were nearly as numerous as those of the Romans, and their offices and attributes were mystified by the worst inventions of priestcraft. They worshipped the sun and moon among their principal divinities, and they personified the seasons and various phenomena of nature, giving to each its place in their mythological series: they had a god of war, a god of peace, a god of mirth, and in fact a god for almost every imaginable contingency, together with household divinities (answering to the penates of the ancients) almost without

---

"Los hombres son de buena statura, mas blancos que loros; las cabeças à tolondrones con un hoyo en medio por hermosura, i por asiento, i por carga."—*Hist. de las Indias*, Dec. III, Lib. IV.

* See Plate 64.

† Since this paragraph was written I have received a letter from Dr. John Macartney, of the city of Mexico, who speaks of the "singular forms" of the skulls in the ancient cemetery of Santiago de Tlatelolco. I wait with great interest for the facts these relics may develope. The cemetery asserted to have been lately discovered at Durango, in the Mexican states, may also throw much additional light on this subject.

‡ Hist. of Mexico, B. VI. (Cullen.)

number. It is asserted that, after the conquest by the Spaniards, the Franciscan monks, alone, destroyed in eight years, more than twenty thousand idols.* Their temples were in proportion; Torquemada estimated them at forty thousand, and Clavigero thinks this estimate is much within bounds. They had their fasts, penances and feasts, their monks, vestals and priests of different orders. But what is most surprising in a nation possessing any claim to refinement, was their numberless human sacrifices; men, women and children were put to death by every possible variety of suffering, and there seems to be no doubt that the blood of no less than twenty thousand human beings was annually devoted to the gods of the Mexicans. When to this account we add the appalling fact that the bodies of the victims were devoured at the feasts of the people, we are compelled to acknowledge that no nation on the earth has ever presented such a combination of revolting enormities.† It is but justice, however, again to remark, that these abominations were not practised by the Toltecas and the other ancient nations of Anahuac, but by their successors and perhaps conquerors of the Aztec family.

We pass over other traits of barbarism, which prove, that while the intellectual character of the Mexicans was far exalted above that of the other nations of North America, their moral perceptions appear to have been blunted in proportion: all their institutions, religious and civil, were established and maintained with bloody rites, which must have constantly operated to deaden and obliterate the finer feelings of our nature. Familiarity with death leads to indifference of life, and hence, perhaps, the superior courage of the Mexicans: for notwithstanding the aspersions of De Pauw and others, these people yielded to the Spaniards only after a valiant struggle. De Pauw asserts that Mexico was conquered by Cortez with 450 vagabonds, and fifteen horses, badly armed. This is a great error; for every reader of American history is aware, that Cortez enlisted against the doomed empire, the people of various tributary and discontented provinces; so that in place of attacking Mexico with 450 men, he commenced his invasion with 200,000. Cortez acknowledges the multitude of his allies, and admits that at the siege of the capital, they fought against the Mexicans with even greater ardor than the Spaniards themselves. The siege of the city lasted seventy-four days, during which time the inhabitants defended themselves with the utmost bravery; nor did they surrender until 50,000 of their number had been destroyed by famine and the sword, and seven of the eight parts of their city had fallen into the hands of the enemy.

* Hist. of Mexico, B. VI, p. 26. (Cullen.) † CLAVIGERO, Hist. of Mexico, p. 59.

THE MEXICANS.

Let us now turn to the more pleasing part of the picture, that which considers the progress these people had made in the refinements of civilised life.

The state of civilisation among the Mexicans, when they were first known to the Spaniards, was much superior to that of the Spaniards themselves on their first intercourse with the Phenicians, "or that of the Gauls when first known to the Greeks, or that of the Germans and Britons when first known to the Romans. —Their understandings are fitted for every kind of science, as experience has actually shown. Of the Mexicans who have had an opportunity of engaging in the pursuit of learning—which is but a small number, as the greater part of the people are always employed in the public or private works—we have known some good mathematicians, excellent architects, and learned divines."*

The architectural taste of the Mexican nation is chiefly seen in the Palace of Mitla, and the ruins of Palenque. The first of these remains is situated in the province of Oaxaca, and belongs to the era of the Zapotecas: it embraces five separate buildings, disposed with great regularity, courts, terraces, columns, arabesques and subterranean vaults. The columns, which are the only ones hitherto found in America, are without capitals, and indicate the infancy of this department of art.†

If we go southward to Guatemala, which was a province of Mexico under nearly all the dynasties that governed that country, we find other architectural remains of an elaborate and imposing character, which tend still more strongly to impress the mind with the genius of the ancient people of Anahuac. "The cave of Tibulca," says Juarros, "appears like a temple of great size hollowed out of the base of a hill, and is adorned with columns, having bases, pedestals, capitals and crowns, all accurately adjusted according to architectural principles."‡ Juarros also describes the cavern temple at Mixco in yet more extraordinary details; which remind us, says an ingenious author, of the rock caverns and temples of Ellora, Elephanta, and other similar monuments of Hindoo workmanship.§ Are these the works of the Toltecas, or of their cultivated progenitors the Olmecas?

In the same region of country, near the village of Palenque, are the ruins of a city of which we have already spoken, in which the massive edifices, the inclined

---

* CLAVIGERO, *ut supra*. † HUMBOLDT, Monuments, II, p. 156.
‡ Hist. of Guatemala, p. 57.
§ M'CULLOH, Researches, p. 316.—The monumental treasures of New Spain have been for centuries hidden from investigation by a singularly selfish policy. It is matter of congratulation, however, that the time is rapidly approaching when the Anglo Saxon race will control the destinies of Mexico, and throw open her buried monuments to the scrutiny of art and science.

walls, the bas-reliefs and hieroglyphic sculpture, belong obviously to a remote age, and are by pretty general consent attributed to the Toltecas.

The gigantic monuments of Anahuac are also seen in the pyramids of Cholula, Teotihuacan and Papantla. When the Aztecs took possession of this country in the 12th century, they found these monuments already existing, and referred them to the Toltecas. The pyramid of Cholula has a base twice the breadth of that of Cheops, yet is low in proportion.* It is built of unbaked bricks, is four stories or terraces in height, and is constructed in the direction of the four cardinal points.—The pyramids of Teotihuacan are eight leagues north of the city of Mexico: two of these are dedicated to the Sun and Moon, and these again are surrounded by hundreds of others of smaller size, which form streets in lines from north to south, and from east to west. Lastly in this series of monuments, is the pyramid of Papantla, built of hewn stones of Cyclopean dimensions, and ornamented with hieroglyphics.

Suffice it to add, that the year of the Mexicans consisted like our own, of three hundred and sixty-five days, but instead of twelve it was divided into eighteen months, each of twenty days: they possessed a distinct system of hieroglyphic writing, and their annals went back more than eight centuries and a half before the arrival of the Spaniards.

Their knowledge of arithmetic and astronomy, as we have already noted, was both extensive and accurate. They had constructed considerable aqueducts, of which the remains yet exist, and numerous canals for irrigation, of which one is asserted to have extended a distance of one hundred and fifty leagues. "They were able to extract, separate and fuse metals; to give copper the hardness of steel, for the fabrication of their weapons and instruments; to make mirrors of this hardened copper, or of hard stone; to form images of gold and silver, hollow within; to cut the hardest precious stones with the greatest nicety; to manufacture and dye cotton and wool, and work and figure the stuffs in various ways; and to spin and weave the fine hair of hares and rabbits, into fabrics resembling and answering the purposes of silks."† Such are the people whom certain closet authors in Europe have stigmatised as barbarians, incapable of the arts and refinements of civilised life.

Clavigero, speaking of the present descendants of the Aztecs, observes that

---

* HUMBOLDT, Monuments, I, p. 89.—This traveller states the side of the base to be, 1,423 feet, while its height is only 177 feet.

† CARLI, quoted in Lawrence's Lect. on Zoology, &c. p. 480.

they possess both the imitative and inventive faculties; and although slow in their motions, they show extraordinary perseverance in those works that require long continued attention. They are taciturn and severe in their manners, and seldom exhibit those transitions of passion so common in other nations. They are generous and disinterested, setting little value on gold, and giving, without reluctance, what has cost them much labor to obtain.

But it will still be asked, where are now the descendants of the civilised Mexicans? Where is the genius of that people? A passage from Humboldt will sufficiently answer these questions. "As to the moral faculties of the Indians, it is difficult to appreciate them with justice, if we only consider this long oppressed caste in their present state of degradation. The better sort of Indians, among whom a certain degree of intellectual culture might be supposed, perished in great part at the commencement of the Spanish conquest, the victims of European ferocity. The Christian fanaticism broke out in a particular manner against the Aztec priests; and the Teopixqui, or ministers of the divinity, and all those who inhabited the Teocalli, or houses of the gods, who might be considered as the depositories of the historical, mythological and astronomical knowledge of the country, were exterminated; for the priests observed the meridian shade in the gnomons, and regulated the calendar. The monks burned the hieroglyphic paintings, by which every kind of knowledge was transmitted from generation to generation. The people, deprived of these means of instruction, were plunged in ignorance so much the deeper, inasmuch as the missionaries were unskilled in the Mexican languages, and could substitute few new ideas in the place of the old. The remaining natives then consisted of the most indigent race, poor cultivators, artizans, among whom was a great number of weavers, porters, who were used as beasts of burthen, and especially those dregs of the people, those crowds of beggars, who bore witness to the imperfection of the social institutions, and the existence of feudal oppression, and who, in the time of Cortez, filled the streets of all the great cities in the Mexican empire. How shall we judge then, from these miserable remains of a powerful people, of the degree of civilisation to which it had risen from the twelfth to the sixteenth century, and of the intellectual development of which it is susceptible? If all that remained of the French or German nation were a few poor agriculturists, could we read in their features that they belonged to nations which had produced Descartes and Clairaut, Kepler and Leibnitz?"*

* Polit. Essay, B. II, Chap. VI.

CRANIA AMERICANA.

In addition to these remarks, we will merely note the moral and political resemblance that exists between the ancient and modern Mexicans on the one hand, and the Egyptians of the age of Pharaoh and the present Copts on the other. Slavery has degraded the faculties of both, and it would require centuries of the most favorable circumstances to resuscitate the dormant genius of either.

PLATE XVI.

MEXICAN.

 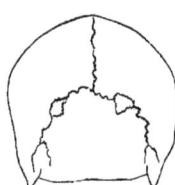

A skull of large and massive developments, with a full, broad but retreating forehead, and great width between the parietal bones. The head is more oval and elongated than is usual in this race, and there is a remarkable fulness of the phrenological region of constructiveness. The face is large and projecting, and the lower jaw broad and ponderous. This is a relic of the genuine Toltecan stock, having been exhumed from an ancient cemetery at Cerro de Quesilas, near the city of Mexico. It was accompanied by numerous antique vessels, weapons, &c., indicating a personage of distinction. This cranium was brought from Mexico by the Hon. J. R. Poinsett, and by him presented to the Academy of Natural Sciences of Philadelphia.

MEASUREMENTS.

Longitudinal diameter,	7.1 inches.
Parietal diameter,	5.7 inches.
Frontal diameter,	4.4 inches.
Vertical diameter,	5.2 inches.
Inter-mastoid arch,	15.9 inches.
Inter-mastoid line,	4. inches.

THE MEXICANS.

Occipito-frontal arch,	14. inches.
Horizontal periphery,	20.5 inches.
Internal capacity,	83. cubic inches.
Capacity of the anterior chamber,	39. cubic inches.
Capacity of the posterior chamber,	44. cubic inches.
Capacity of the coronal region,	17.5 cubic inches.
Facial angle,	72 degrees.

PLATE XVII.

MEXICAN.

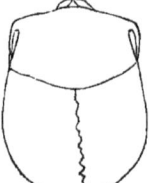 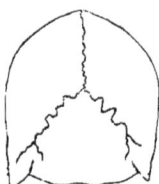

With a better forehead than is usual, this skull presents all the prominent characters of the American race—the prominent face, elevated vertex, vertical occiput, and the great swell from the temporal bones upward. Of the particular tribe to which this individual belonged I am not informed; and I should have hesitated to present it as a genuine Mexican had I not received, through Mr. Joseph Smith, late of this city and now of Mexico, a skull which corresponds with it in almost every particular, from an ancient tomb at Tacuba. Of the latter I subjoin, at the end of the following measurements, three diagrams for the purpose of comparison.

MEASUREMENTS.

Longitudinal diameter,	6.8 inches.
Parietal diameter,	5.5 inches.
Frontal diameter,	4.6 inches.
Vertical diameter,	6. inches.
Inter-mastoid arch,	15.6 inches.

Inter-mastoid line,	4.4 inches.
Occipito-frontal arch,	14.6 inches.
Horizontal periphery,	19.9 inches.
Internal capacity,	89.5 cubic inches.
Capacity of the anterior chamber,	33.5 cubic inches.
Capacity of the posterior chamber,	56. cubic inches.
Capacity of the coronal region,	19.5 cubic inches.
Facial angle,	80 degrees.

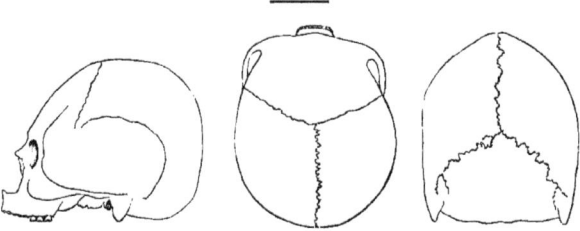

The skull represented in the above diagrams came too late to be lithographed: but in a future part of this work are inserted three heads from Otumba, which will materially assist in completing this section of the illustrations. (See Plates 59, 60, 61.)

PLATE XVII.—A.

MEXICAN.

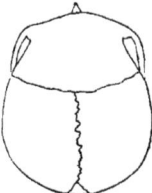 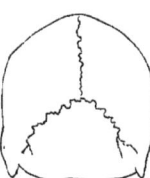

This is the cranium of a Mexican Indian of the Pames tribe, whose location is at the hamlet of San Lorenzo, not far from the city of Mexico. It was exhumed at the particular request of the late Dr. Antommarchi, Physician to

THE MEXICANS.

Napoleon, and by that gentleman deposited in my collection at the request of my friend Dr. M. Burrough, United States Consul at Vera Cruz. The certificates which accompanied this skull go to prove that it belonged to an Indian of the unmixed race, but of whose history nothing is stated. It therefore only remains to subjoin the usual

MEASUREMENTS.

Longitudinal diameter,	6.6 inches.
Parietal diameter,	5.3 inches.
Frontal diameter,	4.3 inches.
Vertical diameter,	5.2 inches.
Inter-mastoid arch,	14.6 inches.
Inter-mastoid line,	4.1 inches.
Occipito-frontal arch,	13.6 inches.
Horizontal periphery,	19. inches.
Internal capacity,	74. cubic inches.
Capacity of the anterior chamber,	28. cubic inches.
Capacity of the posterior chamber,	46. cubic inches.
Capacity of the coronal region,	11.5 cubic inches.
Facial angle,	77 degrees.

PLATE XVIII.

MEXICAN.

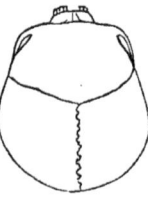 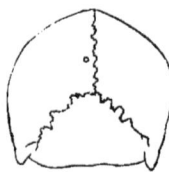

A remarkably well characterised Toltecan head, from an ancient tomb near the city of Mexico, whence it was exhumed with a great variety of antiques, vessels, masks, ornaments, &c. It is preserved in the collection of the American Philosophical Society; and I am indebted for its use on this occasion to the estimable Librarian of that institution, John Vaughan, Esq. The forehead is low, but not very receding; the face projects, and the whole cranium is extremely unequal in its lateral proportions.

MEASUREMENTS.

Longitudinal diameter,	6.4 inches.
Parietal diameter,	5.7 inches.
Frontal diameter,	4.5 inches.
Vertical diameter,	5.4 inches.
Inter-mastoid arch,	14.6 inches.
Inter-mastoid line,	4.5 inches.
Occipito-frontal arch,	13.5 inches.
Horizontal periphery,	20.2 inches.
Internal capacity,	77. cubic inches.
Capacity of the anterior chamber,	30. cubic inches.
Capacity of the posterior chamber,	47. cubic inches.
Facial angle,	78 degrees.

PLATE XVIII.—A.

MEXICAN.—TLAHUICA?

 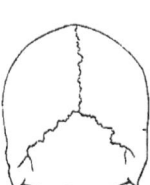

This is a female skull, obtained from Acapacingo, in the valley of Cuernavaca, about fifty miles south of the city of Mexico. It was obtained and presented to me by that distinguished friend and patron of science, William Maclure, Esq., President of the Academy of Natural Sciences of Philadelphia. Mr. Maclure did not inform me to what tribe this individual belonged; but as Clavigero* states

---

* Hist. of Mexico, I, p. 7. (Cullen's Tr.)

THE NATCHEZ.   157

that all the tribes of that section of Mexico belonged to the great Tlahuica nation, I have designated this specimen accordingly. We recognise in this skull the projecting face, the retreating forehead and the flat occiput of the Toltecan family, although the whole head is more elongated than usual. The styloid process exceeds any similar appendage I have ever seen, and touches the lower jaw in a way that must have impeded the opening of the mouth.

MEASUREMENTS.

Longitudinal diameter,	6.9 inches.
Parietal diameter,	5.2 inches.
Frontal diameter,	4.2 inches.
Vertical diameter,	5.4 inches.
Inter-mastoid arch,	14.5 inches.
Inter-mastoid line,	4.1 inches.
Occipito-frontal arch,	14. inches.
Horizontal periphery,	19.2 inches.
Internal capacity,	78. cubic inches.
Capacity of the anterior chamber,	30. cubic inches.
Capacity of the posterior chamber,	48. cubic inches.
Capacity of the coronal region,	14.25 cubic inches.
Facial angle,	76 degrees.

THE NATCHEZ.

The traditions of the Natchez state, that they migrated from Mexico at two different periods: and their singular usages lead to the belief that they were a branch of the great Toltecan family, which, as we have seen, was subjected to great vicissitudes, and ultimately, in a great measure, expatriated from Anahuac.

The more obvious analogies between the Natchez and the Toltecas, consist in the worship of the sun, the practice of human sacrifices on the death of eminent persons, hereditary distinctions, and fixed institutions, in which respect they differed from all the other nations of Florida.

The Natchez not only worshipped the sun, but kept what they termed the eternal fire; which last they accomplished by slowly burning a torch made of three pieces of wood joined at one end.*

Their hereditary usages were very remarkable, and constituted, in fact, a feudal system of the most exclusive kind. They called their principal chief the *Great Sun*, and the nobles and their children were called *suns;* while all that portion of the tribe not allied to these dignitaries, were stigmatised by an epithet equivalent to the English word rabble. Yet what is even more singular, nobility was derived and transmitted exclusively through the female sex.

The character of these people was more pacific than that of most other American tribes. They rarely make wars, says Charlevoix, nor place their glory in destroying their fellow creatures; but, once excited to revenge by repeated provocation, their resentment is appeased only by the extermination of their enemies. The fate of the first French colony in their nation is a tragical illustration of this fact, and may be told in a few words. The French, by repeated aggressions, aroused the vengeance of a people who had assiduously cultivated their friendship. A plan was concerted by the Indians for destroying their enemies in a single night; and with such fidelity was this secret maintained, that on the eve of St. Andrew, A. D. 1729, they fell upon the hapless colony, and of seven hundred Europeans, all except a mere handful were massacred without mercy.

We have only to add the uniform result of such resistance on the part of the Indians. The French entered the country of the Natchez in great force, and this injured people, after a valiant struggle, was at last dispersed and almost exterminated in the year 1730.†

It is a singular circumstance in the character of these people, that they were in the practice of funeral sacrifices to an extent unknown elsewhere in America

---

* Charlevoix, Voy. de l'Amerique, Let. XXX.

† The French sold their Natchez prisoners, including a chief, into slavery in the West India Islands. Such of the Natchez as escaped the fate of their country, fled up Red River, in Louisiana, and encamped six miles below the town of Natchitoches. Monsieur St. Dennie, a French Canadian, was then Commandant at Natchitoches: he collected what soldiers and militia he had at his disposal, and these being joined by the Natchitoches Indians, the Natchez were attacked in their camp by the whole force. The besieged "defended themselves desperately for six hours, but were at length totally defeated by St. Dennie, and such of them as were not killed in battle, were driven into the lake, where the last of them perished, and the Natchez as a nation became extinct."—Sibley, *Message from the President of the U. S.*, 1806, p. 80.

excepting in Peru. My friend Mr. Nuttall has embodied the more striking features of this usage in the following paragraph. "When either the male or female Sun died, all their *allouez*, or intimate attendants, devoted themselves to death, under a persuasion that their presence would be necessary to maintain the dignity of their chief in the future world. The wives and husbands of these chiefs were likewise immolated for the same purpose, and considered it the most honorable and desirable of deaths. More than a hundred victims were sometimes sacrificed to the manes of the Great Chief. The same horrible ceremonies, in a more limited degree, were also exercised at the death of the lesser chiefs.

"At the death of one of their female chiefs, Charlevoix relates, that her husband not being noble, was, according to their custom, strangled by the hands of his own son. Soon after, the two deceased being laid out in state, were surrounded by the dead bodies of twelve infants, strangled by order of the eldest daughter of the late female chief, and who had now succeeded to her dignity. Fourteen other individuals, were also prepared to die, and accompany the deceased. On the day of interment as the procession advanced, the fathers and mothers who had sacrificed their children, preceding the bier, threw the bodies on the ground at different distances, in order that they might be trampled upon by the bearers of the dead. The corpse arriving in the temple where it was to be interred, the fourteen victims now prepared themselves for death by swallowing pills of tobacco and water, and were then strangled by the relations of the deceased, and their bodies cast into the common grave and covered with earth."[*]

Among other singular customs of the Natchez, was that of distorting the head by compression. Du Pratz mentions, the women place their newborn infant in a cradle which is about two feet and a half long, nine inches broad, and six inches deep, stuffed beneath with a kind of mattrass, with the plant called Spanish beard. "The infant is laid on its back in the cradle, and fastened to it by the shoulders, the arms, the legs, the thighs and the hips; and over its forehead are laid two bands of deer-skin, which keep its head to the cushion, and render that part flat:" and he adds, that they never place their children on their feet until they are a year old.[†]

During the invasion of Florida, by Ferdinand de Soto, the Spaniards met with some Indians whose heads were moulded precisely into the form above described. "Their heads are incredibly long," (high) observes the historian, "and

---

[*] Travels in Arkansas, p. 271.—CHARLEVOIX, Voy. de l'Amerique, Let. XXX.
[†] Hist. of Louisiana, p. 323.

pointed upwards, owing to a custom of artificially compressing them from the period of the child's birth, until it attains the age of nine or ten years."* The people thus described are said to inhabit the province of Tula; and it is curious to observe, that this name was also that of the Toltecan capital of Anahuac, and signified a *place of reeds*. The same name is found in Texas and Guatemala, indicating the migrations of the Toltecan nation. It is, therefore, a reasonable presumption, that the Natchez were a colony of the old Toltecan stock.†

The Natchez lived very much excluded from intercourse with the adjacent nations, excepting the Chetimaches. They inhabited the banks of the Mississippi in three principal villages near the city which now bears their name; but the last remnant of the nation not long since occupied a small village on the Talipoosa river, in Alabama. During the late war between the United States and the Creek Indians, these Natchez joined the army of General Jackson, but since that period their name appears to exist only in history.‡

PLATES XX AND XXI.

NATCHEZ.

The extraordinary cranium of which two views are given on the annexed plates, was obtained from a mound near the city of Vicksburg, state of Mississippi, by Dr. W. Byrd Powell, of New Orleans, who has furnished me with the following brief memorandum.

"This skull is a fac-simile of another obtained at Natchez, but in a better state of preservation. It was obtained from a mound which was full of bones for the most part in a decomposed state. The drawings I send you are remarkably accurate; and the following are a few of the most remarkable phrenological measurements, derived from the skull itself:

"From individuality to occipital spine 5½ inches.

"From destructiveness to destructiveness 5¾ inches.

"From cautiousness to cautiousness 6½ inches.

---

* GARCILASO DE LA VEGA, Hist. de la Florida, Lib. IV, cap. 13.—Instead of nine or ten years, (nueve à diez anòs,) the time employed in the process was probably that number of months.

† M'CULLOH, Researches, p. 271.—Mr. Nuttall thinks that the place called *Quigalta* in De Soto's narrative, and the place where that brigand expired, was within the Natchez territory.—*Trav. in Arkansas*, p. 263.

‡ NUTTALL, Trav. p. 234.

"From secretiveness to secretiveness 6¼.

"From constructiveness to constructiveness 4½."

Mr. Dorfeuelle, of Cincinnati, has kindly presented me with a cast of another skull obtained near the city of Natchez, and which corresponds in most of its details with that here figured, and of which I subjoin two diagrams.

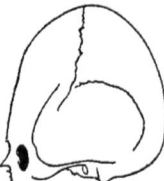 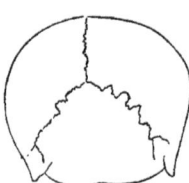

I am further informed that five at least of these extraordinary crania, have been obtained from different mounds in the ancient territory of the Natchez. It is now well ascertained, however, that several other tribes of our southern Indians also practised the art of changing the form of the skull. Among these were the CHOCTAWS. "They flatten their heads with a bag of sand," says Adair, "which with great care they keep fastened to the skull of the infant, while it is in its tender and imperfect state."* Bartram is more explicit. "The Choctaws are called by the traders Flats, or Flatheads, all the males having the fore and hind part of their skulls flattened or compressed, which is effected in the following manner. As soon as the child is born, the nurse provides a cradle or wooden case, where the head reposes, being fashioned like a brick mould. In this part of the machine the little boy is fixed, a bag of sand being laid on its forehead, which, by continual gentle compressure, gives the head somewhat the form of a brick from the temples upwards, and by these means they have high and lofty foreheads, sloping off backwards."† The Choctaws, therefore, moulded their heads in the same style or form with the Natchez. I subjoin diagrams of an admirably preserved cranium from a mound high up the Alabama river, and which has been

* Hist. of the Amer. Indians, p. 284.   † Trav. p. 517.

kindly lent me by Dr. O. H. Fowler, of this city. Whether it be a Choctaw or a Natchez, I cannot determine, but it is probably the latter.

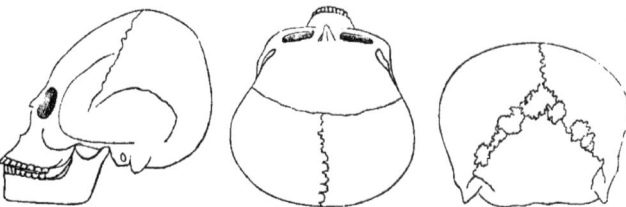

The WAXSAWS, according to Lawson, resorted to a somewhat similar device. "They use a roll which is placed on the babe's forehead, it being laid with its back on a flat board, and swaddled down hard thereon, from one end of this engine to the other." "The instrument," he adds, "is a sort of press that is let out and in, more or less, according to the discretion of the nurse, in which they make the child's head flat: it makes the eyes stand a prodigious way asunder, and the hair hang over the forehead like the eaves of a house, which seems very frightful."* Finally, it seems certain that the Katawbas on the east, and the Attakapas on the west side of the Mississippi, practised a similar usage.

THE CHETIMACHES.

Near the Natchez was another powerful though not numerous nation, called the Chetimaches. Du Pratz states that the latter are a branch of the Natchez, who have always looked upon them as their brethren.† But this affinity appears to have been of a social nature only, for Mr. Gallatin observes that he could find no analogies in their respective languages, and their customs appear to have been altogether dissimilar.

* Hist. of Carolina, p. 33.   † Hist. of Louisiana, p. 314.

They formerly inhabited the vicinity of the Lake Barataria, but, though once a warlike people, were subdued by the Europeans early in the last century; for Charlevoix, writing in the year 1722, says that the Chetimaches were nearly all destroyed at that time, and that the few of the tribe then remaining were slaves to the French colony.

PLATE XIX.*

CHETIMACHES.

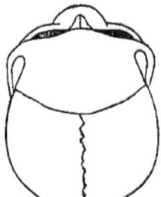 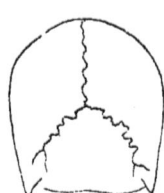

The late Dr. Justus Le Beau, of New Orleans, presented me with two genuine skulls of this tribe, which were exhumed from a cemetery in the Parish of St. Mary, in Louisiana. Of these heads I have figured the largest, which presents a singularly massive development. The nearly vertical occiput, the great height of the skull, and the size and strength of the bones of the face, are not surpassed by those of any Indian cranium I have seen. The measurements are as follow:

MEASUREMENTS.

Longitudinal diameter,	6.9 inches.
Parietal diameter,	5.6 inches.
Frontal diameter,	4.2 inches.
Vertical diameter,	5.9 inches.
Inter-mastoid arch,	15.5 inches.
Inter-mastoid line,	4.3 inches.
Occipito-frontal arch,	14. inches.

* In the regular order the Chetimaches should have preceded the Natchez.

Horizontal periphery,	20.	inches.
Internal capacity,	85.	cubic inches.
Capacity of the anterior chamber,	39.25	cubic inches.
Capacity of the posterior chamber,	45.75	cubic inches.
Capacity of the coronal region,	13.25	cubic inches.
Facial angle,	71	degrees.

THE MUSKOGEES OR CREEKS, AND SEMINOLES.

The Muskogee or Creek confederacy is composed of several nations or remnants of nations, among which the most prominent, at the present time, are the Seminoles. I am indebted to the politeness of Dr. Forry, of the United States Army, for some interesting particulars in reference to this coalition.

MUSKOGEES. "Among the great nation of Creek Indians," says he, "the principal and original tribe was the Muskogee, by whom the claim of having always occupied the country recently in their possession is boldly asserted. Long known as a powerful and restless confederacy, its sway extended over the present limits of Georgia, Alabama and Florida. It consisted of a community of tribes, which, having become reduced in numbers, incorporated themselves with the ruling band. In progress of time these various clans or tribes became, in some measure, a homogeneous people.

"The SEMINOLES, who have a similar origin, consist chiefly of Muskogees. The ancient possessors of the soil have become extinct, or at least have lost their identity among the wars, and changes and confusion incident to our aborigines. The collective appellation of *Seminoles*, in its Muskogee acceptation, has a signification expressive of the character of the Bedouin Arab. Detaching themselves from the main body of the Creeks, they wandered wherever a greater abundance of game or undisturbed possession of the soil might offer inducements. The Yamassees, a powerful people of whom much is said in our early colonial history, were, after long wars with their ancient enemies the Creeks, completely broken up, and under the elder king Payne, the Seminoles reduced as tributaries all refractory tribes. Thus from this nucleus of a people, there gradually arose

THE CREEKS.

by natural increase and accessions from other tribes, a nation of *Seminoles, or wanderers.**

Mr. Bartram describes the Creek women as of short stature but well formed: their visage, says he, is round, their features regular and beautiful: the brow is high and arched; the eye large, black and languishing, and expressive of modesty, and diffidence. "They are, I believe, the smallest race of women yet known, seldom above five feet high, and the greater number never arrive to that stature: their hands and feet are not larger than those of Europeans of nine or ten years of age; yet the men are of gigantic stature, a full size larger than Europeans; many of them above six feet, and few under that, or five feet eight or ten inches."† He adds that their complexion is much darker than that of any tribe he had seen to the north of them.

Bernard Romans observes, that they are remarkably well shaped and a very hardy race. "What deserves notice here is, that their thorax is very shallow, so that a savage of this race may appear almost a giant by the breadth of his shoulders, yet not measure so much in circumference as an ordinary European; but whether this is the effect of art or nature, I cannot pretend to decide." Their women, he adds, are handsome, and the whole nation so hospitable that they are always ready to share their pipe and board with a stranger. On the other hand they are adepts in cruelty when they wreak their vengeance on a captive enemy.‡

Bartram confirms this picture, by stating that they are fond of their wives and children, and kind to travellers who pass through their country with pacific intentions. "I have been weeks and months amongst them in their towns," says he; "I never observed the least sign of contention or wrangling; never saw an instance of an Indian beating his wife or reproving her in anger. In this case they stand as examples of reproof to the most civilised nations, as not being deficient in justice, gratitude and a good understanding."§

Bartram has justly characterised the Creeks as a proud and arrogant people, "valiant in war, ambitious of conquest, restless, and perpetually exercising their arms, yet magnanimous and merciful to a vanquished enemy, when he submits, and seeks their friendship and protection." They habitually unite the subjected

---

* Sketch of the Indian Tribes known under the appellation of Muskogee, with some general remarks on the Manners and Customs, &c., of the American Aborigines. By Samuel Forry, M. D., Medical Staff, U. S. Army. MS.

† Trav. in Florida, p. 484. ‡ Nat. Hist. of Florida, I, p. 92.
§ Trav. in Florida, p. 490.

tribes into their own confederacy, and give them all the rights possessed by themselves.

Hence the present Creek nation is said to embrace the remains of no less than fifteen different tribes, which they have conquered at various times. "This confederacy of remnants," says Romans, "is a race of very cunning fellows, and with regard to us the most to be dreaded of any nation on the continent, as well for their indefatigable thirst for blood, (which makes them travel incredibly for a scalp or prisoner) as for their being truly politicians bred."*

All these details go to prove that the Creeks possess, in a remarkable degree, those seemingly incompatible extremes that compose the Indian character.

PLATE XXII.

SEMINOLE.

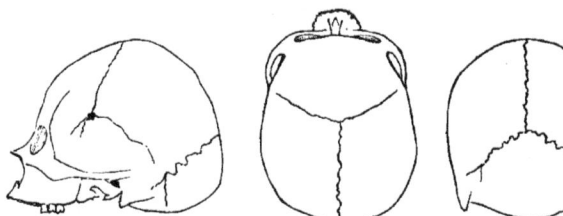

This remarkably characteristic Indian head was presented to me by my friend Dr. G. Emerson of this city, who at the same time favored me with the following historical memorandum. "Seminole warrior, slain at the battle of St. Joseph's, thirty miles below St. Augustine, in June 1836, by Captain Justin Dimmick, of the First Regiment United States Artillery. At the commencement of the action Captain Dimmick rode forward, and received the fire of the Indians at a distance of about thirty yards. The Captain's horse being struck on the neck and flank, he dismounted; and the Indians, supposing him to be badly wounded, rushed towards him to scalp him. At that moment Captain D. raised his gun, (a double-barrel fowling piece,) and shot both of the Indians in succession: he

* Nat. Hist. of Florida, I, p. 91.

then seized the musket of a soldier who stood near him, and sprang upon his enemies, one of whom (the subject of the annexed drawing) he found already dead, by a ball through the head, while the other was merely wounded. The latter was at once despatched by a thrust of the bayonet; and thus by the singular bravery of Captain Dimmick, these two savages lay dead, and side by side, in a few moments after the action began."

The accompanying lithograph, and the preceding wood outlines, convey an exact representation of this interesting relic, which presents a lofty, though retreating forehead, great breadth between the parietal bones, and remarkable altitude of the whole cranium. The orbits of the eyes show the medium size and quadrangular form, noticed when speaking of the Creek Indians. The fatal ball is observed to have entered the skull at the coronal suture, at its junction with the sphenoid bone; and it passed out through the opposite parietal bone.

MEASUREMENTS.

Longitudinal diameter,	7.3 inches.
Parietal diameter,	5.9 inches.
Frontal diameter,	4.6 inches.
Vertical diameter,	5.8 inches.
Inter-mastoid arch,	15.9 inches.
Inter-mastoid line,	4.4 inches.
Occipito-frontal arch,	15.3 inches.
Horizontal periphery,	20.7 inches.
Internal capacity,	93. cubic inches.
Capacity of the anterior chamber,	35.5 cubic inches.
Capacity of the posterior chamber,	57.5 cubic inches.
Capacity of the coronal region,	25. cubic inches.
Facial angle,	72 degrees.

PLATE XXIII.

SEMINOLE.

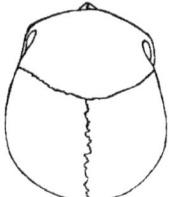 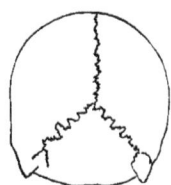

A Seminole warrior, of whose history nothing is known. The skull was obtained in Florida twelve miles south of the Suwannee river, and presented to me by Dr. Eugene H. Abadie, of the United States Army, to whom I am indebted for various similar obligations. It is a large head, with the Indian characters very strongly marked, and having a remarkably well developed forehead.

MEASUREMENTS.

Longitudinal diameter,	7.1 inches.
Parietal diameter,	5.6 inches.
Frontal diameter,	4.7 inches.
Vertical diameter,	5.5 inches.
Inter-mastoid arch,	15. inches.
Inter-mastoid line,	4.1 inches.
Occipito-frontal arch,	14.8 inches.
Horizontal periphery,	20.3 inches.
Internal capacity,	89. cubic inches.
Capacity of the anterior chamber,	52.? cubic inches.
Capacity of the posterior chamber,	37.? cubic inches.
Capacity of the coronal region,	19.? cubic inches.
Facial angle,	78 degrees.

THE SEMINOLES.

PLATE XXIV.

SEMINOLE.

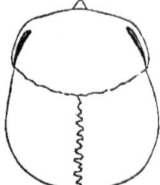 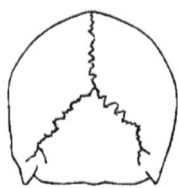

This Seminole skull was sent me by the late lamented Henry B. Croom, Esq. It possesses the strong traits of the other crania of this nation.

MEASUREMENTS.

Longitudinal diameter,	7. inches.
Parietal diameter,	5.9 inches.
Frontal diameter,	4.5 inches.
Vertical diameter,	5.8 inches.
Inter-mastoid arch,	14.7 inches.
Inter-mastoid line,	4.6 inches.
Occipito-frontal arch,	14.2 inches.
Horizontal periphery,	20.5 inches.
Internal capacity,	91.5 cubic inches.
Capacity of the anterior chamber,	44. cubic inches.
Capacity of the posterior chamber,	47.5 cubic inches.
Capacity of the coronal region,	18.1 cubic inches.
Facial angle,	81 degrees.

PLATE XXVI.

MUSKOGEE, OR CREEK.

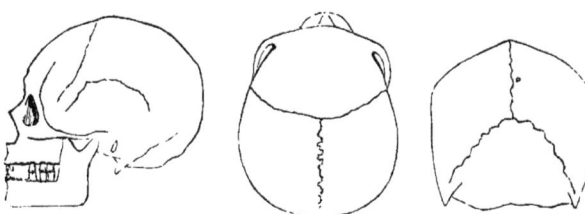

This plate is taken from the skull of Athlaha Ficksa, a full-blood chief of the Creek nation. He fought with great bravery in the United States service, and against the majority of his own countrymen in the present Florida war. He died at Mobile, in 1837, whence I received his cranium through the kindness of Dr. Henry S. Rennolds, of the United States Navy. The broad but low forehead, and the width between the parietal bones, are highly characteristic in this head: a front view is given of it, in order to convey an accurate idea of the osteology of the Indian face. Thus we see the large and projecting cheek bones, an arched and prominent bridge of the nose, powerfully developed jaws and remarkably perfect teeth. The distance between the eyes is even greater than is usual, yet the orbits themselves are not large in proportion. The following are the measurements of this remarkably fine head.

MEASUREMENTS.

Longitudinal diameter,	7. inches.
Parietal diameter,	5.7 inches.
Frontal diameter,	4.6 inches.
Vertical diameter,	5.3 inches.
Inter-mastoid arch,	15.3 inches.
Inter-mastoid line,	4.5 inches.
Occipito-frontal arch,	14.4 inches.
Horizontal periphery,	20.8 inches.
Internal capacity,	94.75 cubic inches.

Capacity of the anterior chamber,	42.5 cubic inches.
Capacity of the posterior chamber,	52.25 cubic inches.
Capacity of the coronal region,	15.6 cubic inches.
Facial angle,	72 degrees.

THE CHEROKEES.

The Cherokees, says Bartram, are even taller and more robust than the Muskogees, and by far the largest race of men he had seen. Their complexion is brighter than that of the succeeding tribes, and somewhat of an olive cast, while some of their young women are nearly as fair as Europeans.

The same traveller, who was much among the Cherokees towards the close of the last century, describes them as grave and circumspect in their deportment, and slow and reserved in conversation; tenacious of their rights, and impatient of aggression, yet more humane than most of their Indian neighbors. Mr. Bartram speaks of them as a warlike nation, "ready always to sacrifice every pleasure and gratification, even their blood, and life itself, to defend their territory and maintain their rights."* This last statement, however, is rather at variance with history, for the Cherokees have been remarked for their pacific disposition, and their preference of agriculture to war. Mr. Bartram himself mentions the fact of their doing homage to the Creeks in open council; and he adds that this vassalage was arrogantly imposed and passively submitted to.†

It is also certain that some of the southern tribes, and especially the Congarees, Yamassees and Esaws, made incursions into the Cherokee country for the mere purpose of making prisoners, whom they subsequently sold as slaves in Charleston, South Carolina; nor was this practice abolished until the year 1695.‡

It is obvious from the preceding facts that the arts of peace are more congenial to the Cherokees than those of war. They are not only more docile, but far more intelligent and capable of instruction, than the surrounding tribes; and in proof of this we need but instance the syllabic Cherokee alphabet, which

---

* Trav. in Florida, &c., p. 485.   † Loco citat.
‡ GALLATIN, in Archæolog. Amer. II, p. 92.

was invented by a native Indian of that tribe, and by means of which any individual of the nation can be taught to write his own language in three weeks.

Mr. Gallatin records the following interesting observation. "The only well ascertained instance, among our own Indians, of their having, at least in part, become an agricultural nation, (meaning thereby that state of society in which the men themselves do actually perform agricultural labor,) is that of the Cherokees. and it is in proof, that, in this case also, cultivation was at first introduced through the means of slavery. In their predatory incursions they carried away slaves from Carolina; these were used to work, and continued to be thus employed by their new masters. The advantages derived by the owners were immediately perceived. Either in war, or in commercial intercourse, slaves of the African race became objects of desire; and gradually, assisted by the efforts of the government and the beneficial influence of the missionaries, some among those Indians who could not obtain slaves, were induced to work for themselves. Accounts vary as to the extent of that true civilisation, but it is believed that it embraces nearly one third of the male population."*

The same learned author observes that the late Dr. Barton thought the Cherokee language belonged to the Iroquois family, "and on this point," he adds, "I am inclined to the same opinion. The affinities are few and remote; but there is a similarity in the general termination of the syllables, in the pronunciation and accent, which has struck some of the native Cherokees."†

PLATE XXV.

CHEROKEE.

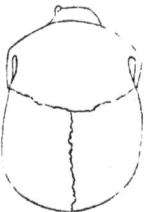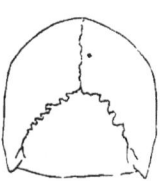

The head of a Cherokee warrior who was known in the army by the name

* Archæolog. Amer. II, p. 157. † Ibid. p. 91.

of John Waring. I have sought in vain for any particulars of his history, nor indeed is there any thing remarkable in the conformation of the skull. It only remains, therefore, to add the

MEASUREMENTS.

Longitudinal diameter,	7.2 inches.
Parietal diameter,	5.3 inches.
Frontal diameter,	4.3 inches.
Vertical diameter,	5.3 inches.
Inter-mastoid arch,	14.1 inches.
Inter-mastoid line,	4.5 inches.
Occipito-frontal arch,	14.7 inches.
Horizontal periphery,	19.1 inches.
Internal capacity,	82. cubic inches.
Capacity of the anterior chamber,	35. cubic inches.
Capacity of the posterior chamber,	47. cubic inches.
Capacity of the coronal region,	12.25 cubic inches.
Facial angle,	77 degrees.

The preceding skull belongs to the Phrenological Society of this city, and I have been allowed the use of it on this occasion by my friend Dr. John Bell. I have in my collection four Cherokee heads for which I am indebted to the zeal and kindness of Dr. J. Martin, of the United States Army. On comparing these with the one belonging to the Phrenological Society, I find them all small, the largest not equalling the average of European skulls, and the mean of the series giving but seventy-nine cubic inches of internal capacity, while the mean of the facial angle is seventy-six degrees.

THE UCHEES.

The Uchees, though now incorporated in the Creek confederacy, were primitively a distinct nation, and spoke a different language. They were originally established east of the Coosa river, and they consider themselves the most ancient inhabitants of the country. Mr. Gallatin* thinks the Uchees may have been the *Apalaches* of De Soto: no tribe in Florida gave that miscreant more trouble; they disputed every inch of ground, and kept up an untiring warfare against the Spaniards, until the latter had left their territory. The valor of the Spaniards, says Garcilaso de la Vega, only redoubled the courage of the Indians.†

PLATE XXVII.

UCHEE.

I received this well-characterised Indian head from my friend Dr. Z. Pitcher, of the U. S. Army, who accompanied it with the following memorandum. "This man spoke the English language, and played well upon the fife, from which circumstance he was known as *Bill the Fifer*. He was attached to the U. S. Army during the Creek war, and was regarded as a dauntless warrior. He died at Fort Gibson, Arkansas, in 1833."

MEASUREMENTS.

Longitudinal diameter,	6.8 inches.
Parietal diameter,	5.4 inches.
Frontal diameter,	4.3 inches.
Vertical diameter,	5.5 inches.
Inter-mastoid arch,	15. inches.
Inter-mastoid line,	4.4 inches.
Occipito-frontal arch,	14.3 inches.
Horizontal periphery,	20.1 inches.
Internal capacity,	81.5 cubic inches.
Facial angle,	75 degrees.

On measuring nine heads of Indians of the Creek and Seminole nations, I find the internal capacity unusually large, being no less than 94.75 cubic inches in the largest, and 81.5 in the smallest skull; and the mean of the series is 87.5 cubic inches, which is a near approach to the Caucasian. The mean facial angle, however, is but seventy-five degrees.

* Archæolog. Amer. II, p. 95.   † Conquete de la Florida, I, p. 150.

THE ALGONQUIN-LENAPÉ.

The Algonkin and Lenapé nations are grouped by philologists under the collective name of Algonquin-Lenapés; yet we observe some physical differences in people of this great family, and they were still more separated by those perpetual hostilities which every where characterise the American tribes.

When the Europeans first became acquainted with the Algonquin-Lenapé nations, they possessed a vast tract of North America, extending from Labrador and Hudson's Bay on the north, to the country of the Florida tribes on the south, while the Mississippi and Atlantic bounded them west and east. It is well known, however, that at the present day many of these tribes inhabit west of the Mississippi, while to the east of that river they are in a geat measure superseded by the white population. It is necessary to remark, however, that in the midst of the Algonquins, and surrounded by them on every side, lived the Iroquois or Five nations.

It will be observed in the course of this work, that I possess an extensive series of the crania of this widely extended nation, and it may therefore be admissible to give a brief enumeration of the principal communities of which it is composed, arranged in a geographical manner: and I take this occasion to acknowledge that these facts are chiefly derived from the published labors of Mr. Gallatin.*

The *Northern group* of the Algonquin-Lenapé embraces the Knistenaux or Crees, the Chippeways, the Ottawas, the Potawatomies, the Missasaugas, and the Algonquins proper. All these nations speak dialects so nearly allied, that they may be rather considered as dialects of the same than as distinct languages. The Knistenaux language is less allied to the general type than any of the others, but even here the affinity is very obvious. The *Northeastern group* included the Micmaks, the Etchemins and the Abenakis, which tribes inhabited the seacoast, and some extent of inland country, from Labrador to the present state of Maine. Among the southernmost of these communities, was the Penobscots, of whom some degraded remains are yet existing.

The *Eastern or Atlantic group*, embraces the New England Indians, or in other words those between the Abenakis and Hudson river; the Long Island

* Archæolog. Amer. II, p. 23, etc.

tribes; the Delaware and Minsi of Pennsylvania and New Jersey; the Nanticokes of Maryland; the Susquehannocks; the Powhattans of Virginia, and the Pamlicoes of North Carolina.* The northern tribes of this great family are familiar in our colonial history by the names of Mohegans or Pequods, Narragansets, Wampanoags and Pawtuckets. The Delawares, less belligerent than those nations, occupy a prominent place in the early annals of Pennsylvania, while the Powhattans hold the same relative position to Virginia.

The *Western group* of Lenapé includes the Menominees, the Miamis, the Illinois, the Ottigamies or Foxes, the Sauks, Kickapoos and Shawnoes, together with some subordinate tribes. They occupied a wide tract of country, extending from the Cumberland river on the south to the Great Lakes.

It is only necessary to add, that these numerous and often remote nations speak dialects of a single language, and that philologists have grouped them on account of this affinity. In physical character there is also an obvious resemblance, and their social habits are much alike; but these points will be considered more in detail hereafter.

We may here add from Mr. Gallatin, that "it is difficult to ascertain whether the name of Algonkins or Algoumekins, did belong to any particular tribe, or was used as a generic appellation." The tribes living on the Ottawa river were more especially distinguished by the name of Algonquins.

THE CHIPPEWAYS.

This powerful nation roves in bands over an extensive tract of country, embracing the whole of the Lakes Superior and Winnepeck, and the Lake of the Woods. Their camps are also seen on Lake Pepin, on the Spirit Lake, on the Assinaboin and Saskatchawan rivers, and at the Sault St. Marie. They are, however, a thinly scattered people, whose numbers have been rapidly diminished by war and the small pox, those two fatal enemies of Indian life.

Mr. Keating gives the following physical traits of this nation. "The

* GALLATIN, Loco citat.

THE CHIPPEWAYS.

Chippeways are not naturally very strong, but they are active; they will walk, swim, paddle, &c., for a length of time without any apparent fatigue. They are inured to exercise, and heedless of exposures of all kinds; they make good hunters and skilful fishers. They are generally tall and thin, and are easily distinguished from the Missouri Indians by the absence of the aquiline nose, which may be considered characteristic of the latter. Their bodies and shoulders are well set and well proportioned: their legs are not very good, generally destitute of calf, with thick knees and ankles: their feet are large; their arms and hands small and well shaped; they possess great strength in the wrist. Their voice is strong and harmonious, and many of them sing, and their ear appears good."* They seem to be among the most intelligent of the northern tribes; brave in war, and faithful to the obligations of friendship.

PLATE XXVIII.

CHIPPEWAY.

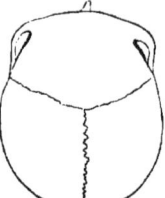 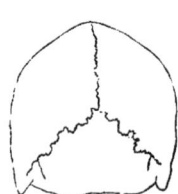

I received this head from Henry R. Schoolcraft, Esq., the distinguished traveller and naturalist, and United States Indian agent at Michillimackinack. Of its history nothing is known, excepting the fact of its having belonged to a genuine Chippeway Indian. The general characters are those of the American race; but the frontal region presents an unusual development.

MEASUREMENTS.

Longitudinal diameter,	7.3 inches.
Parietal diameter,	5.8 inches.

* Exped. II, p. 166.

Frontal diameter,	4.8 inches.
Vertical diameter,	5.5 inches.
Inter-mastoid arch,	15.1 inches.
Inter-mastoid line,	4.6 inches.
Occipito-frontal arch,	14.2 inches.
Horizontal periphery,	20.9 inches.
Internal capacity,	94. cubic inches.
Capacity of the anterior chamber,	43. cubic inches.
Capacity of the posterior chamber,	51. cubic inches.
Capacity of the coronal region,	14.75 cubic inches.
Facial angle,	84 degrees.

THE MENOMINEES.

The Menominees formerly inhabited the country about Green Bay, in Wisconsin, where they were early visited by the Jesuit missionaries, from whom they received the name of *Folles Avoines;* because, with more prudence than the adjacent tribes, they collect in summer a quantity of wild-rice to serve them for subsistence in winter.

Charlevoix and others, says General Pike, have all borne testimony to the beauty of this nation. "From my own observation I had sufficient reason to confirm their information, for the men are all straight and well made, about the middle size, and their complexion fair for savages. In short, he adds, they would anywhere be considered handsome, and the women are even handsomer." Such is the testimony of nearly all travellers. Charlevoix calls them very fine men, and the best shaped in all Canada. Mr. Keating remarks also that the few Menominees he met with, were of a light color, much resembling the white mulattoes of the United States; and he adds, that "they are naturally so much fairer than the neighboring tribes, that they are sometimes called the white Indians."[*] Although a small nation "they are respected by all their neighbors for their bravery and

---

[*] Exped. to the St. Peter's River, I, p. 174.

THE MENOMINEES.

independent spirit, and esteemed by the whites as their friends and protectors. When in the country I have heard their chief assert, in council with the Sioux and Chippeways, that although they were reduced to a few in number, yet they could say—we never were slaves."*

Their bravery is so much respected by the Chippeways, that the latter permit the Menominees to hunt on their grounds on the Mississippi and Lake Superior.†

"Their language, though of the Algonkin stock, is less similar to that of the Chippeways, their immediate neighbors, than almost any dialect of the same stock. As no other tribe speaks it, and they generally speak Chippeway, it is almost impossible to find good interpreters. It is probably owing to that circumstance that they were for a long time supposed to have a distinct language, belonging to another stock than the Algonkin."‡

PLATE XXIX.

MENOMINEE.

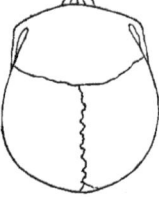 

By the kindness of Dr. Satterlee, of the United States Army, and J. A. Lapham, Esq., I have received a series of Menominee skulls, embracing eight specimens. They are something larger than the average of Indian crania; and although for the most part they present a rather oval shape, they are all marked by a gently flattened occiput.

The annexed plate was drawn from the cranium of a young Menominee woman, probably not more than twenty years of age. The symmetry of this skull, and its equal proportions, are more remarkable than in any other Indian

---

* PIKE, Exped. p. 53, 89.
† WARDEN, United States, III, p. 540.—BELTRAMI, Trav. II, p, 175.
‡ GALLATIN, Archæolog. Amer. II, p. 60.

head I have examined. I received it from Dr. Satterlee, to whom I am much indebted for the practical interest he has shown in this work.

MEASUREMENTS.

Longitudinal diameter,	6.8 inches.
Parietal diameter,	5.6 inches.
Frontal diameter,	4.2 inches.
Vertical diameter,	5.5 inches.
Inter-mastoid arch,	14.7 inches.
Inter-mastoid line,	4.1 inches.
Occipito-frontal arch,	14.1 inches.
Horizontal periphery,	19.9 inches.
Internal capacity,	86.5 cubic inches.
Capacity of the anterior chamber,	36.5 cubic inches.
Capacity of the posterior chamber,	50. cubic inches.
Capacity of the coronal region,	15.5 cubic inches.
Facial angle,	79 degrees.

THE MIAMIS.

The territory claimed by the Miamis and Piankeshaws (two tribes speaking one language) may be generally stated as having been bounded eastwardly by the Maumee river of Lake Erie, and to have included all the country drained by the Wabash. The Piankeshaws occupied the portion bordering on the Ohio. On the east they bordered on the Illinois; the boundary line being the dividing ridge which separates the waters emptying into the Sabine creek, and the Kaskaskia river, from those which fall into the Wabash.*

In physical character the Miamis do not differ from the other western tribes of the great Algonquin-Lenapé stock. Their fine athletic forms, aquiline noses, and strongly marked angular faces, are noticed by all travellers. In intellectual

* GALLATIN, Archæolog. Amer. II, p. 63.

THE MIAMIS.   181

capacity they yield to no tribes in the west. Little Tortoise, the Indian philosopher and friend of Volney, was a Miami: so also, according to Captain Carver, was the celebrated Pontiac, so long the artful and implacable enemy of the English during the past century.

Little Tortoise gave Volney the following account of the acute perceptions of his tribe. "We can distinguish every nation," said he, "at first sight: the face, the complexion, the shape, the knees, the legs, the feet, are to us certain marks of distinction. By the print of the foot we can distinguish not only men, women and children, but also tribes."*

With some admirable traits the Miamis mingle others that are truly deplorable. They are excessively sensual, and like the adjacent tribes, their fondness for spirituous liquors has reduced them to a very low state of degradation: the graphic picture which Volney drew of their social condition fifty years ago, is sufficient evidence of this fact.†

Their revenge was remarkable even among Indians; and to such excess was this demoniac passion indulged, that the Miamis and Kickapoos once embraced a society of men whose office it was to appease the spirit of revenge, whether national or individual, by devouring prisoners taken in war. It is further stated that the members of this inhuman fraternity held their office by hereditary privilege, and that their last celebration took place so recently as the year 1780, since which time it has been discontinued.

Some of the Miami tribes have resisted every attempt at civilisation and conversion, and remain uncompromising Pagans to this day.‡ Even the Jesuits, during the French ascendancy, could make no impression on them; for one of these missionaries declares that the tribes of the Illinois can only be converted by a miracle from heaven.§

---

* View of the Climate of the U. S. p. 412.   † Loco citat.
‡ Morse, Indian Report, Ap. p. 109.   § Lettres Edifiantes, XI, p. 304.

PLATE XXX.

MIAMI.

 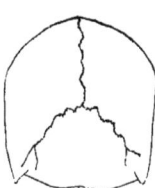

I received this skull from Dr. J. W. Davis, of Thorntown, Indiana, who politely favored me with the following memorandum of the history of the individual.

"The man to whom this cranium belonged was a Miami chief of the Eel river village. This fraction of the tribe was established on Augar river, a tributary of the Wabash, where they held a beautiful section of country known as the 'Thorntown Reserve.' They acknowledged the authority of two individuals as their chiefs, one of whom had received from the whites the name of *Captain Jim*. This man had acquired a great ascendancy over his people by his bravery, his success in the chase, and his uncompromising hostility to the *white faces*. By his cunning and eloquence he several times defeated the project of his colleague and rival, who was as anxious to sell the *reservation* as the whites were to purchase it. In the year 1830 a general council was called once more to deliberate on the propriety of selling their land. The *Captain* again opposed the sale, and in a long and forcible speech depicted the beauty and fertility of the country they then held, and the folly of parting with it for any consideration. No sooner had he ceased, than his rival denounced him as the enemy of his tribe, and wishing its destruction. The *Captain* then sprang upon his feet, retorted the charges, and called his colleague *a white man's dog*, upon which the latter seized a knife in each hand, and rushed furiously upon his opponent, who, with a single weapon of the same kind, willingly joined in combat. The tragedy was short and bloody. Each belligerent received the stab of his adversary, and both fell dead on the spot. They were buried side by side, with a pole bearing a flag placed between them.

The *Captain*, at the time of his death, was forty-five years of age, of a commanding appearance and unconquerable spirit."

MEASUREMENTS.

Longitudinal diameter,	7.3 inches.
Parietal diameter,	5.5 inches.
Frontal diameter,	4.3 inches.
Vertical diameter,	5.5 inches.
Inter-mastoid arch,	14.6 inches.
Inter-mastoid line,	4.6 inches.
Occipito-frontal arch,	14.9 inches.
Horizontal periphery,	21. inches.
Internal capacity,	90. cubic inches.
Capacity of the anterior chamber,	33.5 cubic inches.
Capacity of the posterior chamber,	56.5 cubic inches.
Capacity of the coronal region,	13.5 cubic inches.
Facial angle,	75 degrees.

THE OTTIGAMIES.

The Ottigamie or Fox tribe, and the Sauks, constitute in language, feature and usages, a single nation, and the social and political alliance which now exists between them has continued for centuries. When first observed by Europeans their territory was at the southern extremity of Green Bay, in Wisconsin, but they have more recently occupied large tracts on both sides of the Mississippi. The Sauks and Foxes are a finely formed people, and are said to combine in their characters both valor and generosity. Perhaps no tribes in North America are more warlike than these, and they possess an uncommon share of the perseverance and craftiness of their race. Charlevoix, who wrote early in the last century, after speaking in praise of the warlike spirit of the Iroquois, (who were ever the bitter enemies of the French,) thus characterises the Ottigamies. "It was not long," says he, "before we met with a new enemy, equally brave as the Iroquois, less politic, but much more ferocious, and whom it was impossible to conquer or to surprise. They might be compared to those insects which appear to have as many lives as limbs; for they were no sooner dispersed than they reappeared, and when reduced to a mere handful of brigands, they were still to be encountered every where, and for twenty-five years interrupted commerce, and infested the roads, over a tract more than five hundred leagues in circumference. These were the OTTIGAMIES, commonly called Foxes."* A late traveller remarks that these people still retain their ancient character, being "constantly embroiled in wars and disputes with their neighbors, the results of which show that they have more courage in battle than wisdom in council."†

PLATE XXXI.

OTTIGAMIE.

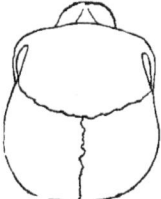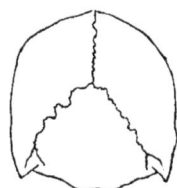

A large and ponderous skull of a full-blood Fox Indian, for which, and various similar favors, I am indebted to the kindness of Dr. B. B. Brown, of St. Louis, Missouri. It is one of the largest aboriginal skulls in my collection, as will be seen by the following

MEASUREMENTS.

Longitudinal diameter,	7. inches.
Parietal diameter,	5.9 inches.
Frontal diameter,	4.7 inches.
Vertical diameter,	5.5 inches.

* Hist. Generale de la Nouv. France, IV, p. 94. † SCHOOLCRAFT, Trav. p. 348.

Inter-mastoid arch,	15.3 inches.
Inter-mastoid line,	4.7 inches.
Occipito-frontal arch,	14.2 inches.
Horizontal periphery,	20.9 inches.
Internal capacity,	91.5 cubic inches.
Capacity of the anterior chamber,	40. cubic inches.
Capacity of the posterior chamber,	51.5 cubic inches.
Capacity of the coronal region,	12.75 cubic inches.
Facial angle,	82 degrees.

THE POTOWATOMIES.

"The Potowatomies are for the most part well proportioned, about five feet eight inches in height, possessed of much muscular strength in the arm, but rather weak in the back, with a strong neck, and endowed with considerable agility. Their voice is feeble and low, but excited, very shrill. Their teeth are sound and clean, but not remarkable for regularity. Their complexion is very much darkened by exposure to the sun and wind, while those parts which are kept covered are observed to retain their native brightness. Their sight is quick and penetrating, but blindness is frequent from the intense application of the eye in still hunting, and from exposure to the alternate, and in some cases, united action of the sun and snow; doubtless also on account of the constant smoke in their huts."[*] The same intelligent traveller adds, what has been already observed of the Indians in general, that although their endurance of cold and hunger are very extraordinary, they are absolute gluttons when freely supplied with food, and will eat ten and twenty times in the day. The Potowatomies, though a brave nation, are much more tractable in temper than some of the neighboring tribes; and Charlevoix, after eulogising their fine exterior, declares that he received more kindness from them, infidels as they were, than from the Christian Hurons.[†]

[*] KEATING, Exped. I, p. 136.   [†] Voy. a l'Amer. Let. XVII.

PLATE XXXIV.

POTOWATOMIE.

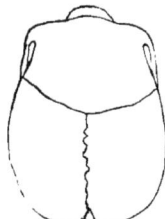 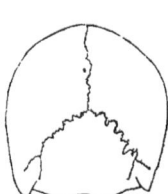

A skull of a genuine Potowatomie, of whose history, however, nothing is known. It is remarkable for its capacity behind the ears, and for the great length and flatness of the coronal region. I received it from my friend Dr. Walker, of the United States Army, who obtained it while stationed in Michigan, which is the native seat of this tribe.

MEASUREMENTS.

Longitudinal diameter,	7.8 inches.
Parietal diameter,	5.7 inches.
Frontal diameter,	4.4 inches.
Vertical diameter,	5.3 inches.
Inter-mastoid arch,	16.8 inches.
Inter-mastoid line,	4. inches.
Occipito-frontal arch,	15.8 inches.
Horizontal periphery,	22.1 inches.
Internal capacity,	98. cubic inches.
Capacity of the anterior chamber,	35.5 cubic inches.
Capacity of the posterior chamber,	62.5 cubic inches.
Capacity of the coronal region,	19. cubic inches.
Facial angle,	80 degrees.

THE NAUMKEAGS.

The Naumkeags constituted one of the many subordinate tribes of the Lenapé nation in Massachusetts. They were governed by the Sagamore of Pawtucket, and their villages occupied the site of the present town of Salem, in Massachusetts. All the New England tribes are said to have been very much alike. "They were tall, straight, of a red complexion, with black eyes, and of a vacant look when unimpassioned." The same author adds, what is more apocryphal, that they "possessed a natural understanding, sagacity and wit, equal to the same attributes in other men."* Had this been the fact they would not have been so easily duped, nor so speedily annihilated, by the Europeans.

PLATE XXXIII.

NAUMKEAG.

I received this head from Dr. A. L. Pearson, of Salem, Mass., near whose residence it was exhumed, together with thirty other skulls and the corresponding skeletons. They were all placed in the sitting posture a short distance below the surface of the ground, but were, for the most part, in a state of decomposition.

MEASUREMENTS.

Longitudinal diameter,	6.9 inches.
Parietal diameter,	5. inches.

* Dwight, Trav. in New England and New York, I, p. 113.

Frontal diameter,	4.2 inches.
Vertical diameter,	5.3 inches.
Inter-mastoid arch,	14.3 inches.
Inter-mastoid line,	3.9 inches.
Occipito-frontal arch,	14.4 inches.
Horizontal periphery,	19.8 inches.
Internal capacity,	71. cubic inches.
Capacity of the anterior chamber,	26. cubic inches.
Capacity of the posterior chamber,	45. cubic inches.
Facial angle,	80 degrees.

THE DELAWARES.

The Lenapé nations have a common tradition that they came from the far west; and migrating towards the east, arrived at the Mississippi river, called by them *Nimesi-sipu*, or the River of Fish. Here they found the Iroquois, who had also migrated, and were encamped on the banks of the river. These restless people found the country east of the river inhabited by numerous warlike tribes called *Alligewi*, and requested permission to establish themselves in their territory. This was denied them, but they were allowed to pass through the country. "They accordingly began to cross the Nimesi-sipu, when the Alligewi, seeing that their numbers were so very great, and, in fact, that they consisted of many thousands, made a furious attack on those who had crossed, threatening them all with destruction if they dared to come over to their side of the river. Fired at the treachery of these people, and the great loss of men they had sustained, and besides not being prepared for a conflict, the Lenapé consulted what was to be done: whether to retreat in the best manner they could, or to try their strength." The latter plan was adopted, and the Iroquois joined them on condition that the conquered country should be shared between the two nations. A fierce conflict ensued; no mercy was shown to the vanquished, and "the Alligewi at last finding that their destruction was inevitable if they persisted in their obstinacy, abandoned the country to the conquerors and fled down the Mississippi, from whence they

THE DELAWARES.

never returned."* The country was divided according to the stipulation; the Iroquois making choice of the lands near the great lakes and their tributary streams, while the Lenapé occupied the region to the south. When the European colonies arrived, the Delawares were the possessors of the southern portion of New Jersey, and parts of the present states of Pennsylvania and Delaware. They received the strangers with confidence and kindness, and for many years this mutual good faith remained unbroken. The Delawares were less warlike than the Iroquois, to whom they finally became in a manner subservient. "In person they were upright, and straight in their limbs, beyond the usual proportion in most nations: their bodies were strong, but of a strength rather fitted to endure hardship than to sustain much bodily labor; their features were regular; their countenances sometimes fierce, in common rather resembling a Jew than a Christian."†

PLATE XXXIV.

LENAPÉ, OR DELAWARE.

 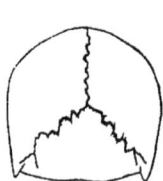

The few Delaware skulls in my possession are more elongated than is usual in the American tribes; they are also narrower in proportion in the parietal diameter, and less flattened on the occiput. The annexed drawing is taken from a skull presented by Dr. Pitcher, U. S. A., who accompanied it with the following memorandum: "I know this to be genuine. The country at present assigned to the Delawares lies north of the Kanzas, between it and the Missouri river. There are some wandering bands of these proud foresters in the Cherokee country, on the Neosho and Canadian rivers, in Arkansas. The individual whose cranium I

---

* HECKEWELDER, Historical Account, &c., p. 31.   † SMITH, Hist. of New Jersey, p. 242.

send you was a female, who died at the little colony on the Neosho river, near Fort Gibson. This is all I can learn of her, as most of the nations of the stock called Algonquin by the philologists, have an aversion to speak of their deceased relatives, and shudder at the idea of calling them by name."

MEASUREMENTS.

Longitudinal diameter,	7. inches.
Parietal diameter,	5.5 inches.
Frontal diameter,	4.6 inches.
Vertical diameter,	5.1 inches.
Inter-mastoid arch,	14.4 inches.
Inter-mastoid line,	4.2 inches.
Occipito-frontal arch,	14.5 inches.
Horizontal periphery,	20. inches.
Internal capacity,	78.5 cubic inches.
Capacity of the anterior chamber,	33. cubic inches.
Capacity of the posterior chamber,	45.5 cubic inches.
Capacity of the coronal region,	16.25 cubic inches.
Facial angle,	76 degrees.

THE IROQUOIS, OR FIVE NATIONS.

The *Iroquois Confederacy* consisted originally of five nations, the Mohawks, Oneidas, Onondagas, Cayugas and Senecas. The French gave them the name of Iroquois, but they called themselves *Mengwe*, or Mingoes. These nations constituted the eastern division of this powerful family, while to the west were several other tribes of the same stock, as the Hurons, Erigas, Andastes, &c., but the latter formed no part of the confederacy. In the year 1712, the Tuscaroras, flying from their own hunting grounds in North Carolina, took refuge among the Iroquois, and were admitted as a sixth nation.*

* Colden, Hist. of the Five Nations, I, p. 1.

History affords ample evidence of the intellectual superiority of the Iroquois over the surrounding nations. They were passionately devoted to war, and were every where formidable and victorious. "The Five Nations," observes Mr. Gallatin, "had already acquired a decided superiority over the other Indians before the arrival of the Europeans. They were at that epoch at war with all the surrounding tribes, with perhaps the single exception of the Andastes on the west. That in which they were engaged on the north, with the Hurons and Algonquins, was still attended with alternate success on each side. But southwardly they had already carried their arms as far as the mouth of the Susquehanna, and the vicinity of New Castle on the Delaware."* In fact they loved war for itself, and all other employments and pastimes were held to be contemptible in comparison; and they gloried most in their assumed appellation of *Ongwe Honwe, The Greatest of Men*. Their language is both energetic and melodious, destitute of labials, but having the guttural aspirate.†

They possessed all the other Indian characteristics in strong relief. They forced their women to work in the field and to carry burthens; they paid little respect to old age; they were not much affected by the passion of love, and singularly regardless of connubial obligations; and they unhesitatingly resorted to suicide as a remedy for domestic and other evils. They were proud, audacious, and vindictive, untiring in the pursuit of an enemy, and remorseless in the gratification of their revenge. In matters of religion their ideas appear to have been extremely vague; and their national observance consisted chiefly in the annual sacrifice of a dog, which they subsequently ate. Their cautiousness and cunning were proverbial even among the Indian nations: thus Colden observes that if they be sent with any message, though it demand the greatest despatch and portend imminent danger, they never tell it at once, but sit down a minute or two in silence, lest they should betray themselves by a hasty expression.‡ Hence they assumed a vacant and even stupid expression of countenance, when they were most awake to what was passing around them.§ It is but justice to add to these traits of the Iroquois, that in their long intercourse with the English colonies before the revolution, they were remarkable for their regard to treaties, and their good faith on all occasions wherein their pledge was once given. Early in the American Revolution they attached themselves strongly to the English interest, and committed horrible ravages in their incursions into the neighboring

---

* Archæolog. Amer. II, p. 75.   † Dwight, Trav. IV, p. 209.
‡ Hist. of the Five Nations, I, p. 20.   § Dwight, Trav. IV, p. 210.

states. Measures were accordingly taken for their subjugation, which was effected in 1779, and the few subsequent years. The remains of this once powerful confederacy are yet seen scattered through the state of New York, subdued in spirit, and debased by their fondness for intoxicating drinks. Some remnants of tribes, however, have assumed agricultural habits, and do comparatively well; but the Iroquois are rapidly diminishing in number, and will soon be known only in history.

PLATE XXXV.

CAYUGA.

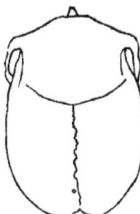 

The skull of a Cayuga chief which I received from Dr. Pitcher, U. S. A., with the following note: "This man was one of the original emigrants, with his tribe, from the state of New York to Ohio, and lastly to Arkansas, where he died at the age of nearly one hundred years, A. D. 1834. His name was Wan-yùn-ta; and he was also long known to the government of New York, in their treaties with the Iroquois, by the name of the *Tall Chief*. He was a good speaker, and a firm, shrewd, sensible man, whose merit alone raised him from a plebeian origin to be chief of his tribe."

MEASUREMENTS.

Longitudinal diameter,	7.8 inches.
Parietal diameter,	5.1 inches.
Frontal diameter,	4.2 inches.
Vertical diameter,	5.4 inches.
Inter-mastoid arch,	14.2 inches.
Inter-mastoid line,	4.5 inches.

THE ONEIDAS.

Occipito-frontal arch,	15.5 inches.
Horizontal periphery,	20.8 inches.
Internal capacity,	93.5 cubic inches.
Capacity of the anterior chamber,	35. cubic inches.
Capacity of the posterior chamber,	58.5 cubic inches.
Capacity of the coronal region,	11.5 cubic inches.
Facial angle,	78 degrees.

PLATE XXXVI.

ONEIDA.

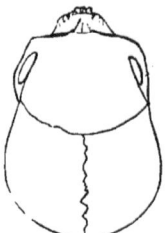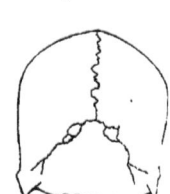

Head of a full-blood Oneida warrior, aged about forty years. He was killed in a fray at the Seneca Reserve, in Ohio, in 1830. He was buried in the Indian cemetery on Sandusky river, below Tiffin, whence his skull was removed and presented to me by my friend Benjamin Tappan, M. D., of Steubenville, Ohio.

MEASUREMENTS.

Longitudinal diameter,	7.5 inches.
Parietal diameter,	5.6 inches.
Frontal diameter,	4.1 inches.
Vertical diameter,	5.8 inches.
Inter-mastoid arch,	14.4 inches.
Inter-mastoid line,	4.3 inches.
Occipito-frontal arch,	14.9 inches.
Horizontal periphery,	20.8 inches.

194   CRANIA AMERICANA.

Internal capacity,	92.5 cubic inches.
Capacity of the anterior chamber,	36. cubic inches.
Capacity of the posterior chamber,	56.5 cubic inches.
Capacity of the coronal region,	18.4 cubic inches.
Facial angle,	74 degrees.

PLATE XXXVII.

HURON.

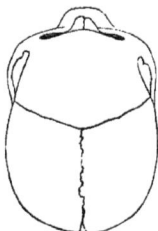 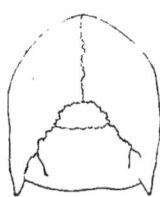

The Hurons call themselves *Wyandots;* and although of the same stock as the Iroquois, the two nations were engaged in deadly and constant war with each other, the Hurons espousing the French, the Iroquois the British interest. At length, about the year 1650, the Hurons were nearly exterminated, and from that time to the present have remained a feeble band. In all the striking traits of Indian character, they were in no respect inferior to the other nations of this stock. The annexed drawing was made from a skull obtained near Detroit by the late Dr. Sturm, the German traveller, of whose executor I purchased it. The only further information I can obtain respecting it, is the statement that it was the head of a chief, who was slain in a broil with his son-in-law. It is a ponderous cranium, and one of the most strongly marked in my collection.

MEASUREMENTS.

Longitudinal diameter,	7.2 inches.
Parietal diameter,	5.3 inches.
Frontal diameter,	4.3 inches.

Vertical diameter,	5.5 inches.
Inter-mastoid arch,	15. inches.
Inter-mastoid line,	4.4 inches.
Occipito-frontal arch,	14.2 inches.
Horizontal periphery,	19.8 inches.
Internal capacity,	74. cubic inches.
Capacity of the anterior chamber,	32.5 cubic inches.
Capacity of the posterior chamber,	41.5 cubic inches.
Capacity of the coronal region,	9.5 cubic inches.
Facial angle,	73 degrees.

On comparing five Iroquois heads, I find that they give an average internal capacity of 88 cubic inches, which is within two inches of the Caucasian mean. The largest of them gives no less than 98.5 cubic inches, and the smallest (the Huron above described) seventy-four. The mean of the anterior chamber is 35.5 cubic inches, while that of the posterior chamber is 52.5. The mean of the coronal region gives 15 cubic inches.

THE PAWNEES.

The Pawnees consist of two nations, the Pawnees proper, and the Ricaras or Aricaras, which last are also called Black Pawnees. The former inhabit the country on the river Platte, and the Ricara villages are below the Mandans, on the Missouri. These tribes speak a language different from any other on this continent. They do not differ much, in their physical character and belligerent habits, from the surrounding nations, but they have until lately practised the singular custom of sacrificing human victims to Venus, "The Great Star." This ceremony was performed annually, and immediately preceded their harvest labors, the success of which it was designed to promote. The practice is said to be an anomaly among the North American nations.[*]

[*] Exped. to Rocky Mountains, I, p. 357.—GALLATIN, Archæolog. Amer. II, p. 128.

PLATE XXXVIII.

PAWNEE.

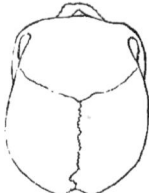 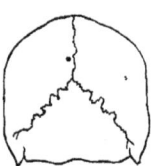

This head appears to have been that of a female, and was brought from the Platte river, about two hundred miles from its junction with the Missouri, by the expedition under Major Long to explore the Rocky Mountains. I am indebted to Mr. T. R. Peale for permission to use it on this occasion, which I do with the more interest because it is the only Pawnee skull I have seen.

MEASUREMENTS.

Longitudinal diameter,	6.6 inches.
Parietal diameter,	5.4 inches.
Frontal diameter,	4.4 inches.
Vertical diameter,	4.9 inches.
Inter-mastoid arch,	13.7 inches.
Inter-mastoid line,	4.3 inches.
Occipito-frontal arch,	13. inches.
Horizontal periphery,	19.1 inches.
Internal capacity,	70.5 cubic inches.
Capacity of the anterior chamber,	31. cubic inches.
Capacity of the posterior chamber,	39.5 cubic inches.
Capacity of the coronal region,	10.6 cubic inches.
Facial angle,	75 degrees.

THE DACOTAS.

This collective appellation embraces many tribes or rather nations of Indians, allied to each other by affinity of language, and in some measure by community of customs and feelings. They are also called Sioux and Naudowessies, and the "Seven Fires," in allusion to their confederacy of seven bands or tribes. They are established on both sides of the Mississippi, and on the western side of that river their hunting grounds extend from the Arkansas to the remote northern plains, and are only bounded on the west by the Rocky Mountains.

In the month of September 1837, I saw twenty-six chiefs and braves of the Sioux nation, then in Philadelphia, on their way to the seat of government. Every man of them had a broad face, high cheek bones, the large Roman nose expanded at the nostrils, a wide but low forehead, and flat occiput. Their complexion was cinnamon brown; several of them were naked to the waist, so that I was not deceived by the color of their faces, which were all painted. Their figures were rather tall, very muscular, and well proportioned. The Sioux are proverbial for their belligerent and sanguinary character. General Pike, who was much among them, says that from his knowledge he does "not hesitate to pronounce them the most warlike and independent nation of Indians within the boundaries of the United States, their every passion being subservient to that of war."*

The Dacota language is said to be less sonorous than the Algonquin, which abounds in labials. "It is certain," says a late traveller, "that their manners and customs differ essentially from those of any other tribe; and their physiognomy, as well as their language and opinions, marks them as a distinct race of people. Their sacrifices and their supplications to the unknown God—their feasts after any signal deliverance from danger—their meat and their burnt offerings—the preparation of incense, and certain customs of their females, offer too striking a coincidence with the manners of the Asiatic tribes before the commencement of the Christian era, to escape observation."†

---

* Exped. Appendix, p. 62.   † SCHOOLCRAFT, Narr. Journal, &c., p. 310.

PLATE XXXIX.

DACOTA.

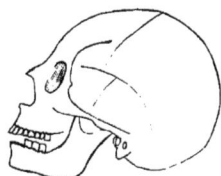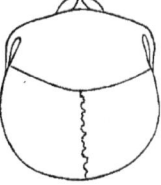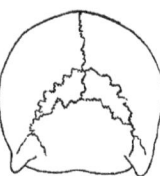

I received this skull from the late Dr. Poole, of this city, but could obtain no particulars, excepting the fact of its having belonged to a Sioux warrior of bad character, and who was killed by some act of violence on the northwestern frontier. The small squared head, the great comparative breadth between the parietal bones, and indifferent frontal development, correspond precisely with those features as observed in the individuals of the Sioux delegation already mentioned.

MEASUREMENTS.

Longitudinal diameter,	6.7 inches.
Parietal diameter,	5.7 inches.
Frontal diameter,	4.2 inches.
Vertical diameter,	5.4 inches.
Inter-mastoid arch,	14.7 inches.
Inter-mastoid line,	4.4 inches.
Occipito-frontal arch,	13.5 inches.
Horizontal periphery,	19.8 inches.
Internal capacity,	85. cubic inches.
Capacity of the anterior chamber,	36. cubic inches.
Capacity of the posterior chamber,	49. cubic inches.
Capacity of the coronal region,	16.6 cubic inches.
Facial angle,	77 degrees.

PLATE XLI.

OSAGE.

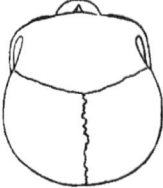 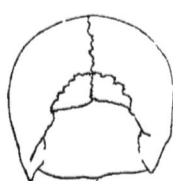

The Osages, Minetaris, Mandans, Assinaboins, and many cognate tribes, are more or less connected with the great Sioux nation, although they are often inveterate enemies to each other. The Osages are now chiefly found in the western part of Arkansas, and are yet a powerful tribe. "They are so tall and robust," says a late traveller, "as almost to warrant the application of the term gigantic; few of them appear to be under six feet, and many are above it."* Among the Osages who visited Boston some years ago, Dr. Warren remarked some very fine looking men: he particularises two, of whom he says that their heads could not be distinguished from those of Europeans.† It is said of these people, that they are fond of war without being remarkable for bravery. They consider horse-stealing a meritorious achievement, and at one time scarcely left a horse to turn a mill in the town of St. Genevieve. They are credited with one virtue, however, which is rare among savages, and that is mercy; for they rarely take the lives of those who fall into their hands."‡

The annexed drawing is derived from the skull of a young warrior named

---

* BRADBURY, Trav. p. 42. † Compar. View of Nervous System, &c., p. 93.

‡ BRECKENRIDGE, Views of Louisiana, p. 147.—On this subject Mr. Gallatin makes the following remarks: "Whether erratic or agricultural, there is a marked difference between the habits and character of all the Indians who dwelt amidst the dense forest which extends from the Atlantic to the Mississippi, and those of the inhabitants of the western prairie. These last are every where less ferocious than those of the eastern side of the Mississippi. Like all savages they put to death the prisoners taken in battle; but the horrid practice of inflicting on them the most excruciating torture for days together, does not appear to have prevailed anywhere beyond the Mississippi."—*Archæolog. Amer.* II, p. 129.

the *Buffalo Toil*. He was arrested in Arkansas on a charge of murder, and placed under guard at Fort Gibson. He soon determined to destroy himself, and succeeded by an excess of gluttony. Dr. Pitcher, to whom I am indebted for this relic, adds, that " as the Osages, Omahas, Kansas, Missouris and Quapaws all speak a language so nearly allied that they can severally converse with each other without an interpreter, you will find this specimen a fit representation of these several tribes."

MEASUREMENTS.

Longitudinal diameter,	6.5 inches.
Parietal diameter,	5.9 inches.
Frontal diameter,	4.6 inches.
Vertical diameter,	5.3 inches.
Inter-mastoid arch,	15.1 inches.
Inter-mastoid line,	4.1 inches.
Occipito-frontal arch,	13.4 inches.
Horizontal periphery,	19.5 inches.
Internal capacity,	83. cubic inches.
Capacity of the anterior chamber,	37.5 cubic inches.
Capacity of the posterior chamber,	45.5 cubic inches.
Capacity of the coronal region,	14.1 cubic inches.
Facial angle,	77 degrees.

"The Missouri Indians of the male sex," says Mr. Gallatin, "exceed in height the ordinary average of the Europeans; but the women are in proportion shorter and thicker. The average facial angle is 78 degrees; the transverse line of the direction of the eyes is rectilinear; the nose aquiline; the lips thicker than those of Europeans; the cheek bones prominent but not angular. The women marry very young, bear children from the age of thirteen to forty, and have generally from four to six."* My measurements of eleven skulls of Missouri tribes gives 77 degrees as a mean of the facial angle, which is confirmatory of that stated by Mr. Gallatin. The mean internal capacity of the skull is eighty cubic inches, and but one head comes up to the European average.

* Archæolog. Amer. II, p. 130.

COTONAY? BLACKFEET.

The Blackfoot nation is one of the most powerful in the northwestern region of this continent; for, notwithstanding their long and desperate conflicts with all the surrounding tribes, they yet number thirty thousand souls. They are composed of three principal divisions, of which the *Cotonay* is the most celebrated and best known. They are proverbial for their uncompromising hostility to the trappers, whom they attack and destroy whenever opportunity offers. They never ask for mercy and rarely award it to their captives. Fierce, crafty and courageous, they hold little communication with other tribes, and revenge themselves on all strangers who intrude, whether for good or evil, within the limits of their hunting grounds.

PLATE XL.

BLACKFOOT.

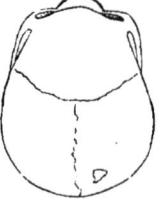 

The only two heads I have ever seen of this isolated nation, were brought to this city by Mr. George Catlin, and by him presented to George Combe, Esq. The latter gentleman has politely placed them at my disposal, and I have had the largest of them figured on the annexed plate. It is the skull of a man who appears to have received a mortal blow on the top of the head, near the junction of the parietal bones, which has penetrated into the cavity of the cranium. This skull has great breadth between the parietal bones, and the phrenological organ of firmness is strikingly prominent.

MEASUREMENTS.

Longitudinal diameter,	7.1 inches.
Parietal diameter,	5.4 inches.
Frontal diameter,	4.3 inches.
Vertical diameter,	5.1 inches.
Inter-mastoid arch,	13.8 inches.
Inter-mastoid line,	4.3 inches.
Occipito-frontal arch,	14. inches.
Horizontal periphery,	19.9 inches.
Internal capacity,	77. cubic inches.
Capacity of the anterior chamber,	33.? cubic inches.
Capacity of the posterior chamber,	44.? cubic inches.
Capacity of the coronal region,	18.2 cubic inches.
Facial angle,	78 degrees.

THE FLAT-HEAD TRIBES OF COLUMBIA RIVER.

The Indians of the Columbia river were little known until the remarkable expedition of Lewis and Clark, since which period they have been visited and described by several intelligent travellers. These tribes are established on both sides of the river, and to a distance of many miles from its mouth. "They are commonly of diminutive stature, badly shaped, and their appearance by no means prepossessing. They have broad, thick, flat feet, thick ankles, and crooked legs: the last of which deformities is to be ascribed, in part, to the universal practice of squatting or sitting on the calves of their legs and heels, and also to the tight bandages of beads and strings, worn round the ankles by the women, which prevent the circulation of the blood, and render the legs of the females particularly ill shaped and swollen. The complexion is the usual copper colored brown of the

North American tribes, though rather lighter than the Indians of the Missouri and the frontier of the United States: the mouth is wide and the lips thick; the nose of a moderate size, fleshy, wide at the extremities, with large nostrils, and generally low between the eyes, though there are rare instances of high aquiline noses; the eyes are generally black, though occasionally we see them of a dark yellowish brown, with a black pupil."*

But the most remarkable feature among them is the almost universal flattening of the head by mechanical contrivances: various means are resorted to to effect this end; but the model of deformity is the same throughout, consisting in a depression of the forehead and consequent elongation of the whole head, until the top of the cranium becomes, in extreme cases, a nearly horizontal plane. This custom obtains among many tribes, among which are the Klickatats, Kalapooyahs and Multnomahs of the Wallamut river, and its vicinity; and the Chinouks, Clatsaps, Klatstonis, Cowalitsks, Kathlamets, Killemooks and Chelakis of the lower Columbia and its vicinity.† It is also stated that several tribes of the coast, both north and south of the river, are in the same practice, but they are all said to speak dialects of the Chenouk language.‡

"The mode by which the flattening is effected," says Mr. Townsend, "varies considerably with the different tribes. The Wallamet Indians place the infant, soon after birth, upon a board, to the edges of which are attached little loops of hempen cord or leather, and other similar cords are passed across and back, in a zigzag manner, through these loops, enclosing the child and binding it firmly down. To the upper edge of this board, in which is a depression to receive the back part of the head, another smaller one is attached by hinges of leather, and made to lie obliquely upon the forehead; the force of the pressure being regulated by several strings attached to its edge, which are passed through holes in the board upon which the infant is lying, and secured there."§

"The mode of the Chinouks, and others near the sea, differs widely from that of the upper Indians, and appears somewhat less barbarous and cruel. A sort of cradle is formed by excavating a pine log to the depth of eight or ten inches. The child is placed in it on a bed of little grass mats, and bound down in the manner above described. A little boss of tightly plaited and woven grass is then applied to the forehead, and secured by a cord to the loops at the side. The

---

* LEWIS and CLARK, Exped. II, p. 130.
† TOWNSEND, Jour. to the Columbia River, p. 175.   ‡ IRVING, Astoria, II, p. 88.
§ Ut supra, p. 175.

infant is thus suffered to remain from four to eight months, or until the sutures of the skull have in some measure united, and the bone become solid and firm. It is seldom or never taken from the cradle, except in case of severe illness, until the flattening process is completed."* My friend Mr. Townsend was so kind as to bring me one of these cradles, of which the subjoined drawing furnishes an accurate idea.

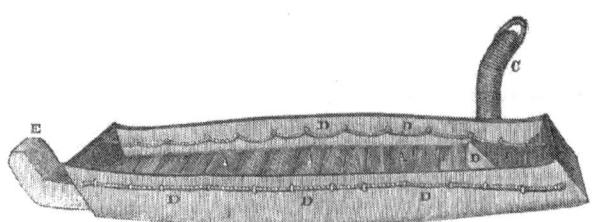

This cradle is formed by excavating a single piece of wood about three feet long. Midway between the top and bottom, inside, are little slats of light wood, A, A, A, in a transverse direction, on which are placed a grass mat or bed. The head of the cradle, B, is an excavated chamber, bounded towards the foot by an inclined plane, D, the rounded margin of which supports the child's neck, while the head itself is received into the concavity at B. Attached to the side of the cradle is the pad, C, made of grass, with a loop at the end: this is drawn down over the child's forehead, keeps it in place, and causes the flatness of that part so universal in these people. The lateral loops, D, D, D, are for the purpose of attaching other cords for the purpose of keeping the child's body in a fixed position. The projecting end, E, is rounded, and answers for rocking the cradle, when poised on it, by a rotary motion applied at the opposite end. The head and neck rest on a grass mat or pillow.

Either of the preceding processes must be very painful, often giving rise to ulceration of the scalp, and perhaps not unfrequently to death itself; yet so highly is this deformity valued among the Columbia river tribes, that their slaves (who are for the most part derived from the adjacent tribes) are not allowed to practise it. The appearance of the infant during the process, is described as both ludicrous

---

* TOWNSEND, Journey, &c., p. 176.

and frightful, "and its little black eyes, forced out by the tightness of the bandages, resemble those of a mouse choked in a trap."* Besides the depression of the head, the face is widened and projected forwards by the process, so as materially to diminish the facial angle; the breadth between the parietal bones is greatly augmented, and a striking irregularity of the two sides of the cranium almost invariably follows; yet the absolute internal capacity of the skull is not diminished, and, strange as it may seem, the intellectual faculties suffer nothing. The latter fact is proved by the concurrent testimony of all travellers who have written on the subject.

"We find them," say Lewis and Clark, "inquisitive and loquacious, with understandings by no means deficient in acuteness, and with very retentive memories; and though fond of feasts and generally cheerful, they are never gay. Every thing they see excites their attention and inquiries, but having been accustomed to see the whites, nothing appeared to give them more astonishment than the air-gun. To all our inquiries they answered with great intelligence, and the conversation rarely slackens.—The dispositions of these people seem mild and inoffensive, and they have uniformly behaved to us with great friendship. They are addicted to begging and pilfering small articles, when it can be done without danger of detection, but do not rob wantonly nor to any large amount.—In traffic they are keen, acute and intelligent, and they employ in all their bargains a dexterity and finesse which, if it be not learnt from their foreign visiters, may show how nearly the cunning of savages is allied to the little arts of more civilised trade. They begin by asking nearly double or treble the value of their merchandise, and lower the demand in proportion to the ardor or experience in trade of the purchaser; and if he expresses any anxiety, the smallest article, perhaps a handful of roots, will furnish a whole morning's negotiation. Being naturally suspicious, they of course conceive that you are pursuing the same system. They, therefore, invariably refuse the first offer, however high, fearful they or we have mistaken the value of the merchandise, and therefore cautiously wait to draw us on to larger offers. In this way, after rejecting the most extravagant prices, which we have offered for mere experiment, they have afterwards importuned us for a tenth part of what they had before refused. In this respect they differ from almost all Indians, who will generally exchange in a thoughtless moment the most valuable article they possess for any bauble which happens to please their fancy."†

* Ross Cox, Columbia River, &c., p. 146.
† Lewis and Clark, Exped. &c., II, p. 136, 138, 141.

"The appearance produced by this unnatural operation," says Mr. Townsend, "is almost hideous, and one would suppose that the intellect would be materially affected by it. This, however, does not appear to be the case, as I have never seen (with a single exception, the Kayouse) a race of people who appeared more shrewd and intelligent."*

In the month of January of the present year, (1839,) I was gratified with a personal interview with a full-blood Chenouk, then on a visit to this city in the hospitable care of my friend Dr. William Blanding. This Indian was a young man twenty years of age. He had been three years in charge of some Christian missionaries, and in that period had acquired great proficiency in the English language, understanding it when spoken to, and replying with a good accent and general grammatical accuracy. He appeared to me to possess more mental acuteness than any Indian I had seen, was communicative, cheerful and well-mannered. Mr. Townsend knew this young man (who is now called William Brooks) in his own country, and they recognised each other when they met in Philadelphia. He possessed marked Indian features, a broad face, high cheek bones, large mouth, tumid lips, a large nose, depressed at the nostrils, considerable width between the eyes, which, however, were not obliquely placed, a short stature, and robust person. His complexion was neither copper colored nor brown, but reasonably fair, such as are seen in white men who have been exposed in the harvest field. What most delighted me in this young man, was the fact that his head was as much distorted by mechanical compression as any skull of his tribe in my possession, and presented the very counterpart to the Kalapooyah figured on the annexed plate.† He cheerfully consented to such measurements of his head as I desired to take, and of which the following are the results:

Longitudinal diameter 7.5 inches.
Parietal diameter 6.9 inches.
Frontal diameter 6.1 inches.
Breadth between the cheek bones 6.1 inches.
Facial angle about 73 degrees.

At the time of Lewis and Clark's expedition, the Sokulks, at the western base of the Rocky Mountains, also flattened the heads of their children. "Their stature is low, their face broad, and their heads flattened in such a manner that

---

* Journey to the Columbia River, &c., p. 175. † See Plate 47.

THE CHINOUKS.

the forehead is a straight line from the nose to the crown of the head."* They are represented as a mild and peaceable people, who live in comparative happiness. There is also near the sources of the Columbia river a tribe still called by the name of Flatheads, who have long since abandoned the custom from which they derived their present designation. Their true name is *Salish*, and they are in no way connected with the Columbia river tribes.†

PLATE XLII.

CHINOUK.

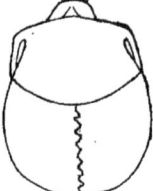 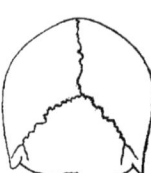

This plate represents a Chinouk skull of the natural form: it was that of a slave, and was obtained by Mr. J. K. Townsend during his late sojourn on the Columbia river. "I have occasionally seen both Chinouks and Chickitats," says Mr. Townsend, "with round or ordinary shaped heads, sickness having prevented the usual distortion while young: but such individuals can never attain to any influence, or rise to any dignity in their tribe, and are not unfrequently sold as slaves."‡

It has been thought by some philosophers, that were the artificial modification of the cranium persisted in for several successive generations, it would at length become congenital and perpetual. This hypothesis is proved to be wholly gratuitous by the evidence derived from the American nations, among whom the characteristic form of the skull is always preserved, unless art has directly interfered to distort it.

---

* Lewis and Clark, Exped. II, p. 12.—Walknaer, Cosmog. p. 583; quoted in Humboldt's Pers. Narr. VI, p. 32.

† Townsend, Journey to the Columbia River, p. 175.—Ross Cox, Trav. &c., p 120

‡ Extract of Letter addressed to me from Fort Vancouver, Sept. 26, 1835.

CRANIA AMERICANA.

This head differs in nothing from that of the Indians in general, from one end of the continent to the other: but it is gratifying to be able to present a perfectly natural skull of a people among whom a round, or naturally formed head, is considered a degradation.

MEASUREMENTS.

Longitudinal diameter,	6.7 inches.
Parietal diameter,	5.4 inches.
Frontal diameter,	4.4 inches.
Vertical diameter,	5.3 inches.
Inter-mastoid arch,	14. inches.
Inter-mastoid line,	4.2 inches.
Occipito-frontal arch,	14. inches.
Horizontal periphery,	19.4 inches.
Internal capacity,	74. cubic inches.
Capacity of the anterior chamber,	33. cubic inches.
Capacity of the posterior chamber,	41. cubic inches.
Capacity of the coronal region,	14. cubic inches.
Facial angle,	76 degrees.

PLATE XLIII.

CHINOUK.

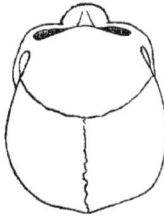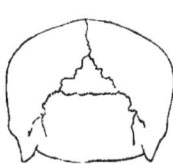

Mr. Townsend, through whose kindness I received this skull, accompanied it with the following memorandum: "The skull of the Chinouk is that of a high chief, as was manifest in the superior style in which his canoe was decked out, the unusual fineness of the wrappings with which the body was covered, and the evident care and attention which had been bestowed on the whole arrangement." This head is small but compact, and has had its full share of artificial compression. The Chinouks inhabit the northern shore of the Columbia river, near its mouth. In common with the adjacent cognate tribes, they appear to possess less courage than the Indians of other nations. Mr. Ross Cox gives a sorrowful account of them. "The good qualities of these Indians," says he, "are few, their vices many. Industry, patience, sobriety and ingenuity, nearly comprise the former; while in the latter may be classed thieving, lying, incontinence, gambling and cruelty."* Lewis and Clark, at an earlier period, made much the same observations. "They seem to be inferior to their neighbors in spirit. No ill treatment or indignity on our part seems to excite any feeling except fear; nor, although better provided than their neighbors with arms, have they enterprise enough to use them advantageously against the animals of the forest, nor offensively against their neighbors, who owe their safety more to the timidity than the forbearance of the Chinouks."† They fashion their canoes and domestic implements with considerable ingenuity, but have no fondness for the sea beyond the mere acquisition of food for their families.

MEASUREMENTS.

Longitudinal diameter,	6.7 inches.
Parietal diameter,	5.9 inches.
Frontal diameter,	4.7 inches.
Vertical diameter,	4.6 inches.
Inter-mastoid arch,	14.2 inches.
Inter-mastoid line,	4. inches.
Occipito-frontal arch,	12.9 inches.
Horizontal periphery,	20. inches.
Extreme length of head and face,	8.3 inches.
Internal capacity,	69. cubic inches.
Capacity of the anterior chamber,	32.5 cubic inches.
Capacity of the posterior chamber,	36.5 cubic inches.
Capacity of the coronal region,	9.9 cubic inches.
Facial angle,	72 degrees.

* Columbia River, &c., p. 147.   † Exped. II, p 116.

PLATE XLIV.

KLATSTONI.

Another one of the tribes of the Oregon, received also from my friend Mr. J. K. Townsend. It will be observed that the longitudinal and parietal diameters are nearly the same, and the forehead very much depressed.

MEASUREMENTS.

Longitudinal diameter,	6.2 inches.
Parietal diameter,	6. inches.
Frontal diameter,	4.6 inches.
Vertical diameter,	5.3 inches.
Inter-mastoid arch,	14.4 inches.
Inter-mastoid line,	4.2 inches.
Occipito-frontal arch,	13.4 inches.
Horizontal periphery,	19. inches.
Extreme length of head and face,	8.3 inches.
Internal capacity,	70. cubic inches.
Capacity of the anterior chamber,	30. cubic inches.
Capacity of the posterior chamber,	40. cubic inches.
Facial angle,	70 degrees.

PLATE XLV.

KILLEMOOK.

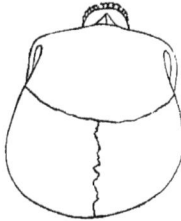 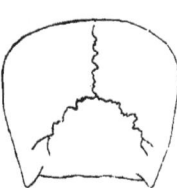

The head of a chief, of very large dimensions and ponderous structure, the

THE CLATSAPS.

jaws and teeth being of enormous size, and the face protruding. The internal capacity is greater than that of any other individual of this series in my possession. I am indebted for this skull also to Mr. J. K. Townsend.

MEASUREMENTS.

Longitudinal diameter,	6.9 inches.
Parietal diameter,	6.3 inches.
Frontal diameter,	4.9 inches.
Vertical diameter,	4.8 inches.
Inter-mastoid arch,	15.7 inches.
Inter-mastoid line,	4. inches.
Occipito-frontal arch,	14. inches.
Horizontal periphery,	21. inches.
Extreme length of head and face,	8.5 inches.
Internal capacity,	92. cubic inches.
Capacity of the anterior chamber,	34. cubic inches.
Capacity of the posterior chamber,	58. cubic inches.
Capacity of the coronal region,	19.3 cubic inches.
Facial angle,	73 degrees.

PLATE XLVI.

CLATSAP.

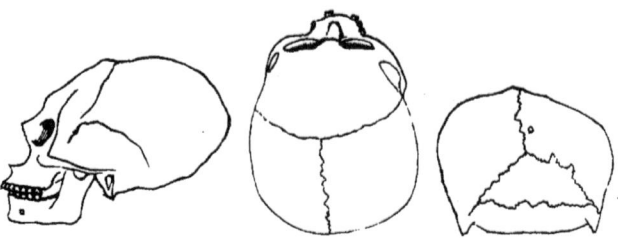

The Clatsaps reside on the southern shore of the bay at the mouth of the Columbia river, and along the sea coast on both sides of Point Adams. Owing to the destroying effects of malignant diseases, especially the small pox, this tribe is reduced to a mere handful of people. The annexed plate is drawn from a skull brought me by Mr. Townsend: I have had a front view taken of it in order to show at one view the great width and inequality of the skull, and the extreme depression of the frontal bone.

MEASUREMENTS.

Longitudinal diameter,	6.7 inches.
Parietal diameter,	6. inches.
Frontal diameter,	5. inches.
Vertical diameter,	4.5 inches.
Inter-mastoid arch,	14.9 inches.
Inter-mastoid line,	4.2 inches.
Occipito-frontal arch,	13. inches.
Horizontal periphery,	19.8 inches.
Extreme length of head and face,	8.3 inches.
Internal capacity,	78. cubic inches.
Capacity of the anterior chamber,	26. cubic inches.
Capacity of the posterior chamber,	52. cubic inches.
Capacity of the coronal region,	8.75 cubic inches.
Facial angle,	70 degrees.

PLATE XLVII.

KALAPOOYAH.

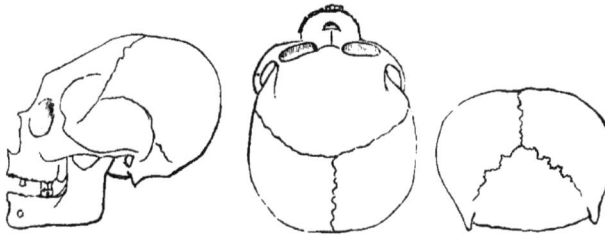

THE KALAPOOYAHS.

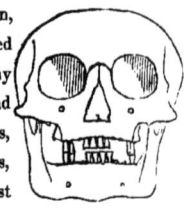

The Kalapooyahs reside on the shores of the Oregon, some distance above its mouth, but they are now a dwindled and degenerate tribe. This fine head is among the many valuable contributions rendered to this work by my friend Mr. Townsend. It strongly resembles, in all its details, the Killemook head already figured. The enormous orbits, and the massive and protruded face, are among its most striking characters.

MEASUREMENTS.

Longitudinal diameter,	6.8 inches.
Parietal diameter,	6.3 inches.
Frontal diameter,	5.2 inches.
Vertical diameter,	4.9 inches.
Inter-mastoid arch,	14.8 inches.
Inter-mastoid line,	4.3 inches.
Occipito-frontal arch,	13. inches.
Horizontal periphery,	20.4 inches.
Extreme length of head and face,	8.6 inches.
Internal capacity,	87. cubic inches.
Capacity of the anterior chamber,	35.5 cubic inches.
Capacity of the posterior chamber,	51.5 cubic inches.
Capacity of the coronal region,	11.2 cubic inches.
Facial angle,	68 degrees.

PLATE XLVIII.

CLICKITAT.

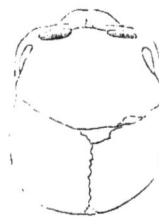 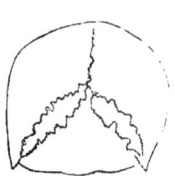

Clickitat skull, from the Columbia river, sent me by Mr. Townsend. It is greatly flattened on the frontal region, and irregular in its proportions. It is also remarkable for the remains of an extensive fracture, commencing above the middle of the left parietal bone, and extending downwards to the base of the skull. This fracture has been followed by evident depression of the bone, and yet the cicatrization has been complete.

MEASUREMENTS.

Longitudinal diameter,	6.6 inches.
Parietal diameter,	5.8 inches.
Frontal diameter,	4.8 inches.
Vertical diameter,	5. inches.
Inter-mastoid arch,	14.2 inches.
Inter-mastoid line,	4.2 inches.
Occipito-frontal arch,	13. inches.
Horizontal periphery,	19.5 inches.
Extreme length of head and face,	7.9 inches.
Internal capacity,	79. cubic inches.
Capacity of the anterior chamber,	36.5 cubic inches.
Capacity of the posterior chamber,	42.5 cubic inches.
Facial angle,	70 degrees.

PLATES XLIX AND L.

COWALITSK.

 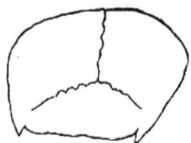

This extraordinary relic was also brought from the Columbia river by my friend Mr. Townsend. Deformed as the other skulls of this series are, this one surpasses them all in those factitious proportions which result from mechanical pressure to the forehead. Thus the vertical diameter is reduced to little more than four inches—the top of the cranium presents a flattened arch not far removed from a horizontal plane, and the face is protruded until the facial angle is reduced to sixty-six degrees, the lowest grade which I have observed in any human skull. I have represented both profile and vertical views of this head; but the latter represents it as possessed of too much regularity, especially about the zygomæ. The first or profile drawing is perfectly accurate in all its proportions, but the artist has inadvertently drawn it one sixth of an inch too small in each of its diameters.

MEASUREMENTS.

Longitudinal diameter,	7. inches.
Parietal diameter,	6.1 inches.
Frontal diameter,	4.9 inches.
Vertical diameter,	4.1 inches.
Inter-mastoid arch,	13.9 inches.
Inter-mastoid line,	4. inches.
Occipito-frontal arch,	12.7 inches.
Horizontal periphery,	20.2 inches.
Extreme length of head and face,	8.6 inches.

216   CRANIA AMERICANA.

Internal capacity,	75. cubic inches.
Capacity of the anterior chamber,	28. cubic inches.
Capacity of the posterior chamber,	47. cubic inches.
Capacity of the coronal region,	6.25 cubic inches.
Facial angle,	66 degrees.

Eight flattened skulls of the Columbia river tribes in my possession (seven of which are figured in the preceding plates) give the following results of measurement.

Mean of the internal capacity, 80 cubic inches.

Mean capacity of the anterior chamber, 31.8 cubic inches.

Mean capacity of the posterior chamber, 46.8 cubic inches.

Mean capacity of the coronal region, 11.8 cubic inches.

Mean facial angle, 70 degrees.

It therefore appears that the operation of flattening and otherwise distorting the head in infancy by artificial contrivances, does not diminish the capacity of the cranium, or the whole volume of brain; neither does it materially affect the relative proportions of brain in the two chambers of the cranium, inasmuch as the lateral expansion of the frontal region compensates for the loss of vertical diameter. The coronal region, however, is very much reduced by the process, and the facial angle is diminished at least five degrees.

The external anatomical measurements are extremely distorted, especially the several diameters, and the length of the head and face conjoined; for example, the eight crania give the following results:

Mean longitudinal diameter, 6.7 inches.

Mean parietal diameter, 6. inches.

Mean frontal diameter, 4.9 inches.

Mean vertical diameter, 4.8 inches.

Mean of inter-mastoid arch, 14.6 inches.

Mean of inter-mastoid line, 4.1 inches.

Mean of occipito-frontal arch, 13.1 inches.

Mean of horizontal periphery, 20. inches.

Mean of extreme length of head and face, 8.3 inches.

SKULLS FROM THE TUMULI OR MOUNDS.

It is designed on this occasion briefly to inquire into the geographical distribution of the mounds, their uses, and the race of people by whom they were constructed.

In North America there are very few mounds east of the Alleghany mountains. They are extremely unfrequent, if not wholly deficient, throughout the New England states, New York, Pennsylvania, and other states as far as South Carolina, where they are common in the interior: the latter remark is also applicable to Georgia and Florida, and all the country which skirts the Gulf of Mexico. Throughout the valley of the Mississippi they are very numerous. Dr. James took measurements of no less than twenty-seven immediately north of the town of St. Louis; Mr. Say counted upwards of thirty on the Kishwaka river, in the north of Illinois; and the bluffs which border the Wisconsin, about four miles above its mouth, are covered with them.* They abound much farther north, and are seen as far as the vicinity of Lake Travers, in lat. 46°, which is probably the northern limit of these remains. They are observed up the Ohio and its tributaries to the base of the Alleghanies, diminish in frequency westward of the Mississippi, and are not seen beyond the Rocky Mountains. To the south, they are common in Arkansas, and in Mexico are vastly numerous. In Peru and its ancient dependencies they are also seen in great number, and even as far south as the country of the Araucos, in Chili. East of the Andes they are rarely seen; and Humboldt is of the opinion that there is not a tumulus in all Guiana.

Most of these structures are mere circular mounds of earth, from twelve to twenty or thirty feet in diameter, and six or eight feet high. Others are of large dimensions and imposing appearance; such is Mount Joliet, in Wisconsin, which is described by Mr. Schoolcraft as of an elliptical form, four hundred and fifty yards in length, seventy-five in breadth, and sixty feet in height.† Mr. Breckenridge mentions another near the Mississippi and Cahokie rivers, eight hundred yards in circumference at base, and ninety feet elevation; and from the top of this mound no less than forty-five others are within range of sight.‡ The Etowee mound, in the Cherokee country, is still larger,§ and that on Grave creek, in

---

* Keating, Exped. I, p. 239.   † Trav. in the Valley of the Mississippi, p. 330.
‡ Views of Louisiana, p. 187.   § Amer. Jour. of Science and Art, I, p. 324.

Virginia, (which will be particularly noticed hereafter,) is also of gigantic size. But the most curious mounds are those constructed into rude resemblances of men and animals, which abound in Wisconsin territory; and these also are proved to be sepulchral monuments by the quantity of human remains embraced in them.*

The mounds are variously shaped, circular, elliptical, and pyramidal, while some of them are formed in parapets, like the pyramid of Medoun, in Egypt.

The uses of these structures were various, as will appear from the position they occupy, and the articles contained in them; nor can there be a question that they were mainly designed for receptacles for the dead. In almost all instances in which they have been carefully examined, human bones have been found in them, and sometimes many skeletons together, and regularly disposed. The remarkable group of pyramids at Teotihuacan, north of the city of Mexico, is situated on a plain that bears the name of Micoatl, or *The path of the dead*, obviously indicating at least one of the uses of those structures, which, in that locality alone, are several hundred in number.† In Peru the mounds are called *Huacas*, which, in the Quichua language, singnifies *to weep*, a designation not less expressive than that of the Mexicans.‡

Besides human remains, the mounds often contain the bones of the bear, otter, beaver and other animals,§ together with stone hatchets and arrow heads, vessels of various kinds, fragments of obsidian and mica, and, more rarely, implements of copper, and ornaments of ivory. It is also not unusual to find ashes, cinders and burnt bones, resting on a platform of stones, showing that the body had been first consumed by fire. There can be no doubt, however, that the mounds were also devoted to other purposes; 1st, as observatories and fortifications in time of war. Thus we are told that when the last remains of the Natchez were pursued by the French, (A. D. 1728,) they threw up a mound on Red river, in Louisiana, occupied it as a fortification, and defended it with the utmost bravery until overcome by the superior tactics of their enemies.|| In like manner the Cherokees, in their late war with the Creeks, surrounded the summit of the Etowee mound with pickets, placed their families in the enclosure, and thus defended themselves from the assaults of their enemies.¶ 2d, As places of

---

* Taylor, in Amer. Jour. of Science, XXXIV, p. 96, with diagrams.
† Humboldt, Monuments, I, p. 91.   ‡ Ruschenberger, Three Years in the Pacific, p. 400.
§ Archæolog. Amer. I, p. 168. || Sibley, in Report, &c., 1806, p. 80.
¶ Cornelius, in Amer. Jour. of Science and Art, I, p. 324.

worship or of sacrifice. The pyramidal structures of Mexico are called TEOCAL-LIS, or houses of the gods, indicative of at least one of the purposes to which they were devoted. 3d, As the foundations of dwellings. This fact has been observed in the low grounds of Louisiana, where the villages were liable to inundation;* and Lewis and Clark appear to refer to a similar use of mounds among the Ottoes of Missouri.†

Of what race were the people who constructed these tumuli? It appears to me that if we examine this question in reference to the cranial remains and other relics found in the mounds, there can be no difficulty in tracing their origin. The first step in the inquiry, however, will consist in an examination of the following series of skulls from localities remote from each other; merely premising, that I have not in this instance admitted any specimens which are not perfectly authenticated by the places and circumstances in which they were obtained.

PLATE LI.

SKULL FROM A MOUND NEAR CIRCLEVILLE, OHIO.

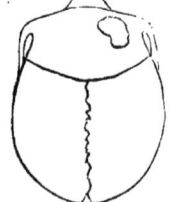 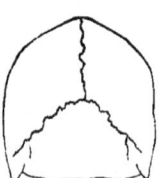

This relic was presented to me by my friend Dr. S. P. Hildreth, of Marietta, Ohio, who has furnished me with the following note. "Cranium of an aboriginal inhabitant of the Sciota valley, taken from an ancient mound constructed on a small natural elevation in the present town of Circleville. Several other skeletons were found, but none of them in a better state of preservation. The os frontis is cut through or beaten in, probably by a blow from a battle axe; and no less than five arrow-heads were found sticking in and about the skeleton. The tumulus is constructed of loam and coarse limestone gravel, which doubtless assisted in

---

* BRINGIER, Amer. Jour. of Science and Art, III, p. 37. † Exped. I, p. 35.

220   CRANIA AMERICANA.

preserving the bones from decay.—The ancient works at Circleville are extensive, and when first discovered were in a fine state of preservation. Trees, the growth of many centuries, covered the ground, bearing evidence of the antiquity of these remains of a former race. Large quantities of human bones, in different stages of decomposition, are found in the gravelly plain about half a mile north of Circleville, showing that this had long been the burial place of a numerous people."*

MEASUREMENTS.

Longitudinal diameter,	7.3 inches.
Parietal diameter,	5.8 inches.
Frontal diameter,	4.4 inches.
Vertical diameter,	5.4 inches.
Inter-mastoid arch,	14.6 inches.
Inter-mastoid line,	4.2 inches.
Occipito-frontal arch,	14.1 inches.
Horizontal periphery,	20.3 inches.
Internal capacity,	86.5 cubic inches.
Facial angle,	76 degrees.

PLATE LII.

SKULL FROM A MOUND ON THE UPPER MISSISSIPPI.

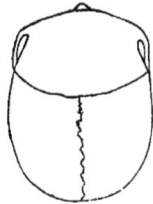 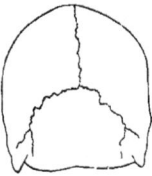

I am also indebted to Dr. Hildreth for this specimen, together with the following memorandum. "Skull taken from a mound seated on the high bluff

---

* The admirable preservation of this skull, is owing to its having been washed with spirit-varnish immediately after exhumation, a process by which these relics may be readily and permanently preserved.

which overlooks the Mississippi river, one hundred and fifty miles above the mouth of the Missouri. There were six mounds placed near each other in a right line, commencing with a small one only a few feet in height, and terminating in another of eight or ten feet elevation, and twenty feet diameter. This skull was obtained from the fifth mound in the series." It is a large cranium, very full in its vertical diameter, and broad between the parietal bones.

MEASUREMENTS.

Longitudinal diameter,	7.1 inches.
Parietal diameter,	5.3 inches.
Frontal diameter,	4.8 inches.
Vertical diameter,	5.5 inches.
Inter-mastoid arch,	14.6 inches.
Inter-mastoid line,	4.2 inches.
Occipito-frontal arch,	14.6 inches.
Horizontal periphery,	20. inches.
Internal capacity,	85.5 cubic inches.
Facial angle,	79 degrees.

PLATE LIII.

SKULL FROM THE GRAVE CREEK MOUND, IN VIRGINIA.

The great mound on Grave creek, Virginia, is about twelve miles from Wheeling, and not far from the Ohio river. As it is one of the largest and most perfect works of the kind in North America, and as it has been excavated with great care and success, I have endeavored to obtain whatever particulars have any connection with the present inquiry. For these I am indebted to James W. Clemens, M. D., of Wheeling, Virginia, from whose memoir, drawn up at my request, I extract the following facts.

"The GRAVE CREEK MOUND is eight hundred and thirty-seven feet in circumference at its base, and seventy feet in height, and is situated on a natural elevation of eighty or one hundred feet above the lowwater mark of the Ohio river. The mound has been for more than half a century in possession of the family of Mr. Tomlinson, whose son accomplished a complete examination of it during the summer of 1838. He commenced digging on the north side of the mound, and about four feet above the trench that surrounds it, from which point a horizontal shaft was excavated to the centre. At a distance of twelve or fifteen feet from the surface were found numerous masses composed of charcoal and burnt bone. Before reaching the centre a passageway was discovered to a vault at the base: this passage had an inclination of ten or fifteen degrees, and had been covered with timber, of which the impression on the earth alone remains; and the vault itself was partially filled up by these timbers giving way, and admitting the soil from above, and many loose stones which appear to have formed part of the covering of this chamber. After removing all this rubbish from the vault, two skeletons were found covered with sand, one on the east, the other on the west side. The former was the smaller and most perfect of the two, and its cranium is figured on the annexed plate.* In this sepulchral chamber, and chiefly in connection with the larger skeleton, was found a great number of trinkets of various kinds, but principally six hundred and fifty *ivory*† beads, perforated in the centre.

"On carrying a shaft upwards from this vault, another was discovered above it, and extending eighteen feet in length and eight in width. In it was found a solitary skeleton in a state of extreme decay, and which appeared, like those in the vault beneath, to have been placed in a standing position. With the bones were also obtained no less than seventeen hundred ivory beads, like those already mentioned, five hundred marine shells of the genus Oliva?, and about one hundred and fifty small plates of mica; the latter being perforated at their sides and corners. Five copper bands or bracelets were found on the bones of the arms, together with various articles of minor interest.

"Mr. Tomlinson next dug a shaft from the top of the mound (which is concave, as if sunk in) down to the lowest vault; but he had first to remove an oak tree two feet and a half in diameter, and numbering three hundred growths from centre to circumference. Within three feet of the surface was found a skeleton in complete decomposition. On reaching the lowest vault it was determined to enlarge it for the more easy access of visiters, and it was accordingly extended to a diameter of twenty-eight feet. During this operation ten more skeletons were

---

* See Plate 53.

† Dr. Clemens assures me that these beads are genuine *ivory*, and not bone; and adds, that as he had himself wrought much in ivory, he could not be mistaken in the material.

discovered, all in the sitting posture, but in so fragile a state as to defy all attempts at preservation."*

The antiquity of the skull from the lower vault is sufficiently established by the preceding circumstances; and I add it to these illustrations with the greater satisfaction on account of the authentic character of all the facts mentioned by Dr. Clemens. The occurrence of *ivory*† beads is a matter of much interest; for it will be at once inquired, where did the ancient Americans procure this material? A glance at the drawing reveals the characteristic traits of the American skull, as seen in the full superciliary ridge, the salient nose, the rounded head, the flattened occiput, and the broad and ponderous lower jaw. Every tooth in this head is perfect; but a part of the occipital bone is deficient, and the dotted line is probably an approximation to the original outline. The following are the only measurements I have been able to obtain.

Longitudinal diameter, ...	6.6? inches.
Horizontal diameter, (from superciliary ridge to occiput,)	6.5 inches.
Parietal diameter, ...	6. inches.
Vertical diameter, ...	5. inches.
Facial angle, about	78 degrees.

PLATE LIV.

SKULL FROM A MOUND ON THE ALABAMA RIVER.

This very interesting cranium has been already mentioned in this work, (page 162,) where three views are given in wood outlines. It is there mentioned as the property of Dr. O. H. Fowler, who, having politely allowed me the use of it, I have gladly made room for it in this place. It is supposed to be a Natchez head, which is altogether probable; but I insert it here as a genuine mound skull. It is flattened on the occiput and os frontis in such manner as to give the whole head a sugar-loaf or conical form, whence also its great lateral diameter, and its

---

* Mr. Tomlinson, the proprietor, has been at great pains and expense to fit up the lower vault of this mound, in which the articles found in it are preserved for the gratification of strangers.

† I am also informed by Dr. Clemens, that he has found *porcelain* beads in a small mound a mile and a half from the greater one.—For an early and interesting account of this mound, see Dr. J. Morton's memoir in the Amer. Jour. of Science and Art, VI, p. 166.

224   CRANIA AMERICANA.

narrowness from back to front. I shall merely repeat that it was exhumed from a mound high up the Alabama river.

MEASUREMENTS.

Longitudinal diameter,	5.9 inches.
Parietal diameter,	6.6 inches.
Frontal diameter,	4.4 inches.
Vertical diameter,	5.1 inches.
Inter-mastoid arch,	15.6 inches.
Inter-mastoid line,	4.4 inches.
Occipito-frontal arch,	12.4 inches.
Horizontal periphery,	19.6 inches.
Internal capacity,	80. cubic inches.
Facial angle,	72 degrees.

PLATE LV.

SKULL FROM A MOUND IN TENNESSEE.

 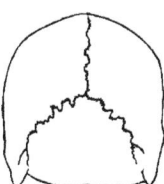

This cranium was exhumed by my friend Dr. Troost, of Nashville, Tennessee, from a mound in that state, at the junction of French-Broad and Holston rivers. Dr. Troost kindly forwarded it to Philadelphia for my use. The section of Tennessee above mentioned, and especially the Holston river, abounds in mounds, one of which covers an acre of ground and is thirty feet high. Six others are seen on that river a short distance above its mouth, which, on being opened, contained nothing but ashes and charcoal.* The present skull is remarkable for

---

* Silliman's Amer. Jour. of Science and Art, I, p. 429.

SKULLS FROM THE MOUNDS.

its vertical and parietal diameter, and flatness and elevation of the occiput. The facial angle is also unusually great.

MEASUREMENTS.

Longitudinal diameter,	6.6 inches.
Parietal diameter,	5.6 inches.
Frontal diameter,	4.1 inches.
Vertical diameter,	5.6 inches.
Inter-mastoid arch,	15.2 inches.
Inter-mastoid line,	4.4 inches.
Occipito-frontal arch,	14. inches.
Horizontal periphery,	19.5 inches.
Internal capacity,	87.5 cubic inches.
Facial angle,	80 degrees.

PLATE LVI.

SKULL FROM A TUMULUS AT SANTA, IN PERU.

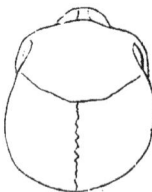 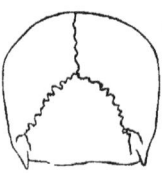

This cranium was obtained from a mound near the town of Santa, in Peru, by Waters Smith, M. D., of the U. S. Navy, who kindly added it to my collection. The body was found in a flexed or sitting posture, accompanied by a number of vessels of baked clay, of fine workmanship and ingenious construction. One of them, which is in my possession, is a quadruple vase with a single tubular mouth.

226   CRANIA AMERICANA.

This is a small, thin skull, covered, when I received it, with very long, black hair, which was removed to make the drawing.

MEASUREMENTS.

Longitudinal diameter,	6.2 inches.
Parietal diameter,	5.4 inches.
Frontal diameter,	4.3 inches.
Vertical diameter,	4.9 inches.
Inter-mastoid arch,	14.6 inches.
Inter-mastoid line,	3.8 inches.
Occipito-frontal arch,	13.3 inches.
Horizontal periphery,	18.5 inches.
Internal capacity,	74.5 cubic inches.
Capacity of the anterior chamber,	30. cubic inches.
Capacity of the posterior chamber,	44.5 cubic inches.
Capacity of the coronal region,	14.5 cubic inches.
Facial angle,	71 degrees.

PLATE LVII.

SKULL FROM A TUMULUS IN THE VALLEY OF RIMAC, IN PERU.

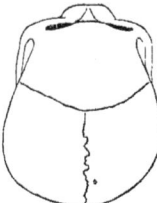 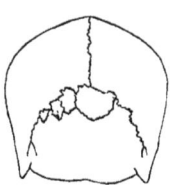

The tumulus from which this relic was obtained is about a mile and a half to the south of Lima. It is nearly two hundred feet in height, and was opened a few years since by the French consul, in search of antiquities. During the progress of excavation several skulls were thrown out, four of which were obtained

SKULLS FROM THE MOUNDS.

by my friend Dr. Henry S. Rennolds, of the U. S. Navy, who politely transferred them to me. The cranium now figured has been much compressed by art, so that the forehead, from the superciliary ridge to the crown of the head, presents a very inclined plane. The bones are large and ponderous throughout.

MEASUREMENTS.

Longitudinal diameter,	6.9 inches.
Parietal diameter,	5.6 inches.
Frontal diameter,	4.4 inches.
Vertical diameter,	5.1 inches.
Inter-mastoid arch,	15.3 inches.
Inter-mastoid line,	4.3 inches.
Occipito-frontal arch,	14. inches.
Horizontal periphery,	19.7 inches.
Internal capacity,	79. cubic inches.
Capacity of the anterior chamber,	29.5 cubic inches.
Capacity of the posterior chamber,	49.5 cubic inches.
Capacity of the coronal region,	14.1 cubic inches.
Facial angle,	72 degrees.

PLATE LVIII.

SKULL FROM A TUMULUS IN THE VALLEY OF RIMAC, IN PERU.

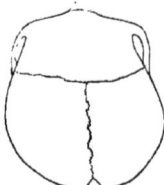 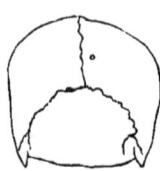

A cranium found with the preceding, also presented to me by Dr. H. S.

Rennolds. It is a small head, with a very retreating forehead, but little if at all altered by art.

MEASUREMENTS.

Longitudinal diameter,	6.5 inches.
Parietal diameter,	5.6 inches.
Frontal diameter,	4.5 inches.
Vertical diameter,	5. inches.
Inter-mastoid arch,	14.7 inches.
Inter-mastoid line,	3.8 inches.
Occipito-frontal arch,	13.2 inches.
Horizontal periphery,	19.2 inches.
Internal capacity,	76.5 cubic inches.
Capacity of the anterior chamber,	34. cubic inches.
Capacity of the posterior chamber,	42.5 cubic inches.
Capacity of the coronal region,	13.75 cubic inches.
Facial angle,	74 degrees.

The preceding illustrations embrace eight genuine mound skulls, and no one, I think, can examine them without being struck with their resemblance to the other crania figured in this work. They have the low forehead, high cheek bones, small facial angle, massive lower jaw, prominent vertex, flat occiput, and rounded head of the American race; and when we recur to the geographical distribution of the mounds as already noticed, they will be found scattered over those parts of both Americas which were inhabited by the demi-civilised nations embraced in the Toltecan family. Wherever these tumuli are found, whether in Peru, Mexico, Florida, or the Valley of the Mississippi, they are observed to be similarly constructed, and to contain analogous remains. Skeletons in the sitting posture are every where characteristic of them: the ashes and burnt bones indicate the practice of consuming the body with fire, which was still practised at the invasion of Mexico by the Spaniards; and when Ulloa visited Peru so recently as the middle of the past century, he saw and described the manner in which mounds were constructed as sepulchral monuments. "The Indians," says he, "having laid the body, without burial, on the ground, environed it with a rude arch of stones or bricks, and earth was thrown upon it as a tumulus, which they call *guaca*. In general they are eight or ten toises high, and about twenty long, and the breadth rather less; but some are larger. The plains near Cyambé are covered with them."* It will be observed from the preceding plates, that the people who interred their dead in the mounds were in the practice of distorting the skull by art, both in the horizontal and vertical methods; and if I may judge from the nine adult mound skulls now in my possession, and sufficiently perfect for measurement, the people whom they represent were one and the same with the American race, and probably of the Toltecan branch. Thus, the mean internal capacity of these heads is but eighty-one cubic inches, or a little more than the mean of the American race, while the facial angle does not exceed the average of that people, or seventy-five degrees. These facts, together with an inspection of many of the long bones found in the mounds, satisfy me that the constructors were neither a gigantic race as asserted by some writers, nor a diminutive people as averred by others;† but of the ordinary stature of the American Indians. The preceding data are to me also conclusive evidence that the occupants of the mounds were not Mongols, nor Hindoos, nor Jews: yet there are two articles found in these sepulchres which are not readily accounted for. One of these is the *ivory beads* described by Dr. Clemens: that gentleman declares that he is not mistaken in the material, and from his account the ornamental use of it must have been by no means inconsiderable. The other objects to which I allude are stones of a discoidal form, with or without a central hole, between which and the margin is a circular groove; the periphery being mostly convex. Now it is remarkable that these quoit-like stones (which moreover closely resemble the *calculi* of the Romans) are not unfrequently found among the antiquities of Scandinavia.‡ Those found in Europe and America differ in nothing from each other, but the uses to which they were put are unknown. The discovery and partial occupancy of this country by the Scandinavians, long before the time of Columbus, is now well established; and this fact may possibly account for the occurrence, in the mounds, of the apparently exotic articles of which we have just spoken.

That the fortifications and other ancient structures of our western country, belong to the same era and people with the mounds, seems probable from the circumstance of their almost constantly occurring together; nor is there any thing

---

* Voy. I, p. 366.—For recent mounds in Florida, see BARTRAM, Trav. in Florida, p. 517.—Bossu, Trav. p. 298.

† ATWATER, Silliman's Amer. Jour. of Science and Art, II, p. 224.

‡ See Journal of the Antiquarian Society of Denmark, published in Copenhagen in the Danish language, Vol. I, Tab. II, Fig. 52, 53.

in the mode of their construction that points to a higher civilisation. In fact, a careful review of all the circumstances will lead almost unavoidably to the conclusion, that the ancient mounds of America owe their origin to the various branches of the great Toltecan family, which was spread, as we have seen, from the confines of Chili to the shores of Lake Superior. Wherever that people made their sojourn we find their monumental traces, presenting, it is true, different degrees of contrivance and ingenuity, but for the most part far exceeding those faculties as possessed by the barbarous tribes. Some of the latter, it is true, have occasionally formed sepulchral mounds, but the instances are rare; and it will probably be hereafter established that all the tribes which erected mounds as a national usage, belonged to the Toltecan stock.* That they once occupied Florida and the valley of the Mississippi, there can be no doubt, but whether it was before or after their dispersion from Mexico is not yet ascertained. It seems more than probable, however, that the *Alligewi* who, according to Indian tradition, were driven southward by the Iroquois and Lanapé, were Toltecan communities—the people who constructed the mounds for their sepulchres, and erected the fortified towns to defend themselves from the barbarous tribes by whom they were surrounded.

SKULLS FROM ANCIENT TOMBS IN MEXICO.

Through the kindness of Mr. Joseph Smith, late of this city, and now resident in Mexico, I have received a series of Mexican skulls, among which are six from the ancient tombs of Tacuba and Otumba. One of these has been already represented in outline,† and three others are lithographed on the annexed plates. They came too late for insertion in their proper place in the series, but possess too much interest to be omitted.

---

* It is not unusual for the modern Indians to bury their dead in the ancient mounds, which they accomplish by slight excavation of the surface. They very rarely construct mounds of their own; they merely recognise the old ones as sepulchres.

† See page 153, 154.

PLATE LIX.

SKULL FROM AN ANCIENT TOMB AT OTUMBA, IN MEXICO.

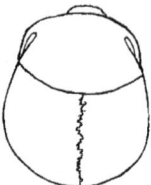 

The present illustration is derived from a small, rounded cranium, with the projecting face and consequent low facial angle characteristic of the Toltecan nations. In fact, its striking resemblance to the Peruvian skulls already figured, will occur to every one.

MEASUREMENTS.

Longitudinal diameter,	6.3 inches.
Parietal diameter,	5.3 inches.
Frontal diameter,	4.4 inches.
Vertical diameter,	5.4 inches.
Inter-mastoid arch,	14.3 inches.
Inter-mastoid line,	4.2 inches.
Occipito-frontal arch,	13.5 inches.
Horizontal periphery,	19.2 inches.
Internal capacity,	74. cubic inches.
Facial angle,	76 degrees.

PLATE LX.

SKULL FROM AN ANCIENT TOMB AT OTUMBA, IN MEXICO.

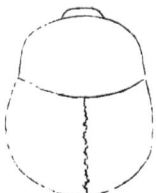 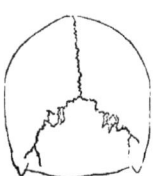

This head was obtained with the preceding, is a little larger and not so spherical: the frontal region is also better developed, yet the projecting face gives a low facial angle.

MEASUREMENTS.

Longitudinal diameter,	6.6 inches.
Parietal diameter,	5.3 inches.
Frontal diameter,	4.4 inches.
Vertical diameter,	5.4 inches.
Inter-mastoid arch,	14. inches.
Inter-mastoid line,	4. inches.
Occipito-frontal arch,	14. inches.
Horizontal periphery,	19.3 inches.
Internal capacity,	76. cubic inches.
Facial angle,	77 degrees.

PLATE LXI.

SKULL FROM AN ANCIENT TOMB AT OTUMBA, IN MEXICO.

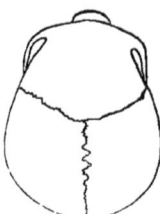 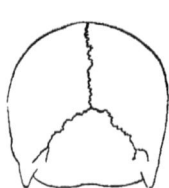

Found with the two preceding heads, but larger, and approaching nearer to the Caucasian model, both in its proportions and facial angle.

MEASUREMENTS.

Longitudinal diameter,	7.1 inches.
Parietal diameter,	5.6 inches.
Frontal diameter,	4.6 inches.
Vertical diameter,	5.5 inches.
Inter-mastoid arch,	15.5 inches.
Inter-mastoid line,	4.1 inches.
Occipito-frontal arch,	15. inches.
Horizontal periphery,	20.2 inches.
Internal capacity,	87. cubic inches.
Facial angle,	80 degrees.

The subjoined wood-cuts will serve to convey an idea of another of these Mexican skulls, remarkable for a low, narrow forehead, and unusual development of the whole posterior region of the cranium.

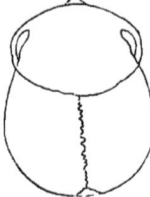 

SKULLS FROM CAVES IN THE VALLEY OF THE OHIO.

It was a custom of many American nations to deposite their dead in caves. The body was sometimes placed entire in these receptacles; but in other instances the bones were exhumed after the decomposition of the body, and then removed to a cave as a final resting place. The two skulls figured on the annexed plates have so much interest that I have thought best to insert them, although the circumstances in which they were found afford us no clue to their national affiliation.

PLATE LXII.

SKULL FROM A CAVE AT GOLCONDA, IN ILLINOIS.

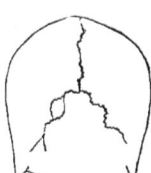

Some few years ago a cave containing many human skeletons, was discovered near the town of Golconda, on the Ohio river. A considerable number was transmitted to this city; of these one is preserved in the Academy of Natural Sciences, and the other in the University of Pennsylvania. The former is figured on the accompanying plate. In general configuration, especially in the frontal region, it approximates to the Caucasian form, but with a small facial angle and full parietal diameter. The other heads from this locality are still more like the Toltecan model, and leave little doubt of their origin and their antiquity.

MEASUREMENTS.

Longitudinal diameter,	6.7 inches.
Parietal diameter,	5.4 inches.

SKULLS FROM CAVES IN OHIO.

Frontal diameter,	4.3 inches.
Vertical diameter,	5.5 inches.
Inter-mastoid arch,	14.5 inches.
Inter-mastoid line,	4.1 inches.
Occipito-frontal arch,	14. inches.
Horizontal periphery,	19.3 inches.
Internal capacity,	81. cubic inches.
Capacity of the anterior chamber,	35.25 cubic inches.
Capacity of the posterior chamber,	45.75 cubic inches.
Capacity of the coronal region,	18. cubic inches.
Facial angle,	76 degrees.

PLATE LXIII.

SKULL FROM A CAVE NEAR STEUBENVILLE, OHIO.

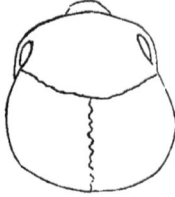 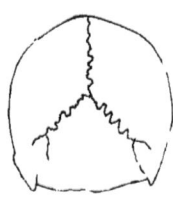

In the month of May 1835, a cavern cemetery was discovered on the bank of the Ohio river, opposite to Steubenville. The cemetery is a fissure formed by a huge mass of rock which has fallen from the side of a hill, and lodged upon other rocks so as to leave an intervening space, of which the circumference is thirty or forty feet, and the entrance two feet and a half in diameter. Judge Tappan, of Steubenville, informs me in a note, that "the bones appear to have been deposited at different periods of time, those on top being alone in good preservation. They were of all ages, and thrown in indiscriminately after the removal of the flesh; for it is well known that some tribes were accustomed to gather, at times, all the bones of their deceased relatives, and place them in a common receptacle." These heads are thoroughly characteristic of the race to which they pertain. They bear no evidences of great age, and no doubt belonged to individuals of the barbarous tribes. Some have thought them *Mingoes*, who were affiliated to the Iroquois: but the form of the head does not support this surmise. Of the great number of skulls found in this place, but few were perfect, of which last I have received eight. For these I am indebted to Dr. Hildreth of Marietta, Ohio; Dr. Andrews and Judge Tappan of Steubenville, in that state; and to Dr. M'Dowell of Pittsburg. The annexed drawing is taken from a remarkably fine head of this series sent me by Dr. Andrews. All these skulls, however, are surprisingly alike—the vertex elevated, the occiput flat, the parietal diameter very great, and the lower jaw massive. They are also of singularly large capacity, and in this respect approach nearer to the Sauks and Foxes, and the Muskogees, than to any other tribes that have come under my notice. For example, the mean internal capacity gives upwards of eighty-five cubic inches, and the facial angle rises seventy-eight degrees. The anterior chamber gives 38.3 cubic inches, the posterior 49.2: but notwithstanding the proportion of the former, there can be little doubt that these skulls belong to the savage tribes, and not to the Toltecan stock.

THE CHARIBS.

That part of the American race called *Charibs*, was at one period a numerous and widely distributed people. Their native seats were the northern regions of South America, almost from the river of Amazons northward to the sea, including the great valley of the Orinoco, and much of the present provinces of Guyana and Venezuela. From thence they extended their migrations to all the Antilles, from Trinidad to Santa Cruz.* They made a valorous opposition to the Europeans who first attempted to colonise their country; and Peter Martyr, the companion of Columbus, declares, that so fierce and menacing was the appearance of the Charibs whom they took in their skirmishes, that no one could look on them without a sensation of horror. In the year 1578, the Charibs of the Orinoco made a desperate and successful incursion into the Spanish province of Valentia,

* The Charib Islands were Trinidad, Grenada, St. Vincent, Dominica, Guadaloupe, Martinique, Santa Cruz, St. Thomas, Nevis, Montserrat, Antigua, St. Kitts, and the Virgin Isles.

THE CHARIBS.

but they were soon after subdued, and have since been kept in check without much difficulty. They are still, however, a numerous people, for Humboldt states that those of the pure race who yet inhabit the banks of the Coronè and Cayuni, and the mountains west of Cayenne and Pacaraymo, are not less than forty thousand in number.* The same traveller observes that the Charibs of Chari, in Venezuela, and those of the lower Orinoco, differ from the other Indians by being taller, and having more regular features. "Their nose is not so large, and less flattened; the cheek-bones are not so high, and their physiognomy has less of the Mongol cast." Their heads are naturally rounded, as in the other tribes; but many of the Charib nations long practised the flattening process, in such manner as to depress the os frontis, and thus elongate the head from front to back. Let us now glance separately at the Continental and the Insular Charibs.

PLATE LXIV.

CHARIB OF VENEZUELA.

When Humboldt visited the continental Charibs, towards the close of the last century, he saw no remains of the custom of distorting the head, which was once so common among them, and even existed in recent times.† Speaking of the Indians of Cumana, Gomara says, "They compress the heads of their children gradually, and for a long time, between two little cushions made of cotton, in order to render the face broad, which they esteem a beauty."‡ A stronger evidence on this subject, however, is derived from the annexed drawing, which was taken from a skull sent me by that distinguished gentleman and scholar, Don Joseph Maria Vargas, of Caraccas. It was found in a terra cotta vessel, wherein it had probably been preserved for centuries. It is much dilapidated, and admits of but a part of the usual

MEASUREMENTS.

Longitudinal diameter,	7. inches.
Parietal diameter,	5.3 inches.
Frontal diameter,	4.8 inches.

* Person. Narr. VI, p. 11.—IV, p. 466. † BARRERE, p. 239.
‡ Hist. de las Indias, cap. LXXIX.

Vertical diameter,	5.1 inches.
Inter-mastoid arch,	14.6 inches.
Inter-mastoid line,	4. inches.
Occipito-frontal arch,	14. inches.
Horizontal periphery,	20.2 inches.
Facial angle,	70 degrees.

PLATE LXV.

CHARIB OF ST. VINCENT.

That the Charibs of the Antilles were derived from the southern continent, and not from Florida, is proved by their traditions, their customs and their language.* The original inhabitants of these islands were a docile people called IGNERIS, allied no doubt to the Indians who occupied Cuba and the other larger islands on the arrival of Columbus. The Igneris, however, were exterminated by the Charibs, who at that period held undisturbed possession.

These Charibs were among the most ferocious and brutal of the American nations. They were without laws and almost devoid of religious observances. Suspicious and revengeful to the last degree, they conducted all their enterprises with singular craftiness. They were morose and even melancholy, and looked upon the other natives as mere beasts to be slain and devoured. To such an excess was their cannibalism carried, that it gave rise to a law in 1504, by which the Spaniards were authorised to make slaves of all the individuals of the Charib nation who should fall into their hands.† It is even gravely asserted that, having tasted the flesh of all the nations who visited them, they pronounced the Frenchman to be most delicate, and the Spaniard the hardest of digestion ‡ To persuade the Charibs to civilisation, or to reduce them to servitude, seemed alike impracticable. "If they did any thing it was only what they chose, how they chose, and when they chose; and when they were most wanted it often happened that they

---

* The Red Charibs (of St. Vincent) had a tradition that their forefathers came from the banks of the Orinoco, whence coasting Trinidad and Tobago to Grenada, and thence by the Grenadines, they arrived at St. Vincent, subdued the native inhabitants called Galibeis, (or Igneris,) and possessed themselves of the Island."—SIR W. YOUNG, *Account of the Charibs*, p. 5.

† HUMBOLDT, Pers. Narr. V, p. 426.

‡ British Emp. in America, II, p. 277.—ROCHEFORT, p. 537.

would not do what was required, or any thing else. When desired to hunt or shoot game, they chose to fish, and probably would neglect the very employment they chose."* Chanvallon declares that their stupid eyes were the mirror of their souls, and that "their reason is not more enlightened than the instinct of brutes." They kept their women in the vilest servitude, and instilled into the minds of their children the love of cruelty and slaughter.

One of the most remarkable facts connected with these people, was their custom of flattening the skulls of their offspring. That which has been often doubted, is now reduced to certainty: yet it must be admitted as a singular circumstance, that Peter Martyr makes no mention of it; and even Humboldt thinks that it was confined to the Black Charibs, who were of Negro descent.† That this is an error is proved by the fact of the continental ancestors of the Insular Charibs having practised the custom in very distant times; by its being recorded by Rochefort, who wrote his account before the Black Charibs were known in St. Vincent;‡ and by the personal testimony of several later voyagers. M. Amic, who was in Guadaloupe in 1791, saw both Charibs and Negroes with flattened heads, and obtained from them the apparatus by which the deformity was effected.§ Mr. Lawrence has figured the head of a Red Charib chief who was well known in St. Vincent;|| and Humboldt has represented both the natural and artificial configuration, the former differing in nothing from the ordinary Indian head.

The annexed illustration of the Charib skull, is derived from a cast in the possession of the Phrenological Society of this city: the original is preserved, I believe, in the Royal Museum at Paris; and it is the same which Gall and Spurzheim have figured in their great work on the Nervous System. A few diameters are all the measurements that can be obtained from the cast.

MEASUREMENTS.

Longitudinal diameter,	7.2 inches.
Parietal diameter,	5.7 inches.
Frontal diameter,	4.5 inches.
Vertical diameter,	5.1 inches.

* Sheldon, in Archæolog. Amer. I, p. 411.   † Pers. Narr. VI, p. 31.
‡ Histoire des Antilles, published in 1671.
§ Journal de Physique, Tome XXXIX, for 1791. || Lectures on Zoology, &c., Plate X.

We shall merely add that the genuine Charibs of St. Vincent were reduced in 1763 to one hundred families; and thirty years later they scarce numbered that many individuals.*

THE BLACK CHARIBS. The Black Charibs of St. Vincent were the descendants of a cargo of slaves of the Moco tribe which were shipwrecked on the island of Bequia, near St. Vincent, about the year 1675. The Charibs first reduced them to slavery; but finding their numbers increase, resolved to destroy all the male children; whereupon the blacks revolted, slew great numbers of their masters, and soon became the most numerous and dominant family on the island.† They flattened the heads of their children, like the natives; a practice which was also adopted by the runaway slaves, in order to stamp their offspring with a badge of freedom. Towards the close of the past century the Black Charibs, joined by the feeble remains of the native Indians, rebelled against the English authorities, and for some time held possession of the island; but being finally subdued, they were, in 1795, exiled to the island of Rattam, in the Bay of Honduras.

THE ARAUCANIANS.

The Araucanians, the most celebrated and powerful of the Chilian tribes, inhabit the region between the rivers Bio-bio and Valdivia, and between the Andes and the sea, and derive their name from the province of Arauco. They are a robust and muscular people, of a lighter complexion than the surrounding tribes. Endowed with an extraordinary degree of bodily activity, they reach old age with few infirmities, and generally retain their sight, teeth and memory unimpaired. They are brave, discreet and cunning to a proverb, patient in fatigue and enthusiastic in all their enterprises, and fond of war as the only source of distinction. Hence their successful opposition to the encroachments of the Spaniards: three centuries of almost constant warfare have neither subdued nor tamed them; and

---

* EDWARDS, Hist. of the West Indies, B. III, chap. 3.
† SIR W. YOUNG, Account of the Charibs, p. 42.

although occasionally driven to their mountain fastnesses, they have always reappeared as formidable and unconquerable as ever. Their vigilance soon detected the value of the military discipline of the Spaniards, and especially the great importance of cavalry in an army; and they lost no time in adopting both these resources, to the dismay and discomfiture of their enemies. Thus in seventeen years after their first encounter with Europeans, they possessed several strong squadrons of horse, conducted their operations in military order, and, unlike the Americans generally, met their enemies in the open field. Nothing, indeed, could surpass their valor; and their wars with the Spaniards are replete with those chivalric exploits which constitute the charm and romance of history.

The Araucanians are highly susceptible of mental culture, but they despise the restraints of civilisation; and those of them who have been educated in the Spanish colonies, have embraced the first opportunity to resume the haunts and habits of their nation. They possessed some of the useful arts before their intercourse with Europeans: thus they extracted and purified the ores of gold, silver, copper and lead; they formed utensils of clay, had a process for varnishing them, and they even constructed vessels of marble. They had invented numbers to express any requisite quantity, and preserved the memory of important events by means of knotted cords, in the manner of the Peruvians; and it is probable that they derived most of these advantages from the latter people. There was, however, but little intercourse between the two nations, as is proved by the fact that there are but fifteen or twenty words common to their languages.*

---

* The preceding facts are derived from Molina's History of Chili, Vol. II, passim.

PLATE LXVI, LXVII.

ARAUCANIAN CHIEF.

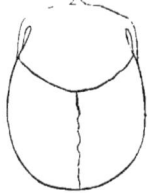 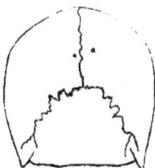

These plates give two views of an Araucanian chief named Bampuni, who was slain in an encounter with the Chilian army under General Bulnes, in 1835. The skull was obtained by my friend Dr. Casanova, who could only furnish the above brief particulars in reference to it. It is a symmetrical head; the frontal region is lofty, but narrow, the whole posterior cranium is full, and the internal capacity is not much short of the Caucasian mean. The details are so well expressed on the accompanying plates, that it only remains to add the anatomical

MEASUREMENTS.

Longitudinal diameter,	6.9 inches.
Parietal diameter,	5.4 inches.
Frontal diameter,	4.1 inches.
Vertical diameter,	5.4 inches.
Inter-mastoid arch,	15. inches.
Inter-mastoid line,	4.1 inches.
Occipito-frontal arch,	14.2 inches.
Horizontal periphery,	19.5 inches.
Internal capacity,	84.5 cubic inches.
Capacity of the anterior chamber,	32.5 cubic inches.
Capacity of the posterior chamber,	52. cubic inches.
Capacity of the coronal region,	19. cubic inches.
Facial angle,	76 degrees.

THE ARAUCANIANS.

PLATE LXVIII.

ARAUCANIAN CHIEF.

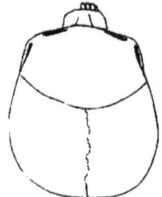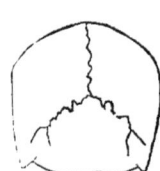

This is the cranium of another Araucanian chief named Chilicoi, who was killed in the same battle with the subject of the preceding plate. I received it also from Dr. Casanova, who could give no additional particulars. The eye is struck with the projecting face and consequent small facial angle, the low forehead, the flattened vertex, and the smallness of the whole head.

MEASUREMENTS.

Longitudinal diameter,	6.7 inches.
Parietal diameter,	5.4 inches.
Frontal diameter,	4.7 inches.
Vertical diameter,	4.9 inches.
Inter-mastoid arch,	14.2 inches.
Inter-mastoid line,	4.9 inches.
Occipito-frontal arch,	13.4 inches.
Horizontal periphery,	19.5 inches.
Internal capacity,	77. cubic inches.
Capacity of the anterior chamber,	32. cubic inches.
Capacity of the posterior chamber,	45. cubic inches.
Capacity of the coronal region,	11.9 cubic inches.
Facial angle,	72 degrees.

The three Araucanian skulls in my collection give a mean internal capacity of seventy-nine cubic inches, which is much more than that of the Peruvians, and a little less than the average of the collective American race. The mean facial angle gives barely seventy-five degrees.

USUAL POSITION OF THE BODY IN INDIAN SEPULTURE.

As an additional evidence of the unity of race and species in the American nations, I shall now adduce the singular fact, that from Patagonia to Canada, and from ocean to ocean, and equally in the civilised and uncivilised tribes, a peculiar mode of placing the body in sepulture has been practised from immemorial time. This peculiarity consists in the *sitting posture*, and will be best understood by reference to the annexed drawing.

PLATE LXIX.

NATURAL MUMMY OF A MUYSCA INDIAN OF NEW GRENADA.

It will be observed in this instance that the body is in the sitting posture, the legs being flexed against the abdomen, and the feet turned inwards. The arms are also flexed so as to touch the chest, the chin being supported on the palms of the hands, and the fingers received into the hollow beneath the cheek bones. This interesting relic was brought from New Grenada, in South America, by the late Charles Biddle, Esq., who presented it to the Academy of Natural Sciences of this city, where it is now preserved. The body is not embalmed, but only desiccated; yet the muscles are so well preserved as to render it probable that some antiseptic fluid may have been applied to them.

Let us now trace this singular custom from south to north. The Moluches and Pampas of Patagonia bury their dead in large square pits. "They are placed in a row, *sitting*, with all the weapons and other things which belonged to the dead."—FALKER's *Patagonia, quoted in Appendix to Molina*.—Dobrizhoffer also observes that the equestrian tribes of that country "compose the corpse in such manner that the knees touch the face."—*Hist. Abipones*, I, p. 132.

The Indians of Chili had the same custom, but they exposed their dead on a stage above ground.—FORSTER, *Obs. During a Voy. Round the World*, p. 564.

The Coroados of Brazil place the body in a sitting posture in a large pot, which is buried in the ground amidst cries and lamentation.—SPIX and MARTIUS, *Trav. in Brazil*, II, p. 250.

MODE OF SEPULTURE.

The Paraguas of Paraguay place their dead in a similar attitude.—DE AZARA, *Voy. dans l'Amerique*, II, p. 143. This custom, as practised among the Atures, in the Valley of the Orinoco, has already been stated, (page 134.)

Garcilaso de la Vega states that in the year 1560, he saw five embalmed bodies of Peruvian Incas, three men and two women. "They were seated in the manner of Indians, with the hands across upon the breast, and their eyes towards the earth."—*Comment.* Book V, Chap. 29.—"The mountain Indians," says Herrera, "commonly built their tombs high, like towers, and hollow; and they buried their dead bowing the body, their thighs bound and in the sitting attitude." —*Hist.* Dec. III, Lib. 9, Cap. 3.—Dr. Ruschenberger, who personally exhumed several mummies near Arica, states that "the body was placed in a squatting posture, with the knees drawn up and the hands applied to the side of the head." (See page 109 of this work.) I have myself examined the desiccated bodies of six Peruvians, all of which were in the same position.

The Indians of New Grenada followed the same custom, as is proved by the annexed illustration. The Spanish residents of that republic have a tradition that the natives, flying from the violence of their conquerors, died in caves and other obscure places, in an attitude which truly seems indicative of despair. Some very ancient monuments are said by Herrera to have been discovered by the early Spaniards near Zenu, in Venezuela: "These graves or tombs were magnificent, adorned with broad stones, into which the bodies were placed in a sitting posture." —*Hist. Amer.* IV, p. 221.

The Mexicans sometimes burned and sometimes buried their dead: when they buried them it was "in deep ditches formed of stone and lime, within which they placed the bodies in a sitting posture, on low seats, or *icpalli*."—CLAVIGERO, *Hist. of Mexico*, B. VI.—The same author adds, that Quinetzin, one of the early Chechemecan kings of Mexico, was embalmed "and afterwards placed in a great chair, clothed in royal habits."—*Idem*, B. II.

When a Charib died his body was placed in the grave in an attitude "resembling that in which they crouched round the fire or the table when alive, with the elbows on the knees, and the palms of the hands against the cheeks."—SHELDON, in *Archæolog. Amer.* I, p. 378.—SIR W. YOUNG, *Account of the Charibs*, p. 8.

The Muskogees or Creeks had a similar usage.—BARTRAM, *Trav.* p. 515.— ROMANS, *Hist. of Florida*, I, p. 98.—The latter author adds that the Arkansas were in the same practice, "with the addition of tying the head down to the knees."—*Idem*, p. 101.

The Alibamons bury their dead in a sitting posture; in order to justify this custom they say that man is upright, and has his face turned towards heaven, which is to be his habitation.—LE Bossu, *Trav. in Louisiana*, I, p. 157.

On the discovery of the Mammoth cave, in Kentucky, a woman was found in a state of complete desiccation. "She was buried in a squatting form, the knees drawn up close to the breast, the arms bent, with the hands raised, and crossing each other about the chin."—*Archæolog. Amer.* I, p. 359.

I am informed by Mr. Nuttall, that such also was the custom of the Osages of Missouri.—Of the Omahaws. JAMES, *Exped.* I, p. 224.—Of the Mandans. LEWIS and CLARK, *Exped.* I, p. 163.—Of the Potowatomies. KEATING, *Exped.* I, p. 115.—Of the Chippeways. BETRAM, *Trav.* II, p. 266.—Of the Delawares. SMITH, *Hist. of New Jersey*, p. 137.—Of the Nahants and other tribes of Lenapé in New England. WARREN, *Compar. View, &c.*, p. 134.—The present town of Salem, in Massachusetts, is the site of the old village of the Naumkeags: on making an excavation a few years since, many skeletons were found, "placed very near each other, with the knees drawn up to the breast, and the hands laid near the face, which was directed to the east." *Dr. Pearson's Letter to the Author.*— Dr. Pearson had a drawing made of the skeletons *in situ*.

In respect to the Canadian Indians, Charlevoix observes: "The dead man is painted, enveloped in his best robe, and with his weapons beside him, is exposed at the door of his cabin in the posture which he is to preserve in the grave; and this posture is that which a child has in the bosom of its mother."—*Journal d'un Voyage, &c.*, VI, p. 107.

Some excavations at Goat Island, at the Falls of Niagara, have revealed the same fact.—*Ingram's Manual, &c.*, p. 63.

Finally, I am assured by Dr. Troost that the mounds he opened in Tennessee contained skeletons in the same attitude; and Lieutenant Mather has made a similar communication to me in reference to a mound examined by him in Wisconsin.

Thus it is, that notwithstanding the diversity of language, customs and intellectual character, we trace this usage throughout both Americas, and affording, as we have already stated, collateral evidence of the affiliation of all the American nations.*

---

* I am aware that this practice is not exclusively American. Mr. Edwards, (Hist. of the West Indies, Book I, Append.,) cites Herodotus for its prevalence among the Nassamones, a people who inhabited northern Africa between Egypt and Carthage; and Cicero records it as a usage of the ancient Persians. The modern Circassians, on the death of a nobleman, "set up a high wooden bed

THE MONGOL-AMERICANS.

PLATE LXX.

ESKIMAUX.

Since writing the chapter on the Polar Family, (page 50,) I have been favored by George Combe, Esq., with the use of four genuine Eskimaux skulls, which are figured on the annexed plate. The eye at once remarks their narrow, elongated form, the projecting upper jaw, the extremely flat nasal bones, the expanded zygomatic arches, the broad, expanded cheek bones, and the full and prominent occipital region.

MEASUREMENTS.

	Longitud. diameter.	Parietal diameter.	Frontal diameter.	Vertical diameter.	Intermast. arch.	Intermast. line.	Occipito-frontal arch.	Horizontal periphery.	Facial angle.	Internal capacity.
1.	7.5	5.4	4.6	5.4	14.3	4.1	15.2	20.4	72°	93.
2.	7.3	5.5	4.4	5.3	14.1	4.3	14.4	20.3	75°	80.
3.	7.5	5.1	4.3	5.5	14.8	3.9	15.5	20.3	73°	87.5
4.	6.7	5.	4.4	5.	13.6	4.	13.9	18.9	71°	

The extreme elongation of the upper jaw contracts the facial angle to a mean of seventy-three degrees, while the mean of three heads of the four, gives an internal capacity of eighty-seven cubic inches, a near approach to the Caucasian average. The following diagrams will enable the reader to make his comparisons still more in detail.

in the open air, upon which they place the body of the deceased in a sitting attitude after the bowels have been taken out;" but the interment, which is eight days later, is in the recumbent posture.—KLAPROTH, *Caucasian Nations*, p. 337.—The New Hollanders sometimes bury their dead in this attitude.—BARTON, *N. South Wales*, p. 203.—The Hottentots, says Kolbein, double up the corpse "neck and heels, much in the manner of a human fœtus."—*Present State of Cape of Good Hope*, p. 315.—The people of the Tonga Islands, Pacific Ocean, inter their dead in this position.—MARRINER, *Tonga Islands*, p. 211; and Kotzebue has also observed it at the islands of Radack and Ulea.—*Voy. of Discovery*, III, p. 173, 211.

No. 1.—From Davis's strait; the largest head in the series, and the best frontal development. The nasal bones are so flat as to be scarcely perceptible.

 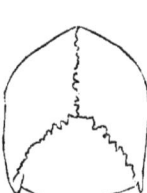

No. 2.—On this skull is written the brief memorandum, "Found in the snow by Captain Parry." In every particular a well characterised Eskimaux head.

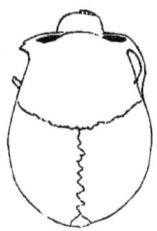 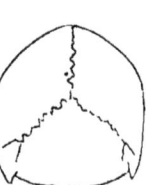

No. 3.—"Found by Mr. John Turnbull, Surgeon, upon Disco Island, coast of Greenland, in the summer of 1825."

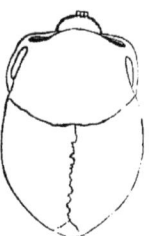 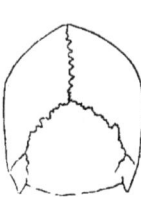

No. 4.—This skull was obtained at Icy Cape, the northwest extremity of America, and is marked "from A. Collie, Esq., Surgeon of H. M. Ship Blossom."

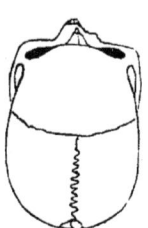 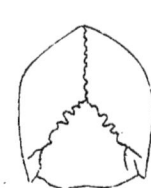

The great and uniform differences between these heads and those of the American Indians, will be obvious to every one accustomed to make comparisons of this kind, and serve as corroborative evidence of the opinion that the Eskimaux are the only people possessing Asiatic characteristics on the American continent.

ANATOMICAL MEASUREMENTS.

These measurements are derived from one hundred and forty-seven skulls of American Indians of forty different nations and tribes; and the crania are all of adult persons, and unaltered by art. The table is itself sufficiently explanatory for general purposes, but it is necessary to premise the manner in which the measurements have been taken.

The *longitudinal diameter* is measured from the most prominent part of the os frontis, between the superciliary ridges, to the extreme end of the occiput.

The *parietal diameter* is measured between the most distant points of the parietal bones, which are, for the most part, the protuberances of these bones.

The *frontal diameter* is taken between the anterior inferior angles of the parietal bones.

The *vertical diameter* is measured from the fossa between the condyles of the occipital bone, to the top of the skull.

The *inter-mastoid arch* is measured, with a graduated tape, from the point of one mastoid process to the other, over the external table of the skull.

The *inter-mastoid line* is the distance, in a straight line, between the points of the mastoid processes.

The *occipito-frontal arch* is measured by a tape over the surface of the cranium, from the posterior margin of the foramen magnum to the suture which connects the os frontis with the bones of the nose.

The *horizontal periphery* is measured by passing a tape around the cranium so as to touch the os frontis immediately above the superciliary ridges, and the most prominent part of the occipital bone.

The *length of the head and face* is measured from the margin of the upper jaw, to the most distant point of the occiput.

CRANIA AMERICANA.

The *zygomatic diameter* is the distance, in a right line, between the most prominent points of the zygomæ.

The *facial angle** is ascertained by an instrument of ingenious construction

---

* The facial angle, which was first proposed by the learned Professor Camper, is measured in the following manner: a line called the facial line, is drawn from the anterior edge of the upper jaw, (or, if the tooth projects beyond the jaw, from the tooth itself,) to the most prominent part of the forehead, which is usually the space between the superciliary ridges. A second or horizontal line, is drawn through the external opening of the ear (meatus auditorius) till it touches the base of the nostrils, between the terminal roots of the front incisor teeth, and from this point it is still prolonged until it meets with the facial line already described: hence the two lines may meet at, or very near, the nasal spine, or base of the nose; but in other instances the decussation of the lines occurs at a point considerably anterior to the bone. It is obvious that an angle will be formed where these lines thus intersect each other, and this is the facial angle. For example, notice the annexed wood cut, (No. 1,) which represents the skull of the Cowalitsk already figured in this work, (see Plate 50.) The line A, B, is the facial line, extending, as just observed, from the anterior margin of the upper jaw to the most prominent part of the os frontis; the second or horizontal line, is represented between the points C and D, and for the purpose of having a fixed point for its anterior termination, I have uniformly carried it to the *nasal*

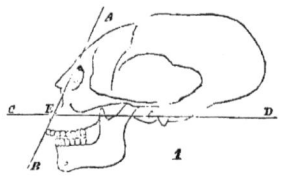

spine, above and between the roots of the two front incisor teeth. The point E, where these lines decussate each other, is the facial angle, which in the present instance will be found to measure about sixty-six degrees.—The second wood cut (No. 2) represents the lines as drawn on a much better formed head, that of a Peruvian Indian, in which the angle at E measures seventy-six degrees.

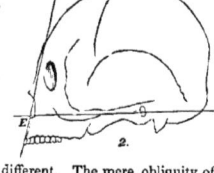

The most casual inspection of these diagrams will satisfy any one that the facial angle is no criterion of mental intelligence; and in justice to Camper we must add that he does not assert it to be so. In fact it chiefly gives the projection of the face in relation to the head, without conveying the least idea of the capacity of the cranium, which is often the same in heads whose diameters are altogether different. The mere obliquity of the teeth contracts the angle; and what is yet more important, the space between the eyes from whence the facial line is drawn, may be very prominent, so as to give an angle of eighty degrees, while the forehead itself retreats so rapidly, that if the facial line were made to touch it, the resulting angle would not perhaps exceed sixty-five degrees.

"The maximum angle that can be embraced by the facial lines," says Camper, "is 100°: if we advance these lines still further, the head becomes preternaturally large, as in hydrocephalus. But it is surprising to observe that the most ancient Greek artists have chosen the very maximum of the facial angle, while the best Roman graveurs were satisfied with the angle of 95°.

"I have thus established the two extremes of obliquity in the facial line, viz: from 70° to 100°.

and ready application, which has received so many additions from the suggestions of different individuals, that its invention cannot be ascribed to any one person. The original idea, however, originated with my friend Dr. Turnpenny; and I have much pleasure in explaining it, inasmuch as it appears to me to supersede

These embrace all the gradations, from the head of the Negro to the sublime beauty of the ancient Greek models. If we descend below 70° we have an orang outang, or a monkey; if we descend still lower we have a dog or a bird—a snipe, for example, of which the facial line is almost parallel with a horizontal plane."—(*Dissertation sur les différence réelles, &c.*, p. 42, &c.)

Professor Blumenbach has denied that the genuine antique heads present an angle of 95° or 100°, and supposes that such measurements could only be derived from incorrect copies. Dr. Wiseman, on the other hand, remarks, "that whoever will examine the heads of Jupiter in the Vatican Museum, particularly the bust in the large circular hall, or the more defaced heads of the Elgin marbles, will be satisfied that Camper is accurate in this respect."—(*Twelve Lectures, &c.*, p. 105.)

Another mode of comparing skulls was devised by Professor Blumenbach, called the *norma verticalis*, or vertical method; and consists in supporting the head on the lower jaw, and then looking down upon it from above and behind. If, however, several skulls are to be compared, they are to be stood each one on its occiput, the jaw being vertical and resting against a board or other plane surface. To make the comparison complete, the occipital ends should be so elevated as to bring the cheek bones on a line, as in the following diagram, which is copied from Blumenbach.—(*De Generis Humani Var. Nat.* p. 204, *et tab.* 1.)

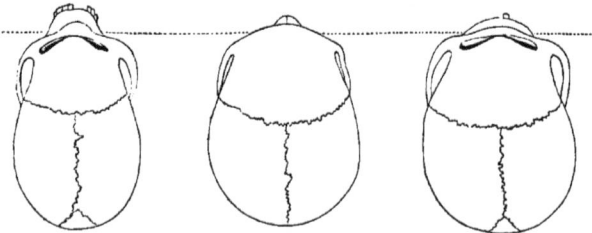

The *first* of these figures represents a Negro head, elongated, and narrow in front, with expanded zygomatic arches, projecting cheek bones, and protruded upper jaw. The *second* is a Caucasian skull, in which those parts are nearly concealed in the more symmetrical outline of the whole head, and especially by the full development of the frontal region. The *third* figure is taken from a Mongol head, in which the orbits and cheek bones are exposed, as in the Negro, and the zygomæ arched and expanded; but the forehead is much broader, the face more retracted, and the whole cranium larger. Having been at much pains to give the *norma verticalis* of the skulls figured in this work, the reader will have ample opportunity to compare for himself. He will see that the American head approaches nearest to the Mongol, yet is not so long, is narrower in front, with a more prominent face and much more contracted zygomæ.

all other modes of ascertaining the facial angle. The following diagram represents the instrument, which may be called the *Facial Goniometer*, as applied to a cranium for the purpose of measurement.

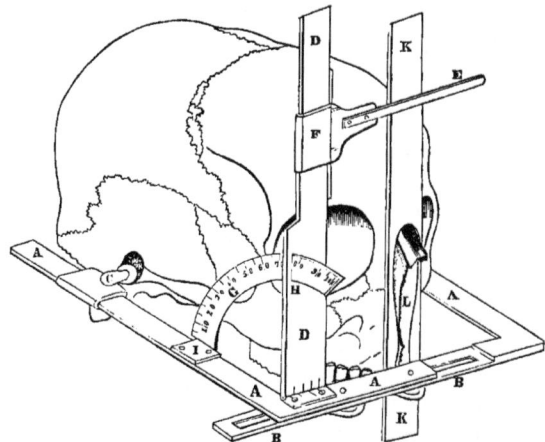

The letters A, A, A represent the rectangular basal limbs of the instrument, (which is made of brass,) the front limb sliding at B, so as to increase or diminish the distance between the right and left limbs. In order to fix the goniometer to a skull, there is attached to each of the lateral limbs a slide with a conical pivot attached, C, which enters the meatus of the ear. The limb D, D, is attached by a hinge to the base, and can be brought to form any angle with it. G is a scale of one hundred degrees, attached by a hinge at I, and let through the limb D, D, at H. E is a horizontal limb, at right angles with D, D, on which it slides at F. The thin piece of wood, K, K, has an opening at L, to admit the nasal bones to pass through it. Now this piece of wood necessarily touches the most prominent parts of the forehead and upper maxillary bone, and therefore represents the *facial line*. To measure the facial angle, bring the upper surface of the anterior basal limb of the instrument on a horizontal plane with the nasal spine; then let the limb D, D, fall back until the lateral limb E, touches the facial line K, K, when the facial angle will be at once designated on the scale. For the purpose of greater accuracy the lateral basal limbs of the instrument are graduated in inches and parts of inches,

ANATOMICAL MEASUREMENTS.

(not represented in the diagram,) and the sliding parts of the anterior limb are fixed by screws (as seen on each side of A) whenever the instrument is properly adjusted. With this apparatus the facial angle of any skull may be ascertained with exactness in the brief space of two or three minutes.

Internal capacity.—An ingenious mode of taking this measurement was devised by Mr. Phillips, viz: a tin cylinder was provided about two inches and three-fourths in diameter, and two feet two inches high, standing on a foot, and banded with swelled hoops about two inches apart, and firmly soldered, to prevent accidental flattening.—A glass tube hermetically sealed at one end, was cut off so as to hold exactly five cubic inches of water by weight, at 60° Fahrenheit. A float of light wood, well varnished, two and a quarter inches in diameter, with a slender rod of the same material fixed in its centre, was dropped into the tin cylinder; then five cubic inches of water, measured in the glass tube, were poured into the cylinder, and the point at which the rod on the float stood above the top of the cylinder, was marked with the edge of a file laid across its top; and the successive graduations on the float-rod, indicating five cubic inches each, were obtained by pouring five cubic inches from the glass tube *gradatim*, and marking each rise on the float-rod. The graduations thus ascertained, were transferred to a mahogany rod fitted with a flat foot, and these subdivided, with compasses for the cubic inches and parts. In order to measure the capacity of a cranium, the foramina were first stopped with cotton, and the cavity was then filled with *white pepper seed*[*] poured into the foramen magnum until it reached the surface, and pressed down with the finger until the skull would receive no more. The contents were then transferred to the tin cylinder, which was well shaken in order to pack the seed. The mahogany rod being then dropped down with its foot resting on the seed, the capacity of the cranium in cubic inches is at once read off on it.

Nearly all the preceding measurements were taken with my own hands.

Coronal, sub-coronal, anterior and posterior chambers of the cranium.—An apparatus was devised by my friend Mr. Phillips to obtain these capacities, which

---

[*] White pepper seed was selected on account of its spherical form, its hardness, and the equal size of the grains. It was also sifted to render the equality still greater.

will be best understood with the aid of the annexed diagram. A, A, represent the top and bottom, and B, B, the ends of the instrument, dovetailed into each other to prevent warping. C, C, C, are sliders and screws, the latter being fitted with collars on each side of the sliders where they pass through it, in order that the screw may carry the slider along with it when moved backward and forward. D, cranium to be measured. E, F, is an iron straight-edge, standing on two legs welded to it and filed to the same length, so

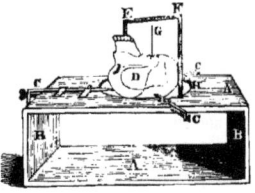

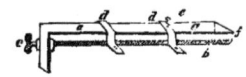

that when they rest on a horizontal plane, the straight-edge is also horizontal. G is a rod attached to a float of cork, small enough to drop into the foramen magnum; it is cut to such a length that when the base of the float is raised to the level of the plane on which rest the legs of the straight-edge E, F, the top of the rod shall rise to the upper margin of the straight-edge. H is an oval hole cut in the top of the frame A, (which is of stout mahogany plank,) large enough to admit the free adjustment of the largest cranium. *In the lower figure,* c, is the screw moving the slider a, a, the former, when in place, working into a nut through a hole in the mahogany top-piece. d, d, are clamps to confine the slide in a regular direction: f, the point of the slider as shown in the lower figure, is bevilled off on the top and two sides; but the lower side of the slider is carried out straight to the point, which is thus kept in the same plane as the top of the frame on which it is bound by the pinching-screw e, tapped into the clamp nearest the point of the slider.

Capacity of the coronal region.—This measurement is the space included between an imaginary plane drawn through the centres of ossification of the parietal and frontal bones, and the inner surface of the portion of cranium above it. To obtain this measurement, the instrument was first adjusted so as to bring the top of the frame A, A, to coincide with the plane of the horizon. The sutures and small foramina on the top of the skull being stopped with wax or putty, and when necessary, the inside of the cranium having been well varnished, the centres of ossification of the parietal bones were marked with a cross, and a line was drawn between the centres of ossification of the os frontis: the cranium was then placed inverted in the oval hole H, and the point of the slider at the end of the frame being pressed against the drawn line between the centres of ossification of the frontal bone, the sliders at the sides of the instrument are then brought in contact with the centres of ossification of the parietal bones, the slider at the end being moved backward or forward to bring the cranium into the proper place. The float C is then dropped into the foramen magnum, and the frame E, F, held over it, as shown in the figure: mercury is then poured into the cranium until the top of the float-rod rises to the straight-edge E, F, thus indicating the surface of the mercury to stand at the level of the top surface of the frame A, A; and as the adjustment of the centres of ossification to the points of the sliders has brought them into the same plane as the top of the frame, the surface of the mercury must coincide with an imaginary plane, drawn through the centres of ossification. The mercury is then transferred to a graduated glass tube, and the capacity of the coronal region read off in cubic inches and parts.

The *sub-coronal region* is obtained by deducting the capacity of the coronal region (obtained as above stated) from the total capacity.

Capacity of the anterior chamber of the cranium.—This measurement is the capacity of the space contained between an imaginary plane, at right angles to the anterior and posterior diameter of the cranium, coinciding with, or let fall from the anterior margin of the foramen magnum, and passing at right angles through the imaginary plane (drawn through the centre of ossification) which formed the dividing line between the coronal and sub-coronal regions. It is thus taken: the cranium being placed in the frame exactly as in taking the capacity of the coronal region, the straight-edge of a slip of wood is laid across it over the anterior margin of the foramen magnum and at right angles to the anterior and posterior diameter of the skull. One side of a carpenter's square is then laid on the mahogany surface, so that the other side of the square, which would then be upright, would stand with its flat surface pressing against the side of the cranium; and another square is adjusted in the same manner on the other side of the skull, each having one of their vertical edges pressing against the straight edge of the ruler laid over the anterior margin of the foramen magnum; and a pencil mark is drawn on each parietal bone along the perpendicular edges of the squares adjusted to the straight edge; these pencil marks will be at right angles to the plane passing through the centres of ossification, and indicate the position of the plane dividing the anterior and posterior chambers, as described in the definition of that capacity. The cranium is then taken from the instrument, and a hole, eighth of an inch in diameter, drilled through the pencil marks in each parietal bone, about two inches from the meatus auditorius: a piece of stiff, straight wire is then passed through these two holes, and the cranium nearly filled with white pepper seed. The skull is then held in the left hand, with the face resting on the palm; the seed being well packed with the finger or steel strike, and a candle placed nearly between the eye and foramen magnum, all the seed above the inserted wire is drawn out through the foramen by means of a strike made of a piece of stiff steel, half an inch wide, first filed straight on the edge, and then bent laterally so as to draw out the seed from the sides of the cranium. By working the strike about until it rested on both the wire and anterior margin of the foramen magnum, and examining how the surface of the seed coincided with these two points of the measurement, by inspection through the foramen with a due management of the light, the capacity can be obtained in a much more satisfactory manner than was at first anticipated. The seed is then transferred to the tin tube, and its quantity ascertained as in measuring the total capacity.

The *capacity of the posterior chamber* is obtained by deducting the capacity of the anterior chamber from that of the whole cranium.

The points through which the plane was drawn in the two last measurements, was preferred to one drawn from the meatus auditorius, so that it should be vertical when the head was placed in its natural position when in life; because the irregular form of the meatus prevented its being a fixed starting point; and the difficulty of determining the living position of the head (which must have depended entirely on the eye, and might have been materially affected by the disposition of the light,) would have thrown a degree of uncertainty and irregularity over the results. A line drawn through the centre of the meatus, however, and the one adopted, generally coincided within a quarter of an inch.

NOTE.—It will be observed that all the measurements have not been obtained in respect to every skull, which has chiefly arisen from the imperfection of some of the crania, while a few others came to hand so late as to preclude the possibility of taking the more difficult measurements.—All the Peruvians marked with a star are from the Temple of the Sun, (see page 132.) The figures in the first column refer to corresponding numbers in my Catalogue of Crania, and are inserted here for the purpose of reference, and to give greater facility in comparing and correcting the measurements hereafter. The number in the second column refers to the corresponding plate in this work. The Table was considerably extended during the progress of the work through the press, which will explain some slight differences between it and the results as stated in the preceding pages.

TABLE OF ANATOMICAL MEASUREMENTS.

NATIONS OR TRIBES.	No. in Catalogue.	Plate.	Longitud. diameter.	Parietal diameter.	Frontal diameter.	Vertical diameter.	Inter-mast. arch.	Inter-mast. line.	Occipito-frontal arch.	Horizontal periphery.	Length of head and face.	Zygomatic diameter.	Facial angle.	Internal capacity in cubic inches.	Capacity of anterior chamber.	Capacity of posterior chamber.	Capacity of coronal region.	Sub-coronal region.
*Peruvian.	75		6.	6.	4.6	5.1	15.5	4.1	13.5	19.8	7.8	5.5	72°	83.5	36.5	47.	14.5	69.
*Peruvian.	76		6.5	5.	4.1	4.9	14	4.	13.5	18.6	7.8	4.7	73°	64.	23.	41.	11.9	11.9
*Peruvian.	77		6.6	5.7	4.2	5.2	15.5	4.4	13.	19.4	7.8	5.5	75°	75.	35.	30.	12.25	62.75
Peruvian.	79		6.0	5.7	4.5	5.3	15.	4.4	13.9	19.3	7.9	5.2	74°	74.5	31.5	43.	11.4	63.1
Peruvian.	81		5.9	5.7	4.4	5.3	15.2	4.3	13.3	18.3	7.9	5.1	76°	79.	32.25	46.75	18.	61.
Peruvian.	82		6.6	5.6	4.5	5.4	15.5	4.	13.8	19.2	8.	5.4	79°	75.	31.5	43.50	16.1	58.9
*Peruvian.	85	11-B	6.3	5.8	4.5	5.3	15.	4.	13.2	19.	7.2	5.5	80°	76.5	30.	46.5	12.25	64.25
*Peruvian.	86	11	6.1	6.	4.7	5.5	16.	4.5	14.1	19.5	7.8	5.4	81°	83.	33.5	49.5	15.75	67.25
*Peruvian.	87	8 & 9	5.8	5.7	4.4	5.1	14.5	4.1	12.7	18.4	7.4	5.	75°	71.75	28.75	43.	11.4	60.35
*Peruvian.	699		6.6	5.6	4.4	5.2	14.8	4.	13.6	19.2	7.8	5.2	74°	72.	26.5	45.5	9.25	62.75
*Peruvian.	90		6.3	5.5	4.2	5.	14.5	3.7	13.2	18.5	7.6	4.9	75°	70.	28.5	41.5	12.6	57.4
Peruvian.	91		6.2	5.8	4.3	4.9	14.5	4.1	12.6	18.7	7.4	5.2	73°	66.5	25.	41.5	9.7	58.6
*Peruvian.	92		6.8	5.4	4.5	5.3	14.7	4.2	14.	19.5	7.8	5.7	75°	74.5	34.50	40.	13.5	61.
*Peruvian.	93		6.1	5.9	4.6	5.2	15.2	4.1	13.2	19.2	7.7	5.2	75°	76.5	34.25	42.25	14.2	62.30
*Peruvian.	95	11-A	6.7	6.	4.5	5.6	16.2	4.5	14.5	20.2	8.	5.6	80°	89.5	34.	55.5	20.5	69.
*Peruvian.	96		6.4	5.9	4.5	5.	14.1	4.2	13.4	19.4	7.5	4.9	73°	68.	31.5	36.5	12.2	55.8
*Peruvian.	97	11-D	6.5	5.5	4.6	5.6	14.8	4.5	13.6	19.5	7.9	5	67.5°	68.5	33.	35.5		
*Peruvian.	100		6.2	5.5	4.4	5.	13.6	3.8	12.6	18.7	7.3	5.	70°	60.	27.5	32.5	12.5	47.5
*Peruvian.	400		6.5	5.7	4.4	5.2	14.7	4.3	13.4	19.5	7.8	5.5	76°	70.	30.5	39.5	13.1	56.9
*Peruvian.	697		6.7	5.5	4.6	4.9	14.1	4.	13.4	19.5	8.	6.5	73°	71.	32.5	38.5	10.5	60.5
*Peruvian.	402		6.9	5.6	4.4	5.3	15.2	4.1	14.	20.2	8.	6.5	77°	78.5	34.	44.5	11.8	66.2
*Peruvian.	403		6.6	5.6	4.3	5.3	14.9	3.9	13.8	19.5	7.6	5.2	74°	79.	31.	48.	15.5	63.5
*Peruvian.	405		5.9	5.6	4.3	4.9	14.5	3.9	12.9	18.4	7.4	4.9	75°	62.	23.5	38.5	10.1	51.9
*Peruvian.	406		6.3	5.7	4.3	5.3	15.	3.9	13.7	19.	7.5	4.8	76°	75.5	29.5	46.	12.4	63.5
*Peruvian.	446	11-C	6.	5.9	4.4	5.	15.2	3.2	13.	7.6	5.4	80°	77.	28.	49.	11.3	65.7
Peruvian.	447		6.5	5.0	4.6	5.1	14.9	4.	13.2	19.2	7.8	5.4	74°	71.	29.	42.	10.3	60.7
Peruvian.	448		6.1	5.7	4.5	5.	15.	4.	12.9	18.7	7.9	5.3	74°	74.	32.	42.	14.9	59.1
Peruvian.	449		6.3	0.1	4.9	5.3	16.	4.4	13.2	19.5	8.	5.5	77°	83.5	35.5	48.	19.5	64.
*Peruvian.	450		5.9	6.	4.7	5.	15.	4.1	12.6	19.1	7.6	5.3	75°	74.5	35.	39.5	14.3	60.2
Peruvian.	451		6.8	5.4	4.3	5.6	14.6	4.3	14.3	19.5	7.8	5.2	78°	87.	31.	56.	19.75	67.25
Peruvian.	452		6.3	5.8	4.4	5.3	14.4	4.2	13.2	19.2	7.8	5.4	69°	83.	34.	49.	11.5	71.5
*Peruvian.	685		6.3	5.3	4.4	4.6	14.	3.9	13.	18.7				69.	29.	40.	12.3	56.7
Peruvian.	686		6.4	5.5	4.3	5.2	14.8	4.	13.2	19.	7.6			71.	38.	33.	14.4	56.6
Chimuyan.	11	6	6	5.5	4.4	2.5	2	14.3	3.8	13.4	18.8	7.6	4.9	76°	67.5	28.5	39.	10.25	57.25
Quichua.	637		7.	5.2	4.5	2	14.6	4.	14	19.5	8.2	5.2	70°	79.	33.	46.	17.5	61.5
Atacames.	651		6.6	5.3	3.8	5.2	14.5	3.9	14.	19.2	8.	5.1	73°	75.	29.	46.	14.5	60.75
Atacames.	652		6.6	5.4	1.3	4.8	14.2	4.	13.1	19.5	7.8	5.	74°	74.	27.5	46.5	8.75	65.25
Atacames.	653		7.2	5.5	4.4	5.1	14.8	4.1	13.7	20.2	8.2	5.4	76°	80.	34.25	46.75	13.3	66.7
Araucanian.	654	68	6.7	5.4	4.7	4.9	14.2	4.1	13.4	19.5	7.8	5.	72°	77.	32.	45.	11.9	65.1
Araucanian.	655	66	6.9	5.4	4.1	5.4	15.	4.1	14.2	19.5	8.	5.	76°	84.5	32.5	52.	19.	65.5
Araucanian.	656		6.6	5.3	4.2	5.	14.2	4.	13.8	19.	7.9	4.9	76°	75.	26.	49.	15.25	59.75
Mexican.	714	61	7.1	5.6	4.6	5.5	15.5	4.1	15.	20.2	8.3	5.2	80°	87.				
Mexican.	559	17	6.8	5.5	4.6	6.	15.6	4.4	14.6	19.9	8.1	5.3	80°	89.5	33.5	56.	19.5	70.
Mexican.	715	59	6.3	5.3	4.4	5.4	14.3	4.2	13.5	19.2	7.7		76°	74.				
Mexican.	499		7.1	5.6	4.5	5.4	15.2	4.3	14.2	20.	8.4	5.3	72°	87.5	36.25	51.25	19.25	68.25
Mexican.	716	60	6.6	5.3	4.4	5.4	14.	4.	14.	19.3	7.8		77°	76.				
Mexican.	A.N.S.	16	7.1	5.7	4.4	5.2	15.9	4.	14.	20.5	8.4	5.6	72°	83.	39.	44.	17.5	65.5
Mexican.	717		7.	5	3.4	3.5	3	14.5	4.1	14.	20.			78°	77.				
Mexican.	681	17-A	6.6	5.3	4.3	5.2	14.6	4.1	13.6	19.	7.5	5.4	77°	74.	28.	46.	11.5	62.5
Mexican.	718		6.8	5.5	4.8	5.7	15.9	4.	14.6	19.9	8.	5.4	76°	77.				
Mexican.	682		7.	5.4	4.3	5.3	15.	4.1	14.	19.8	8.	5.4	76°	80.5	36.5	44.	15.5	64.5
Mexican.	720		6.9	5.3	4.5	5.5	14.7	3.9	14.6	19.8	8.1		80°	82.				
Mexican.	A.P.S.	18	6.4	5.7	4.5	5.4	14.6	4.5	13.5	20.2	7.2	5.2	78°	77.	30.	47.		
Mexican.	34	18-A	6.9	5.2	4.2	5.	14.5	4.1	14.	19.2	8.	5.1	76°	78.	30.	48.	14.25	63.75
Chetimaches.	43		6.5	5.7	4.3	5.9	15.5	4.1	14.	19.1	8.	5.1	77°	80.	30.5	49.5	16.25	63.75
Chetimaches.	70	19	6.9	5.6	4.2	5.9	15.5	4.3	14.	20.	8.5	5.7	71°	85.	39.25	45.75	13.25	71.75
Seminole.	C.		6.9	5.6	4.6	5.3	15.	4.2	13.6	19.8			75°	80.				
Seminole.	707	23	7.1	5.6	4.7	5.	15.	4.1	14.8	20.3	8.	5.3	78°	80.				
Seminole.	604	22	7.3	5.9	4.6	5.8	15.9	4.4	15.3	20.7	8.4	5.3	72°	93.	35.5	57.5	25.	68.
Seminole.	708		7.	5.5	4.4	5.4	14.9	4.2	14.6	20.1	8.1	5.	73°	86.				
Seminole.	C.		7.3	5.6	4.2	5.6	15.2	4.7	15.	20.4			73°	82.5				
Seminole.	456	24	7.	5.9	4.5	5.8	14.7	4.6	14.2	20.5	7.9	5.6	81°	91.5	44.	47.5	18.1	73.4

CRANIA AMERICANA.

NATIONS OR TRIBES.	No. in Catalogue.	Plate.	Longitud. diameter.	Parietal diameter.	Frontal diameter.	Vertical diameter.	Inter-mast. arch.	Inter-mast. line.	Occipito frontal arch.	Horizontal periphery.	Length of head and face.	Zygomatic diameter.	Facial angle.	Internal capacity or whole skull.	Capacity of anterior chamber.	Capacity of posterior chamber.	Capacity of coronal region.	Sub-coronal region.
Muskogee.	579	26	7.	5.7	4.6	5.3	15.3	4.5	14.4	20.8	8.3	5.8	72°	94.75	42.5	52.25	15.6	79.15
Muskogee.	441		6.8	5.8	4.2	5.6	15.4	4.3	15.	20.	8.5	5.4	74°	89.5	37.25	52.25	18.8	70.7
Uchee.	39	27	6.8	5.4	4.3	5.	15.	4.4	14.3	20.1			75°	81.5				
Cherokee.	632		7.2	5.2	4.2	5.5	14.5	4.	14.6	20.2			77°	88.	36.5	51.5		
Cherokee.	633		6.8	5.	4.1	5.2	13.7	3.8	13.7	18.9	7.8		76°	74.	33.	41.	16.	58.
Cherokee.	634		7.	5.3	4.1	5.1	14.5	4.	14.	19.5	8.3		74°	81.	32.5	48.5	19.2	61.8
Cherokee.	635		6.6	5.1	3.8	4.9	13.4	3.6	13.8	18.5		4.5		70.		18.		52.
Cherokee.	B.	25	7.2	5.3	4.3	5.3	14.1	4.5	14.	19.1			77°	82.	35.	47.	12.25	69.75
Choctaw.	408		7.2	3.	4.2	5.5	14.6	3.9	14.7	19.2	8.4	5.1	74°	79.	28.	51.	13.7	65.3
Sauk.	561		7.4	3.9	4.6	5.5	15.3	4.3	15.	21.	8.	5.6	81°	90.5	41.5	55.	24.25	72.
Ottigamie.	639	31	7.	3.9	4.7	5.5	15.3	4.7	14.2	20.9	8.1	5.8	82°	91.5	40.	51.5	12.75	78.75
Ottigamie.	413		6.9	3.9	4.7	5.	15.	4.2	14.2	20.2	8.2	5.4	76°	89.5	34.	55.5	19.25	70.25
Potowatomie.	657	34	7.8	5.7	4.4	5.3	16.	4.	15.8	22.1	8.2	5.2	80°	98.	35.5	62.5	19.	79.
Chippeway.	683	28	7.3	5.8	4.1	8.6	15.1	4.6	14.2	20.9	8.	5.5	84°	94.	43.	51.	14.75	79.25
Chippeway.	684		7.2	5.5	4.3	5.5	14.8	4.1	14.6	20.2	8.3	5.5	73°	85.5	35.	50.5	13.2	72.3
Menominee.	35		6.7	5.0	4.2	5.1	14.3	4.4	13.5	19.5	7.9	5.4	72°	72.5	33.	39.	14.1	58.4
Menominee.	44		6.8	5.4	4.3	5.5	14.	3.2	14.	19.7	7.9	5.4	75°	74.				
Menominee.	78		7.3	5.7	4.5	5.3	14.2	4.5	14.2	21.		8.1	5.6	78°	85.25	38.	47.25	13.75	71.5
Menominee.	454	29	6.8	5.3	6.4	2.5	5.	14.7	4.1	14.1	19.0	7.7	5.2	79°	86.5	36.5	50.	15.5	71.
Menominee.	453		7.1	5.8	4.5	5.4	14.9	4.6	14.1	20.6	8.2	5.8	75°	87.	37.5	49.5	13.5	73.5
Menominee.	563		6.9	5.7	4.5	5.3	15.3	4.5	14.	20.4	8.1		76°	83.5	40.	43.5		
Menominee.	W.		7.1	5	6.4	4.5	4	14.8	4.3	15.	20.5			75°	83.5	33.	50.5	21.	62.5
Menominee.	80		0.6	5.4	4.2	4.9	14.2	3.9	13.6	19.3	8.	3.1	74°	71.5	30.	41.5	16.25	55.25
Massasauga.	27		7.	5.2	4.3	5.2	13.8	4.1	14.2	19.5	9.2	5.2	76°	77.5	29.	48.5	13.25	64.25
Lenapé.	40	32	7.	3.5	4.6	5.1	14.1	4.1	2	14.5	20.	8.1	5.	76°	78.5	33.	45.5	16.25	62.25
Lenapé.	630		7.8	5.4	4.1	6.2	15.6	1.3	16.	21.5	8.8		80°					
Minsi.	508		6.7	5.	4.2	5.3	14.	4.1	13.6	19.3	7.6		78°	72.				
Manta.	418		7.	5.1	3.9	5.3	14.6	3.9	14.	19.5	7.9	5.2	79°	74.5	30.	44.5	16.75	57.75
Quinnipiak.	26		7.	5.7	4.7	5.3	15.	4.4	14.1	20.2	7.8			77.	34.5	42.5	15.	62.
Gepepscot.	P.C.		6.8	3.1	4.2	5.6	15.6	4.	14.4	19.	7.9	5.2	76°	77.5	31.	46.5	20.	57.5
Miami.	407		6.9	5.5	4.3	5.5	14.5	4.1	14.	19.8	7.9		75°	79.75	33.25	46.5	17.1	62.65
Miami.	542	30	7.3	5.5	4.3	5.3	14.6	4.6	14.9	21.	8.4	5.5	75°	90.	33.	36.5	13.5	76.5
Miami.	562		7.	5.1	4.2	5.6	14.5	4.2	14.1	19.5	8.		78°	82.5	36.5	46.	15.5	67.
Miami.	541		7.6	5.3	4.3	5.5	15.	4.1	15.5	20.5	8.5	5.1		91.				
Natiek.	38		6.7	5.2	4.1	5.7	14.5	4.1	14.3	19.	8.2		73°	77.75	28.	19.75	13.9	63.85
Natiek.	84		6.9	5.4	4.3	5.3	14.3	3.9	14.9	19.0	7.9	5.1	78°	83.	35.	48.	18.	65.
Natiek.	604		0.9	5.1	4.1	5.1	13.1	4.1	14.	19.2	8.1		70°	77.25	30.	47.25	10.3	66.95
Natiek.	693		6.7	5.2	4.3	5.3	14.2	3.9	14.1	19.1	8.2		78°	77.5	30.	47.5	14.5	63.
Natiek.	498		7.	5.1	4.1	5.2	13.5	4.1	13.9	19.5	8.	5.	75°	77.5	28.	49.5	12.1	65.40
Natiek.	690		6.7	5.3	4.5	5.3	14.	4.	14.4	19.5								
Natiek.	588		7.4	5.7	4.5	5.7	15.	5.	15.	21.5	8.3	5.8	79°	100.	38.	62.	20.1	79.90
Natiek.	689		6.9	5.2	4.2	5.5	13.3	4.1	13.7	19.5			77°	77.				
Natiek.	601		7.	5.1	4.3	5.1	13.5	4.1	14.1	19.6	6.5	5.1	73°	77.	32.5	44.5		
Natiek.	692		6.9	5.1	4.	5.2	13.9	4.1	14.2	19.	8.2	4.9	72°	70.				
Naumkeag.	567	33	6.9	5.	4.2	5.3	14.3	3.9	15.4	19.	8.	4.8	80°	71.	26.	45.		
Naumkeag.	631		7.4	5.5	4.4	5.9	15.	4.3	14.	18.7				93.5	33.	60.5		
Shawnee?	606		6.9	4.9	4.1	4.	13.5	3.9	14.	18.7	7.7		78°	71.			15.4	55.60
Dacota.	605	30	6.7	5.7	4.2	5.4	14.7	4.4	13.5	19.8	7.8	5.2	77°	85.	36.	49.	16.6	68.40
Assinaboin.	659		7.6	5.8	4.6	3.1	14.9	4.3	14.9	21.2	8.4	5.0	79°	97.	40.	57.	18.75	78.25
Minetari.	650		7.3	4.4	4.5	1.	14.1	4.1	14.7	20.2	8.5	5.1	74°	94.5	34.	50.5	18.6	65.90
Mandan.	643		7.1	5.4	4.3	5.1	14.2	3.8	14.6	20.	8.2	4.9	77°	82.	31.	51.	25.	57.
Mandan.	644		7.	5.3	4.1	5.3	13.9	4.2	14.1	19.8	8.1	5.	74°	76.5	31.5	45.	14.	62.5
Ricara.	649		7.	5.2	4.1	5.1	13.5	4.	14.	19.5	8.	4.9	76°	71.5	28.	43.5	16.25	46.5
Osage.	660		7.	5.4	4.2	5.5	14.8	4.1	14.5	20.	8.	5.3	80°	82.5	40.5	42.	17.1	65.4
Osage.	54	41	6.5	5.9	4.6	5.3	15.	4.1	13.4	19.5	7.7	5.7	77°	83.	37.5	45.5	14.1	68.9
Pawnee.	P.	38	6.6	5.4	4.4	4.9	13.7	4.3	13.	19.1	7.5	5.2	75°	70.5	31.	39.5	10.6	59.9
Cotonay.	C.	40	7.1	5.4	4.3	5.1	13.8	4.3	14.	19.9	8.	5.	28°	77.	33.?	44.?	18.2	58.8
Cotonay.	C.		6.9	5.6	4.5	5.3	14.	4.	13.9	20.	8.1	5.1	79°	79.5	38.?	41.5?		
Oneida.	33	36	7.5	5.6	4.1	5.8	14.4	4.3	14.9	20.8	8.5	5.6	74°	92.5	36.	56.5	18.4	74.1
Cayuga.	417	35	7.8	5.1	4.2	5.4	14.2	4.5	15.5	20.8	8.4	5.4	78°	93.5	35.	58.5	11.5	82.
Huron?	P.		6.7	5.6	4.1	5.2	14.5	3.9	14.	19.2	7.9		76°	81.5	33.	48.5	17.	64.5
Huron.	15	37	7.2	5.3	4.3	5.5	15.	4.4	14.2	19.8	8.2	5.8	73°	74.	32.5	41.5	9.5	64.
Iroquois.	16		7.5	5.5	4.4	5.5	15.2	4.5	15.1	20.8	8.8	5.5	74°	98.5	41.25	57.25	20.2	78.3
Iroquois.	A.N.s.		7.1	5.4	4.2	5.3	14.4	4.	14.1	20.								
Mingo.	455		7.1	5.5	4.5	5.2	14.7	4.1	14.5	20.2	8.1	5.4	77°	81.5	36.	45.5	18.75	62.75
Chinouk.	457		6.9	5.8	4.3	5.2	14.5	4.1	14.	19.8	8.1	5.4	73°	80.	34.	46.	13.	67.
Chinouk.	578	42	6.7	5.4	4.4	5.3	14.	4.2	14.	19.4	7.8	5.3	76°	74.	33.	41.	14.	60.

TABLE OF ANATOMICAL MEASUREMENTS.

Skulls from Caves in the Valley of Ohio.	No. in Catalogue	Plate	Longitud. diameter	Parietal diameter	Frontal diameter	Vertical diameter	Inter-mast. arch.	Inter-mast. line.	Occipito-frontal arch.	Horizontal periphery	Length of head and face.	Zygomatic diameter	Facial angle	Internal capacity in cu. inches	Capacity of anterior chamber	Capacity of posterior chamber	Capacity of coronal region	Capacity of sub-coronal region
Steubenville.	420		7.	6.1	4.6	5.6	15.5	5.4	2	14.	20.5	8.3	5.5	80°	90.	39.	51.	19.2	70.8
Steubenville.	437	63	6.7	6.	4.6	5.7	16.	4.4	14.1	20.2	8.1	5.6	79°	92.	33.5	58.5	19.25	72.75
Steubenville.	438		6.7	6.	4.5	5.1	15.	4.1	13.5	20.	8.	5.3	80°	84.5	43.	41.5	14.9	69.6
Steubenville.	658		6.7	6.	4.5	5.2	15.	4.1	13.4	20.	8.3		79°	92.5			22.8	69.7
Steubenville.	436		7.	5.8	4.5	5.7	15.6	4.5	14.2	20.5	8.	5.2	77°	88.	39.	49.	15.4	72.6
Steubenville.	439		6.6	5.5	4.3	5.1	14.	4.1	13.7	19.2	8.	5.5	78°	75.			16.3	58.7
Steubenville.	440		7.1	5.7	4.6	5.6	15.	4.4	14.2	20.2	8.1		76°	89.	40.	59.	18.75	70.25
Steubenville.	687		6.2	6.	4.5	5.	14.8	4.	13.2	19.4				72.	35.5	36.5	15.75	56.25
Golconda.	A.N.S.	62	6.7	5.4	4.3	5.5	14.5	4.1	14.	19.3	7.8	4.9	76°	81.	35.25	45.75	18.	63.
Skulls from the Mounds.																			
Circleville, Ohio.	53	51	7.3	5.5	4.4	5.4	14.6	4.2	14.1	20.3	8.2	5.5	76°	86.5				
Tennessee.	T.	55	6.6	5.6	4.1	5.6	15.2	4.4	14.	19.5	8.1	5.3	80°	87.5			15.3	72.2
†Atakapas.	C.		6.5	5.3	4.3	5.7	14.1	4.1	13.6	18.8	7.3	5.	81°	76.				
†Natchez.	F.	54	5.9	6.6	4.6	5.1	15.6	4.4	12.4	19.6			72°	80.				
Santa, Peru.	73	56	6.2	5.1	4.3	4.9	14.6	4.1	3.	13.3	18.5	7.8	5.1	71°	74.5	30.	44.5	14.5	60.
†Rimac, Peru.	414	57	6.0	5.6	4.4	5.1	15.3	4.3	14.	19.7	8.3	5.5	72°	79.	29.5	49.5	14.1	64.9
Rimac, Peru.	412	58	6.5	5.6	4.5	5.	14.7	3.8	13.2	19.2	7.8	5.4	74°	76.5	34.	42.5	13.75	62.75
Rimac, Peru.	68		7.	5.9	4.7	5.4	15.6	3.9	14	2	20.3	8.3	5.4	74°	89.5	37.	42.5	14.75	74.75
Mississippi.	416	52	7.1	5.3	4.5	5.5	14.6	4.2	14.1	20.			79°	85.5			18.1	67.4
Flatheads of Columbia river horizontally compressed.																			
Clickitat.	461	48	6.6	5.8	4.8	5.	14.2	4.2	13.	19.5	7.9	5.6	70°	79.	36.5	42.5	12.75	66.25
Cowalitsk.	573	49	7.	6.1	4.9	4.1	13.9	4.	12.7	20.2	8.6	5.5	66°	75.	28.	47.	6.25	68.75
Kalapooyah.	574	47	6.8	6.3	5.2	4.9	14.8	4.3	13.	20.4	8.6	6.	68°	87.	35.5	51.5	11.2	75.8
Clatsap.	575	46	6.7	6.	5.	4.5	14.9	4.2	13.	19.8	8.3	5.5	70°	78.	26.	52.	8.75	69.25
Killemook.	578	45	6.9	6.9	4.9	4.8	15.7	4.	14.	21.	8.5	5.7	73°	02.	34.	58.	19.3	72.7
Chinook.	462	43	6.7	5.9	4.7	4.6	14.2	4.	12.0	20.	8.3	5.5	72°	69.	32.5	36.5	0.9	49.1
Klatstoni.	577	44	6.2	6.	4.6	5.3	14.4	4.2	13.4	19.	8	3	5.5	70°	70.	30.	40.	12.75	57.25
Chinook.	721		6.6	6.	5.	5.5	14.9	4.2	13.1	20.	8.3	6.	67°	84.	35.2	18.8	14.25	69.75
Ancient Peruvians.																			
Atacama.	P.	3	6.5	5.2	4.3	5.1	14.5	4.	13.8	18.5	8.3	5.1	68°	72.5	26.	46.5	14.75	57.75
Arica.	67	4	7.3	5.3	4.3	5.3	14.	4.3	15.	19.8	8.7	5.4	73°	81.5	31.5	50.	16.25	65.25
Peru.	R.	5	6.7	4.5	4.1	4.1	11.5	3.6	14.2	18.	8.8	4.9	61°	65.5	19.75	45.75	12.75	52.75

MEAN RESULTS OF THE FOREGOING TABLE.

	Toltecan nations, including skulls from the mounds.		Barbarous nations, with skulls from the Valley of Ohio.		American Race, embracing the Toltecan and barbarous nations.		Flathead tribes of Columbia river.		Ancient Peruvians.	
	No. of skulls	MEAN.	No. of skulls	MEAN.	No. of skulls	MEAN.	No. of skulls	MEAN.	No. of skulls	MEAN.
Longitudinal diameter.	57	6.5	90	7.	147	6.75	8	6.7	3	6.8
Parietal diameter.	57	5.6	90	5.5	147	5.55	8	6.	3	5.
Frontal diameter.	57	4.4	90	4.3	147	4.35	8	4.9	3	4.2
Vertical diameter.	57	5.2	90	5.4	147	5.35	8	4.8	3	4.8
Inter-mastoid arch.	57	14.9	90	14.6	147	14.75	8	14.6	3	13.3
Inter-mastoid line.	57	4.	90	4.2	147	4.15	8	4.1	3	4.
Occipito-frontal arch.	57	13.6	90	14.2	147	13.9	8	13.1	3	14.3
Horizontal periphery.	57	19.4	90	19.9	147	19.65	8	20.	3	18.8
Length of head and face.	53	7.8	78	8.1	131	7.45	8	8.3	3	8.4
Zygomatic diameter.	49	5.3	64	5.3	113	5.3	8	5.7	3	5.1
Facial angle.	55	75° 35′	83	76° 13′	138	75° 45′	8	69° 30′	3	67° 30′
Internal capacity in cubic inches.	57	76.5	87	89.4	144	79.6	8	79.95	3	73.2
Capacity of the anterior chamber.	46	‡32.5	73	34.5	119	33.5	8	32.95	3	25.7
Capacity of the posterior chamber.	46	‡43.8	73	48.6	119	46.2	8	47.	3	47.4
Capacity of the coronal region.	46	‡14.	71	16.2	117	15.1	8	11.9	3	14.6
Capacity of the sub-coronal region.	46	‡61.8	71	66.5	117	64.5	8	67.35	3	58.6
The total capacity being estimated at 100, gives the following proportionate results as parts of 100. { Ant. chamb.		42.6		41.5		42.1		40.62		35.1
Post. chamb.		57.4		58.5		60.		59.37		64.9
Coronal reg.		18.47		19.6		19.		15.		20.
Sub-cor. reg.		81.53		80.4		81.		85.		80.

† These three heads are artificially moulded.

‡ The seeming discrepancy in the sums of these two pairs of measurements, arises from the fact that only 46 of the 48 heads measured, enter into each series.

REMARKS.—In the above scale of results, the skulls from the mounds have been classed with the Toltecan division, and those from the caves of Steubenville, &c., with the Barbarous tribes. The great size of the Steubenville crania has considerably enhanced the mean internal capacity of the heads of the Barbarous Nations, so that it exceeds that of the Flatheads of Columbia river; but the latter, as heretofore stated, compare fairly with the average of the entire race. It is curious to observe, however, that the Barbarous Nations possess a larger brain by five and a half cubic inches, than the Toltecans; while, on the other hand, the Toltecans possess a greater relative capacity of the anterior chamber of the skull, in the proportion of 42.3 to 41.8. Again, the coronal region, though absolutely greater in the Barbarous tribes, is rather larger in proportion in the Demi-civilised tribes; and the Facial Angle is much the same in both, and may be assumed, for the race, at *seventy-five degrees.*

In conclusion, the author is of the opinion that the facts contained in this work tend to sustain the following propositions:

1st. That the American Race differs essentially from all others, not excepting the Mongolian; nor do the feeble analogies of language, and the more obvious ones in civil and religious institutions and the arts, denote anything beyond casual or colonial communication with the Asiatic nations; and even these analogies may perhaps be accounted for, as Humboldt has suggested, in the mere coincidence arising from similar wants and impulses in nations inhabiting similar latitudes.

2d. That the American nations, excepting the Polar tribes, are of one Race and one species, but of two great Families, which resemble each other in physical, but differ in intellectual character.

3d. That the cranial remains discovered in the Mounds, from Peru to Wisconsin, belong to the same race, and probably to the Toltecan family.

NOTE.—*On the Internal Capacity of the Cranium in the different Races of Men.*—Having subjected the skulls in my possession, and such also as I could obtain from my friends, to the internal capacity measurement already described, I have obtained the following results. The mean of the American Race, (omitting the fraction) is repeated here merely to complete the Table. The skulls of idiots and persons under age were of course rejected.

RACES.	No. of skulls.	Mean internal capacity in cubic inches.	Largest in the series.	Smallest in the series.
Caucasian.	52	87.	109.	75.
Mongolian.	10	83.	93.	69.
Malay.	18	81.	89.	64.
American.	147	82.	100.	60.
Ethiopian.	29	78.	94.	65.

ANATOMICAL MEASUREMENTS.

1. The *Caucasians* were, with a single exception, derived from the lowest and least educated class of society. It is proper, however, to mention that but three Hindoos are admitted in the whole number, because the skulls of these people are probably smaller than those of any other existing nation. For example, seventeen Hindoo heads give a mean of but seventy-five cubic inches; and the three received into the table are taken at that average. To be more specific, we will give in detail the number of individuals of each nation as far as ascertained.

Anglo-Americans,	6
Germans, Swiss and Dutch,	7
Celtic Irish and Scots,	7
English,	4
Guanché (Libyan,)	1
Spanish,	1
Hindoo,	3
Europeans, nation not ascertained,	23
	52

2. The *Mongolians* measured, consist of Chinese and Eskimaux; and what is worthy of remark, three of the latter give a mean of eighty-six cubic inches, while seven Chinese give but eighty-two.

3. The *Malays* embrace Malays proper and Polynesians, thirteen of the former and five of the latter; and the mean of each presents but a fractional difference from the mean of all.

4. The *Ethiopians* were all unmixed Negroes, and nine of them native Africans, for which I am chiefly indebted to Dr. McDowell, formerly attached to the colony at Liberia.

5. Respecting the American Race I have nothing to add, excepting the striking fact that of all the American nations the Peruvians had the smallest heads, while those of the Mexicans were something larger, and those of the barbarous tribes the largest of all, viz:

Toltecan nations.	Peruvians collectively,	76 cubic inches.
	Mexicans collectively,	79 cubic inches.
	Barbarous tribes, as per Table,	82 cubic inches.

An interesting question remains to be solved, viz: the relative proportion of brain in the anterior and posterior chambers of the skull in the different races; an inquiry for which I have hitherto possessed neither sufficient leisure nor adequate materials.

During the laborious task of collecting the facts embraced in the preceding measurements, I have great pleasure in acknowledging the occasional attendance and aid of Dr. Goddard, Professor W. R. Johnson, Mr. Townsend, Mr. R. Pearsall, Dr. J. K. Barnes, Dr. Hardy, and Mr. Robert E. Peterson.

PHRENOLOGICAL MEASUREMENTS.

Being indebted to Mr. Phillips for the mode of obtaining many of these measurements, and for the successful accomplishment of them all, I have obtained from him the following explanatory note:

"The measurements in the following table, from amativeness to combativeness inclusive, were taken with the craniometer; amativeness being measured from the point where the external occipital crest intersects the lower semi-lunar line: those from individuality to philoprogenitiveness, to between constructiveness and constructiveness, with the callipers. From causality to causality, and supra orbitar foramen to causality, with dividers. The measurements from the meato-temporal line to the arch from caution to caution, with a graduated strap. The height of benevolence, veneration, firmness, conscientiousness and hope, above the plane drawn through the centres of ossification of the frontal and parietal bones, was obtained by placing the cranium in the frame, foramen magnum downwards, the centres of ossification being adjusted to the points of the sliders as before: a straight-edge, similar to that used with the float-rod except in having the legs shorter for convenience, was held over the spot to be measured, its legs resting on the mahogany surface; a graduated rod was then held vertically against the side of the straight-edge, with its point resting on the part to be measured, when the height of the organ above the plane was shown on the rod where it appeared above the straight-edge.

"The other measurements were taken with the craniometer, callipers, dividers, and the measuring frame, to the centres of the organs as traced on a cast furnished by Mr. Combe, and figured on Plate LXXII. The measurements with the strap were obtained as follows: the meato-temporal line was taken from the centre of the meatus auditorius (the end of the strap being held over the meatus, not pressed down into it) to the middle of the parieto-sphenoidal suture, where the anterior inferior angle of the parietal bone unites with the greater wing of the sphenoid bone. For greater convenience this point will be found marked by a cross on the Cotonay head, Plate XL. The inter-sphenoidal arch, over reflecting organs, was measured from the above described spot marked with a cross, to the corresponding spot on the other side of the cranium, laying the strap over the centres of causality. The inter-sphenoidal arch, over the perceptive organs, was taken between the same points of measurement as the last, placing the strap over the perceptive organs, and keeping it above the superciliary ridge, where this appeared but a mere bony protuberance, as was frequently the case. Meatus to caution was taken from the centre of the meatus auditorius to the centre of ossification of the parietal bone. The arch from caution to caution, by laying the strap from centre to centre of ossification of the parietal bones, over the top of the cranium, and generally a little back of the organ of firmness.

"That some errors may exist in so numerous a series of measurements is not merely possible but probable; but the following facts show the reader how much care was taken to avoid them: a series of measurements with the craniometer and compasses, much more extensive than any we had seen published, had been carefully made on upwards of ninety of the crania, when Mr. George Combe arrived in this city. That gentleman immediately pointed out so many erroneous points of measurement, (arising from the use of a badly marked bust,) that those tables were condemned, together with the labor bestowed on them. I then proposed the strap measurements, the five last under the bracket, and some others, and the work was commenced anew. Dr. Morton took down all the measurements, the whole of which were made by myself; thus avoiding the inaccuracies which must necessarily have occurred, had several different persons contributed their aid."

Nations and Tribes	Plate	No. in Catalogue	Amativeness	Philoprogenitiveness	Adhesiveness	Self-esteem	Approbativeness	Firmness	Conscientiousness	Veneration	Hope	Marvellousness	Ideality	Benevolence	Causality	Individuality	Order	Secretiveness	Cautiousness	Destructiveness	Combativeness	Individuality to philoprogenitiveness	Comparison to concentrativeness	Cautiousness to cautiousness	Ideality to ideality	Secretiveness to secretiveness	Destructiveness to destructiveness	Combativeness to combativeness	Constructiveness to constructiveness	Causality to causality	Supra-orbital foramen to ear cavity	Masto-temporal line	Inter-spheno-arch over reflecting organs	Inter-spheno-arch over perceptive organs	Mastoid to eration	Arch from eristation to caution	Reserotene	Veneration	Firmness	Conscientiousness	Hope
Peruvian.		450	1.95	2.9	3.25	4.4	4.15	4.8	4.6	4.6	4.5	4.3	4.2	4.5	4.2	3.9	3.8	3.4	4.3	3.2	3.3	6.	5.45	5.8	4.7	5.75	5.85	5.3	4.3	2.	1.2	2.35	6.9	6.6	3.35	6.8	1.1	1.6	1.75	1.4	1.4
Peruvian.		91	2.1	3.3	3.7	4.4	4.3	4.5	4.35	4.5	4.25	4.		3.95	4.35	3.95	3.7	3.6	3.1	4.55	3.7	3.4	6.1	5.75	5.75	4.65	5.45	5.3	5.1	4.2	3.85	1.15	2.2	6.3	6.2	3.7	6.3	1.	1.4	1.4	1.1	1.2
Peruvian.	11–A	95	2.5	3.1	4.1	4.75	4.65	5.05	4.85	5.25	5.		4.7	4.35	5.1	4.45	4.1	4.		4.55	2.8	3.7	6.8	6.1	5.85	4.85	5.65	5.75	5.55	4.35	2.05	1.3	2.7	6.75	6.8	3.6	6.8	1.4	1.9	1.75	1.5	1.6
Peruvian.	11–D	97	2.25	2.8	3.7	4.45	4.3	4.75	4.7	4.75	4.5	4.4	4.25	4.65	4.45	4.15	4.		3.2	4.2	2.7	3.4	6.5	5.95	4.4	4.6	5.55	5.45	4.95	4.3	1.7	1.3	2.45	7.	6.7	3.65	5.55	1.1	1.4	1.5	1.15	1.1
Peruvian.		79	2.2	3.2	3.55	4.4	4.9	4.7	4.8	4.8	4.6	4.25	4.7	4.5	4.1	3.9	3.2	4.65	2.7	3.3	6.6	6.1	5.6	4.75	5.5	5.45	5.05	4.2	1.9	1.2	2.4	6.9	6.5	3.6	6.55	1.05	1.45	1.45	1.2	1.4
Peruvian.		402	2.25	3.4	3.6	4.7	4.25	4.9	4.65	4.85	4.7	4.6	4.1	4.8	4.6	4.2	4.3	4.	3.5	6.9	6.4	5.3	4.55	5.5	5.45	4.75	4.3	2.	1.25	2.6	7.2	7.2	3.75	5.9	1.1	1.5	1.3	1.1	1.3
Peruvian.	11–B	85	2.2	3.	3.9	4.4	4.35	4.85	4.75	4.8	4.65	4.6	4.6	4.25	3.9	3.8	3.1	3.35	6.2	5.3	5.7	4.5	5.4	5.4	4.3	1.8	1.2	2.6	6.6	6.25	3.45	6.6	1.05	1.5	1.5	1.35	
Peruvian.		90	2.	3.25	3.65	4.35	4.3	4.6	4.5	4.5	4.4	4.3	4.	4.65	4.15	3.7	3.7	3.1	4.4	2.7	3.25	6.3	6.	5.6	4.5	5.35	5.05	4.4	4.1	1.55	1.15	2.15	6.7	6.2	3.5	6.2	1.1	1.5	1.5	1.15	1.3
Peruvian.	11–C	446	2.	2.85	4.	5.45	4.6	4.9	4.7	4.9	4.65	4.45	4.3	4.7	4.35	3.95	3.8	3.3	4.55	2.8	4.1	6.	5.8	4.85	5.8	5.4	5.2	4.25	1.45	1.15	2.5	6.65	6.6	3.7	6.5	1.	1.5	1.45	1.25	1.3
Peruvian.		405	1.9	3.1	3.65	4.3	4.2	4.65	4.5	4.55	4.4	4.2	4.05	4.35	4.05	3.65	3.6	2.9	4.45	2.75	3.6	6.	5.4	5.4	4.5	5.	5.25	5.3	4.2	1.75	1.2	2.4	6.6	6.45	3.6	6.25	1.	1.35	1.35	1.	1.25
Peruvian.		406	2.1	3.1	3.4	4.4	4.2	4.8	4.7	4.8	4.8	4.1	4.6	4.35	3.95	3.85	3.2	4.2	2.7	3.4	6.3	5.8	5.6	4.6	5.4	5.1	4.9	4.1	1.95	1.3	2.45	6.75	6.4	3.8	6.1	1.	1.4	1.4	1.1	1.3
Peruvian.		81	2.	2.9	3.	4.7	4.1	4.8	4.8	4.75	4.6	4.2	4.5	4.2	3.8	3.65	3.15	4.4	2.8	3.35	5.9	5.75	5.65	4.3	5.45	5.4	5.1	4.3	1.7	1.05	2.25	6.7	6.3	3.6	6.75	1.2	1.7	1.75	1.45	1.5
Peruvian.		77	2.15	3.	3.55	4.4	4.3	4.7	4.6	4.65	4.6	4.5	4.05	4.55	4.45	4.15	4.1	3.4	4.4	3.8	3.6	6.6	5.75	5.55	4.6	5.5	5.4	5.05	4.1	1.75	1.15	2.5	6.5	6.4	3.5	6.2	1.	1.4	1.5	1.2	1.25
Peruvian.	11	86	2.	2.8	3.45	4.5	4.45	5.	4.9	5.	4.8	4.5	4.15	4.75	4.3	4.	3.9	3.25	4.5	2.55	3.45	6.35	6.	5.9	5.1	5.6	5.5	5.45	4.5	2.	1.1	2.75	6.7	6.3	3.65	6.75	1.25	1.65	1.65	1.3	1.4
Peruvian.		400	2.1	3.1	3.6	4.4	4.15	4.7	4.55	4.85	4.55	4.4	4.	4.7	4.3	4.	3.9	3.2	4.4	2.9	3.6	6.35	5.75	5.45	4.7	5.4	5.55	5.45	4.15	1.8	1.2	2.35	6.6	6.3	3.4	6.35	1.1	1.6	1.6	1.2	1.4
Peruvian.		449	2.15	2.8	3.5	4.5	4.7	4.9	4.8	4.85	4.45	3.3	4.15	4.7	4.3	3.95	3.85	3.6	4.5	2.8	3.4	6.1	5.75	6.	5.25	6.05	5.55	5.6	4.7	2.	1.4	2.4	7.1	6.8	3.6	7.	.9	1.6	1.75	1.6	1.45
Peruvian.		413	2.	3.60	3.85	4.4	4.4	4.6	4.55	4.55	4.55	4.4	4.1	4.4	4.15	3.8	3.15	4.2	2.7	3.3	6.3	5.85	5.3	4.85	5.55	5.25	4.9	4.4	1.85	1.3	2.4	6.6	6.7	3.4	6.25	1.	1.55	1.5	1.25	1.4
Peruvian.		452	2.1	3.5	3.6	4.2	4.1	4.6	4.55	4.7	4.4	4.25	4.6	4.25	3.85	3.7	3.15	4.25	2.75	3.2	6.3	5.6	5.5	4.85	5.65	5.5	5.3	4.45	1.95	1.25	2.25	6.56	6.5	3.1	6.58	1.1	1.55	1.45	1.25	1.4
Peruvian.		75	2.1	3.25	3.7	4.35	4.3	4.65	4.6	4.6	4.5	4.4	4.15	4.55	4.3	4.05	3.9	3.15	4.35	2.6	3.5	6.45	6.	5.8	4.9	5.75	5.5	5.55	4.6	1.7	1.25	2.25	7.1	7.	3.25	6.6	1.1	1.5	1.5	1.15	1.3
Peruvian.		76	2.3	3.1	4.05	4.4	4.4	4.5	4.3	4.4	4.25	4.1	3.8	4.4	4.	3.8	3.6	3.	4.25	2.25	3.2	6.5	6.3	5.2	4.3	5.2	4.9	4.3	3.8	1.65	1.05	2.25	6.25	6.3	3.15	6.25	1.2	1.6	1.65	1.3	1.35

TABLE OF PHRENOLOGICAL MEASUREMENTS—Continued.

NATIONS AND TRIBES.	Plate.	No. in Catalogue.	Amativeness.	Philoprogenitiveness.	Adhesiveness.	Self-esteem.	Approbativeness.	Firmness.	Conscientiousness.	Veneration.	Hope.	Marvellousness.	Ideality	Benevolence	Causality	Individuality	Order.	Percepe eases	Cautiousness	Destructiveness	Combativeness	Individuality in philosophical truths	Comparison to	Causationess in [illegible]	Identity to	Recreativeness to electrorestranees	Destructive to destructive	Combativeness as as	Causality to contentiveness trees	Causality to causality	Supra orbital-caru to can	Mecho-temporal line.	Intra spinal it in reflex	Intra spinal reflex over perspective regul-	Medlin to caution.	Arch from cau tion to caution	Believe tence	Veneration	Firmness	Cautious to Cinnamon	Hope.
Peruvian.	8 & 9	87	2.0	2.8	3.25	4.4	4.25	4.05	4.7	4.55	4.6	4.55	4.4	4.53	4.2	3.8	3.75	3.1	4.15	2.7	3.25	5.05	5.4	5.65	4.65	5.35	3.25	5.2	4.35	2.05	1.25	2.23	6.9	6.25	3.55	6.3	1.15	1.4	1.4	1.2	1.3
Peruvian.		100	2.	3.	3.4	3.95	4.	4.4	4.25	4.5	1.4	4.3	4.	4.4	4.2	3.	3.7	3.	1.1	2.6	1.25	6.2	5.65	5.3	4.1	5.25	5.1	5.1	4.1	1.8	1.05	2.45	6.	6.	3.35	6.05	1.05	1.55	1.5	1.15	1.3
Peruvian.		93	2.15	3.	3.3	4.2	4.2	4.85	4.7	1.8	1.6	1.35	3.3	1.7	4.4	3.		3.2	1.4	2.73	2.35	6.1	5.75	3.7	4.8	3.8	5.25	5.25	4.5	1.95	1.15	2.35	6.4	6.63	3.5	6.8	1.25	1.65	1.65	1.4	1.5
Peruvian.		403	2.25	3.1	3.6	4.2	4.1	1.7	4.46	4.8	4.6	4.4	4.35	4.75	1.3	4.	3.8	3.2	4.3	2.4	3.35	6.7	6.	5.4	1.5	3.35	5.1	5.15	3.9	1.6	1.15	2.2	7.2	6	3.3	6.25	1.2	1.05	1.5	1.2	1.5
Peruvian.		96	2.2	3.4	3.5	4.4	4.3	4.6	4.45	4.5	1.4	4.36	4.1	4.5	4.1	3.1	3.7	3.7	1.35	2.65	3.33	6.35	5.9	5.4	4.63	5.45	5.33	5.23	4.33	1.	1.2	2.	7.	6.5	3.6	6.15	1.	1.45	1.4	1.2	1.3
Peruvian.		73	1.8	3.	3.5	4.45	4.4	4.8	4.6	4.6	1.55	4.4	4.3	4.5	1.3	3.9			4.4	1.35	3.5	6.25	6.1	5.35	4.3	5.2	5.23	4.9	4.2	1.8	1.2	2.5	6.6	6.4	2.25	6.1	1.1	1.6	1.6	1.4	1.4
Peruvian, (Mound.)		68	2.2	3.5	3.9	4.5	4.05	4.9	4.8	1.85	4.7	4.63	4.4	4.85	4.4	4.15	3.95	3.2	1.6	2.75	3.7	6.95	6.45	5.6	5.	5.7	5.45	6.6	4.6	2.4	1.35	2.4	7.25	7.1	3.85	6.3	1.3	1.53	1.6	1.25	1.3
Peruvian, (Mound.)	58	412	2.1	3.3	3.7	4.4	4.1	4.6	4.55	4.6	4.5	4.4	4.4	4.85	4.4	3.75	3.95	2.2	1.6	2.6	3.3	6.45	5.75	3.6	5.	5.6	5.25	5.1	4.6	1.8	1.3	2.35	6.7	7.1	3.35	6.3	1.05	1.5	1.5	1.2	1.3
Chimuyan.		11	2.3	3.4	3.5	4.25	4.3	4.5	4.4	4.6	4.33	4.15	4.05	4.5	4.5	3.4	3.8	3.2	4.5	2.55	3.25	6.5	6.1	5.2	4.6	5.6	4.95	4.7	4.35	1.75	1.15	2.15	6.50	6.6	3.63	5.95	1.1	1.5	1.4	1.1	1.35
Mexican.	61	714	2.4	3.5	4.2	4.9	1.7	5.1	4.9	4.95	4.8	4.554.3	4.554.3	4.8	4.5	4.1	4.05	3.3	4.5	2.7	3.5	6.85	3.35	5.4	4.35	5.5	5.2	5.05	1.4	1.85	1.25	2.6	6.75	6.9	3.65	6.5	1.13	1.65	1.7	1.35	1.5
Mexican.	60	716	2.1	3.4	3.8	4.05	4.5	4.85	4.55	4.8	4.6	4.55	4.1	1.6	4.33	3.05	3.8	3.	4.1	2.55	3.1	6.7	6.3	5.25	4.75	5.23	4.9	4.65	4.5	2.05	1.2	2.2	7.4	7.9	3.1	0.4	1.4	1.9	1.7	1.4	1.6
Mexican.	59	715	2.15	2.9	3.5	4.4	4.3	4.6	4.6	4.8	4.6	4.6	4.4	4.6	4.25	3.9	3.	3.8	3.1	2.55	3.2	6.4	0.3	5.1	4.55	3.4	5.	5.1	4.5	1.85	1.15	2.33	6.8	7.	3.5	6.05	1.2	1.05	1.6	1.2	1.4
Mexican.	17	559	2.46	3.25	3.75	4.55	4.4	5.1	5.15	4.85	4.85	1.6	4.1	4.9	4.4	4.05	4.	3.35	4.3	2.7	3.3	6.8	6.4	5.3	4.5	5.3	4.6	4.7	4.55	2.05	1.15	2.33	7.2	7.	2.53	6.8	1.3	1.9	2.	1.5	1.05
Mexican.	16	A.W.	2.1	3.9	4.15	4.75	4.6	4.8	4.6	5.15	4.85	4.65	4.4	4.85	4.3	3.83	3.95	3.35	4.3	2.65	3.6	6.9	4.	5.25	4.5	3.4	1.9	5.4	4.06	1.9	1.3	2.5	7.25	6.63	3.5	6.65	1.	1.6	1.7	1.3	1.8
Mexican.		718	2.3	3.3	3.7	4.6	4.5	5.2	4.8	5.15	4.9	4.6	4.4	4.754.5	4.054.3	3.95	4.	3.2	4.5	4.25	2.6	3.25	6.7	6.25	5.2	4.3	5.35	5.25	4.65	4.45	2.15	1.2	2.9	6.8	6.7	3.5	0.75	1.5	2.	1.9	1.6	1.25
Pawnee.	17—A	681	2.25	3.1	3.5	4.4	4.25	4.7	4.4	4.55	4.5	4.3	4.1	4.4	4.2	3.95	3.9	3.	4.3	2.65	3.3	6.55	5.9	5.2	4.4	5.3	5.1	4.6	4.65	3.83	1.75	3.6	6.8	6.15	3.45	5.9	1.05	1.9	1.4	1.05	1.25
Pawnee.		682	2.3	3.4	3.7	4.8	4.55	4.9	4.7	4.8	4.6	4.554.3	4.554.3	4.75	4.55	4.25	3.95	2.9	3.1	2.7	3.45	7.	6.55	5.3	4.5	5.3	5.3	5.4	4.75	4.2	1.8	1.2	2.7	7.25	6.6	3.55	6.25	1.2	1.53	1.7	1.3	1.45
Lenapé.	32	40	2.2	3.8	4.05	4.8	4.6	4.85	4.4	4.7	4.7	4.54	4.6	4.3	4.5	4.5	2.9	3.15	3.9	2.9	3.45	3.9	3.9	6.15	1.55	5.3	5.5	4.9	4.25	1.8	1.	2.5	6.75	6.4	3.4	6.35	1.4	1.75	1.65	1.25	1.55
Miami.		568	1.	3.4	2.75	4.	4.3	4.7	4.5	4.7	4.5	4.654.15	4.654.15	4.6	1.6	4.1	4.1	3.1	3.15	2.53	3.3	6.05	6.15	4.9	1.33	5.1	5.	5.	4.25	1.5	1.05	2.3	6.6	6.25	3.25	0.25	1.3	1.7	1.65	1.25	1.3
Miami.		569	2.35	2.4	3.9	4.5	4.4	4.85	4.8	4.8	4.7	4.6	4.6	4.	4.5	4.1	3.0	3.15	4.2	2.8	3.25	6.9	6.25	5.16	4.53	5.15	5.15	4.7	4.05	1.75	1.3	2.5	6.75	6.75	3.25	6.1	1.2	1.75	1.6	1.35	1.5

Miami.	30	542	2.7	3.75	4.1	4.7	4.05	4.95	4.8	4.65	4.6	4.2	4.7	4.45	4.15	3.4	3.2	4.4	2.8	3.6	7.3	6.75	5.25	4.5	5.5	5.4	4.8	4.35	2.
Miami.		407	2.2	3.45	4.15	4.7	4.5	4.8	4.05	4.75	4.6	4.5	4.2	4.05	4.4	4.1	3.9	3.	4.3	2.6	3.35	6.85	6.5	4.8	5.45	5.3	5.1	4.25	1.7
†Sauk.		561	2.5	3.7	4.	4.75	4.5	4.95	4.7	4.95	4.7	4.5	4.35	4.95	4.7	4.3	4.05	3.3	4.3	2.6	3.2	7.4	5.85	4.85	5.8	5.6	5.6	4.5	1.9
†Outgamie.		415	2.25	3.75	3.85	4.7	4.55	4.9	4.7	4.05	4.5	4.4	4.4	4.6	4.4	4.1	4.	3.1	4.4	2.7	3.4	7.1	6.25	5.6	5.35	5.35	5.05	4.4	1.9
†Pottowatomie.	32	557	2.5	3.75	4.1	4.95	4.85	5.25	4.7	4.95	4.7	4.05	4.25	4.85	4.6	4.3	4.05	3.25	4.4	2.65	3.65	7.7	0.95	5.7	5.6	5.3	5.45	4.65	1.75
Quinnipiak.		26	2.35	3.2	3.6	4.55	4.3	4.7	4.55	4.7	4.5	4.45	4.2	4.05	4.4	4.15	4.1	3.2	4.3	2.65	3.65	6.9	6.25	5.5	5.55	5.55	5.	4.5	1.9
†Outgamie.		639	2.25	3.45	3.85	4.45	4.35	4.75	4.7	4.8	4.8	4.8	4.55	4.95	4.75	4.45	4.15	3.25	4.55	2.5	3.35	7.	6.4	5.6	6.	5.7	4.8	4.8	2.
Naumkag.		597	2.35	3.6	4.	4.5	4.45	4.85	4.5	4.8	4.5	4.4	4.15	4.7	4.35	4.15	3.55	3.	4.2	2.4	3.3	7.1	5.6	4.6	6.	5.7	4.8	4.1	1.9
Menominee.		454	2.3	3.55	4.	4.55	4.5	4.9	4.8	5.	4.8	4.75	4.45	4.8	4.55	4.2	4.	2.3	4.2	2.4	2.7	8.9	6.	5.6	6.05	4.8	4.6	4.1	1.9
Menominee.		44	2.4	3.4	3.55	4.4	4.2	4.7	4.4	4.7	4.6	4.5	4.2	4.05	4.4	4.1	4.	3.1	4.15	2.05	3.3	0.85	5.6	4.5	5.65	5.4	5.05	4.3	1.75
Menominee.		78	2.2	3.7	4.	4.5	4.35	4.7	4.5	4.75	4.65	4.6	4.5	4.2	4.7	4.6	4.35	4.3	3.	2.8	3.55	7.25	6.25	6.65	4.85	5.8	5.	4.	1.6
Menominee.		563	2.4	3.4	3.7	4.5	4.35	4.8	4.7	4.8	4.05	4.5	4.3	4.75	4.4	4.15	4.1	4.	4.4	2.85	3.4	6.9	6.25	5.	6.85	6.75	5.	5.45	1.85
Menominee.		25	2.1	3.1	3.5	4.3	4.65	4.5	4.55	4.4	4.3	4.16	4.45	4.3	3.95	4.		3.15	4.3	2.8	3.3	6.7	6.	5.35	4.15	5.55	5.6	4.3	1.9
†Chippeway.		683	2.45	3.8	4.	4.6	4.8	4.7	4.85	4.7	4.8	4.7	4.25	4.9	4.7	4.5	4.3	3.4	4.35	2.9	3.5	7.3	6.05	5.25	4.35	5.95	5.25	4.7	2.
Gepepcot.		P.C.	2.3	3.4	3.9	4.65	4.5	4.9	4.55	4.7	4.5	4.6	4.35	4.1	4.15	3.9	3.8	3.15	3.05	2.45	3.25	6.75	6.3	4.95	4.55	5.1	4.75	4.15	1.6
†Naick.		688	2.5	3.85	4.4	4.8	4.9	4.05	4.85	4.9	4.8	4.35	4.75	4.5	4.2	4.25	3.25	2.9	3.75	7.5	6.5	4.55	5.75	5.75	5.25	4.15	1.8		
†Massasaugs.		27	2.2	3.05	3.8	4.5	4.4	4.7	4.5	4.7	4.3	4.4	4.1	4.05	4.35	4.1	3.9	2.9	4.8	2.7	3.3	7.05	6.5	5.	4.25	5.1	5.2	4.7	4.1
†Araucanian.	66	556	2.3	2.5	4.05	4.7	4.45	4.8	4.05	4.7	4.5	4.4	4.4	4.1	4.6	4.15	3.85	2.75	4.3	2.05	3.2	6.8	6.5	5.35	4.2	5.3	5.3	4.06	1.9
†Araucanian.		656	2.25	3.4	3.6	4.8	4.25	4.9	4.6	4.55	4.4	4.3	4.2	4.1	4.45	4.2	3.95	2.8	3.05	4.25	2.55	3.35	6.7	6.25	5.2	4.25	5.25	5.05	4.95	1.65
Atacames.		652	2.5	3.6	3.85	4.05	4.35	4.6	4.45	4.4	4.3	4.2	4.1	4.1	4.3	3.9	3.1	4.2	2.6	3.45	6.7	6.1	4.9	4.2	5.35	5.25	4.05	1.75		
Atacames.		653	2.15	3.7	3.9	4.5	4.3	4.65	4.45	4.6	4.3	4.3	4.2	4.35	4.1	3.1	4.3	2.7	7.15	6.3	5.2	4.15	5.4	5.	4.3	1.75				
Atacames.		551	2.2	3.4	3.55	4.55	4.3	4.75	4.6	4.75	4.6	4.75	4.6	4.05	3.95	3.85	3.15	4.3	2.6	3.4	0.6	6.35	5.2	4.25	5.2	4.9	4.2	1.55		
†Araucanian.	68	664	2.2	3.5	3.9	4.6	4.4	4.45	4.5	4.35	4.4	4.1	4.	4.35	3.95	3.85	3.15	4.4	3.2	2.65	3.2	0.65	6.2	5.2	4.15	5.4	5.05	4.85	2.1

67

TABLE OF PHRENOLOGICAL MEASUREMENTS—Continued.

NATIONS AND TRIBES.	Plate.	No. in Catalogue.	Amativeness.	Philoprogen. itiveness.	Adhesiveness.	Self-esteem.	Approbative-ness.	Firmness.	Conscientious-ness.	Veneration.	Hope.	Marvellousness.	Ideality.	Benevolence.	Causality.	Individuality.	Order.	Recollectiveness.	Cautiousness.	Destructiveness.	Combativeness.	Philoprogen. itiveness of Liveness.	Comparative- ness.	Cautiousness to Cautiousness.	Identity to Identity.	Recretiveness to secretiveness.	Destructiveness to destructive- ness.	Combativeness to combativities.	Causality to Constructive- ness.	Supra-orbital ity in aura to causal ity.	Mean-temporal line.	Infer spheroid arch over reflect ing organs.	Inter-spheroid arch over per ceptive organs.	Hearing to caution.	Arch from ear tion to caution	Benevo- lence.	Venera- tion.	Firmness.	Conscien- tiousness	Hope.
†Seminole.	C.	2.4	3.3	3.8	4.5	4.45	4.8	4.6	4.75	4.6	4.55	4.4	4.7	4.5	4.2	4.1	3.5	4.2	2.6	3.4	6.9	6.1	5.2	4.55	5.5	5.2	4.8	4.25	1.9	1.35	2.75	6.9	7.05	3.75	5.8	1.05	1.55	1.6	1.25	1.3
†Seminole.	C.	2.6	3.8	4.2	4.8	4.8	5.1	4.9	4.93	4.7	4.55	4.35	4.75	4.75	1.45	4.25	3.6	4.35	2.6	3.55	7.25	6.4	5.3	4.5	5.0	5.2	4.9	4.	1.9	1.25	2.65	6.75	6.9	3.75	6.3	1.	1.6	1.75	1.3	1.3
†Seminole.	456	2.3	3.8	3.95	4.7	4.2	5.05	4.7	4.95	4.8	4.7	4.7	4.4	4.8	4.6	4.25	4.1	3.8	4.45	2.9	3.4	6.8	6.25	5.6	5.3	5.8	5.7	5.1	1.85	1.5	2.65	7.	6.9	3.25	6.75	1.3	1.95	1.9	1.5	1.6
†Seminole.	22	604	2.2	3.25	3.85	4.5	4.6	5.	4.8	4.95	4.8	4.7	4.4	4.4	4.9	4.0	4.2	4.1	3.3	4.3	2.7	3.15	7.	5.46	5.45	4.15	4.75	5.55	5.3	4.75	4.4	1.25	2.5	7.2	6.9	3.6	6.6	1.45	2.1	1.8	1.3	1.9
†Seminole.	707	2.3	3.5	4.05	4.7	4.7	5.2	4.9	5.25	5.1	4.65	4.8	4.65	5.	4.55	4.	3.9	3.35	4.3	2.7	3.2	7.2	6.6	5.65	4.75	5.85	5.3	5.	4.55	2.	2.35	7.1	7.	3.6	7.1	1.3	1.8	1.8	1.5	1.4
†Euchee.	30	2.45	3.5	4.	4.9	4.7	4.95	4.75	5.	4.9	1.0	4.7	4.4	4.85	4.3	3.95	3.9	3.25	4.7	2.7	3.65	6.75	6.35	5.45	4.7	5.2	5.85	5.05	4.25	1.75	2.05	6.7	6.75	3.5	6.25	1.5	1.75	1.6	1.2	1.6
†Muskogee.	441	2.2	3.55	3.85	4.75	4.65	5.2	5.	5.05	4.9	4.7	4.4	4.7	4.85	4.3	3.95	3.9	3.25	4.4	2.8	3.5	7.	6.25	5.45	5.2	5.4	5.45	5.1	1.75	1.	2.5	6.75	6.45	3.65	6.9	1.4	1.85	1.85	1.4	1.6
†Muskogee.	26	579	3.7	3.45	3.7	4.05	4.45	4.9	4.7	4.85	4.75	4.7	4.5	4.8	4.9	4.0	4.2	4.05	3.05	1.85	3.	3.4	6.4	5.7	5.7	5.05	5.86	5.05	4.5	1.9	1.2	2.6	7.1	7.2	3.5	6.5	1.1	1.6	1.5	1.25	1.4
Chetimaches.	19	70	2.35	3.4	3.7	4.05	4.15	5.	4.85	5.	4.9	4.7	4.7	4.65	5.	4.23	3.75	4.3	3.75	4.6	3.	2.05	6.8	6.1	5.6	4.3	5.5	5.3	4.95	4.25	1.75	2.65	6.75	6.8	3.6	6.6	1.3	1.65	1.65	1.3	1.45
Chetimaches.	43	2.2	3.6	3.05	4.8	4.5	5.2	4.9	5.1	4.95	4.7	4.7	4.65	4.75	4.4	3.85	4.1	3.4	1.5	3.4	3.45	6.5	5.95	5.45	4.3	5.35	6.1	4.8	4.25	1.75	2.25	6.95	6.5	3.7	6.6	1.3	1.8	1.7	1.4	1.6
Cherokee.	634	2.4	3.7	4.1	4.7	4.5	4.9	4.6	4.9	4.9	4.65	4.35	4.05	4.75	4.0	3.35	4.05	2.9	4.1	2.5	3.2	6.95	6.6	5.2	4.8	6.15	5.	4.55	4.3	1.65	2.5	6.6	6.5	3.25	6.3	1.1	1.8	1.8	1.45	1.6
Cherokee.	632	2.45	3.8	4.25	4.85	4.75	4.9	4.75	4.85	4.65	4.55	4.55	4.	4.6	4.7	4.5	4.1	3.	4.35	2.55	3.3	6.95	6.7	5.06	4.55	5.2	5.1	4.7	4.2	1.55	2.3	6.95	6.75	3.5	6.25	1.15	1.7	1.65	1.3	1.5
†Cayuga.	35	417	2.5	3.8	4.3	4.7	4.5	4.95	4.85	4.75	4.65	4.6	4.35	4.7	4.7	4.55	4.1	4.3	3.15	4.4	2.55	3.3	7.3	6.8	5.	4.23	5.4	5.2	4.65	4.2	2.05	2.5	6.75	6.7	3.7	5.75	1.	1.3	1.4	1.1	1.25
†Oneyda.	33	2.5	3.7	4.1	4.8	4.6	5.15	4.8	5.	4.9	4.8	4.8	4.6	4.95	4.7	4.3	4.3	3.2	4.5	2.7	3.6	7.6	6.8	6.5	4.25	5.5	5.3	4.95	4.3	1.85	1.05	2.8	6.7	6.6	3.5	6.05	1.1	1.8	1.7	1.3	1.6
†Huron.	27	15	2.3	3.66	4.05	4.5	4.4	4.76	4.45	4.7	4.55	4.4	4.3	3.05	3.1	4.05	4.3	3.2	4.1	2.0	3.2	7.5	6.8	5.75	4.8	5.25	5.4	4.7	4.3	1.7	1.4	2.5	6.3	6.7	3.4	5.0	1.05	1.5	1.5	1.1	1.35
Iroquois.	16	2.5	4.1	4.15	4.35	4.7	5.05	4.9	5.	4.7	4.6	4.4	4.05	4.2	4.15	4.15	3.2	2.0	3.7	7.7	0.95	5.35	4.9	5.36	5.4	4.9	4.45	1.75	1.25	2.05	7.05	6.95	3.6	6.6	1.2	1.75	1.85	1.5	1.5
Mingo.	455	2.	3.6	2.0	4.5	4.35	4.8	4.6	4.9	4.55	4.4	4.55	4.2	4.75	4.55	4.25	4.	2.3	7.15	6.66	5.45	4.7	5.45	6.6	5.5	5.06	4.35	1.85	1.25	2.5	7.05	6.95	3.15	6.55	1.3	1.75	1.8	1.5	1.5
†Osage.	54	3.	2.1	2.3	4.6	4.8	4.7	4.9	4.9	4.8	4.7	4.5	4.8	4.5	4.15	4.05	3.4	2.5	4.4	4.75	4.9	4.75	4.1	5.35	4.8	5.7	5.3	4.4	2.05	1.2	2.6	6.9	6.5	3.6	6.3	1.2	1.55	1.6	1.2	1.4
Osage.	660	2.25	3.3	3.8	4.7	4.5	4.9	4.65	4.9	4.75	4.05	4.0	4.4	4.9	4.75	4.45	4.1	3.05	4.35	2.55	3.33	6.1	6.85	5.3	4.4	5.3	5.15	4.75	1.8	1.25	2.5	7.7	7.45	3.45	6.6	1.15	1.65	1.65	1.35	1.45
Mandan.	643	2.1	2.53.	3.8	4.75	4.5	4.8	4.55	4.75	4.65	4.6	4.15	4.7	4.5	4.15	4.5	4.15	3.9	2.1	2.5	3.25	7.15	6.75	6.35	4.25	5.4	5.05	4.85	4.1	1.75	1.	2.45	7.1	7.	3.1	6.9	1.25	1.9	1.9	1.6	1.3

The foregoing Table comprises the measurements of 100 unaltered crania of adult aboriginal Americans: those marked thus † are crania actually ascertained to be males, and by far the greater part of the rest have all the appearance of being males also. In correcting so great a number of measurements and results, (about 7500 in all the Tables,) some errors escaped notice in the last revision of part of the proofs; but the mean and extreme numbers, were obtained from a copy of the Tables corrected after the first four pages had been printed. For the errors see *Errata*.

The two following Tables contain the measurements of American crania artificially moulded; and the last those of four Eskimaux, given for the purpose of comparison.

TABLE OF PHRENOLOGICAL MEASUREMENTS—Continued.

NATIONS AND TRIBES.	Plate.	No. in Catalogue.	Amativeness.	Philoprogenitiveness.	Adhesiveness.	Self-esteem.	Approbativeness.	Firmness.	Conscientiousness.	Hope.	Veneration.	Marvellousness.	Ideality.	Benevolence.	Causality.	Individuality.	Order.	Secretiveness.	Cautiousness.	Destructiveness.	Combativeness.	Individuality to philoprogenitiveness.	Comparison to concentrativeness.	Cautiousness to cautiousness.	Ideality to ideality.	Secretiveness to secretiveness.	Destructiveness to destructiveness.	Combativeness to combativeness.	Constructiveness to constructiveness.	Causality to causality.	Supra orbitar ridge to cautiousness.	Mean-temporal line.	Inter-sphenoid arch over reflective organs.	Inter-sphenoid arch over perceptive organs.	Brain to caution.	Arch from caution to caution.	Reverence.	Veneration.	Firmness.	Conscientiousness.	Hope.
Flathead of Columbia river.																																										
Cowalitsk.	49	573	2.1	4.2	4.5	4.75	4.8	4.55	4.5	4.2	4.05	3.75	3.75	3.7	3.7	3.6	3.2	4.5	2.7	3.8	6.55	5.75	5.75	4.75	6.	5.4	5.05	4.75	1.9	1.3	2.3	6.35	6.4	3.9	6.3	.55	.9	1.	.8	.8
Clatsap.	46	575	2.05	3.55	4.	4.95	5.	4.9	5.	4.6	4.5	4.25	4.		4.1	3.8	3.4	4.65	2.75	3.65	6.25	5.9	5.2	4.8	5.05	5.5	5.85	4.65	2.	1.25	2.3	6.4	6.25	3.6	6.5	.75	1.2	1.25	1.05	.95
Khisioni.	44	577	1.95	3.	3.75	4.55	4.55	4.9	4.7	4.6	4.4	4.1	3.8	3.8	4.	4.25	3.3	4.2	2.65	3.55	6.05	5.75	5.55	4.45	5.85	5.3	6.2	6.9	2.	1.25	2.2	6.45	6.25	3.4	6.75	.9	1.4	1.5	1.1	1.15
Kinpooynh.	47	574	2.2	3.3	3.8	4.2	4.85	4.8	4.8	4.4	4.4	4.3	4.25	4.3	4.2	4.15	3.85	3.85	3.5	3.8	6.45	6.7	5.75	4.65	5.55	5.6	6.2	6.9	1.85	1.5	2.5	6.83	6.9	3.7	6.75	.9	1.2	1.1	1.	1.05
Clickitat.	48	461	2.05	3.25	3.8	4.5	4.45	4.6	4.4	4.55	4.25	4.15	4.	3.9	4.15	3.8	3.85	3.3	2.9	3.6	6.5	5.75	5.45	4.7	5.75	5.3	5.75	4.95	1.9	1.3	2.45	6.55	6.55	3.	6.55	1.85	1.4	1.5	1.2	1.2
Chinouk.		781	2.3	3.4	4.	4.5	4.7	4.6	4.65	4.2	4.	3.9			4.05	3.8	3.7	3.7	2.75	3.7	6.45	5.5	5.8	4.6	6.	5.6	6.	4.95	1.9	1.4	2.35	6.75	6.6	3.6	7.	1.	1.35	1.4	1.1	1.1
Chinouk.	43	462	2.1	3.2	3.95	4.6	4.65	4.7	4.8	4.4	4.05	4.		4.1	3.95	3.55	3.75	3.2	2.7	3.6	6.4	5.75	5.75	4.4	5.85	5.3	5.55	6.	1.85	1.25	2.35	6.6	6.6	3.6	6.55	.9	1.3	1.5	1.15	1.05
Killemook.	42	578	2.1	3.7	4.3	5.3	5.2	5.4	5.25	5.	4.95	4.65	4.3	4.5	4.1	3.95	3.05	3.75	3.25	2.85	6.5	5.9	6.15	4.05	6.	5.65	6.	4.9	1.9	1.4	2.6	6.4	6.5	3.8	7.6	1.1	1.65	1.83	1.5	1.5
		Mean.	2.14	3.45	4.05	4.67	4.77	4.8	4.73	4.5	4.38	4.14		4.07	4.14	3.93	3.8	3.74	3.3	4.4	2.75	3.66	6.30	5.78	5.74	4.65	5.95	5.47	5.45	4.75	1.89	1.31	2.38	6.54	6.54	3.51	6.74	.97	1.3	1.39	1.11	1.1
Ancient Peruvians.	4	67	2.3	4.	4.4	6.1	5.	5.1	4.85	4.7	4.45	4.25	4.05	4.1	4.45	4.15	3.6	3.6	4.4	2.5	3.3	7.25	6.4	5.2	3.85	5.25	5.1	5.1	4.15	2.	1.3	2.35	6.2	6.45	3.05	6.6	1.1	1.65	1.8	1.4	1.3
	3	P.	2.2	3.6	4.1	5.	4.9	5.1	4.9	4.6	4.5	4.2		4.	4.5	3.8	3.8	3.6	3.5	3.5	6.15	5.9	5.15	2.75	3.75	6.	5.05	4.1	1.6	1.15	2.3	6.05	6.3	3.75	6.5	1.2	1.6	1.8	1.3	1.3
		Mean.	2.27	3.8	4.2	5.05	4.97	5.1	4.87	4.7	4.52	4.15		4.05	4.5	4.05	3.9	3.7	3.7	3.05	4.4	2.69	3.5	7.25	6.15	5.17	3.8	6.25	5.05	5.07	4.13	1.7	1.22	2.32	6.12	6.37	3.7	6.55	1.15	1.63	1.35	1.	1.3
Mongol-Americans.																																									
Eskiman.	70-1		2.4	3.8	4.35	4.85	4.75	5.	4.65	4.9	4.55	4.55	4.5	4.95	1.55	4.2	4.	3.3	4.35	2.55	3.2	7.46	6.85	5.2	4.4	5.45	5.1	4.8	4.3	1.9	1.5	2.5	7.25	7.	3.85	5.5	1.2	1.55	1.6	1.1	1.2
Eskiman.	70-2		2.15	3.65	4.25	4.6	4.65	4.8	4.6	4.6	4.5	4.45	4.5	4.25	4.05	3.25	4.	3.6	4.4	2.65	3.5	7.3	6.3	5.05	4.15	5.5	5.3	4.7	4.	2.1	1.6	2.9	7.1	7.5	3.9	5.5	1.	1.45	1.5	1.05	1.05
Eskiman.	70-3		2.2	3.7	4.3	5.	4.8	4.8	4.7	5.	4.6	4.5	4.5	4.2	4.8	4.55	4.1	3.35	4.3	2.4	3.4	7.4	6.95	5.	4.4	5.1	4.8	4.6	4.2	1.75	1.35	2.55	6.5	6.65	3.75	5.8	1.	1.5	1.7	1.2	1.15
Eskiman.	70-4		2.7	3.8	4.15	4.65	4.4	4.6	4.35	4.4	4.2	4.1	4.1	4.	4.4	4.1	3.8	2.7	4.	2.45	3.2	6.7	5.75	4.4	4.5	5.	4.8	4.8	4.3	1.8	1.4	2.3	6.4	6.3	3.5	5.5	.9	1.3	1.5	1.	1.1
		Mean.	2.36	3.74	4.26	4.77	4.65	4.85	4.57	4.73	4.49	4.	4.21	4.72	4.44	4.00	3.9	3.19	4.26	2.51	3.3	7.21	6.46	4.91	4.36	5.26	5.	4.72	4.2	1.89	1.46	2.56	6.81	6.86	3.75	5.59	1.02	1.45	1.57	1.09	1.12

APPENDIX.

Phrenological Remarks on the relation between the natural Talents and Dispositions of Nations, and the Developments of their Brains. By GEORGE COMBE, Esq.*

No object can be presented to the philosophic mind more replete with interest than an inquiry into the causes of the differences of national character. If the causes be natural, do they originate in the organisation of the body, in the development of the brain, in the influence of climate, or on what other physical agents do they depend? If the differences result solely from moral and political circumstances, it is important to trace their nature and modes of operation.

This subject has been investigated by philosophers in general, without any knowledge of, or reference to, the functions of the different parts of the brain. Phrenologists have avoided this error, and have pointed out and pursued a more perfect method of investigation; but they have not published any separate work devoted exclusively to this inquiry. In presenting the following remarks, I aim only at enabling the reader to observe the relative magnitudes of the whole brain, and the relative proportions of the different parts of the brain, indicated by the national skulls delineated by Dr. Morton, and to draw his own conclusions relative to the influence of these on the natural talents and dispositions of the tribes.

---

* Dr. Morton has requested me to furnish the present contribution to his work entitled *Crania Americana*. As I have been greatly pleased with the correctness, as well as the beauty of the lithographic drawings, many of which I have compared with the original skulls; and as I have every reason to expect that the text will equal, in intrinsic value, the workmanship of the plates, I supply the present brief remarks with all the satisfaction that can be felt in presenting to the public so imperfect a sketch. It is proper to mention, that before I arrived in America Dr. Morton had entered into definite arrangements for the publication of his work, by which limits were prescribed both to the number of plates and extent of the letter press, in consequence of which it was not in his power to alter, or in mine to procure a greater space than is occupied by the following observations. I refer the reader to my own *System of Phrenology* for more detailed information, towards the end of which there is a section on National Skulls.

I prepare this memoir without having the advantage of seeing Dr. Morton's descriptions of the natural characters of the different Indian Races. These are not yet printed. The harmony or discord between his historical delineations, and the phrenological inductions which the reader will be enabled to draw by applying the rules now to be laid down, will depend on the degree of approximation of each to nature. Where discrepancies shall appear, one or other of our views must be erroneous. I solicit the reader candidly to investigate both representations, and not to condemn phrenology at once as chargeable exclusively with error. Imperfect historical descriptions have been given of distant nations, and particularly of barbarous and savage tribes, whose manners have been imperfectly observed, and whose language has been scarcely at all comprehended; and it may ultimately be discovered, that the characteristics indicated by the size and forms of their brains have been more correct than the hasty impressions of travellers.

The favorite opinion with philosophers has been, "That the capacities of the human mind have been, in all ages, the same; and that the diversity of phenomena exhibited by our species, is the result merely of the different circumstances in which men are placed." "This," says Dugald Stewart,* "has long been received as an uncontrovertible logical maxim; or rather, such is the influence of early instruction, that we are apt to regard it as one of the most obvious suggestions of common sense. And yet, till about the time of Montesquieu, it was by no means so generally recognised by the learned as to have a sensible influence on the fashionable tone of thinking over Europe."

There is some ambiguity in this passage. The proposition, that the "capacities of the human mind have been in all ages the same," does not necessarily imply that they have been *alike* in all nations. The Hindoo mind may have been the same in the year 100 as in the year 1800, and so may the English and all other national minds; but it does not follow that either in the year 100 or 1800 the English and Hindoo minds were constituted by nature equal in all their capacities; yet this is what I understand Mr. Stewart to mean: for he adds, "that the diversity of phenomena exhibited by our species, is the result *merely of the different circumstances* in which men are placed;" embracing, in this proposition, men of every nation as equally gifted in mental power. There is reason to question this doctrine, and to view it as not merely speculatively erroneous, but as laying the foundation of much hurtful practice.

When we regard the different quarters of the globe, we are struck with the

* Dissertation prefixed to Encyclop. Britt. p. 53.

extreme dissimilarity in the attainments of the varieties of men who inhabit them. If we glance over the history of Europe, Asia, Africa, and America, we shall find distinct and permanent features of character which strongly indicate natural differences in their mental constitutions. The inhabitants of Europe, belonging to the Caucasian variety of mankind, have manifested, in all ages, a strong tendency towards moral and intellectual improvement. As far back as history reaches, we find society instituted, arts practised, and literature taking root, not only in intervals of tranquillity, but amidst the alarms of war. Before the foundation of Rome, the Etruscans had established civilisation and the arts in Italy. Under the Greek and Roman empires, philosophy, literature, and the fine arts were sedulously and successfully cultivated; and that portion of the people whose wealth enabled them to pay for education, attained a high degree of intelligence and refinement. By the irruption of the northern hordes, these countries were subsequently involved in a chaos of ignorance;—but again the sun of science rose, the clouds of Gothic darkness were dispelled, and Europe took the lead of the world in science, morals, and philosophy. In the inhabitants of this portion of the globe, there appears an elasticity of mind incapable of being permanently repressed. Borne down for a time by external violence, their mental energies seem to have gathered strength under the restraint, and at length to have burst their fetters, and overcome every obstacle opposed to their expansion.

While these remarks are strictly correct in regard to the Teutonic race in Europe, varieties also of mental aptitude have been displayed by other tribes inhabiting that region of the globe. In France, Ireland and Scotland, the Celtic race remains far behind the Teutonic in the arts, sciences, philosophy and civilisation.

When we turn our attention to Asia, we perceive manners and institutions which belong to a period too remote to be ascertained, and yet far inferior to the European standard. The people of Asia early arrived at a point comparatively low in the scale of improvement, beyond which they have never passed.

The history of Africa, so far as Africa can be said to have a history, presents similar phenomena. The annals of the races who have inhabited that continent, with few exceptions, exhibit one unbroken scene of moral and intellectual desolation; and in a quarter of the globe embracing the greatest varieties of soil and climate, no nation is at this day to be found whose institutions indicate even moderate civilisation. Some of the African tribes, however, have advanced beyond the savage condition. They have cities, rude manufactures, agriculture, commerce, government and laws; and in these respects they greatly excel several of the tribes of native Americans, who have continued wandering savages from the beginning to the end of their existence.

The aspect of America is still more deplorable than that of Africa. Surrounded for centuries by European knowledge, enterprise, and energy, and incited to improvement by the example of European institutions, many of the natives of that continent remain, at the present time, the same miserable, wandering, houseless and lawless savages as their ancestors were, when Columbus first set foot upon their soil. Partial exceptions to this description may be found in some of the southern districts of North America; but the numbers who have adopted the modes of civilised life are so small, and the progress made by them so limited, that speaking of the race, we do not exaggerate in saying, that they remain to the present hour enveloped in all their primitive savageness, and that they have profited extremely little by the introduction amongst them of arts, sciences and philosophy. The same observations have occurred to a writer in the Edinburgh Review. The following remarks on the native American character appeared in that work in an article on "Howison's Upper Canada," in June 1822.—"From all that we learn," says the reviewer, "of the state of the aborigines of this great continent from this volume, and from every other source of information, it is evident that they are making no advances towards civilisation. It is certainly a striking and mysterious fact, that a race of men should thus have continued for ages stationary in a state of the rudest barbarism. That tendency to improvement, a principle that has been thought more than perhaps any other to distinguish man from the lower animals, would seem to be totally wanting in them. Generation after generation passes away, and no traces of advancement distinguish the last from the first. The mighty wilderness they inhabit may be traversed from end to end, and hardly a vestige be discovered that marks the hand of man. It might naturally have been expected, that in the course of ages, some superior genius would have arisen among them to inspire his countrymen with a desire to cultivate the arts of peace, and establish some durable civil institutions; or that, at least during the long period since the Europeans have been settled amongst them, and taught them, by such striking examples, the benefits of industry and social order, they would have been tempted to endeavor to participate in blessings thus providentially brought within their reach. But all has been unavailing; and it now seems certain that the North American Indians, like the bears and wolves, are destined to flee at the approach of civilised man, and to fall before his renovating hand, and disappear from the face of the earth along with those ancient forests which alone afford them sustenance and shelter."

The theory usually advanced to account for these differences of national character is, that they are produced by diversities of soil and climate. But, although these may reasonably be supposed to exert a certain influence, they are altogether inadequate to explain the whole phenomena. We ought ever to bear in mind, that Nature is constant in her operations, and that the same causes invariably produce the same effects. Hence, when we find exceptions in result without being able to assign differences in causes, we may rest assured that we have not found the true or the only cause; and our diligence ought to be quickened to obtain new light, and not employed in maintaining the sufficiency of that which we possess.

If we survey a map of the world, we shall find nations whose soil is fertile and climate temperate, in a lower degree of improvement than others who are less favored. In Van Diemen's Land and New South Wales, a few natives have existed in the most wretched poverty, ignorance and degradation, in a country that enriches Europeans as fast as they possess it. In America, too, Europeans and native Indians have lived for centuries under the influence of the same physical causes; the former have kept pace in their advances with their brethren on the old continent, while the latter, as we have seen, remain stationary in savage ignorance and indolence.

Such differences are not confined to the great continents alone; but different tribes in the same hemisphere seem to possess different degrees of native minds, and these remain unchanged through numerous ages. Tacitus describes the Gauls as gay, volatile, and precipitate, prone to rush to action, but without the power of sustaining adversity and the tug of strife; and this is the character of the Celtic portion of the French nation down to the present day. He represents the Britons as cool, considerate, and sedate, possessed of intellectual talent, and says that he prefers their native aptitude to the livelier manners of the Gauls. The same mental qualities characterise the English of the nineteenth century, and they and the French may still be contrasted in similar terms.

Tacitus describes the Germans, allowing for their state of civilisation, as a bold, prudent, self-denying, and virtuous people, possessed of great force of character; and the same features distinguish them still. The native Irishman, in manners, dispositions and capacities, is a being widely different from the lowland Scotchman; and if we trace the two nations to the remotest antiquity, the same characteristic differences are found.

These differences between nations living under similar climates, are commonly attributed entirely to the religious and political institutions of the several countries. Presbytery and parish schools, for example, are supposed to have rendered the Scotchman habitually attentive to his own interest; cautious, thoughtful, and honest: while Popery and Catholic priests have made the Irishman free and generous withal, but precipitate and unreflecting—ready in the gust of passion to sacrifice his friend, and in the glow of friendship to immolate himself. It is forgotten that there were ages in which popery and priests had equal ascendancy in all the British isles; and that the Englishman, Irishman, and Scotchman, were beings as specifically distinct then as at present: besides, the more correct, as well as the more profound view, is to regard religious and political institutions, when not forced upon a people by external conquest, as the spontaneous growth of their natural propensities, sentiments and intellectual faculties. Hierarchies and constitutions do not spring from the ground, but from the minds of men. If we suppose one nation to be gifted with much wonder and veneration, and little conscientiousness, reflection and self-esteem; and another to possess an endowment exactly the reverse; it is obvious that the first would be naturally prone to superstition in religion, and servility in the state; while the second would, by native instinct, resist all attempts to make them reverence things unholy, and tend constantly towards political institutions, fitted to afford to each individual the gratification of his self-esteem in independence, and his conscientiousness in equality before the law. Those who contend that institutions came first, and that character follows as their effect, are bound to assign a cause for the institutions themselves. If they do not spring from the native mind, and are not forced on the people by conquest, it is difficult to see whence they can originate.

The phrenologist is not satisfied with these common theories of national character; he has observed that a particular size and form of brain is the invariable concomitant of particular dispositions and talents, and that this fact holds good in the case of nations as well as of individuals.

If this view be correct, a knowledge of the size of the brain, and the proportions of its different parts, in the different varieties of the human race, will be the key to a correct appreciation of the differences in their natural mental endowments, on which external circumstances act only as modifying influences. Such, accordingly, is the light in which I regard this great subject. If the size of the brain and the proportions of its different parts be the index to natural national character, the present work, which represents with great fidelity the skulls of the American tribes, will be an authentic record in which the philosopher may read the native aptitudes, dispositions and mental force of these families of mankind. If this doctrine be unfounded, these skulls are mere facts in Natural History, presenting no particular information as to the mental qualities of the people.

In applying phrenology to the elucidation of character as indicated by national skulls, the most important points to be attended to are the following.

1st. To judge of the *size* of the whole brain. This is indicated by the dimensions of the skull. Magendie, in his Compendium of Physiology, says that "the only way of estimating the *volume of the brain*, in a living person, is to *measure the dimensions of the skull;* every other means, even that proposed by Camper, is uncertain." (Milligan's Translation, p. 104.) Sir Charles Bell observes, "that the bones of the head are moulded to the brain, and the peculiar shapes of the bones of the head are determined by the original peculiarity in the shape of the brain." (Bell's Anatomy, II, p. 390.) Dr. Gordon, in the forty-ninth Number of the Edinburgh Review, admits that "there is in most instances, a general correspondence between the size of the cranium, and the quantity of cerebrum; that large heads usually contain large brains, and small heads small brains." (p. 246.)

The size of the national skulls indicates the dimensions of the brains which they contained. The influence of size in the brain on national character may be judged of from the following facts.

First. The brain of a child is small, and its mind is weak. As the brain grows in size and attains to maturity in structure, the mental manifestations increase in vigor.

Secondly. A small brain is *one* but not the only cause of idiocy. A brain may be enlarged by disease and idiocy ensue; but if this organ be too small, although it be healthy in structure, idiocy is an invariable consequence. Phrenologists have in vain called on their opponents to produce a single instance of the mind being manifested vigorously by a very small brain.

Dr. Gall has laid it down as a fact, to which there is no exception, that where the brain is so small that the horizontal circumference of the head does not exceed thirteen or fourteen inches, idiocy is the invariable consequence. "Complete intelligence," he remarks, "is absolutely impossible with so small a brain; in such cases idiocy, more or less complete, invariably occurs, and to this rule no exception either has been, or ever will be found." To the same effect, Dr. Spurzheim, in his work on Insanity, says: "We are very well aware that a great number of facts, repeated under various circumstances, are necessary before we can draw a general conclusion; but with respect to idiotism from birth, we have made such a number of observations in various countries, that we have no hesitation in affirming that a too small brain is unfit for the manifestation of the mind. I beg to remark, that I do not say that idiotism is the attribute of a too small brain only; idiotism may be the result of different causes, one of which is a too small brain. We are convinced from observation, that the laws of nature are constant; and if we continually observe that the same phenomenon takes place under the same circumstances, we consider our conclusion as certain, till experience shows the contrary. No one, then, has the right to maintain that an inference is too hastily drawn because he has not made a sufficient number of observations. It is his duty to show facts which prove the contrary, if he intend to deny the inference." In the Journal of the Phrenological Society of Paris, for April 1835, Dr. Voisin reports observations made upon the idiots under his care at the Parisian Hospital of Incurables, in order to verify the assertion of Dr. Gall in the passage just quoted; and mentions that he found it substantiated by every one of his cases. In the lowest class of idiots, where the intellectual manifestations were null, the horizontal circumference, taken a little higher than the orbit, varied from eleven to thirteen inches, while the distance from the root of the nose backwards over the top of the head to the occipital spine was only between eight and nine inches. When the size varied from fourteen to seventeen inches of horizontal measurement, and eleven or twelve in the other direction, glimpses of feelings and random intellectual perceptions were observable, but without any power of attention or fixity of ideas. Lastly, when the first measurement extended to eighteen or nineteen inches, although the head was still small, the intellectual manifestations were regular enough, but deficient in intensity. In a full sized head, the first measurement is equal to twenty-two inches, and the second to about fourteen inches. So large was the head of Spurzheim, that even on the skull these two measurements amounted to $22\frac{1}{4}$ and $13\frac{5}{10}$ inches respectively.

Thirdly. Individuals and nations distinguished for great aggregate force of mind, animal, moral and intellectual, have had large brains. King Robert Bruce, Napoleon, Cuvier, Canova, Burns the poet, Dr. Gall and Dr. Spurzheim, among men, and the Teutonic race compared with the Hindoo among nations, may be cited as examples.

I do not adduce these observations as *evidence* to *prove* the influence of size in the brain on the power with which the faculties of the mind are manifested, but merely as a statement of the proposition that such influence exists. The subject will be found more fully expounded in my System of Phrenology, in which also the influence of temperament, health, and exercise, in modifying the

APPENDIX.

effects of size, is explained; because the correct phrenological proposition is, that other conditions being equal, the size of each organ is an indication of the vigor of the mental faculty which it manifests. In examining national *crania*, we are not informed of the temperament and education of the individuals, but left to judge of the natural character chiefly by the size of the brain and the proportions of its different parts. Our additional information rarely extends beyond the condition in which the tribes existed, viz: whether they were savages, barbarians, or civilised. I shall, for these reasons, confine my remarks chiefly to the size of the skulls, and to the proportions of their different regions.

According to these views, the aggregate natural mental power, (animal, moral, and intellectual,) of the individuals composing any nation, will (other conditions being equal) be great or small in proportion to the size of their brains. Plate LXXI represents a Swiss skull, of average size, part of the collection of the Phrenological Society of Edinburgh. I have visited Switzerland and seen many skulls of that people, and this one appears to me to represent fairly the average characteristics. History informs us that in a rude age, before modern civilisation was established, this people, in a wild and inhospitable country, displayed extraordinary mental vigor (animal, moral and intellectual,) in vindicating and maintaining civil and religious liberty; and we know that the same character continues to distinguish them in the present day. They may here be assumed as a specimen of a powerful race, to serve as a standard by which to compare the skulls of the other tribes represented in this work.

The measurements of this Swiss skull, as taken by Dr. Morton and Mr. Phillips, are as follow:

Amativeness,	2.7	Order,		4.2
Philoprogenitiveness,	3.6	Secretiveness,		3.45
Adhesiveness,	4.4	Cautiousness,		4.55
Self-esteem,	4.8	Destructiveness,		2.85
Approbativeness,	4.7	Combativeness,		3.45
Firmness,	5.5	Individuality to philoprogenitiveness,		7.2
Conscientiousness,	4.9	Comparison to concentrativeness,		6.7
Veneration,	5.	Cautiousness to cautiousness,		5.55
Hope,	4.8	Ideality to ideality,		4.75
Marvellousness,	4.9	Secretiveness to secretiveness,		6.
Ideality,	4.5	Destructiveness to destructiveness,		5.4
Benevolence,	5.	Combativeness to combativeness,		5.3
Causality,	4.8	Constructiveness to constructiveness,		4.6
Individuality,	4.4	Causality to causality,		2.1

Supra-orb. foramen to causality,	-	1.5	Arch from caution to caution,	-	6.5
Meato-temporal line, -	-	2.65	Benevolence, -	-	1.3
Inter-sphenoidal line over reflecting organs, - - - -		7.8	Veneration, -	-	1.6
			Firmness, -	-	1.7
Inter-sphenoidal line over perceptive organs, - - - -		7.8	Conscientiousness,	-	1.3
			Hope, -	-	1.2
Meatus to cautiousness, -	-	3.8			

(Height above plane passing through centres of caution and causality.)

The internal capacity of this skull is 95.5 cubic inches; the capacity of the coronal region 21.25 cubic inches; facial angle, 87°.

On comparing these measurements with those of the American skulls as exhibited in Dr. Morton's tables, the differences will be seen: or by comparing the dimensions of this Swiss skull as they appear to the eye in the plate, with those of the other skulls delineated in this work, all being drawn as large as nature, their relative proportions will become apparent.

As, however, different parts of the brain manifest different mental faculties, the *second* object in studying national crania is to judge of the size of the different parts of the brain in relation to each other. This is indispensable to a correct elucidation of mental character as indicated by the brain; but the limits to which I am confined prevent me from entering into minute detail. I, therefore, confine myself to a few directions for estimating the size of each of the three great regions of the brain—that which is the seat of the intellectual faculties; that which is the seat of the moral and religious sentiments; and that which is the seat of the animal propensities, and of the sentiments common to man and the lower animals.

1st. The anterior lobe of the brain is the seat chiefly of the intellectual powers. The lower ridge, and the middle perpendicular portion, manifest the faculties which observe objects that exist, their qualities, actions, and physical relations. The upper anterior ridge manifests the powers which compare, reflect, estimate causes, and draw inferences. The superior *horizontal* portion of the anterior lobe manifests some of the moral sentiments.

The anterior lobe rests on the super-orbitar plates, and these plates indicate its *breadth* from side to side, and its length from front to back. The *breadth* can be estimated by means of callipers applied to the exterior of the skull, at the point where the super-orbitar plate reaches each side, A, Plate LXXI. The *length* of the super-orbitar plate, and of the anterior lobe, from front to back, may be judged of, not with mathematical accuracy, but to a degree closely approximating to truth, by measuring the distance to which the skull extends forward from the point A to B on the superciliary ridge. The point A is located in the middle space between the edge of the suture of the frontal bone and the edge of the squamous suture of the temporal bone, where these two approach nearest to each other, on the plane of the superciliary ridge. On examining a number of open skulls, I find that a line run directly across the skull from the point A on one side, to the corresponding point on the other, on the same level with the superciliary ridges, coincides closely with the transverse posterior margin of the super-orbitar plates. If a perpendicular line be dropped from the point A, when the axis of the eye is parallel to the plane of the horizon, it will be found to coincide closely with the most projecting point of the zygomatic arch; and as this part of the zygomatic arch can be *felt* in the *living* head, it affords a means of appreciating the length of the anterior lobe in living persons. The masks of Napoleon and Canova show very long anterior lobes when measured according to this rule.

The *height* of the anterior lobe, so far as it manifests the intellectual faculties, may be estimated by a line drawn from B on the superciliary ridge, to a point about a quarter of an inch above the centre of ossification of the frontal bone D, Plate LXXI. The point of ossification, D, of the frontal bone corresponds to the centre of the organ of causality on each side.

The space included in D, A, B, denotes the dimensions of the anterior lobe devoted to intellect in the Swiss skull.

The size of the organs devoted to the moral sentiments may be estimated as follows. These organs lie in the coronal region of the head; and when the axis of the eye is parallel with the plane of the horizon, a horizontal line stretched across the forehead at the superior edges of the organs of causality and drawn backward till it touch the superior edges of the organs of cautiousness, would leave all the moral organs above it, and the organs of the propensities common to man and the lower animals, below or behind it. The centre of ossification of each parietal bone, C, is the centre of the organ of cautiousness.

I have drawn a line from the centre of ossification in the frontal bone, D, to the centre of ossification in the parietal bone, C, (the centres of causality and cautiousness respectively,) on the Swiss skull, and assume all the region above this line, or the space included in E, C, D, to manifest the moral sentiments.

The space E, C, F, denotes the seat of the organs of self-esteem, love of approbation, and cautiousness, C being in the centre of cautiousness. These three sentiments are common to man with the lower animals. Self-esteem and love of approbation, take their direction from the predominant faculties with which they are combined in the individual. If we find them combined with a high coronal region, they will assist the moral sentiments. If they be combined with the coronal region small, and the base of the brain (the organs lying below F, C, D,) large, they will give an increased stimulus to the animal feelings.

The following figures will serve as additional illustrations of these measurements.

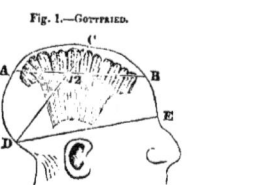
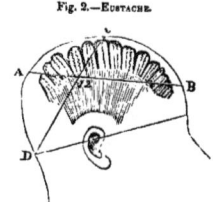

Fig. 1 represents the head of Gesche Margarethe Gottfried, who was executed at Bremen in 1828, for poisining, in cold blood, during a succession of years, both her parents, her three children, her first and second husbands, and about six other individuals.

The line A B commences at the organ of causality B, and passes through the middle of cautiousness, 12. These points are in general sufficiently distinguishable on the skull, and the line can easily be traced. The convolutions lying above the line A B must have been shallow and small, compared with those below, which are devoted to the animal propensities.

Fig. 2 is a sketch of the head of a Negro called Eustache, who was as much distinguished for high morality and practical benevolence, as Gottfried was for deficiency of these qualities. During the massacre of the whites by the Negroes in St. Domingo, Eustache, while in the capacity of a slave, saved, by his address, courage and devotion, the lives of his master and upwards of four hundred other whites, at the daily risk of his own safety. The line A B is drawn from causality B, through cautiousness, 12; and the great size of the convolutions of the moral sentiments may be judged of from the space lying between that line and the top of the head C.

Both of the sketches are drawn from busts, and the convolutions are filled in suppositively for the sake of illustration. The depth of the convolutions, in both cuts, is greater than in nature, that the contrast may be rendered the more perceptible. It will be kept in mind, that I am here merely teaching rules for observing heads, and not proving particular facts. The spaces, however, between the line A B and the top of the head, are accurately drawn to a scale.

APPENDIX. 281

Dr. Abram Cox has suggested, that the size of the convolutions which constitute the organs of self-esteem, love of approbation, concentrativeness, adhesiveness, and philoprogenitiveness, may be estimated by their projection beyond a base formed by a plane passing through the centres of the two organs of cautiousness and the spinous process of the occipital bone. He was led to this conclusion by a minute examination of a great number of the skulls in the collection of the Phrenological Society. A section of this plane is represented by the lines C, D, in Figs. 1 and 2.

To determine the size of the convolutions lying in the lateral regions of the head, Dr. Cox proposes to imagine two vertical planes passing through the organs of causality in each hemisphere, and directly backwards, till each meets the outer border of the point of insertion of the trapezius muscle at the back of the neck. The more the lateral convolutions project beyond these planes, the larger do the organs in the sides of the head appear to be—namely, combativeness, destructiveness, secretiveness, cautiousness, acquisitiveness, and constructiveness; also, to some extent, tune, ideality, wit, and number.

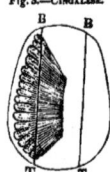 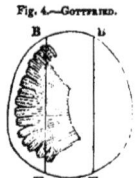

Fig. 3.—CINGALESE.   Fig. 4.—GOTTFRIED.

Fig. 3 represents a horizontal section of the skull of a Cingalese, the lines B T being sections of the planes above described. Fig. 4 represents the same section of the skull of Gottfried, the female poisoner already referred to. The lateral expansion of the head beyond the lines B T in Fig. 4, forms a striking contrast with the size of the same regions in Fig. 3. The Cingalese are a tribe in Ceylon, and in disposition are remarkably mild and pacific.

Dr. Cox suggests farther, that the size of the convolutions lying at the base of the brain, may be estimated by their projection below a plane passing through the superciliary ridges and the occipital spine, (D E, Fig. 1, and D, Fig. 2,) and by observing the distance at which the opening of the ear, the mastoid process, and other points of the base of the skull, lie below that plane.

The number of national crania accessible to any individual is comparatively small, and the conclusions which can be drawn from them must be proportionally imperfect. I, therefore, state the following deductions, not as ascertained scientific results, but as those to which I have been led by such facts as have hitherto fallen under my observation.

1. The *independence* of any tribe or nation, that is to say, its freedom from foreign yoke, is the result of a large development of the organs of self-esteem, firmness, and combativeness or destructiveness, in the majority of the people.

Independence of a foreign yoke may be achieved, *firstly*, by submitting to extermination in preference to subjection; or *secondly*, by successful self-defence.

The former (independence maintained at the expense of existence) is the result of a combination in which the organs of self-esteem, firmness, combativeness and destructiveness are *plus*, and the moral and intellectual organs minus; and the aggregate size of the whole brain is minus, in the nation which is exterminated, compared with that of the nation which attacks it. The Caribs and the Iroquois Indians, (see Plates XXXVII and LXIV,) for example, have never been subdued by the Anglo Saxon race, but have sternly maintained their independence. They, however, have not been able to sustain themselves as independent communities possessing their own territories; but have either been exterminated or removed into distant regions. They have receded before the superior strength, combination, and skill of their invaders, but never bowed the neck and became quietly subject to them. The combination now mentioned occurs in their brains.

Independence secured by successful self-defence, is the accompaniment of an aggregate size of brain, animal, moral and intellectual, equal to that of the invading nation. The Araucanians, (Plates LXVI, LXVII, LXVIII,) in South America, and the Swiss in Europe, (Plate LXXI,) afford examples of this remark.

Permanent subjection to a foreign yoke, is the result of an inferior aggregate development of brain, animal, moral and intellectual, in the people subdued, to that possessed by the conquering tribe; but with the moral and intellectual organs larger in the subdued people in proportion to the organs of combativeness, destructiveness and self-esteem, than they exist in tribes which prefer extermination to submission. The Peruvians and Mexicans, subdued by the Spaniards, and the Hindoos subdued by the British in India, afford examples. In them the aggregate size of the whole brain is less than the aggregate size of the whole brain in the Spaniards and English; but in them also the moral and intellectual regions of the brain are larger in proportion to the animal region, than in the Caribs and the Iroquois Indians. The increased size of the moral and intellectual regions in proportion to the animal region, gives docility, while the deficiency in aggregate size is accompanied by feebleness of character.

Independence accompanied by *civilisation*, is the result of large aggregate size of brain, with the intellectual organs well developed, and the intellectual faculties cultivated.

Independence, civilisation, and *political freedom*, are the results of large aggregate size of brain, the moral and intellectual regions predominating in the majority of the people, aided by long cultivation. This combination characterises the British, Anglo-Americans, and Swiss.

Among the native tribes of North America, the Cherokees and Chippeways have made the greatest advances towards civilisation; and the coronal and intellectual regions in their brains are larger in proportion to that of the animal propensities, than in the brains of the Hurons and other tribes which have constantly receded before the Europeans. These tribes have preserved their independence, and the aggregate size of their brains, including the animal, moral and intellectual regions, is larger than that of the Peruvians of the Inca race, who have submitted to subjection, and larger than that of the Hurons who have resisted subjection, but been exterminated.

As the present work may come into the possession of readers who have not ready access to the common Phrenological works, I subjoin a drawing of the skull having the organs marked on it, Plate LXXI, and a table of the functions of the organs.

The organs are divided into orders and genera as follows:

ORDER I.—FEELINGS.

Genus I. PROPENSITIES—*Common to Man with the Lower Animals.*

*1. AMATIVENESS—produces sexual love.
2. PHILOPROGENITIVENESS.—*Uses:* Affection for young and tender beings.—*Abuses:* Pampering and spoiling children.
3. CONCENTRATIVENESS.—*Uses:* It gives the desire of permanence in place, and renders permanent, emotions and ideas in the mind.—*Abuses:* Aversion to move abroad: morbid dwelling on internal emotions and ideas, to the neglect of external impressions.
4. ADHESIVENESS.—*Uses:* Attachment; friendship and society result from it.

* These numbers refer to the corresponding numbers on Plate LXXI.

—*Abuses:* Clanship for improper objects, attachment to worthless individuals. It is generally strong in women.

5. COMBATIVENESS.—*Uses:* Courage to meet danger and overcome difficulties, tendency to oppose and attack whatever requires opposition, and resist unjust encroachments.—*Abuses:* Love of contention, and tendency to provoke and assault. This feeling obviously adapts man to a world in which danger and difficulty abound.

6. DESTRUCTIVENESS.—*Uses:* Desire to destroy noxious objects, and to kill for food. It is very discernible in carnivorous animals.—*Abuses:* Cruelty, murder, desire to torment, tendency to passion, rage and harshness, and severity in speech and writing. This feeling places man in harmony with death and destruction, which are woven into the system of sublunary creation.

{ THE LOVE OF LIFE.
{ APPETITE FOR FOOD.—*Uses:* Nutrition.—*Abuses:* Gluttony and drunkenness.

7: SECRETIVENESS.—*Uses:* Tendency to restrain within the mind the various emotions and ideas that involuntarily present themselves, until the judgment has approved of giving them utterance; it is simply the propensity to conceal, and is an ingredient in prudence.—*Abuses:* Cunning, deceit, duplicity, and lying.

8. ACQUISITIVENESS.—*Uses:* Desire to possess, and tendency to accumulate articles of utility, to provide against want.—*Abuses:* Inordinate desire of property, selfishness, avarice, theft.

9. CONSTRUCTIVENESS.—*Uses:* Desire to build and construct works of art.—*Abuses:* Construction of engines to injure or destroy, and fabrication of objects to deceive mankind.

Genus II. SENTIMENTS.

I. *Sentiments common to Man and the Lower Animals.*

10. SELF-ESTEEM.—*Uses:* Self-respect, self-interest, love of independence, personal dignity.—*Abuses:* Pride, disdain, overweening conceit, excessive selfishness, love of dominion.

11. LOVE OF APPROBATION.—*Uses:* Desire of the esteem of others, love of praise, desire of fame or glory.—*Abuses:* Vanity, ambition, thirst for praise independently of praise-worthiness.

APPENDIX.

12. CAUTIOUSNESS.—*Uses:* It gives origin to the sentiment of fear, the desire to shun danger, and circumspection; and it is an ingredient in prudence. *Abuses:* Excessive timidity, poltroonery, unfounded apprehensions, despondency, melancholy.
13. BENEVOLENCE.—*Uses:* Desire of the happiness of others, universal charity, mildness of disposition, and a lively sympathy with the enjoyment of all animated beings.—*Abuses:* Profusion, injurious indulgence of the appetites and fancies of others, prodigality, facility of temper.

II. *Sentiments proper to Man.*

14. VENERATION.—*Uses:* Tendency to venerate or respect whatever is great and good; gives origin to religious adoration.—*Abuses:* Senseless respect for unworthy objects consecrated by time or situation, love of antiquated customs, abject subserviency to persons in authority, superstitious awe.
15. FIRMNESS.—*Uses:* Determination, perseverance, steadiness of purpose.—*Abuses:* Stubbornness, infatuation, tenacity in evil.
16. CONSCIENTIOUSNESS.—*Uses:* It gives origin to the sentiment of justice, or respect for the rights of others, openness to conviction, the love of truth.—*Abuses:* Scrupulous adherence to noxious principles when ignorantly embraced, excessive refinement in the views of duty and obligation, excess in remorse or self-condemnation.
17. HOPE.—*Uses:* Tendency to expect future good; it cherishes faith.—*Abuses:* Credulity with respect to the attainment of what is desired, absurd expectations of felicity, not founded on reason.
18. WONDER.—*Uses:* The desire of novelty; admiration of the new, the unexpected, the grand, the wonderful and extraordinary.—*Abuses:* Love of the marvellous and occult; senseless astonishment; belief in false miracles, in prodigies, magic, ghosts, and other supernatural absurdities.—*Note:* Veneration, Hope and Wonder, combined, give the tendency to religion; their abuses produce superstition.
19. IDEALITY.—*Uses:* Love of the beautiful and splendid, desire of excellence, poetic feeling.—*Abuses:* Extravagance and absurd enthusiasm, preference of the showy and glaring to the solid and useful, a tendency to dwell in the regions of fancy, and to neglect the duties of life.
20. WIT.—Gives the feeling of the ludicrous, and disposes to mirth.

21. IMITATION.—Copies the manners, gestures, and actions of others, and appearances in nature generally.

ORDER II.—INTELLECTUAL FACULTIES.

Genus I. *External Senses.*

Genus II. *Knowing Faculties which perceive the Existence and Qualities of External Objects.*

22. INDIVIDUALITY.—Takes cognisance of existence and simple facts.
23. FORM.—Renders man observant of form.
24. SIZE.—Gives the idea of space, and enables us to appreciate dimension and distance.
25. WEIGHT.—Communicates the perception of momentum, weight and resistance; and aids equilibrium.
26. COLORING.—Gives perceptions of colors and their harmonies.

Genus III. *Knowing Faculties which perceive the Relations of External Objects.*

27. LOCALITY.—Gives the idea of direction in space.
28. NUMBER.—Gives the talent for calculation.
29. ORDER.—Communicates love of physical arrangement.
30. EVENTUALITY.—Takes cognisance of occurrences or events.
31. TIME.—Gives rise to the perception of duration.
32. TUNE.—The sense of melody and harmony arises from it.
33. LANGUAGE.—Gives facility in acquiring a knowledge of arbitrary signs to express thoughts, readiness in the use of them, and the power of inventing and recollecting them.

Genus. IV. *Reflecting Faculties which Compare, Judge, and Discriminate.*

34. COMPARISON.—Gives the power of discovering analogies, resemblances, and differences.
35. CAUSALITY.—Traces the dependencies of phenomena, and the relation of cause and effect.

When any organ is deficient in size, the power of manifesting the faculty attached to it is proportionally feeble; when the organ is large, it is powerful.

MODES OF ACTIVITY OF THE FACULTIES.

All the faculties, when active in a due degree, produce actions good—proper—or necessary. Excess of activity and improper direction produce abuses. The smallness of a particular organ is not the cause of its producing abuses. Thus, though the organ of Benevolence be small, this does not produce cruelty. It will be accompanied with indifference to the miseries of others. It may lead to the omission of duties. When one organ is small, abuses may result from another being left without proper direction and restraint. Thus, large Acquisitiveness and Secretiveness, combined with small Conscientiousness, and deficient reflecting faculties, may produce theft. Large Destructiveness, with small Benevolence, may produce cruel and ferocious actions.

Every faculty when in action, from whatever cause, produces the kind of feeling, or forms the kind of ideas, already explained as resulting from its natural constitution.

The PROPENSITIES and SENTIMENTS cannot be excited to activity by a mere act of the will. We cannot conjure up the emotions of fear, compassion, or veneration, by merely willing to experience them. These faculties, however, may enter into action from internal excitement of the organs; and then the desire or emotion which each produces is experienced, whether we will to experience it or not. We have it in our power to permit or restrain the manifestation of them in the action; but we have no option, if the organ be excited, to experience or not to experience the feeling itself. There are times when we feel involuntary emotions of fear, or hope, or awe, arising in us, for which we cannot account; and such feelings depend on the internal activity of the organs of these sentiments.

In the *second* place, these faculties may be called into action independently of the will, by the presentment of the external objects fitted by nature to excite them. When an object in distress is presented, the faculty of benevolence starts into activity, and produces the feelings which depend upon it. In these cases, the power of acting, or of not acting, is dependent on the will; but the power of feeling, or of not feeling, is not so.

In the *third* place, the faculties of which we are now speaking, may be excited to activity, or repressed, *indirectly*, by an effort of the will. Thus, the knowing and reflecting faculties have the function of forming ideas. If these faculties be employed to conceive internally the objects fitted by nature to excite the propensities and sentiments, the latter will start into activity in the same manner, but not in so powerful a degree, as if their appropriate objects were externally present. The vivacity of the feeling, in such cases, will be in proportion to the strength of the conception, and the energy of the propensities and sentiments together. If we conceive inwardly an object in distress, and benevolence be powerful, compassion will be felt, and tears will sometimes flow from the emotion produced. Hence he who has any propensity or sentiment predominantly active from internal excitement, will have his intellect frequently filled with conceptions fitted to gratify it.

These faculties have not the attributes of perception, conception, memory, imagination: they have the attribute of sensation alone; that is to say, when they are active, a sensation or emotion is experienced. Hence sensation is an accompaniment of the activity of all the faculties which feel, and of the nervous system in general; but sensation is no faculty in itself.

The laws of the KNOWING and REFLECTING faculties are different. These faculties form ideas, and perceive relations; they constitute will; and they minister to the gratification of the other faculties which only feel.

1*st*, These faculties, as well as the former, may be active from internal causes, and then the kinds of ideas which they are fitted to form, are presented involuntarily to the mind. The musician feels the notes flowing on him uncalled for. A man in whom Number is powerful and active, calculates by a natural impulse.

2*dly*, These faculties may be excited by the presentment of the external objects fitted to call them into activity; and,

3*dly*, They may be excited to activity by an impulse from the propensities or sentiments.

When excited by the presentment of external objects, the objects are perceived, and this act is called PERCEPTION. Perception is not a separate power, but results from the lowest degree of activity of these faculties; and, if no idea is formed when the object is presented, the individual is destitute of the power of manifesting the faculty whose function is to perceive objects of that kind. Thus, when tones are produced, he who cannot perceive the melody of them, is destitute of the power of manifesting the faculty of tune. Each of Them performs perception in its own sphere.

When these faculties are excited by an act of the will, the ideas which they had previously formed are recalled: this act is named MEMORY, which results from the *activity* of each of these faculties; but it is no faculty in itself. Tune remembers music; Individuality, facts; and so on. Time acting along with any of these faculties gives the impression of the *previous existence* of the ideas recalled, which impression distinguishes Memory from Conception or Imagination.

When these faculties are powerfully active, from internal excitement, the ideas they have previously formed are vividly and rapidly conceived, and the act of forming them, when not associated with the impression of past time, is styled CONCEPTION or IMAGINATION. Each executes conception in its own sphere. When conceptions of absent external objects become vivid and permanent, through disease of the organs, the individual believes in the actual presence of the objects, and is deluded by phantoms or visions. This is the explanation of the cases cited in Dr. Hibbert's work on Apparitions. Great size or disease of the organ of Wonder, contributes especially to this effect.

And, lastly, JUDGMENT, in the philosophical sense, belongs to the reflecting faculties alone. The knowing faculties may be said, in one sense, to judge; as, for example, the faculty of Tune may be agreeably or disagreeably affected, and, in this way, may be said to judge of sounds; but judgment, in the proper sense of the word, is a perception of relation or of fitness, or of the connection between means and an end, and it belongs to the reflecting faculties. These faculties have perception, memory, and imagination also. He who possesses them powerfully, perceives and conceives, remembers and imagines, processes of deduction, or ideas of abstract relations, with great facility.

Practical Judgment in the affairs of life, depends on a harmonious combination of *all* the organs, particularly of the propensities and sentiments, in just proportions. In order to act rightly, it is as necessary to feel correctly as to reason deeply.

ATTENTION is not a faculty of the mind, but merely consists in a vivid application of the faculties which form ideas. Unless an organ be adequately possessed, the objects of which it takes cognisance cannot be attended to by an effort of the will. The intellectual powers are greatly assisted in producing attention by Concentrativeness and Firmness.

ASSOCIATION expresses the mutual influence of the faculties.

The principles of Association must be sought for in the constitution of the faculties, and not in the relations of particular ideas. In using Association as an instrument of artificial memory, we ought to keep always in view, that every individual will associate, with greatest facility, ideas with those particular things which he has the greatest natural facility in perceiving. For example: he who has Number most powerful, will associate words most easily with numbers; he who has Form most powerful, will associate words most easily with shapes; he who has Locality most powerful, will associate words most easily with position;

and he who has Tune most powerful, will associate words most easily with musical notes.

Hence, also, the influence of association on our judgment is easily accounted for. He in whom Veneration is powerful, and to whom the image of a saint has from infancy been presented as an object to be venerated, experiences an instantaneous and involuntary emotion of awe and respect every time the image is presented to him; or a conception of it formed, because it is now a sign which excites in him that feeling, and the latter excludes the reflecting faculties from performing their functions. Hence, until we can break this association, and prevent the conception of the image from operating as a sign to excite the faculty of Veneration into activity, we shall never succeed in bringing his understanding to examine into the real attributes of the object itself, and to perceive its want of every quality that ought justly to be venerated.

Thus, the associations which mislead the judgment and perpetuate prejudices, are associations of words or things with *feelings* or *sentiments*, and not associations merely of ideas with ideas.

PLEASURE and PAIN, and also *Joy* and *Grief*, are affections of the mind arising from the exercise of every faculty. Every faculty, when indulged in its natural action, feels pleasure; when disagreeably affected, feels pain; consequently the kinds of pain and pleasure are as numerous as the faculties.

PASSION is the highest degree of activity of any faculty, and the passions are as different as the faculties: thus, a passion for glory is the result of great energy and activity of the faculty of *Love of Approbation;* a passion for money, of *Acquisitiveness;* a passion for music, of *Tune;* a passion for metaphysics, of *Causality.*

SYMPATHY is not a faculty, nor is it synonymous with moral approbation. The same notes sounded by ten instruments of the same kind, harmonise, blend softly together, and form one peal of melody. The cause of this is to be found in the similarity of the constitution and state of the strings. Each faculty of the human mind has a specific constitution; and, in virtue of it, produces specific kinds of feelings, or originates or suggests specific kinds of ideas; and wherever similar faculties are active in different individuals, similar feelings are experienced by each, and similarity of feeling is sympathy.

Sympathy is not synonymous with moral approbation. We *approve* of the actions produced by the lower faculties of others, only when these are guided by the faculties proper to man: we never approve of Combativeness, when indulged for the mere pleasure of fighting; but we approve of the action of this faculty when directed by justice and understanding. We approve of the action of the sentiments proper to man, unmingled with any other motive, when directed by enlightened intellect.

Habit is defined to be "a power in man of doing a thing, acquired by frequently doing it." Now, before it can be done at all, the faculty and organ on which it depends must be possessed in an available degree; and the more powerful these are, the greater will be the energy with which the possessor will do the thing at first, and the ease with which he will learn to repeat it. Habit, therefore, is the result of facility acquired by exercise. It is the organ which acquires activity and superior facility in performing its functions, by being properly used, just as the fingers of a musician attain increased rapidity and facility of motion by the practice of playing.

TASTE is the result of the *harmonious action* of the faculties generally, in at least a moderate degree of vigor. Thus, the most beautiful poetry is that by which gratification is afforded to the higher sentiments and intellectual powers, without the introduction of any extravagance, absurdity or incongruity, to offend any one of them. If Ideality be in excess, this may produce bombast; if Causality predominate too much, it may introduce unintelligible abstractions; if Wit be excessive, it may run into conceits, epigrams, and impertinences. A picture is in best taste when it delights the Knowing Faculties, Reflection, and the Moral Sentiments, without offending any of them.

GEORGE COMBE.

MARSHALL HOUSE, *Philadelphia, April* 4, 1839.

EXPLANATION OF THE PLATES.

The original of the FRONTISPIECE was painted from life by J. Neagle of this city, a distinguished and well known artist, to whose politeness I am indebted for the privilege of using it on this occasion. The lithographed copy was made by M. S. Weaver, of this city, a young artist of great promise in both accuracy and beauty of delineation. The subject of this portrait, ONGPATONGA, was an Omahaw chief, distinguished in his tribe as a warrior and orator. Among the multitude of Indian portraits which have come under my notice, I know of no one that embraces more characteristic traits than this, as seen in the retreating forehead, the low brow, the dull and seemingly unobservant eye, the large, aquiline nose, the high cheek bones, full mouth and chin, and angular face.

In reference to the MAP at page 95, we may merely add, that a dotted line between the Gulf of Mexico and the great lakes, denotes the principal range of the *mounds*, and consequently the probable ancient seats of the Toltecan tribes in that region.

Plate 1. Embalmed head from the Peruvian cemetery at Arica.
Plate 2. Peruvian child from Atacama.
Plate 3. Peruvian from Atacama.
Plate 4. Peruvian of the Ancient Race.
Plate 5. Peruvian of the Ancient Race.
Plate 6. Chimuyan.
Plate 7. Peruvian child from Santa.
Plate 8 & 9. Peruvian from the Temple of the Sun.
Plate 10. Peruvian child, from the Temple of the Sun.
Plate 11. Peruvian from the Temple of the Sun.
Plate 11—A. Peruvian from the Temple of the Sun.
Plate 11—B. Peruvian from the Temple of the Sun.
Plate 11—C. Peruvian from the Temple of the Sun.
Plate 11—D. Peruvian from the Temple of the Sun.
Plate 12. Aturian of the Orinoco.
Plate 13. Puelche of Patagonia.
Plate 14. Charrua of Brazil.
Plate 15. Botocudo.
Plate 16. Ancient Mexican.
Plate 17. Mexican.
Plate 17—A. Mexican, of the Pames tribe.
Plate 18. Ancient Mexican.
Plate 18—A. Mexican, of the Tlahuica nation.
Plate 19. Chetimaches, of Louisiana.
Plate 20, 21. Natchez.
Plate 22. Seminole.
Plate 23. Seminole.
Plate 24. Seminole.
Plate 25. Cherokee.

EXPLANATION OF THE PLATES.

Plate 26. Muskogee, or Creek.
Plate 27. Uchee, Creek confederacy.
Plate 28. Chippeway.
Plate 29. Menominee.
Plate 30. Miami chief.
Plate 31. Ottigamie, or Fox. This drawing is reduced about two-tenths of an inch.
Plate 32. Lenapé, or Delaware woman.
Plate 33. Naumkeag, of Massachusetts. By an error in taking the facial angle, the face is made too projecting, and the angle therefore too small. This remark is also applicable to Plates 35 and 36.
Plate 34. Pottowatomie.
Plate 35. Cayuga.
Plate 36. Oneyda. Reduced nearly four-tenths of an inch.
Plate 37. Huron, or Wyandot.
Plate 38. Pawnee.
Plate 39. Dacota, or Sioux.
Plate 40. Cotonay. *Blackfoot.*
Plate 41. Osage.
Plate 42. Chinouk of Columbia river; natural form. Reduced nearly four-tenths of an inch.
Plate 43. Chinouk chief. Reduced four-tenths of an inch.
Plate 44. Klatstoni, of Columbia river.
Plate 45. Killemook, of Columbia river.
Plate 46. Clatsap, of Columbia river.
Plate 47. Kalapooyah, of Columbia river.
Plate 48. Clickitat, of Columbia river.
Plate 49, 50. Cowalitsk, of Columbia river. The profile view is reduced nearly three-tenths of an inch.
Plate 51. From a mound at Circleville, Ohio.
Plate 52. From a mound on the Upper Mississippi.
Plate 53. From the Grave creek mound, near Wheeling, Virginia.
Plate 54. From a mound on the Alabama river.
Plate 55. From a mound in Tennessee.
Plate 56. From a Tumulus at Santa, in Peru.
Plate 57. From a Tumulus in the Valley of Rimac, in Peru.
Plate 58. From a Tumulus in the Valley of Rimac, in Peru.
Plate 59. From an Ancient Tomb at Otumba, in Mexico.
Plate 60. From an Ancient Tomb, at Otumba, in Mexico.
Plate 61. From an Ancient Tomb at Otumba, in Mexico.
Plate 62. From a Cave at Golconda, in Illinois.
Plate 63. From a Cave near Steubenville, Ohio.
Plate 64. Charib of Venezuela.
Plate 65. Charib of St. Vincents.
Plate 66, 67. Araucanian chief.
Plate 68. Araucanian chief.
Plate 69. Natural Mummy of a Muysca Indian of New Grenada.
Plate 70. Mongol-Americans, or Eskimaux.

294   CRANIA AMERICANA.

Plate 71. Swiss skull, introduced to illustrate Mr. Combe's Phrenological memoir. See page 277.

Plate 72. Phrenological Chart. Taken from a head furnished to the author by George Combe, Esq. See *Appendix*, p. 283.

The *wood-cuts* of this work were taken from reduced drawings made with my own hands by means of an instrument adapted to the purpose by my friend Mr. Phillips. I had applied to several artists to furnish these drawings, and the camera lucida and graphic mirror were both tried in vain. On being furnished with the annexed drawing apparatus, (which might be called a *Craniograph*,) I was soon able by practice to make my own drawings with great celerity and correctness. Some of my earlier essays, however, are among the last in this work, and will be recognised by their want of finish.

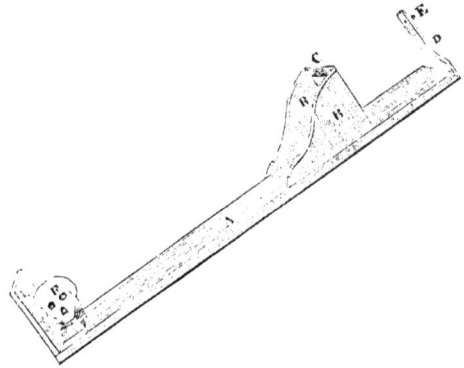

A represents a deal board six feet long and one foot wide; B B two brackets to support two cross pieces one of which is seen at C, having an open space between them about two and a half inches wide, and the centre of the space six inches from the board A; D a piece of board six inches wide dovetailed to the end of the board A, supporting the eye-piece E, the hole at E being six inches from the board A, fifteen inches from the nearest surfaces of the two cross pieces C, and placed perpendicular to the medial line of the board A; G a board dovetailed into the lower end of A. The cranium was adjusted on the board G, with its centre six inches from the surface of A; a piece of glass was then laid over the opening between the cross pieces at C, where it was held down by a screw. By looking down at the cranium F, through the eye-piece E, its outline and markings were seen on the glass at C diminished to one quarter, and were traced out on the glass with a pen and India ink, with great rapidity and accuracy. The drawings thus obtained on the glass, were then traced with a pencil on paper pressed against the glass while held up to the light, after which the drawing was finished with a pen. In the above cut the eye-piece is too high.

INDEX.

A.

Abassians, p. 9.
Abyssinians, p. 26.
Agricultural tribes, p. 73, 172.
Alligewi, p. 188.
Albinos, American p. 69.
Alforian Family, p. 94.
Algonquins, p. 175.
American Race, p. 6.
American Family, p. 62.
Anahuac, p. 141.
Anatomical measurements, p. 249.
Apalachian nations, p. 64.
Apalaches, p. 174.
Araucanians, p. 240.
Architecture of the Peruvians, p. 119.
Arabians, p. 18.
Atacama, p. 96.
Atures, p. 133.
Austro-African Family, p. 90.
Australian Family, p. 93.

B.

Baschkirs, p. 40.
Beard of the Americans, p. 67.
Bedouins, p. 20.
Berbers, p. 22.
Blackfeet, p. 201.
Black Charibs, p. 240.
Botocudos, p. 138.
Brazilian nations, p. 64.
Burats, p. 39.
Burmese, p. 47.

C.

Caucasian Race, p. 5.
Caucasian Family, p. 7.
Calmucks, p. 39.
Caffers, p. 88.
Capacity of the skull in different nations, p. 260.
Cayuga, p. 192.
Celtic Family, p. 15.
Charruas, p. 137.
Chechemecas, p. 142.
Chimù, p. 103, 111.
Chinese Family, p. 44.
Chetimaches, p. 162.
Cholula, p. 150.
Choctaws, p. 161.
Circassians, p. 8.
Chechemecas, p. 142.
Charibs, p. 236.
———— Black, p. 240.

Cherokees, p. 171.
Chinouks, p. 203, 207.
Chippeways, p. 176.
Circleville Mound, p. 219.
Clatsaps, p. 211.
Clickitat, p. 214.
Cochin-China, p. 49.
Collao, p. 102.
Complexions of the Americans, p. 68.
Confusos, p. 85.
Connivos, p. 117.
Copts, p. 24.
Cotonay, p. 201.
Cowalitsk, p. 215.
Creeks, p. 164, 170, 174.
Cuzco, p. 119.

D.

Dacotas, p. 197.
Delawares, p. 189.

E.

Egyptians, p. 24.
Equestrian tribes, p. 74.
Eskimaux, p. 53, 63, 247.
Esmeraldinos, p. 86.
Ethiopian Race, p. 6.

F.

Facial angle, p. 250.
Fellahs, p. 25.
Finns, p. 38.
Five Nations, p. 190.
Flatheads of Columbia river, p. 202.
Fuegians, p. 64.

G.

Gallas, p. 24.
Georgians, p. 8.
Germanic Family, p. 13.
Golconda, Cave at p. 234.
Goths, p. 14.
Greeks, p. 12.
Greenlanders, p. 54, 248.
Guanches, p. 23.

H.

Hindoos, p. 32.
Hiong-nu, p. 43.
Hottentots, p. 90.
Huacas, p. 218.
Huns, p. 42.

I.

Iliyats, p. 10.
Inguches, p. 9.
Indo-European nations, p. 17.
Indostanic Family, p. 32.
Indo-Chinese Family, p. 47.
Iroquois, p. 190.

J.

Japanese, p. 47.
Jews, p. 21.

K.

Kamschatkans, p. 52.
Kanakas, p. 59.
Katawbas, p. 162.
Keralit, p. 52.
Killemooks, p. 210.
Kirgusians, p. 41.
Klatstoni, p. 210.
Koords, p. 11.
Koriaks, p. 52.

L.

Laos, p. 50.
Laplanders, p. 51.
Lenapé, p. 175, 189.
Libyan Family, p. 22.

M.

Malay Race, p. 6.
Malay Family, p. 56.
Map, Explanation of p. 95, 292.
Mandans, p. 199.
Measurements, p. 249.
Menominees, p. 176.
Mexicans, p. 141, 231.
Mitla, p. 149.
Mixed Races, p. 85.
Miamis, p. 180.
Missouri tribes, p. 200.
Mingoes, p. 190.
Minetaris, p. 199.
Moguls, p. 36.
Mongolian Race, p. 5.
Mongol-Tartar Family, p. 38.
Mongol-Americans, p. 241.
Moors, p. 19.
Mound skulls, p. 217.
Muskogees, p. 164, 170.

N.

Natchez, p. 157.
Negro Family, p. 36.
New Zealanders, p. 61.
Nicobar Islands, p. 50.
Nilotic Family, p. 24.
Norma verticalis, p. 251.
Nubians, p. 26.

O.

Oceanic Negroes, p. 91.
Omaguas, p. 118.
Ongpatonga, p. 292.

Osages, p. 199.
Ostiaks, p. 51.
Ottomacs, p. 73.
Otumba, Tombs of p. 230.

P.

Papuas, p. 92.
Patagonians, p. 64, 71.
Pachacamac, p. 132.
Palenque, p. 144, 149.
Pames, p. 155.
Pelasgi, p. 11.
Persians, p. 9.
Peruvians, Ancient p. 96.
———, Inca p. 113.
Phenicians, p. 22.
Phrenological Table, p. 262.
Polar Family, p. 50.
Polynesian Family, p. 59.
Puelches, p. 135, 137.

R.

Rajpoots, p. 34.
Rimac, p. 226.

S.

Salish, p. 207.
Sumoyedes, p. 51.
Sclavonic Nations, p. 15.
Seminoles, p. 164, 174.
Sepulture, Indian p. 244.
Skulls, American p. 65.
Siamese, p. 48.
Sikhs, p. 34.
Singalese, p. 35.
Sioux, p. 197.
Sokulks, p. 206.
Steubenville, Cave at p. 235.

T.

Tartars, p. 39, 42.
Temple of the Sun, p. 132.
Teutonic Nations, p. 14.
Tiaguanico, p. 99.
Tibulca, Cave of p. 149.
Titicaca, p. 97, 100, 103.
Tlahuica, p. 156.
Toltecan Family, p. 83, 84, 141, 228, 230.
Tuariks, p. 22.
Tudas, p. 33.
Tula, p. 160.
Tungusians, p. 51.
Turkish Family, p. 43.

U.

Uchees, p. 173.
Uros, p. 103.

W.

Wahabys, p. 20.
Waxsaws, p. 162.

Y.

Yakuts, p. 41.
Yuncas, p. 103.

TO

JOHN S. PHILLIPS, ESQ.

MEMBER OF THE ACADEMY OF NATURAL SCIENCES OF PHILADELPHIA, &c., &c.

My Dear Sir:—Having now completed a task which has cost me some years of toil and anxiety, it gives me great pleasure to record the many obligations I owe you in the prosecution of these inquiries. To your ingenuity I am almost wholly indebted for the means of obtaining the elaborate measurements appended to this work; which, without your personal aid and untiring perseverance, would have remained in a great measure unaccomplished. It may, perhaps, be thought by some readers, that these details are unnecessarily minute, especially in the Phrenological Table; and again, others would have preferred a work conducted throughout on Phrenological principles. In this study I am yet a learner; and it appeared to me the wiser plan to present the facts unbiassed by theory, and let the reader draw his own conclusions. You and I have long admitted the fundamental principles of Phrenology, viz: That the brain is the organ of the mind, and that its different parts perform different functions: but we have been slow to acknowledge the details of Cranioscopy as taught by Dr. Gall, and supported and extended by subsequent observers. We have not, however, neglected this branch of inquiry, but have endeavored to examine it in connection with numerous facts, which can only be fully appreciated when they come to be compared with similar measurements derived from the other races of men. Yet I am free to acknowledge that there is a singular harmony between the mental character of the Indian, and his cranial developments as explained by Phrenology.

This work has not been composed in that philosophic retirement which is so favorable to investigation and reflection: on the contrary, you can bear witness that I have pursued my course amidst the continued fatigue and anxiety of a professional life; and this must be my apology, if the work I now submit to the public does not embrace all the materials which are called for in such an undertaking.

I am, my dear sir,
Your very obliged friend and servant,

SAMUEL GEORGE MORTON.

PHILADELPHIA, *October* 1. 1839.

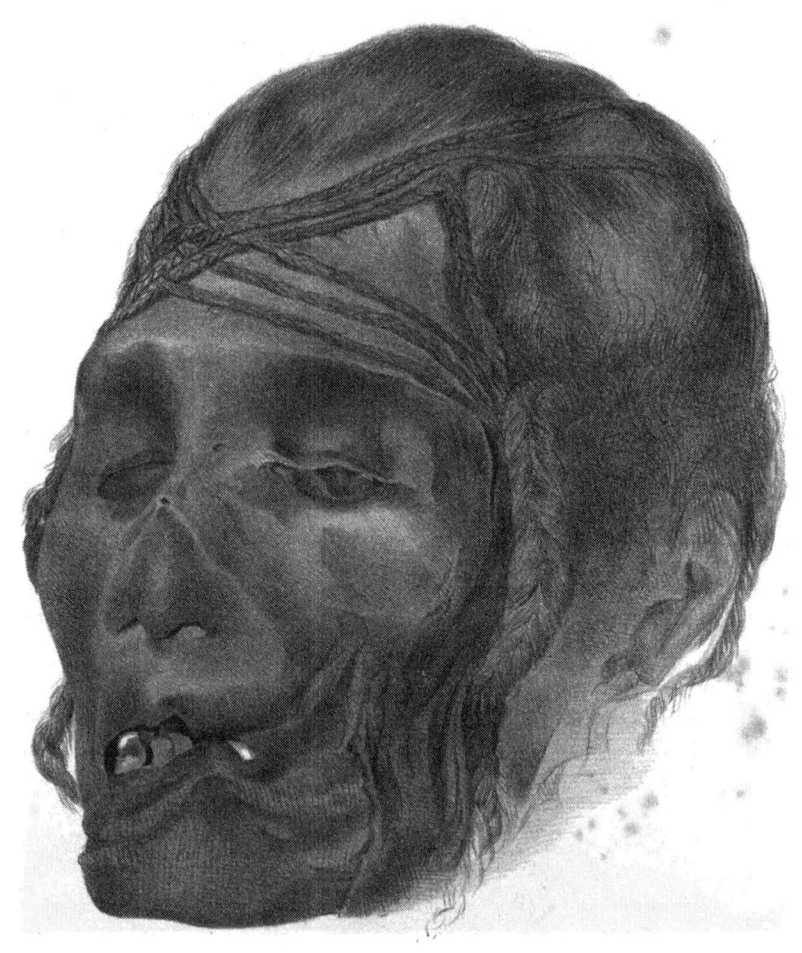

EMBALMED HEAD
FROM THE PERUVIAN CEMETERY AT ARICA.

Drawn from Nature and on Stone by A. Hoffy.
Lith. of T. Sinclair, N° 79 S. Third St. Phil?

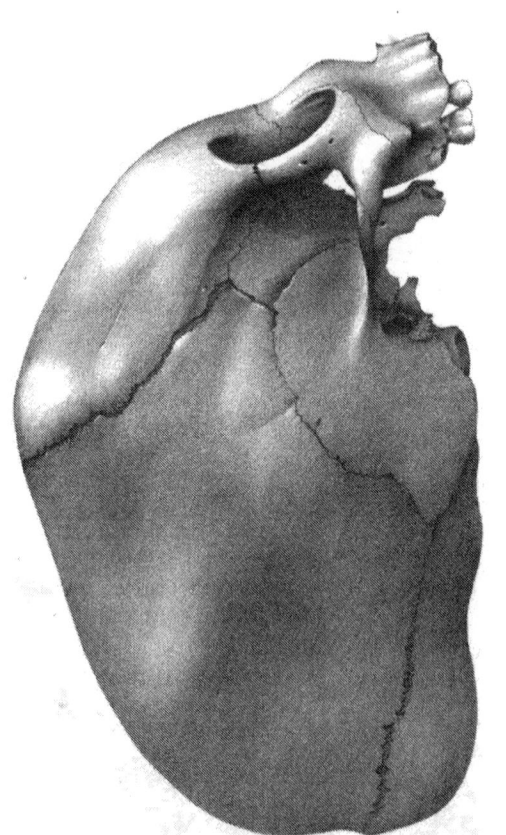

PERUVIAN CHILD
FROM ATACAMA

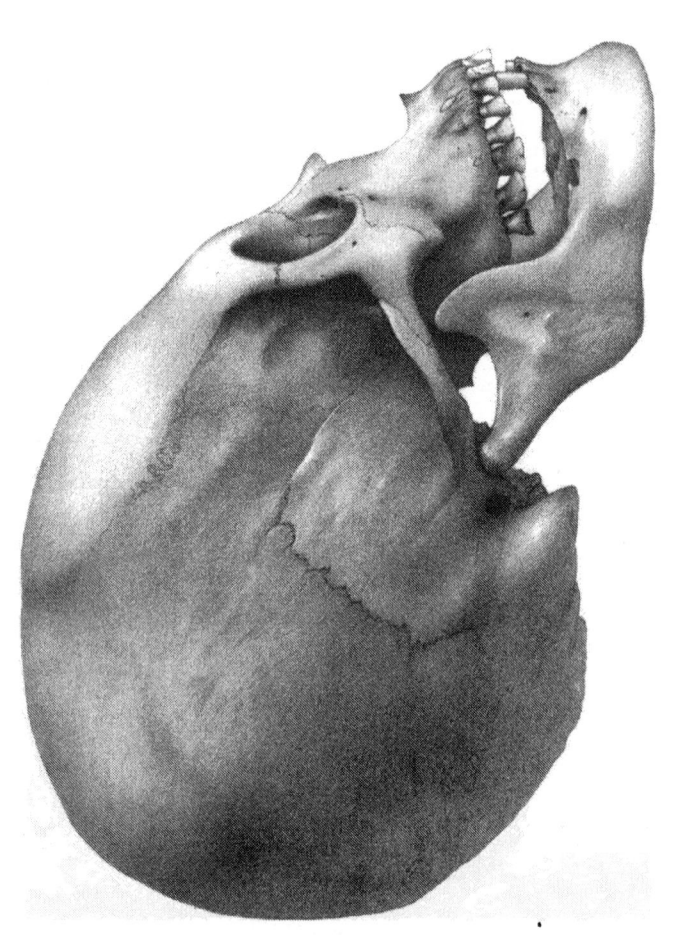

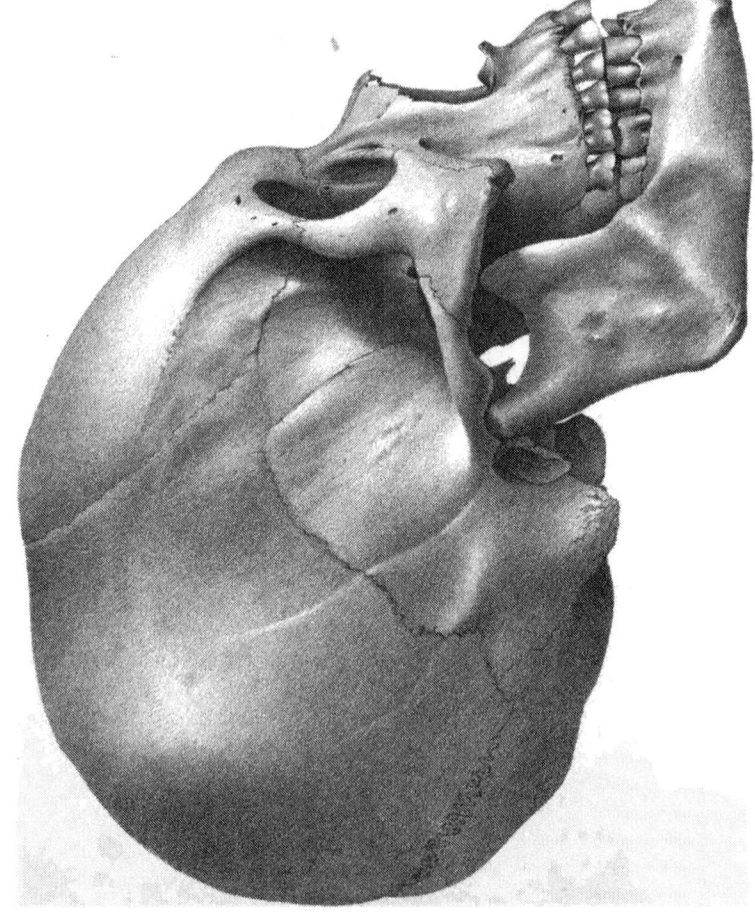

PERUVIAN OF THE ANCIENT RACE.
From Arica.
Drawn from Nature and on Stone by J. Collins

PERUVIAN

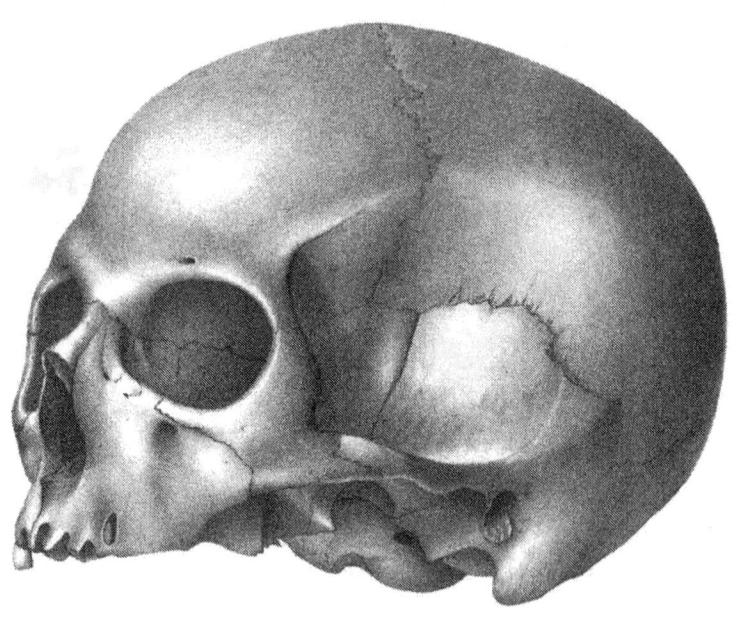

CHIMUYAN.

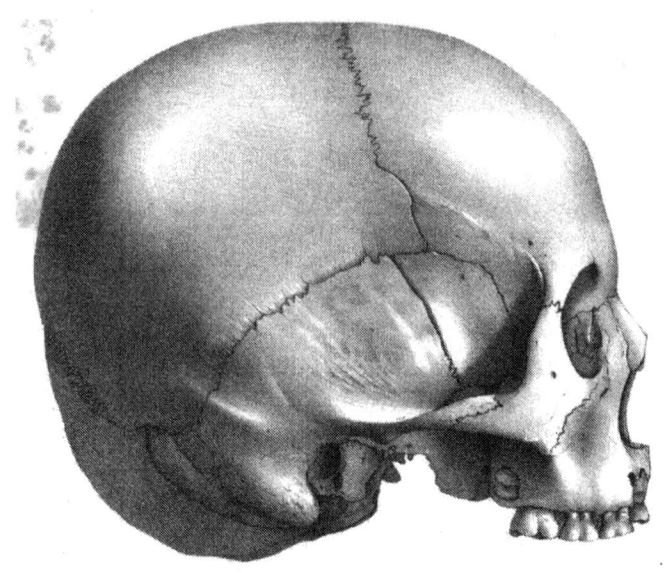

PERUVIAN CHILD

FROM SANTA.

Morton's Crania Americana. PL.8.

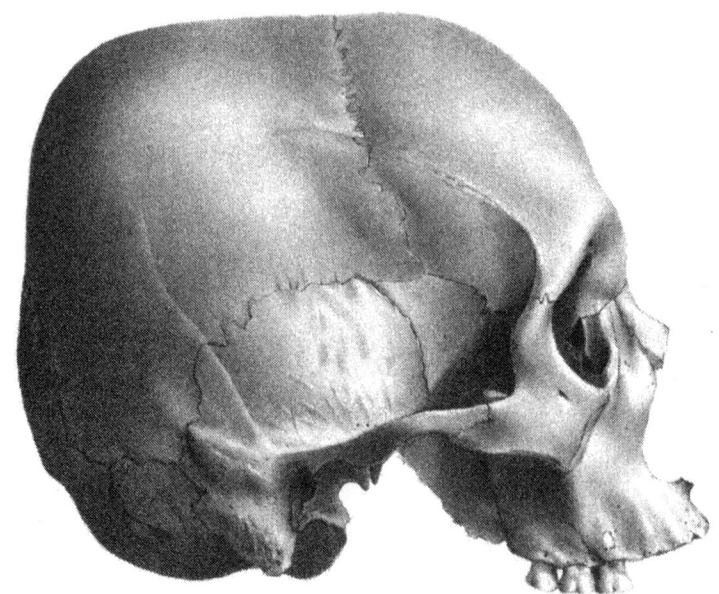

PERUVIAN.
FROM THE TEMPLE OF THE SUN.
Lith. of John Collins N° 79 S.Third St.Phil?

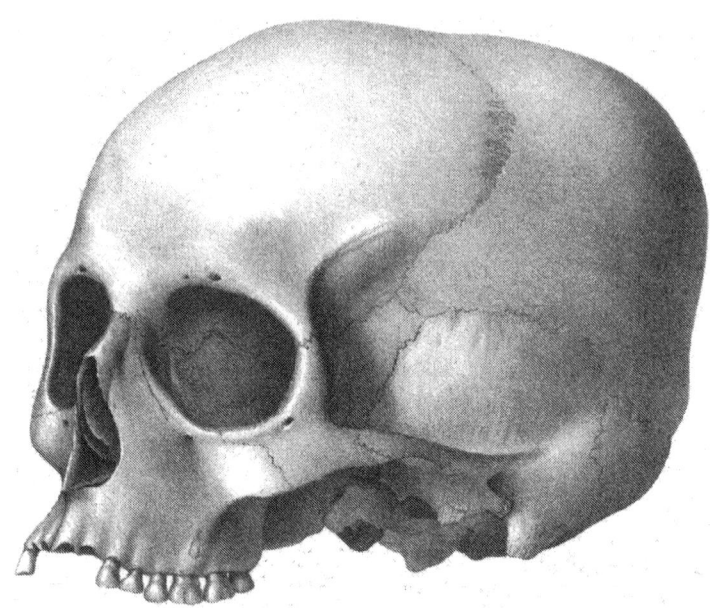

PERUVIAN
FROM THE TEMPLE OF THE SUN
Drawn from Nature and on Stone by John Collins

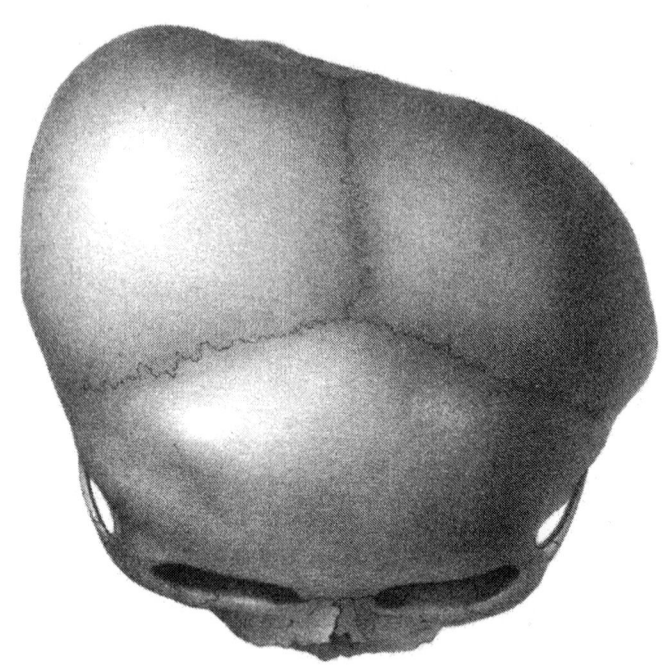

PERUVIAN CHILD

FROM THE TEMPLE OF THE SUN.

Morton's Crania Americana

Pl. II

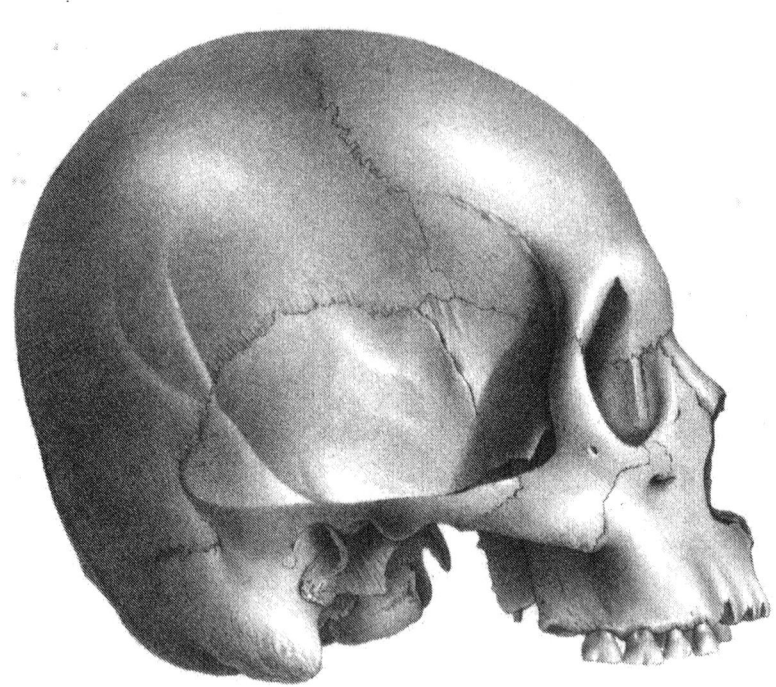

PERUVIAN
FROM THE TEMPLE OF THE SUN.
Lith of John Collins, N° 79 South Third St Philad°

Morton's Crania Americana.

Pl. 11. A.

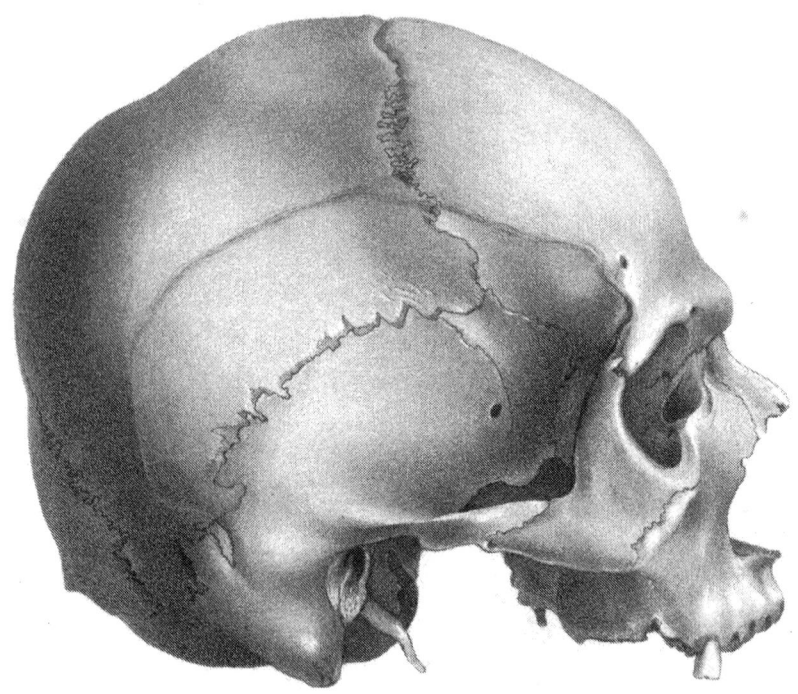

PERUVIAN.

FROM THE TEMPLE OF THE SUN.

Lith. of John Collins, No. 79 S. Third St. Phila.

Morton's Crania Americana. Pl.11.B.

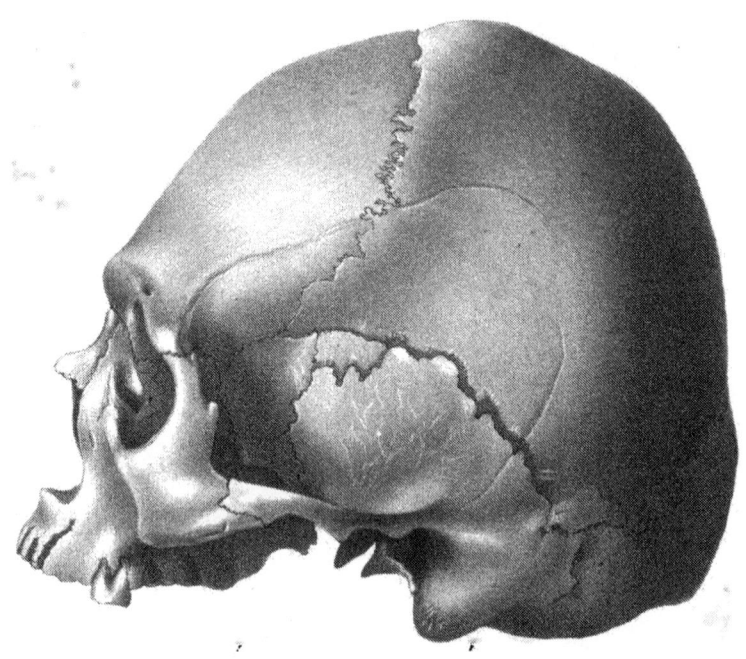

PERUVIAN.
FROM THE TEMPLE OF THE SUN.
Lith. of John Collins, No. 79 S. Third St. Phil.

Mortons' Crania Americana. Pl.11.C.

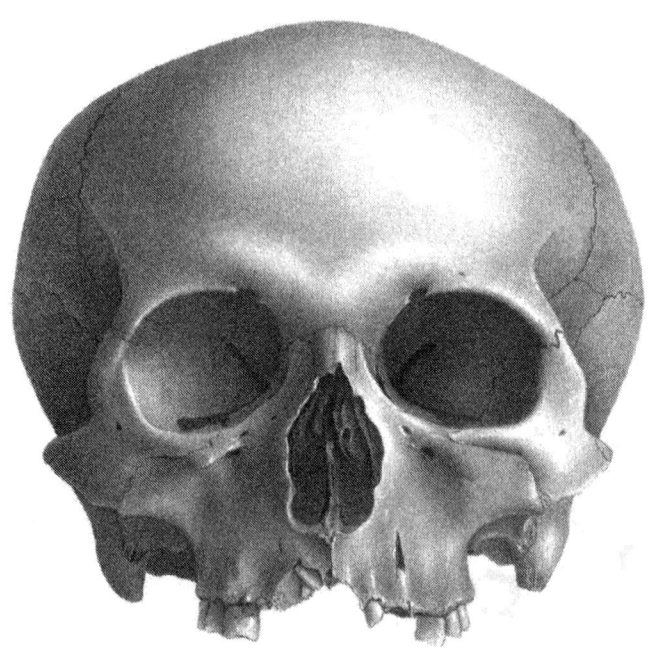

PERUVIAN.
FROM THE TEMPLE OF THE SUN.
Lith. of John Collins, No.79 S.Third St.Phil^a

Morton's Crania Americana. Pl.11.D.

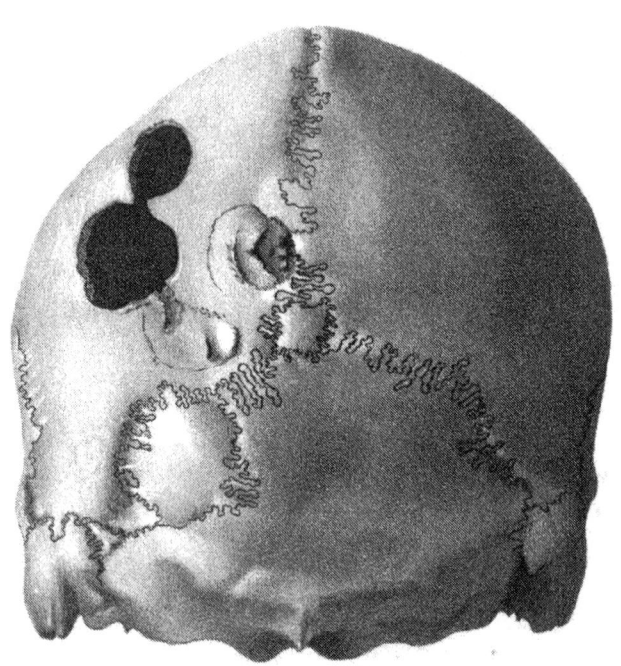

PERUVIAN.
FROM THE TEMPLE OF THE SUN.
Lith of John Collins, No 79 S.Third St. Phila

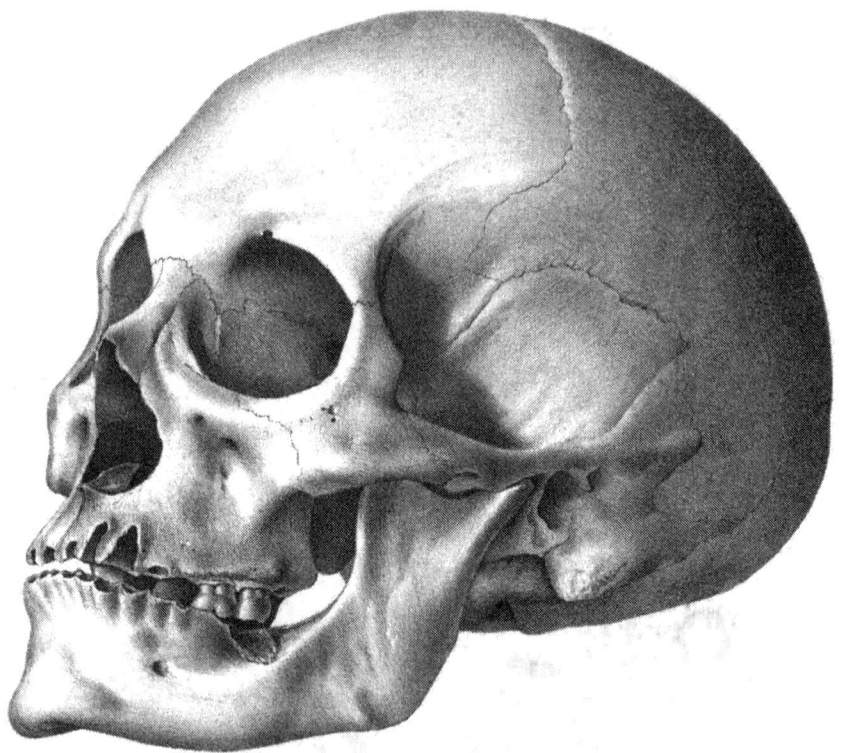

ATURIAN
OF THE ORINOCO.

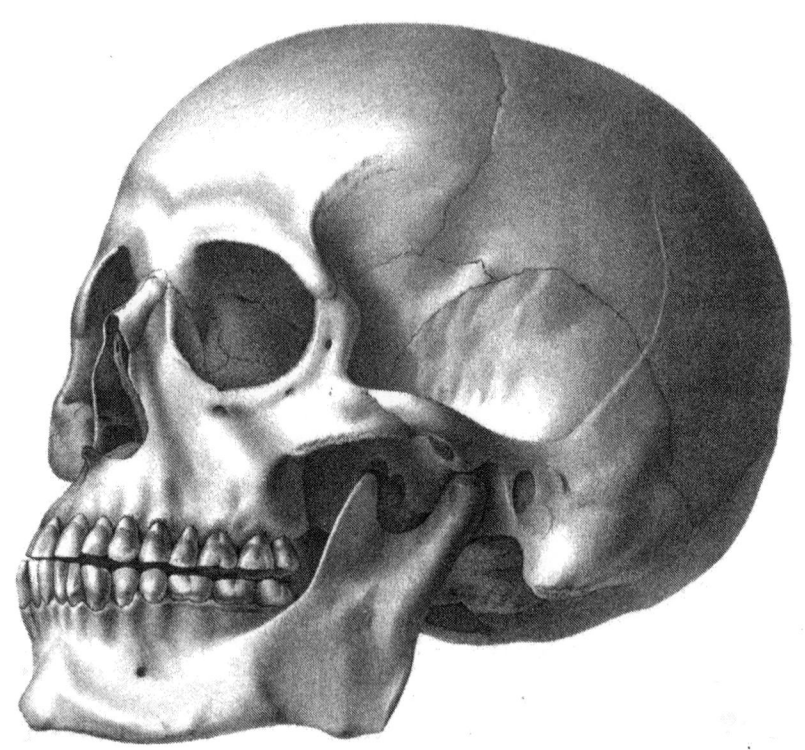

PUELCHE
OF PATAGONIA.

Morton's Crania Americana. Pl. 14

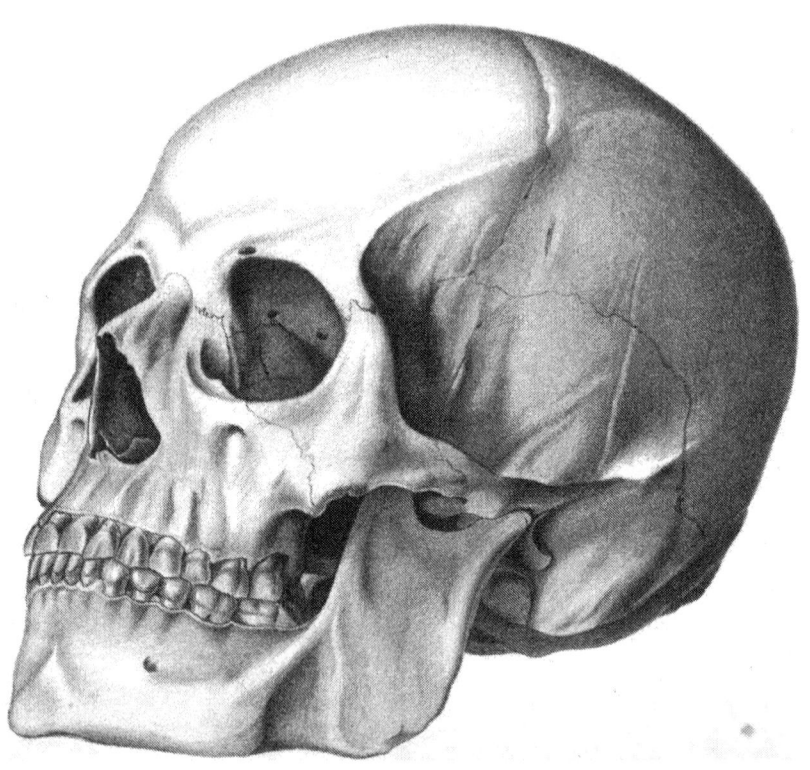

CHARRUA
of Brazil.

From Nature by J.C.Werner. On Stone by T.A.Collins.

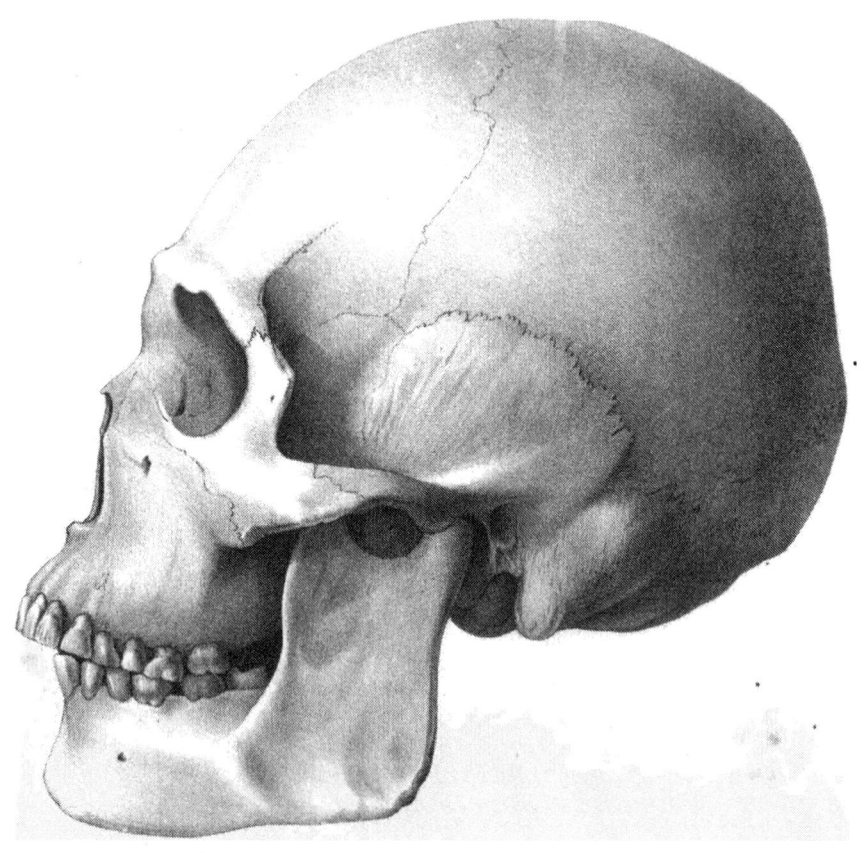

BOTOCUDO

OF BRAZIL.

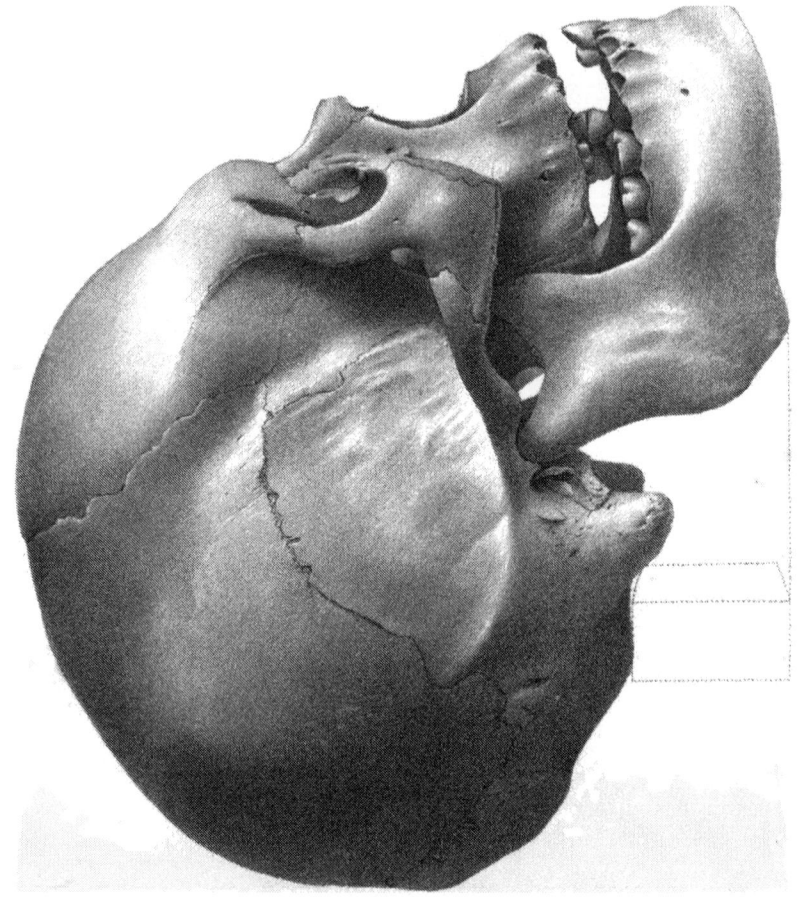

MEXICAN.

Morton's Crania Americana. Pl. 17.

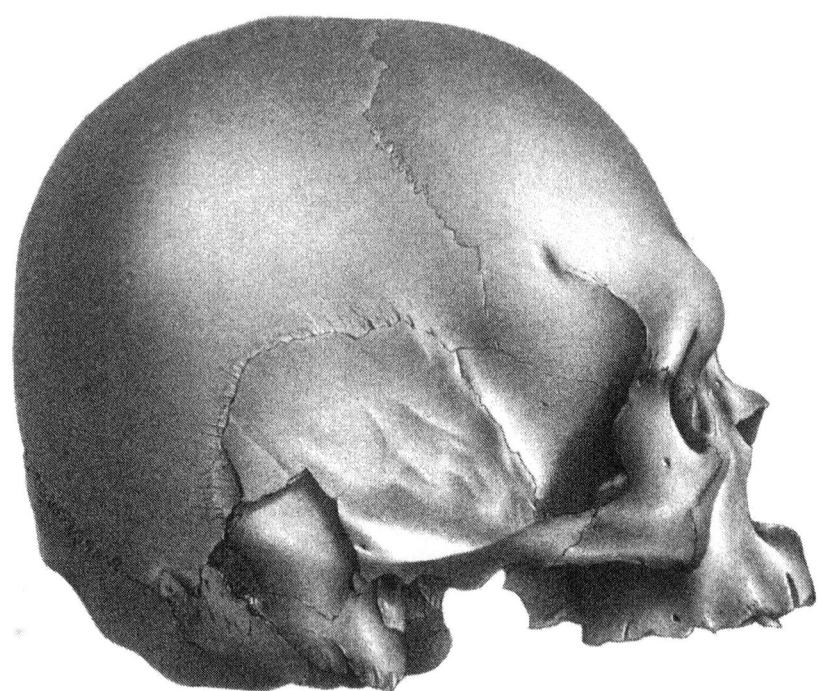

MEXICAN.

Lith. of John Collins No.79 S.Third St Phil.ᵃ

Morton's Crania Americana. Pl.17.A.

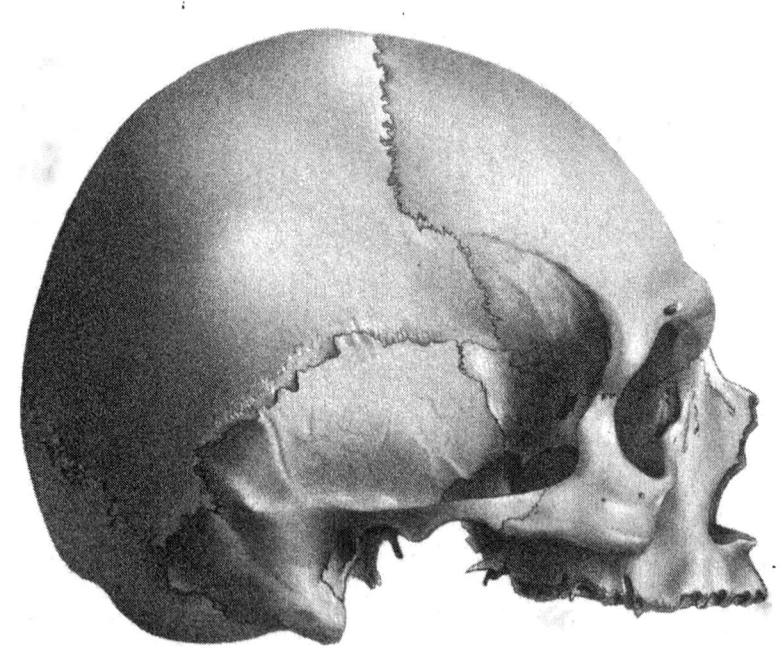

PAMES.
MEXICAN.
Lith of John Collins, N° 79 S. Third St. Phil^a

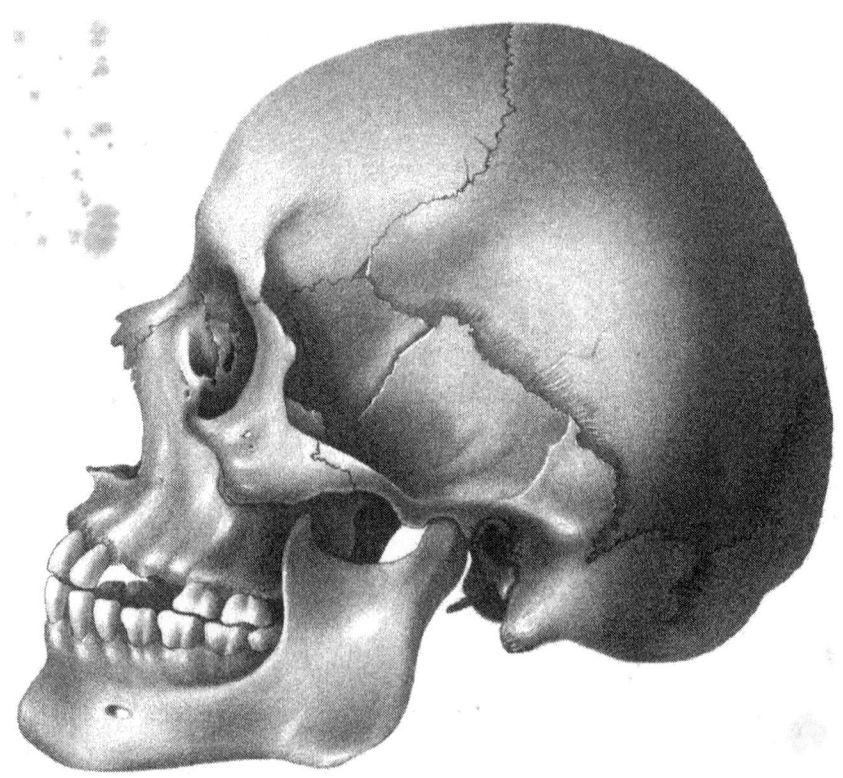

MEXICAN.

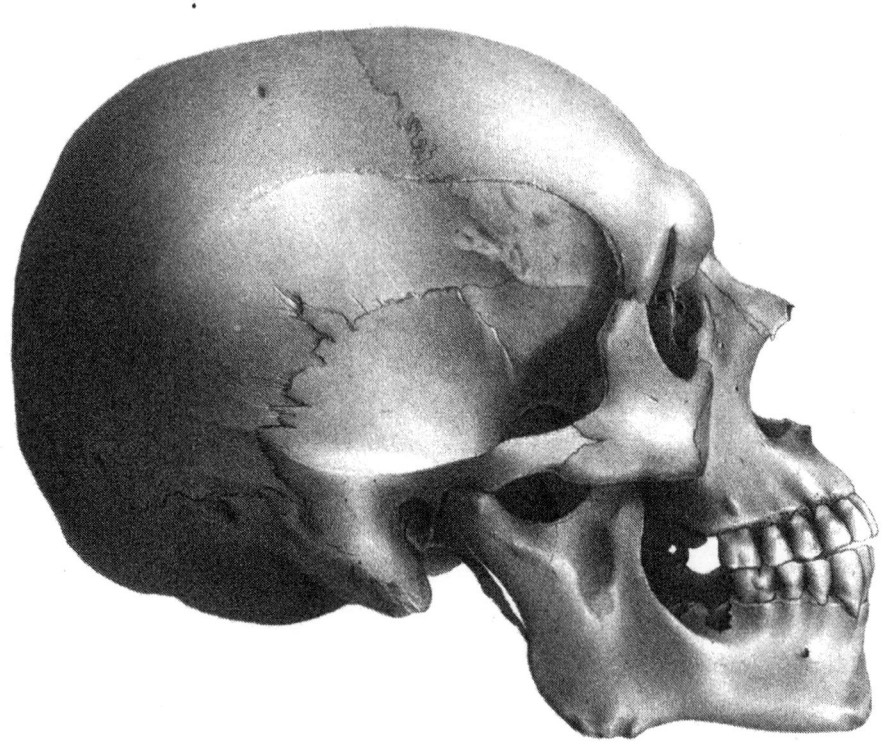

TLAHUICA.
MEXICAN.

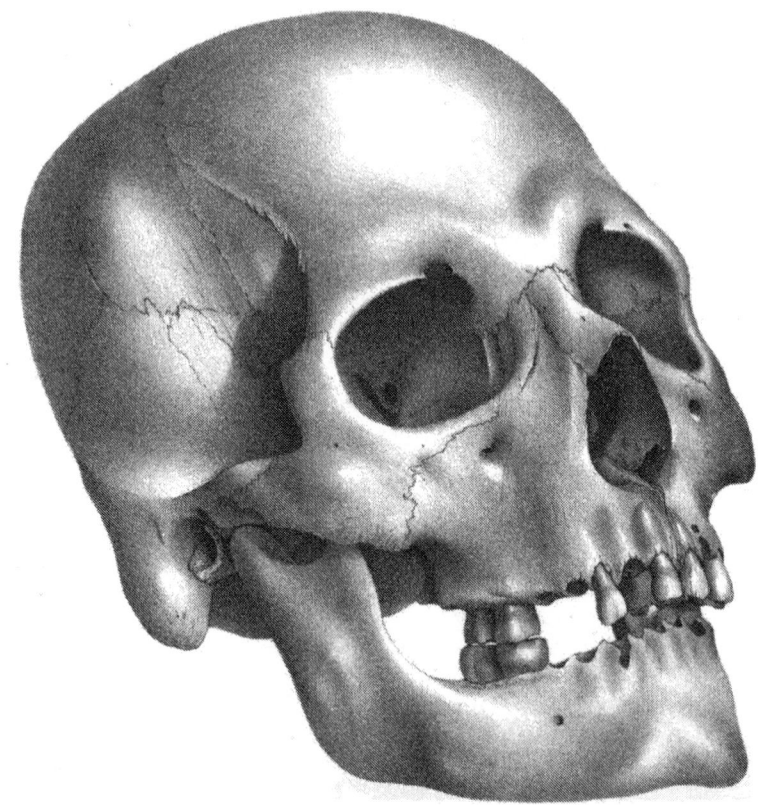

CHETIMACHES:

LOUISIANA.

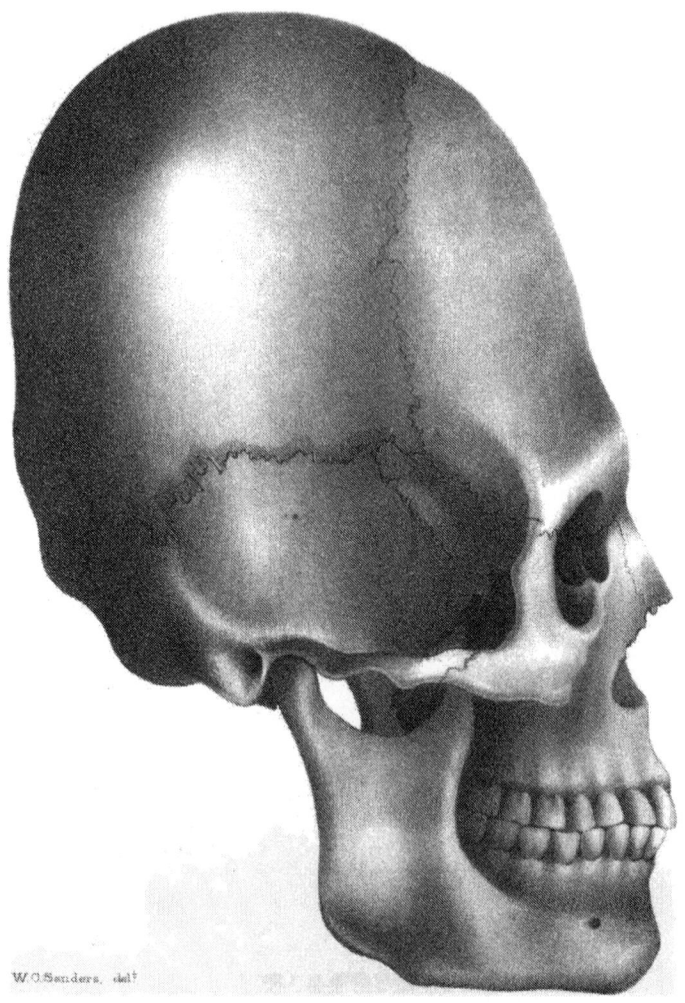

NATCHEZ.
PROFILE VIEW.

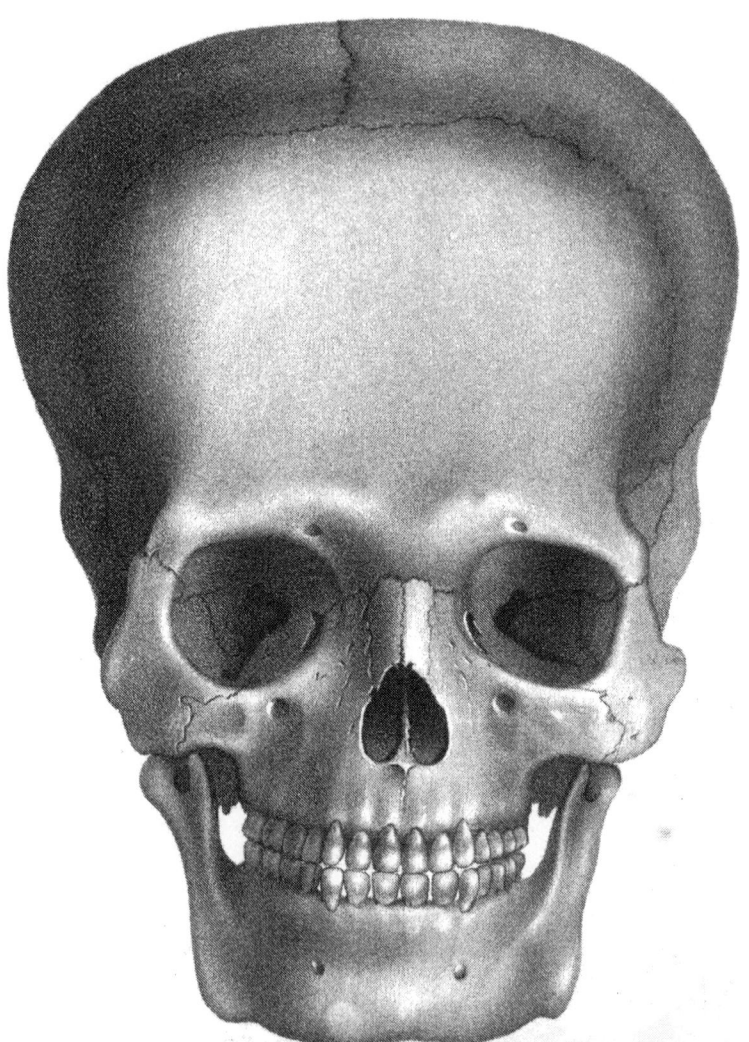

NATCHEZ.
FRONT VIEW.

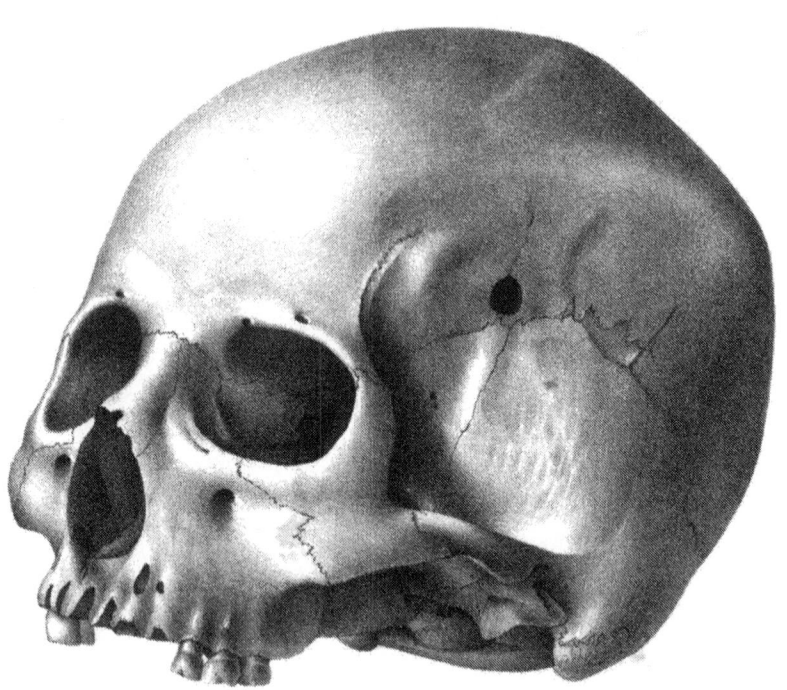

SEMINOLE

Drawn from Nature and on Stone by J. Collins

Morton's Crania Americana. Pl. 23.

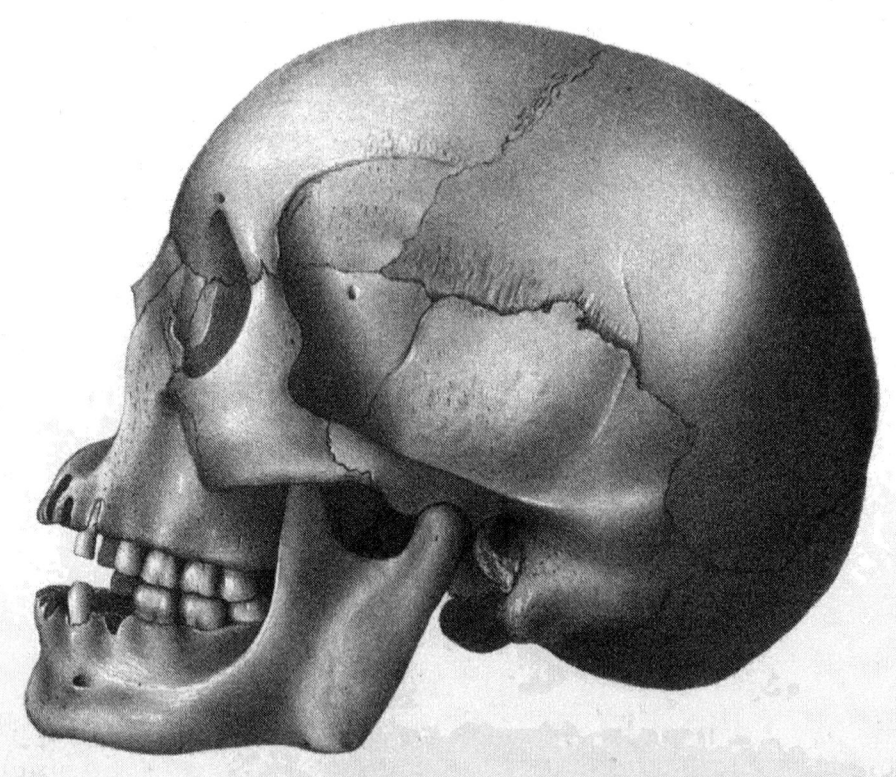

SEMINOLE.

Lith. of John Collins N°79 S.Th'd St. Phil.ᵃ

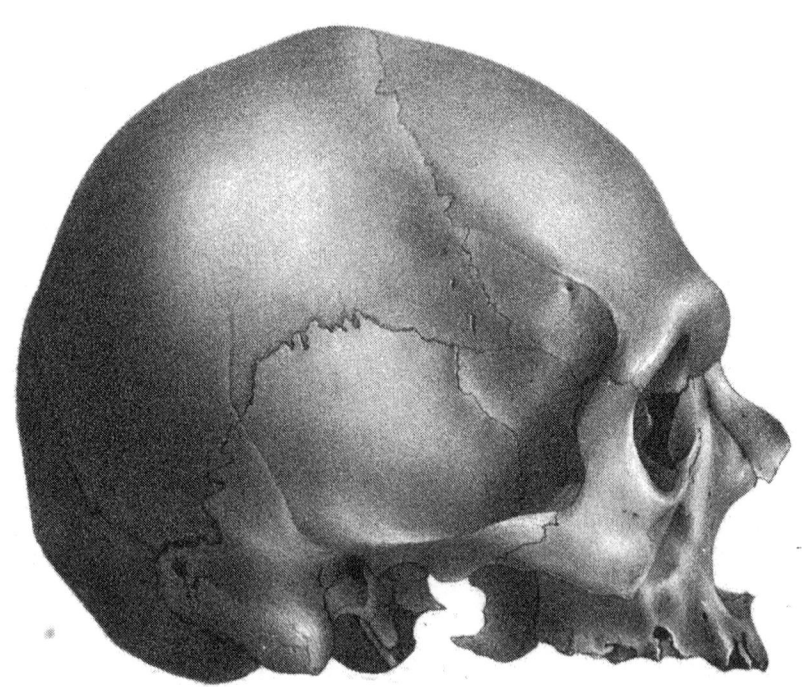

SEMINOLE.

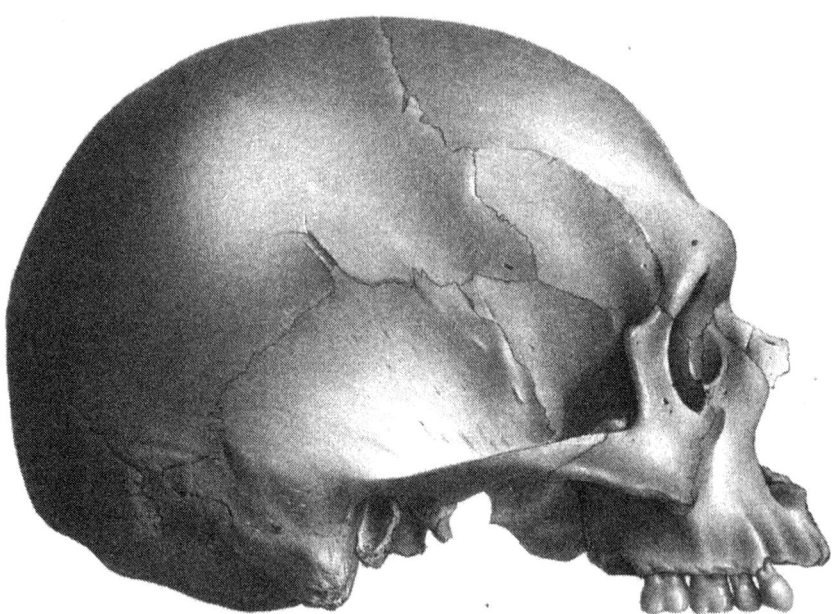

CHEROKEE.

Lith. of John Collins. No 79 S. Third St. Phila

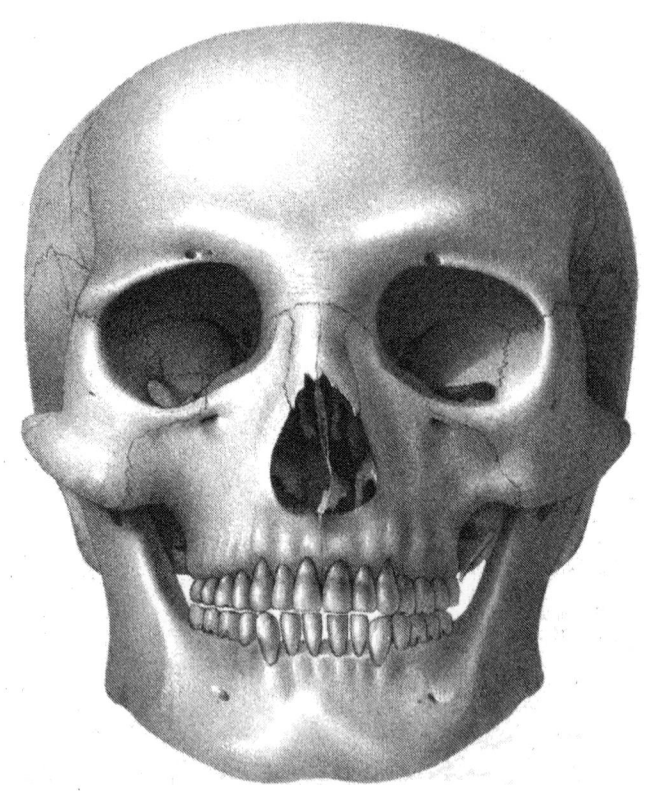

MUSKOGEE.

Morton's Crania Americana. Pl. 27.

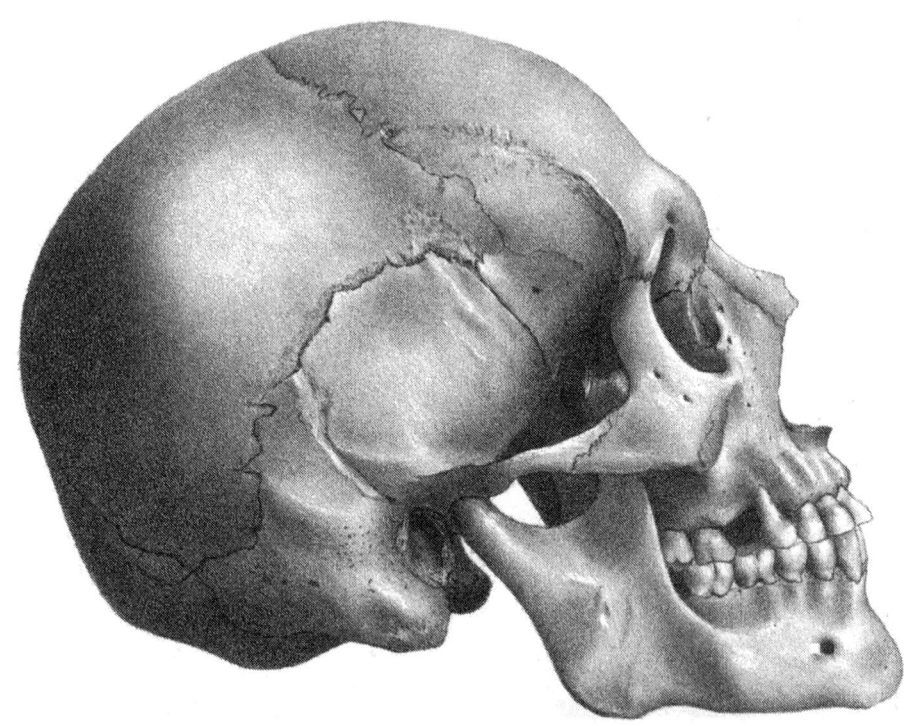

EUCHEE.

Lith. of John Collins N° 79 S Third St Phila

Mortons' Crania Americana.   Pl. 28.

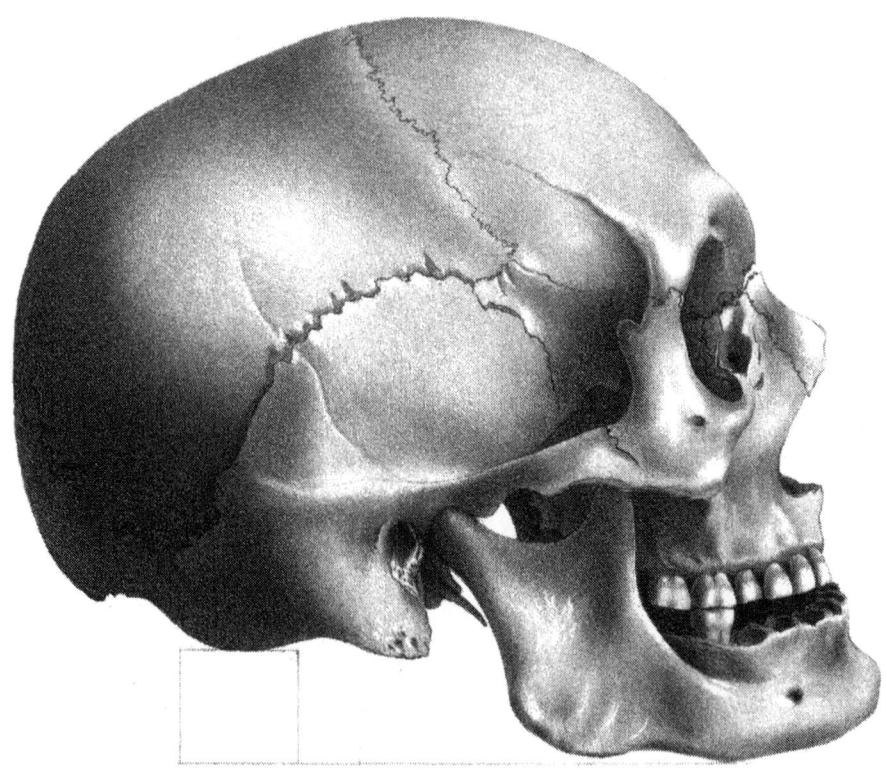

CHIPPEWAY.

Lith of John Collins, N? 79 S. Third St. Phil?

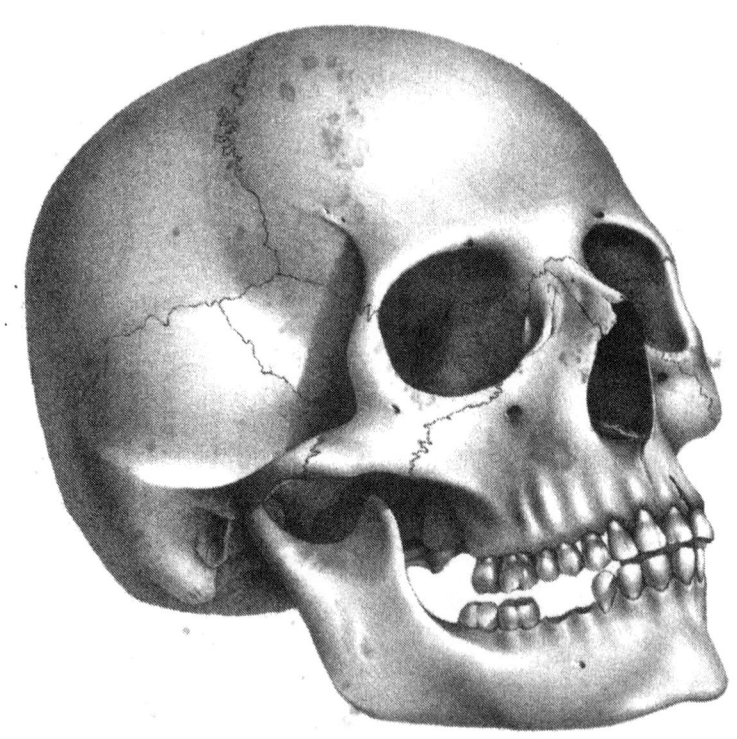

MENOMINEE

Drawn from Nature and on Stone by John Collins.

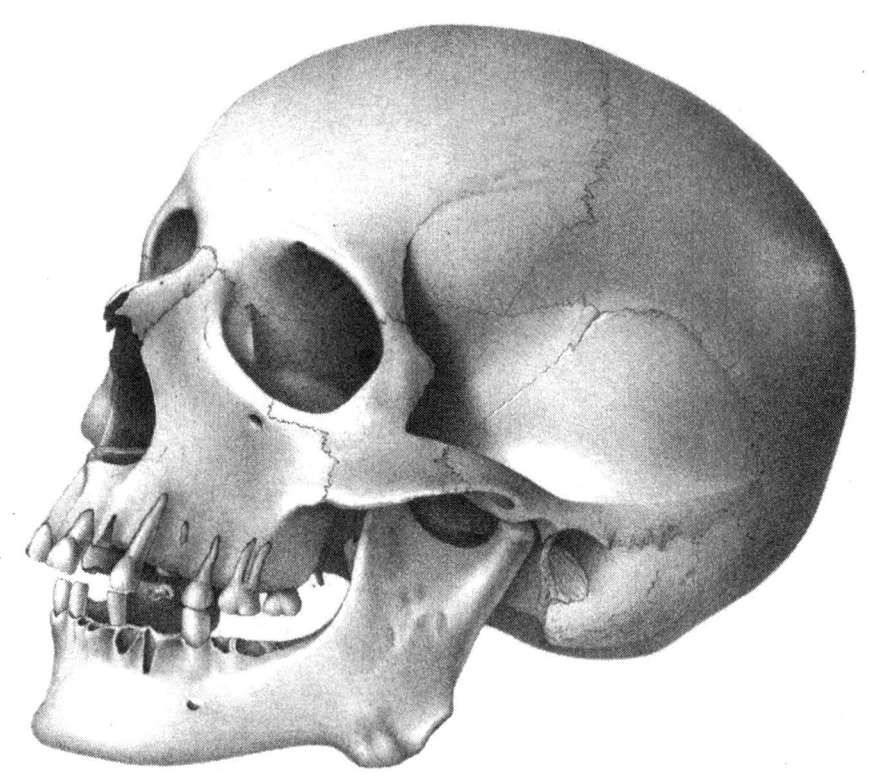

MIAMI CHIEF.

Morton's Crania Americana

Pl. 31

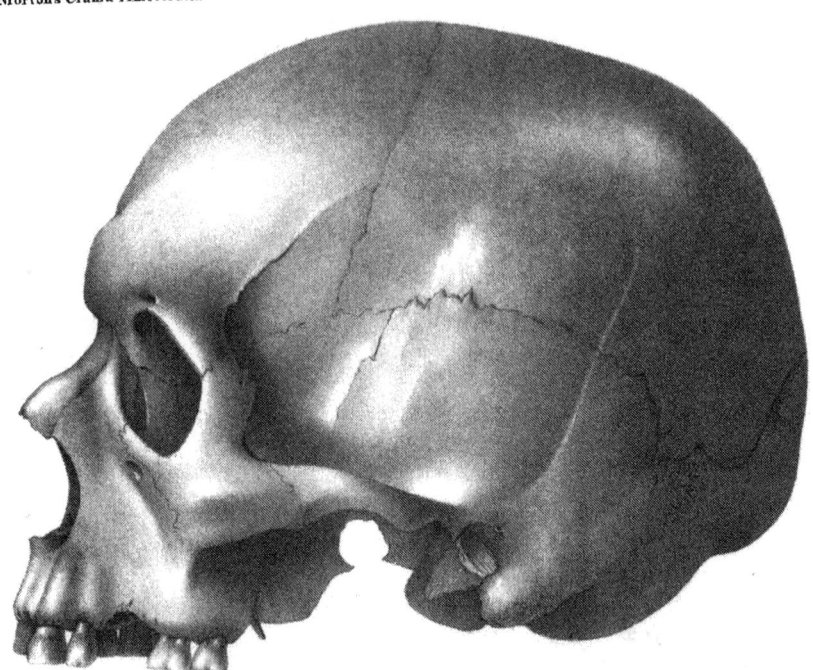

OTTIGAMIE.

Lith of John Collins, N° 79 South Third St Philad.

Morton's Crania Americana   Pl. 32

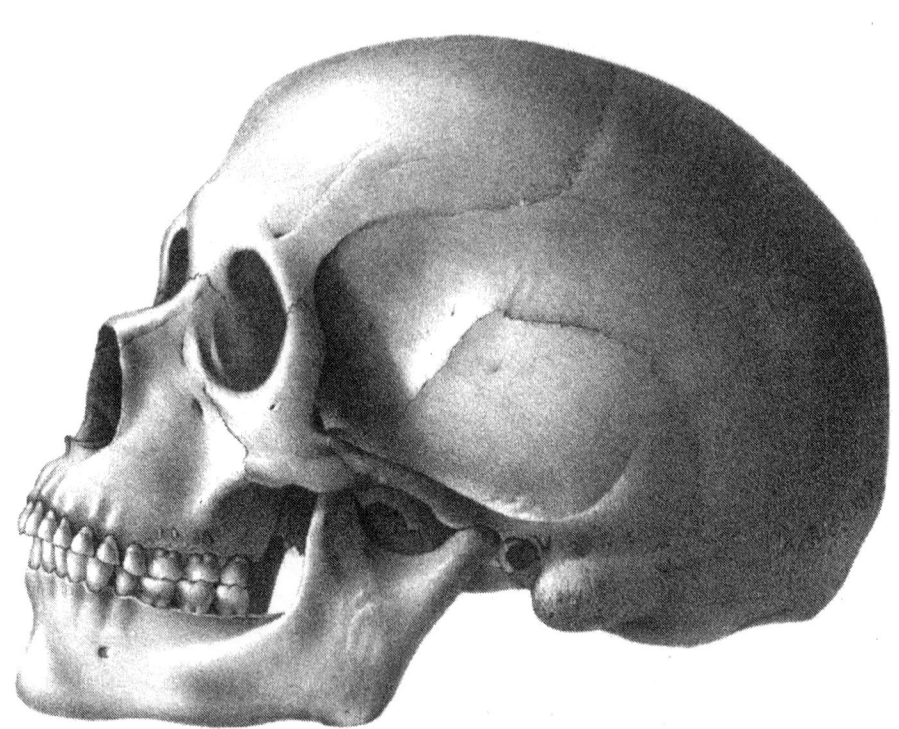

LENNI LENAPE
From Nature and on Stone by John Collins

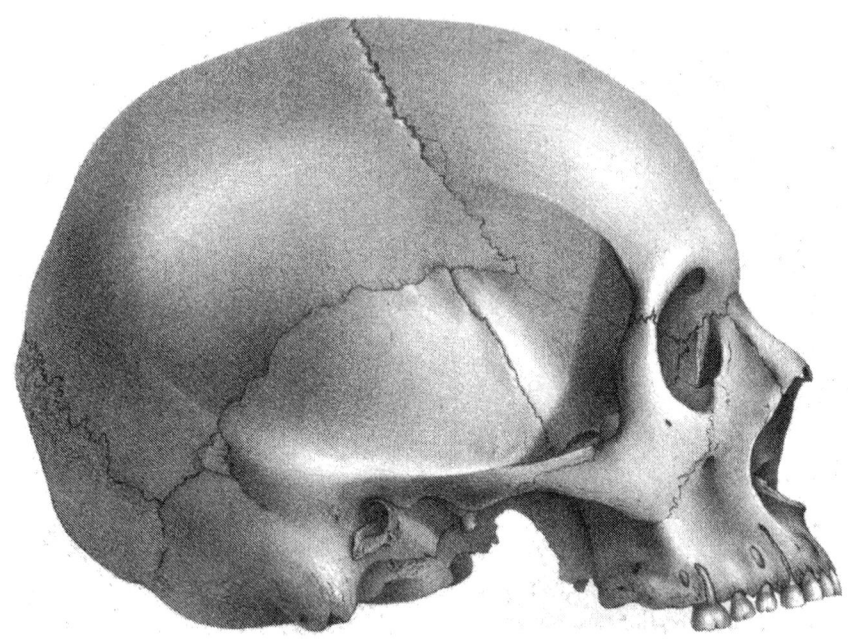

NAUMKEAG

Drawn from Nature and on Stone by John Collins

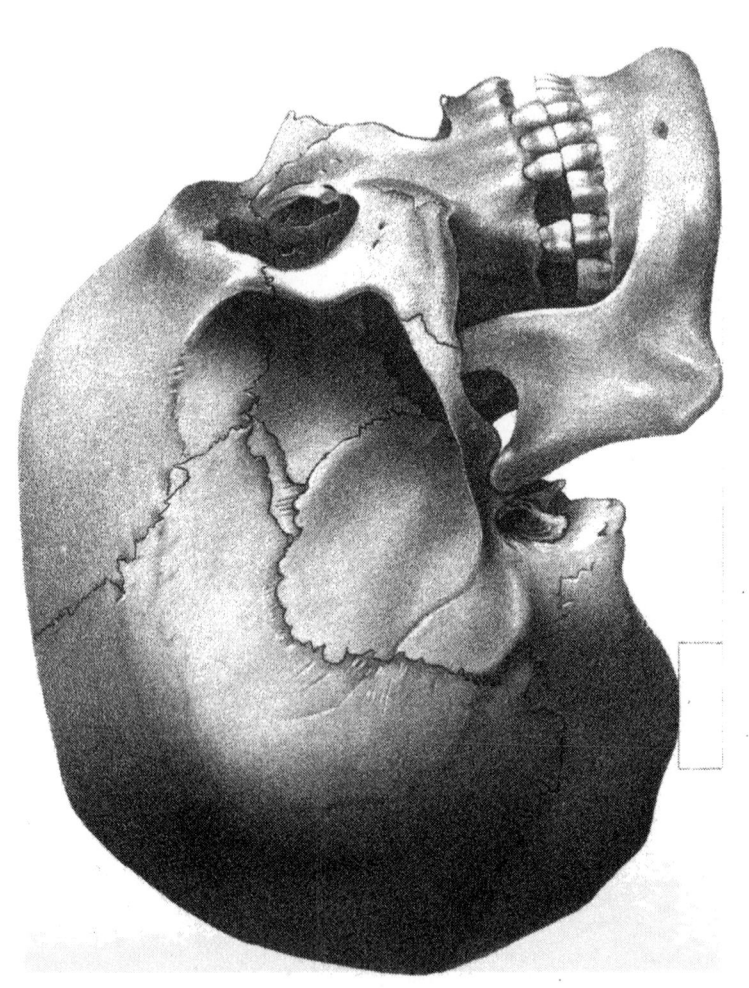

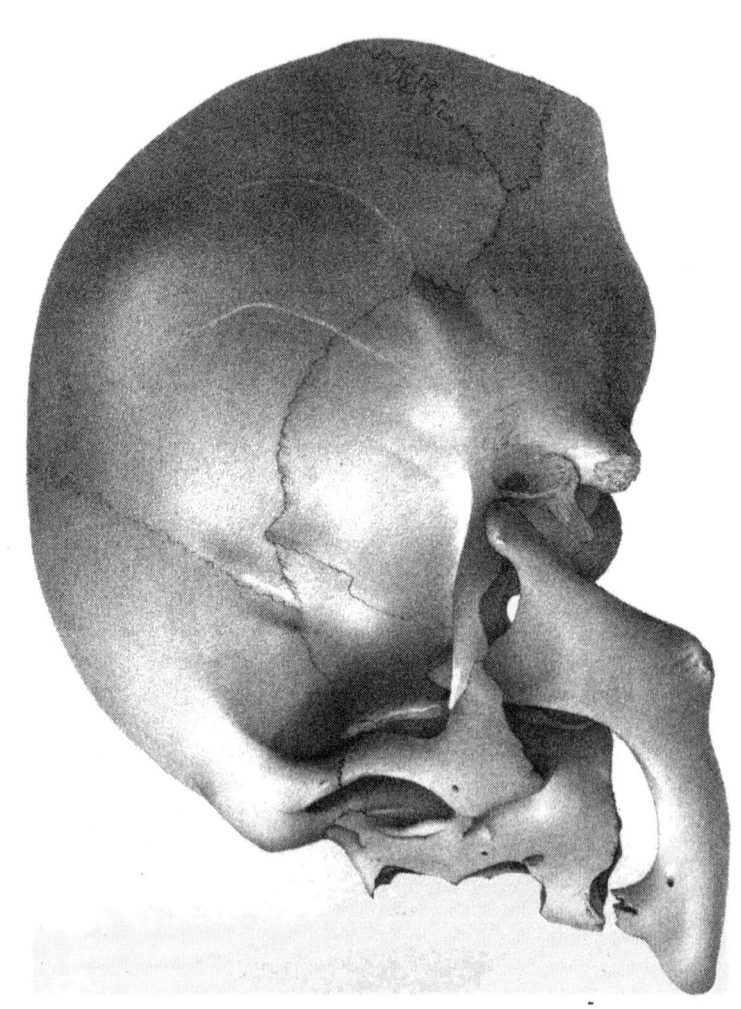

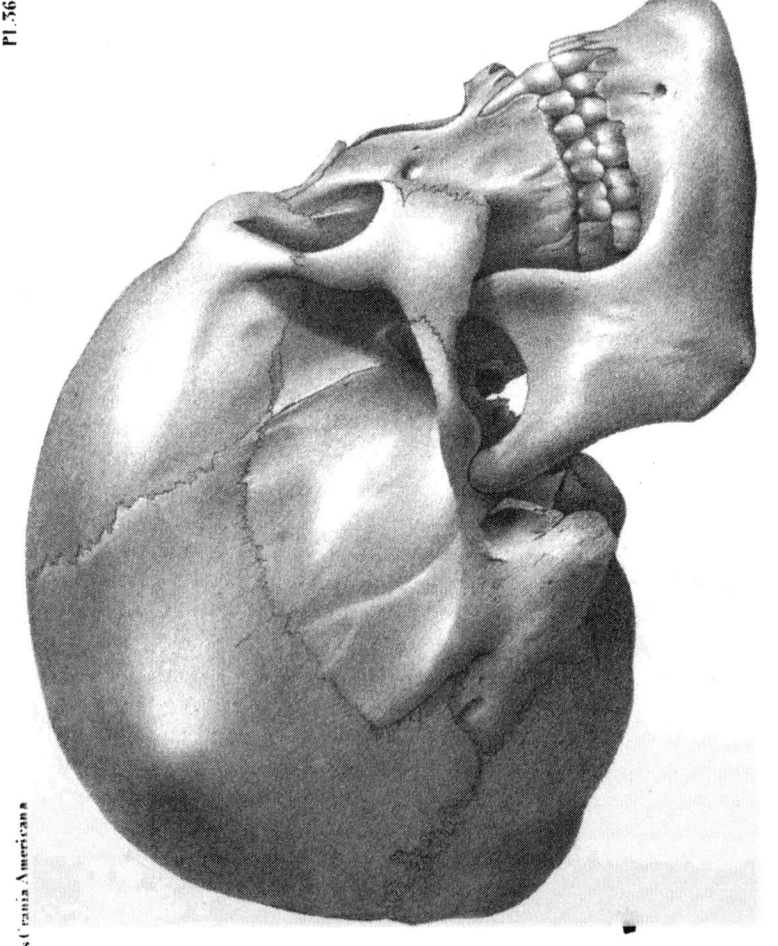

Morton's Crania Americana

Pl. 36

ONEIDA.
IROQUOIS CONFEDERACY.

Lith. of John Collins N°.19 S. Third St. Philadelphia.

Morton's Crania Americana. Pl. 37.

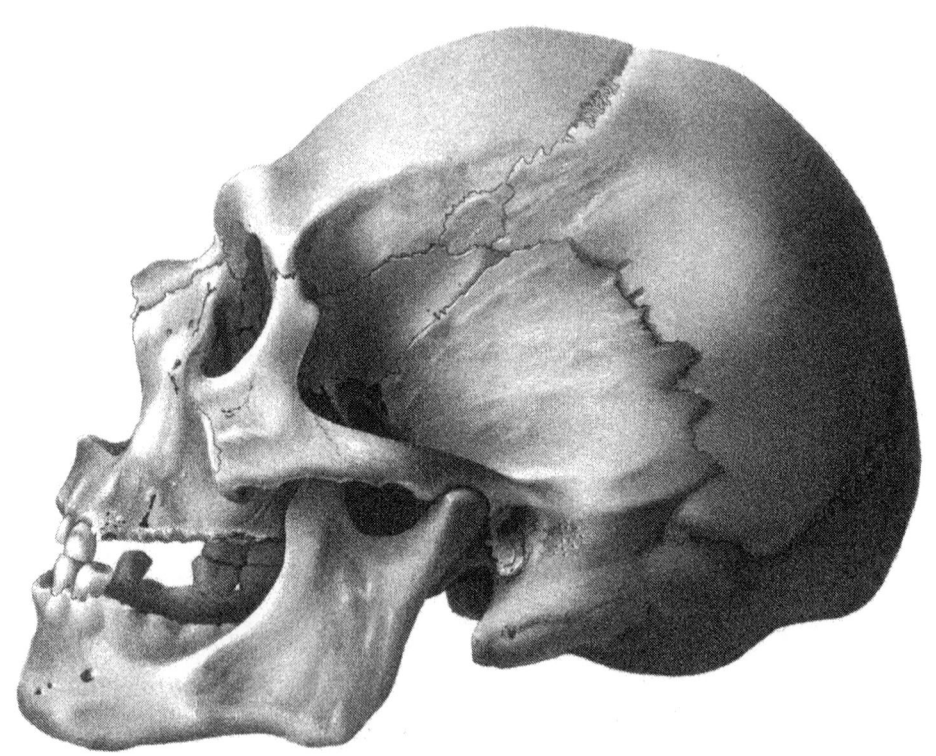

HURON.

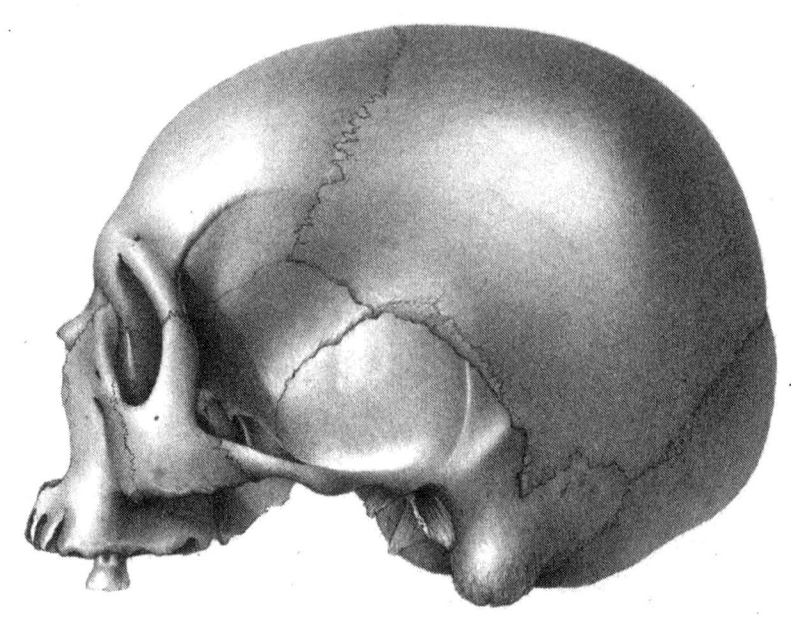

PAWNEE

Morton's Crania Americana

Pl. 39.

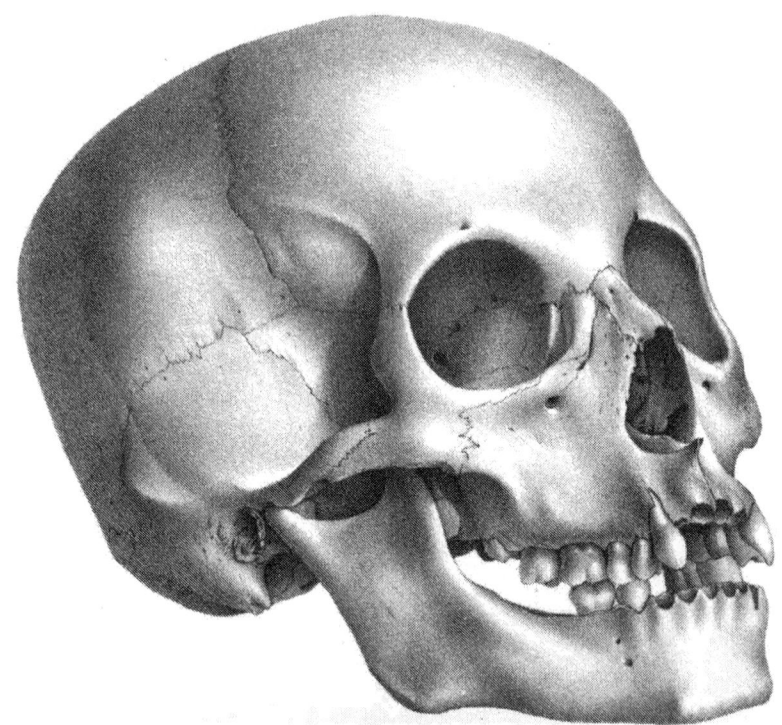

DACOTA

N.W. TERRITORY.

Lith of John Collins, N°20 South Third Street Philadelphia.

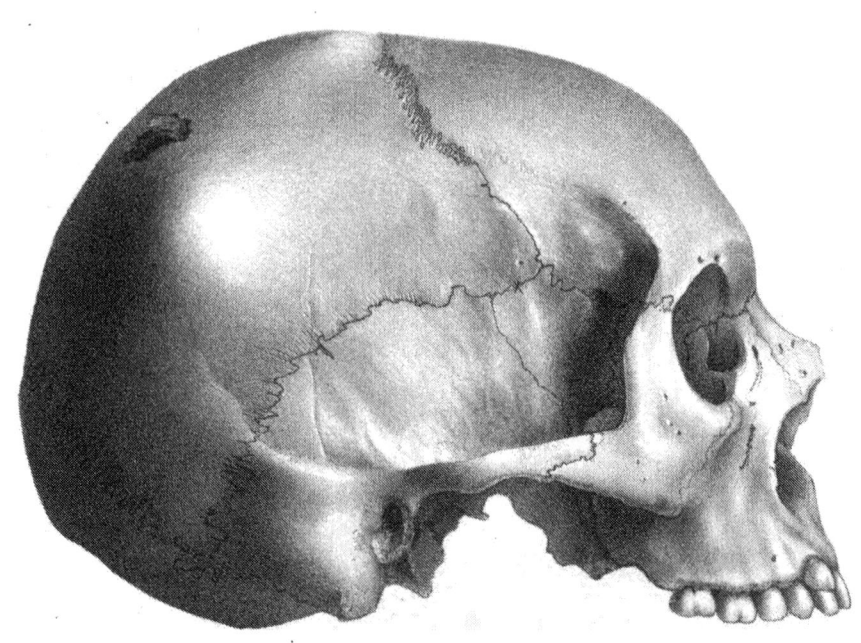

COTONAY.
BLACKFOOT.

Morton's Crania Americana.   Pl. 41

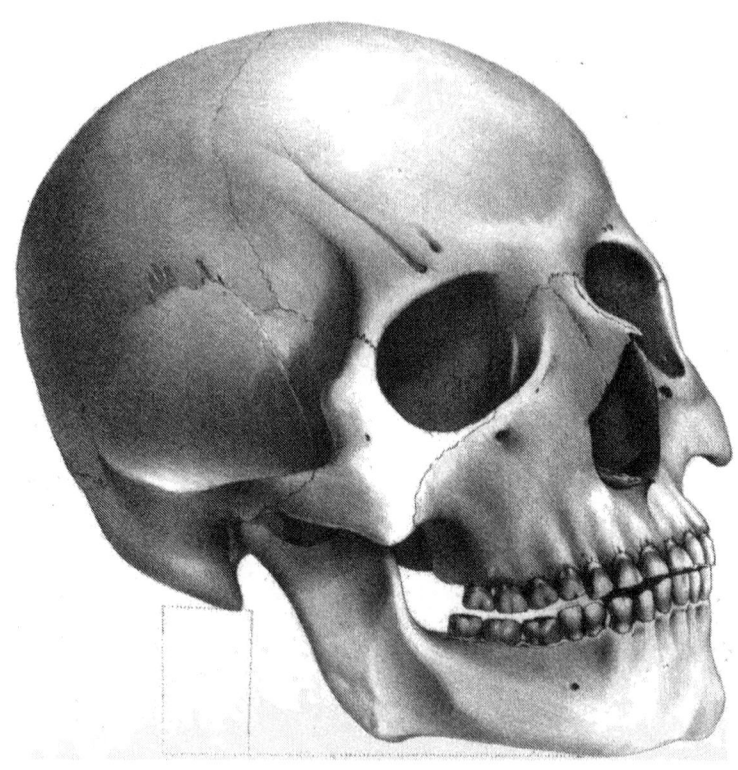

YOUNG OSAGE WARRIOR

Drawn from Nature and on Stone by John Collins

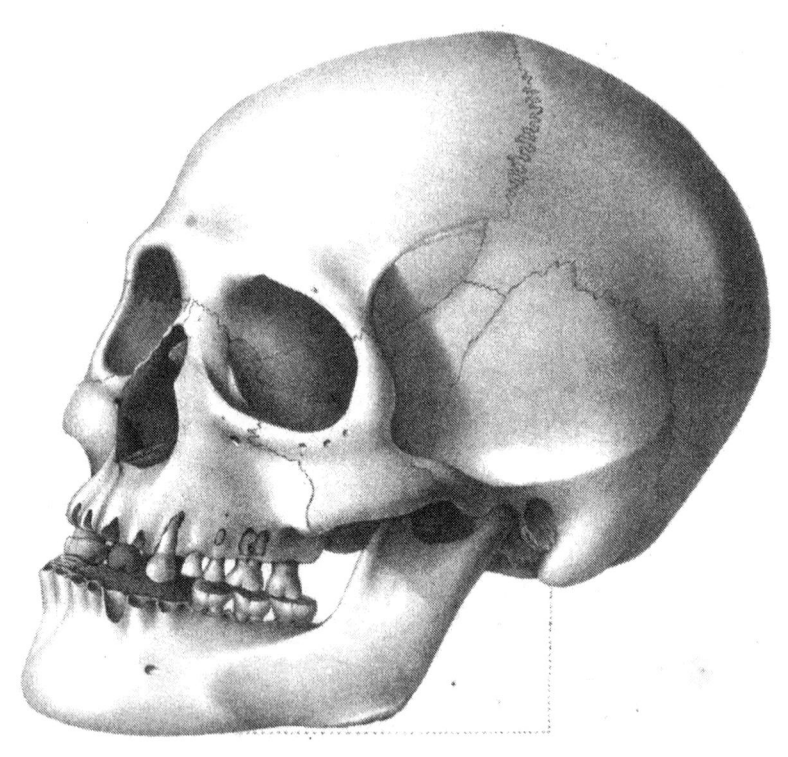

CHINOOK:

OF COLUMBIA RIVER.

Natural Form.

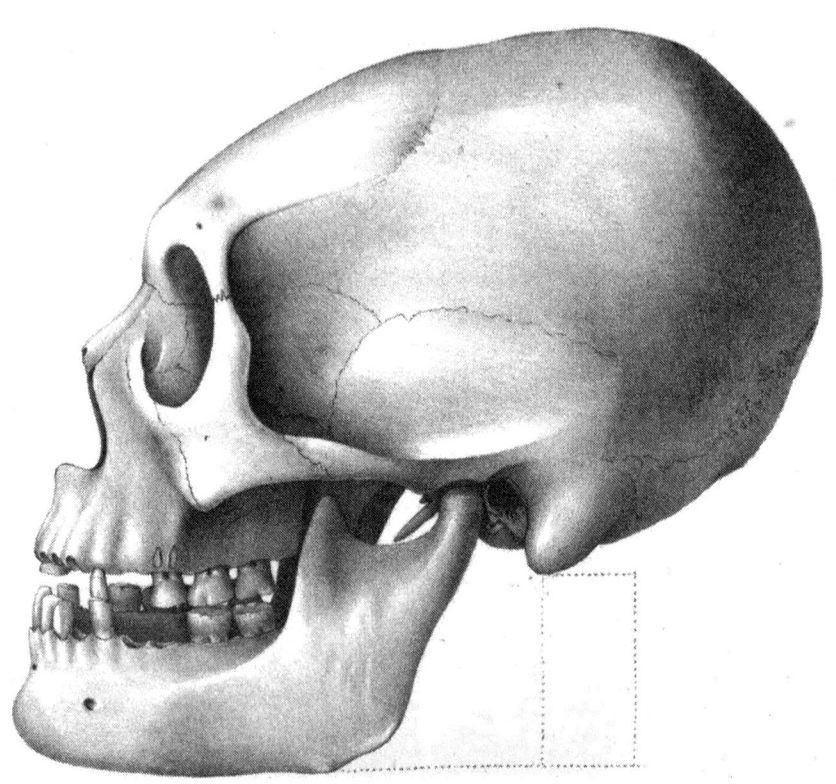

CHINOOK CHIEF.
OF COLUMBIA RIVER
Drawn from Nature and on Stone by John Collins

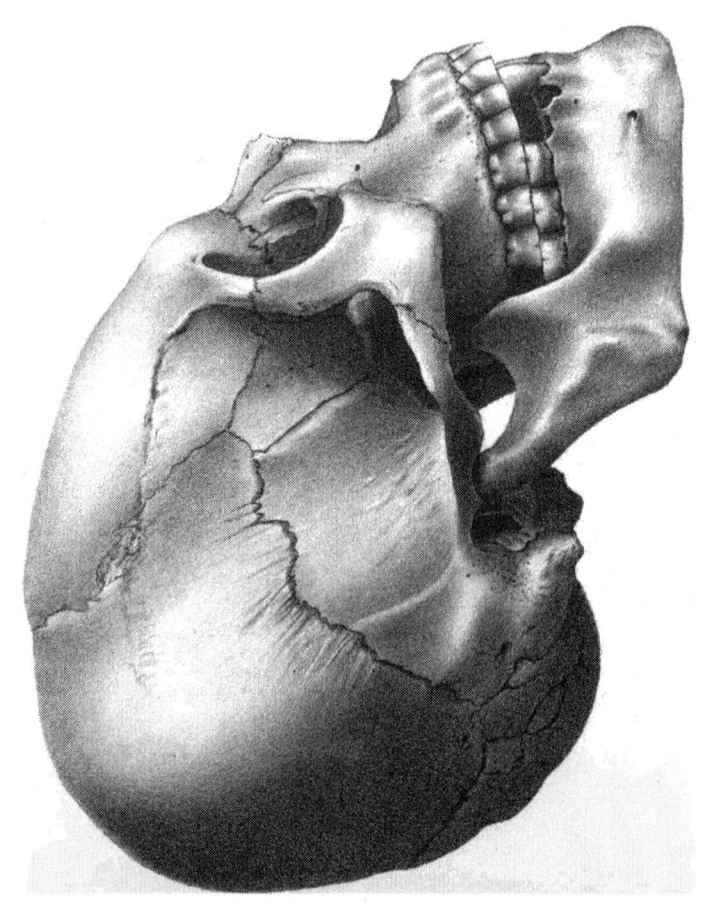

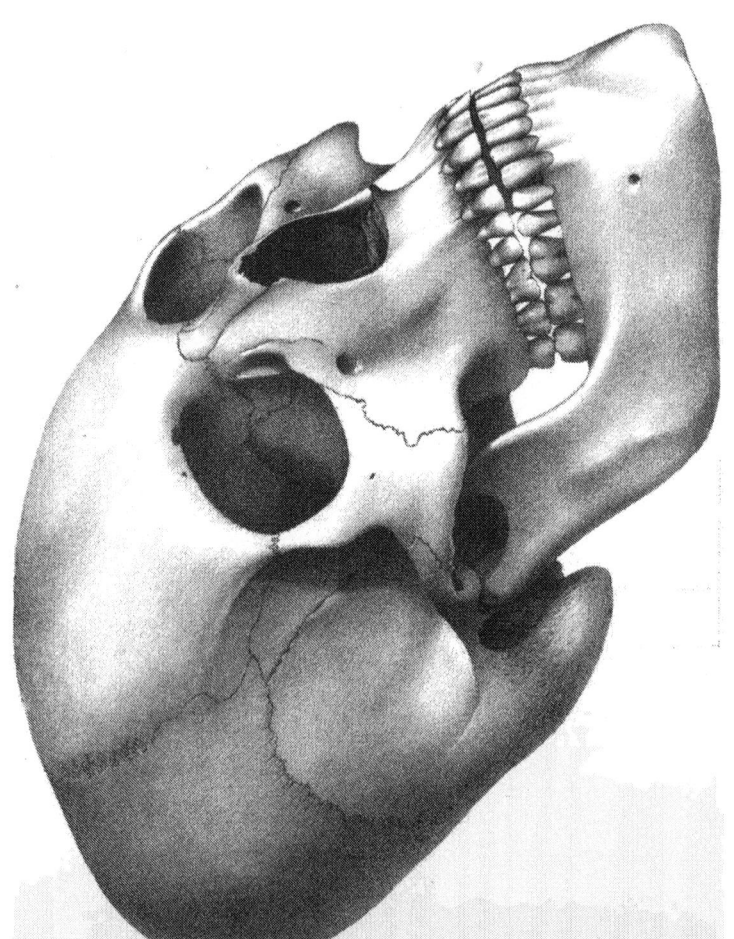

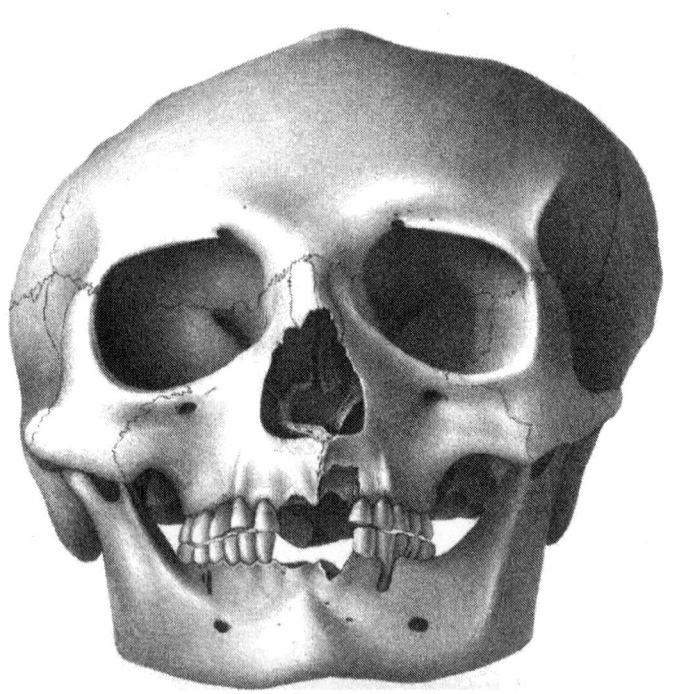

CLATSAP

FROM COLUMBIA RIVER.

Drawn from Nature and on Stone by J. Collins

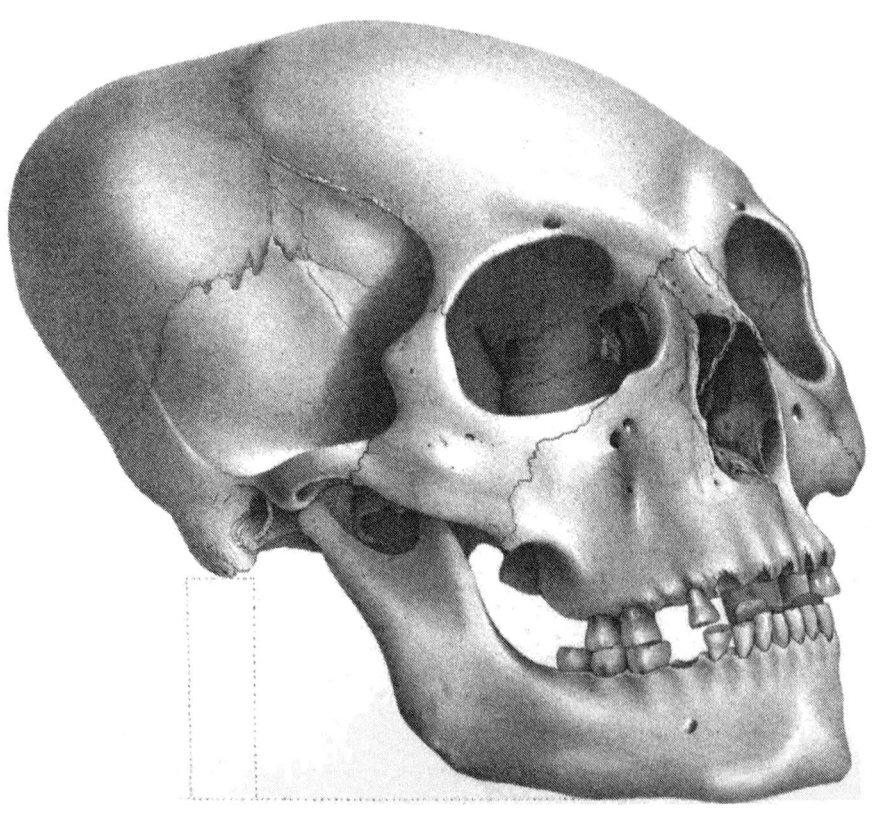

KALAPOOYAH
FROM COLUMBIA RIVER.

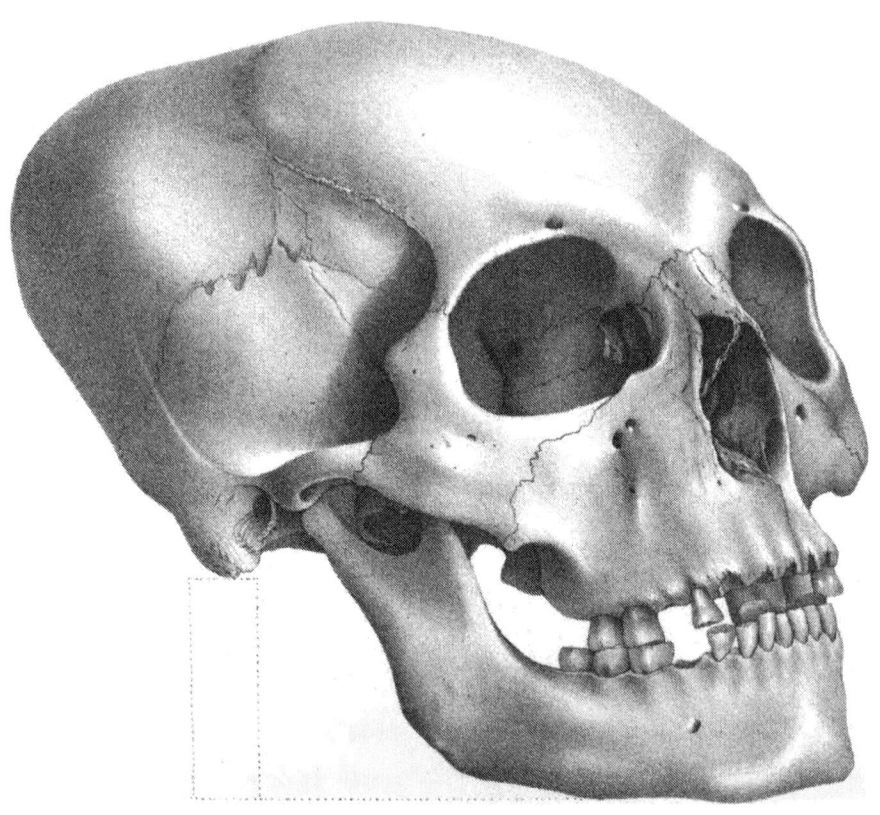

KALAPOOYAH
FROM COLUMBIA RIVER.

Lith. of John Collins N° 79 South Third St Phila.

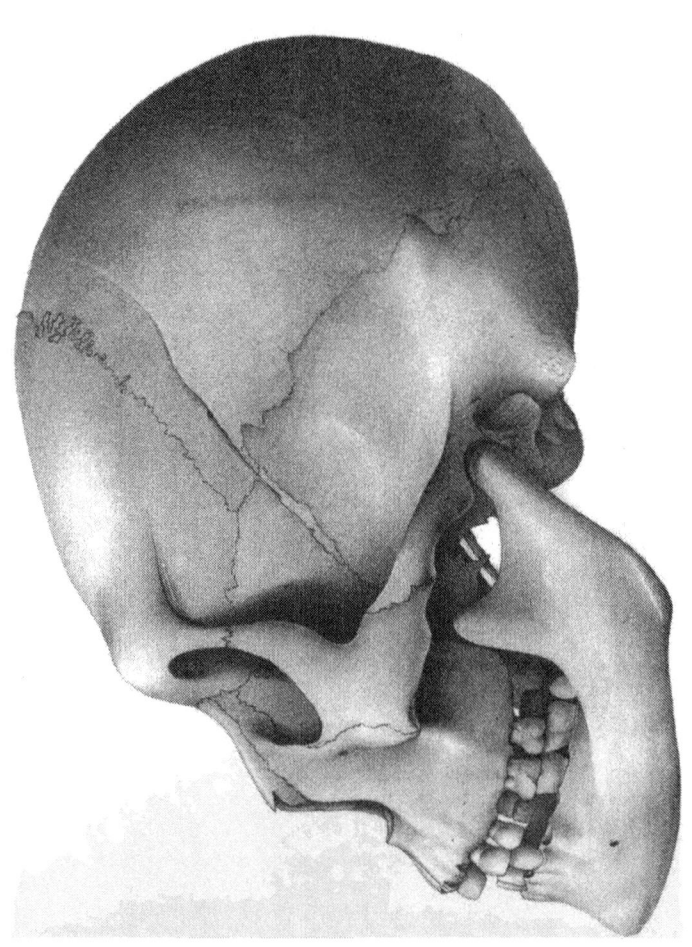

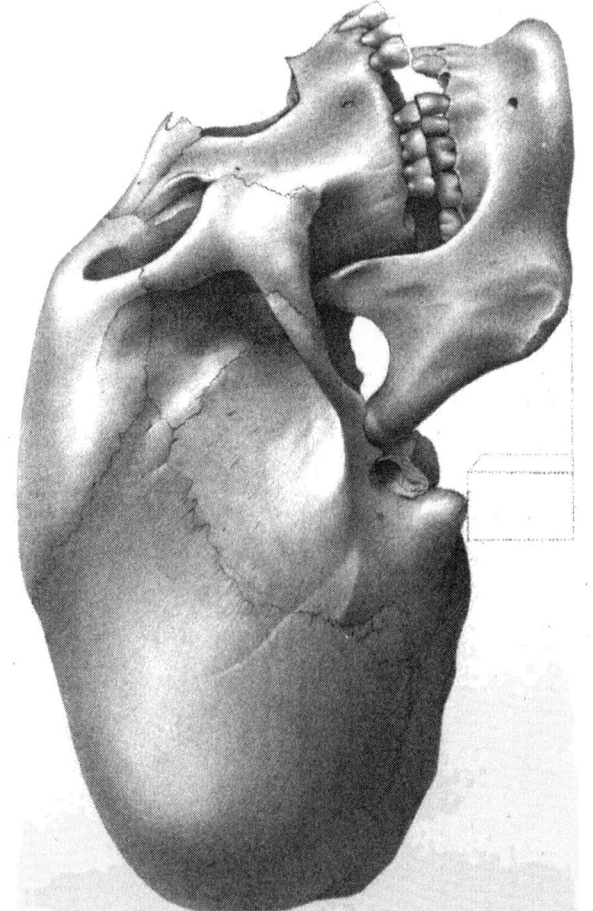

COWALITSK
OF COLUMBIA RIVER.

Lith of John Collins, N° 79 South Third St. Philad.

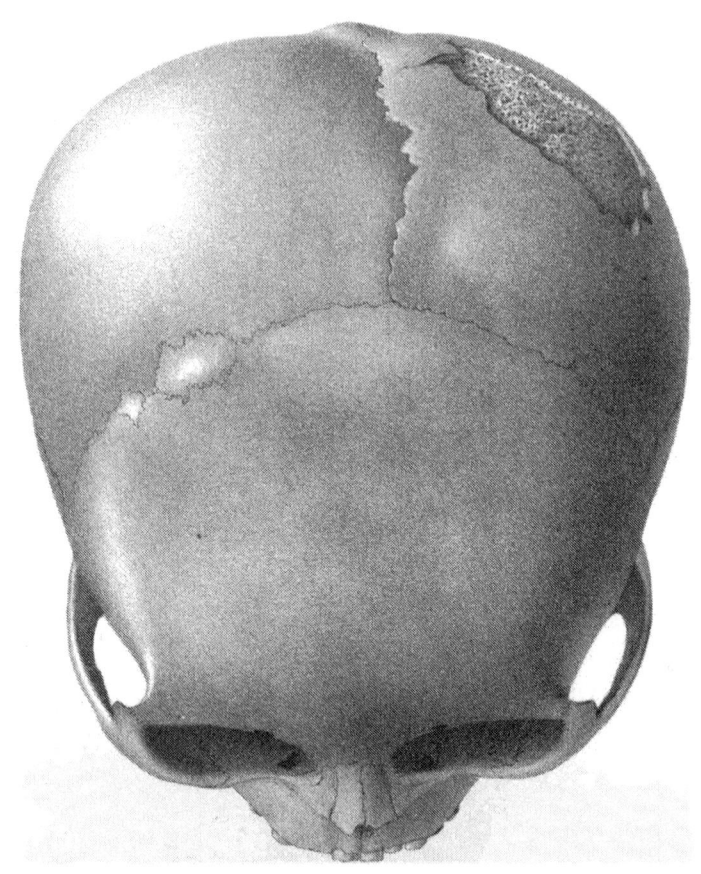

COWALITSK
VERTICAL VIEW

Lith of John Collins No 79 South Third St. Phila

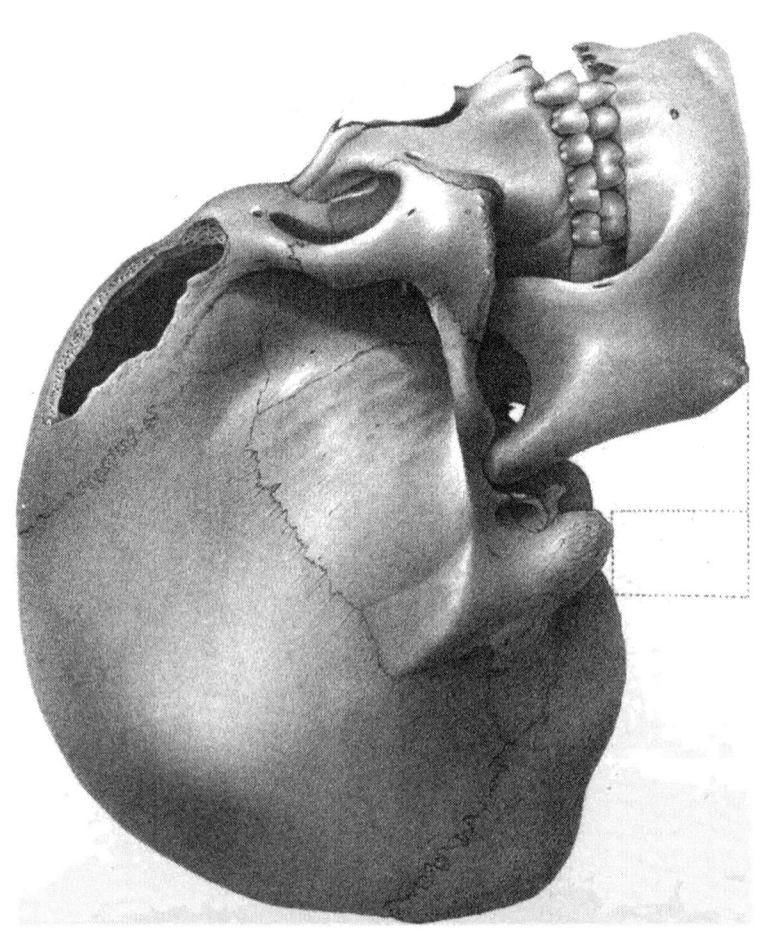

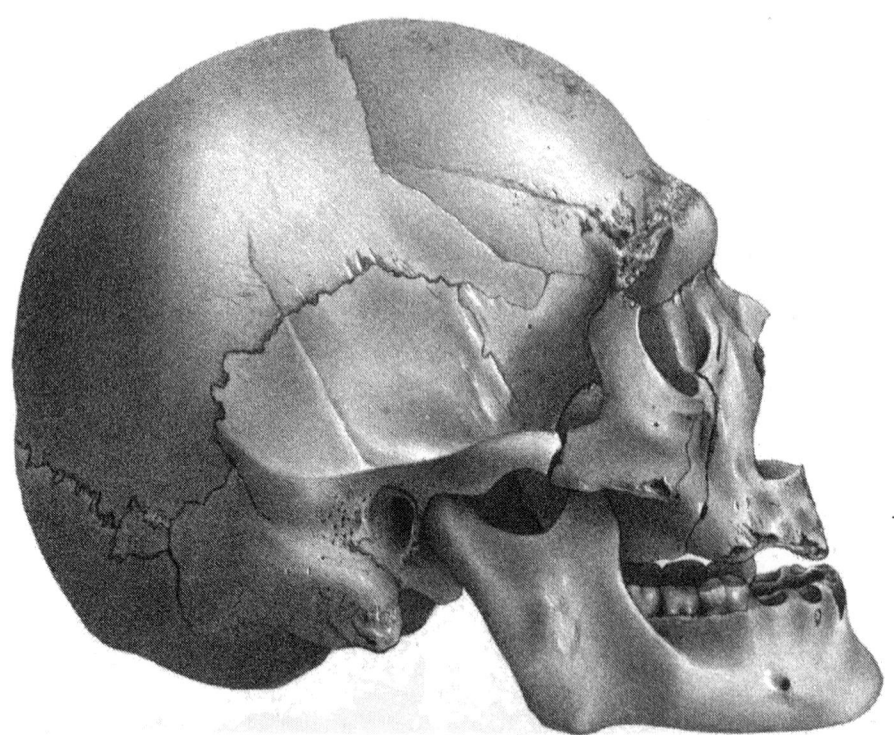

FROM A MOUND
ON THE UPPER MISSISSIPPI.
Lith. of John Collins, N° 79 S. Third St. Phil.ᵃ

Morton's Crania Americana. Pl. 53.

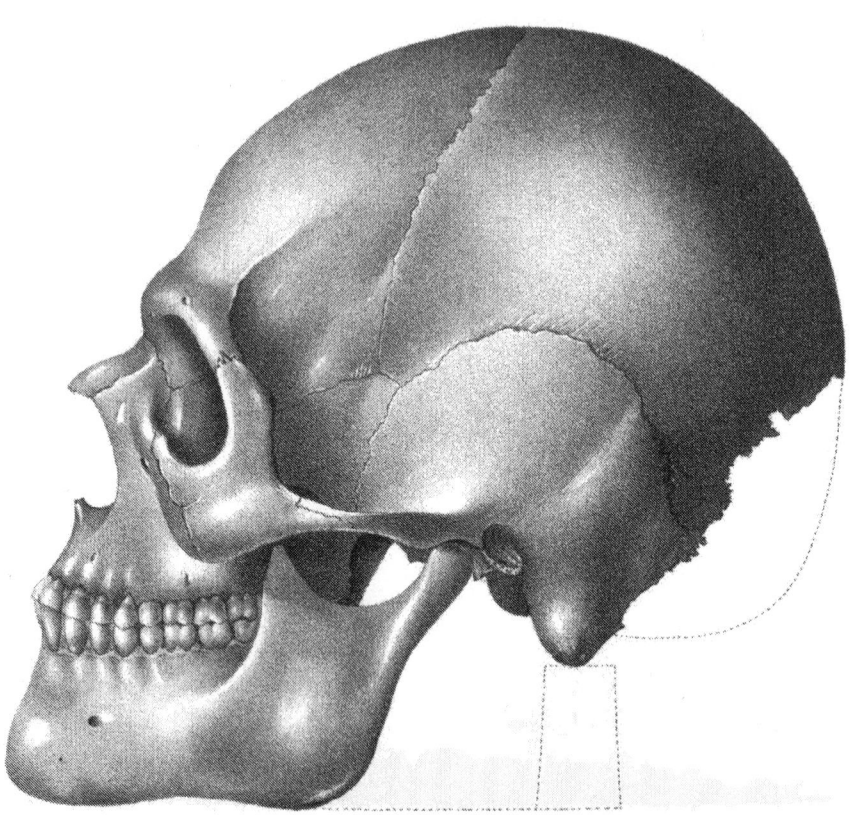

Drawn from Nature by E. Matthews.

FROM THE GRAVE-CREEK MOUND
NEAR WHEELING, VIRGINIA.
Lith. of John Collins, N° 79 S. Third St. Phila.

Morton's Crania Americana. PL.54

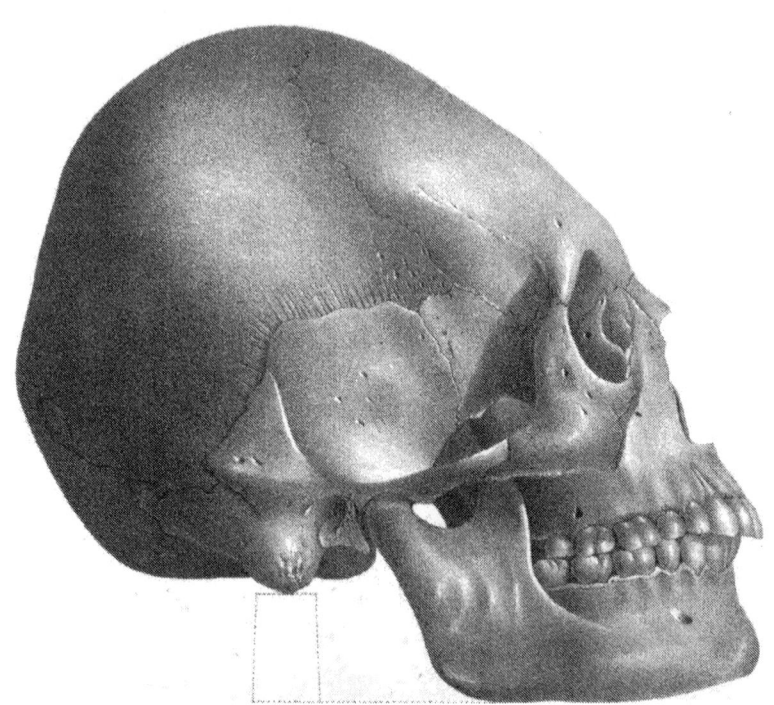

FROM A MOUND
ON THE ALABAMA RIVER.
Lith of John Collins, N° 79 S. Third St. Phil*

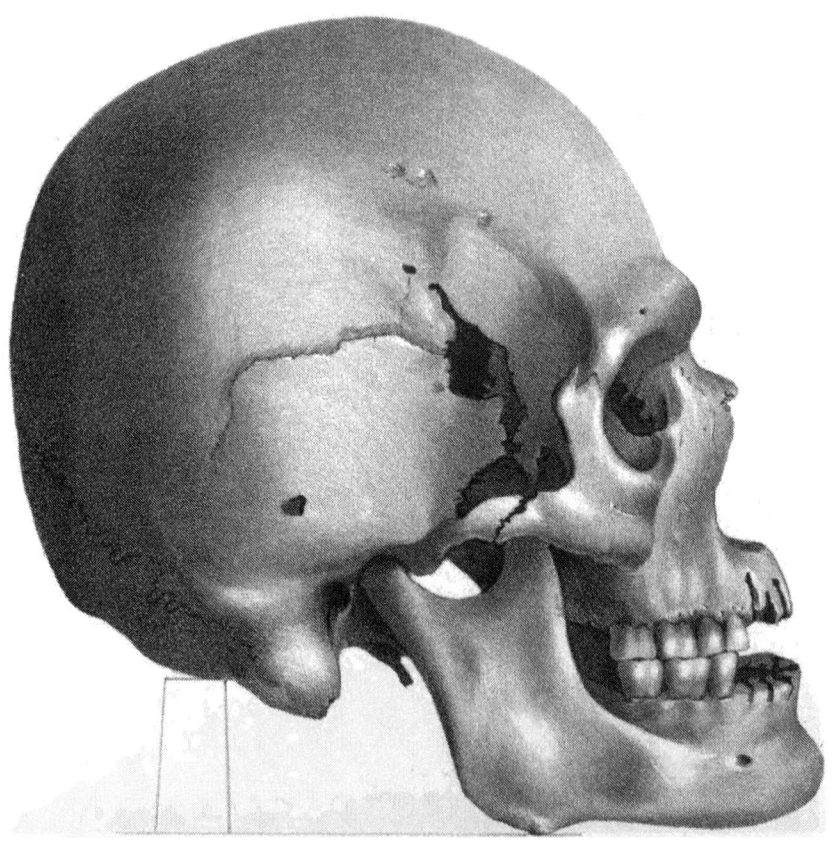

FROM A MOUND
IN TENNESSEE.

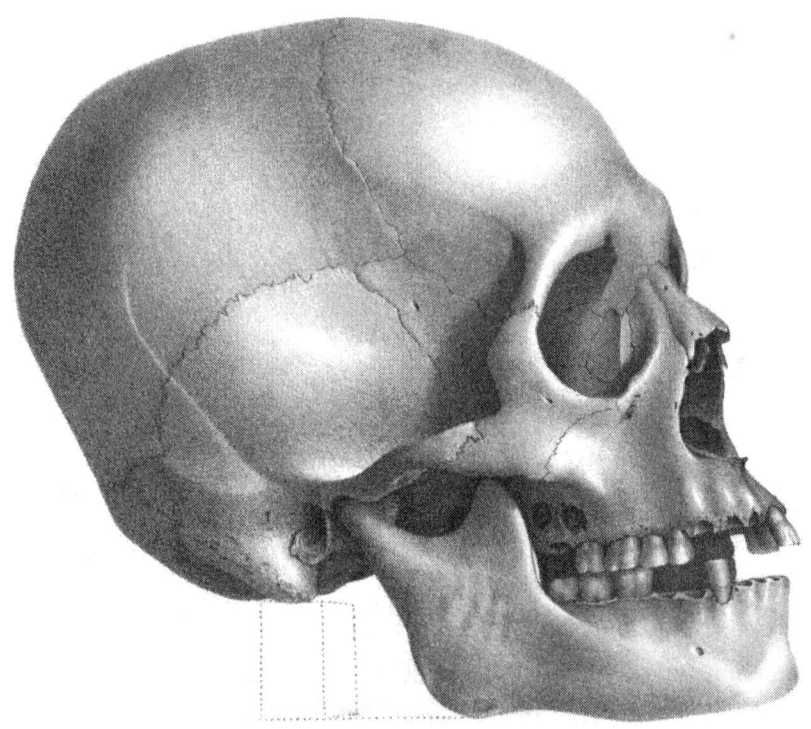

FROM A TUMULUS AT SANTÀ IN PERU.

Morton's Crania Americana

Pl.57

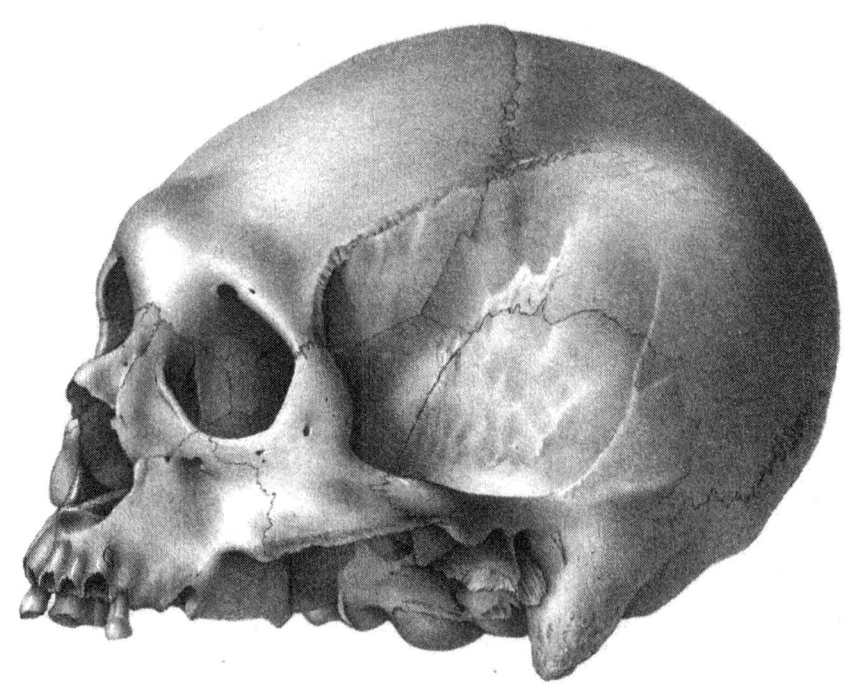

PERUVIAN

FROM A TUMULUS IN THE VALLEY OF RIMAC.

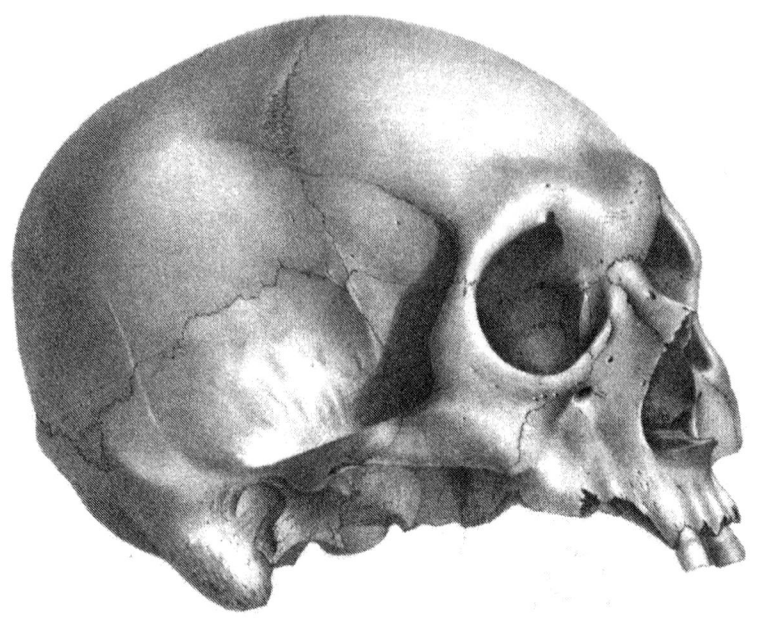

PERUVIAN

FROM A TUMULUS IN THE VALLEY OF RIMAC.

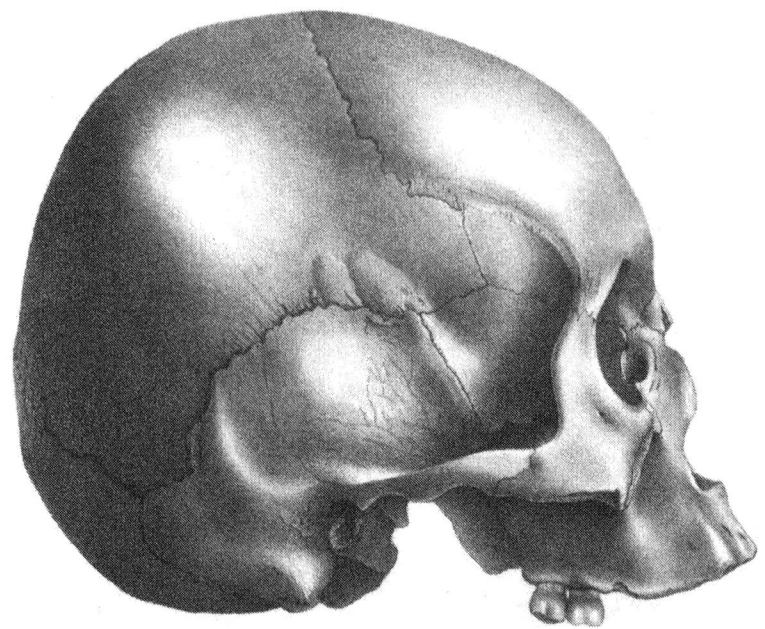

FROM AN ANCIENT TOMB
AT OTUMBA IN MEXICO.

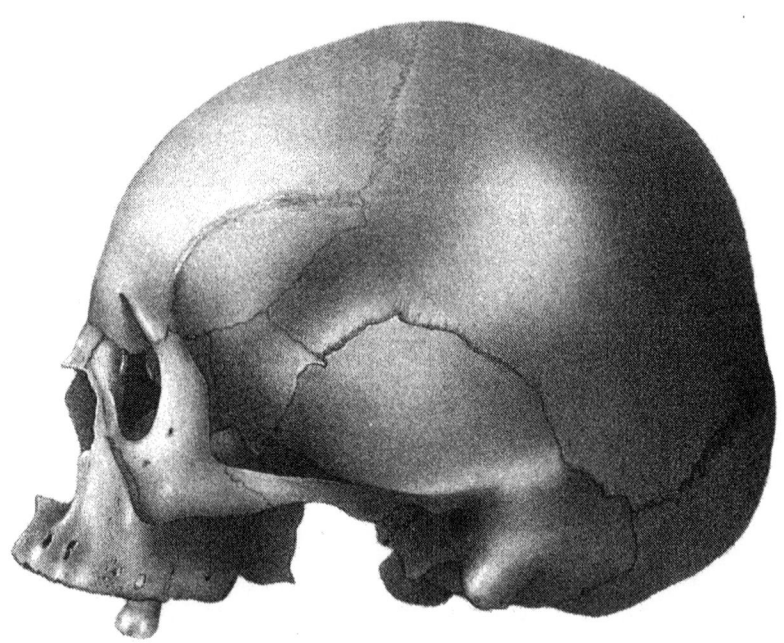

FROM AN ANCIENT TOMB
AT OTUMBA IN MEXICO.

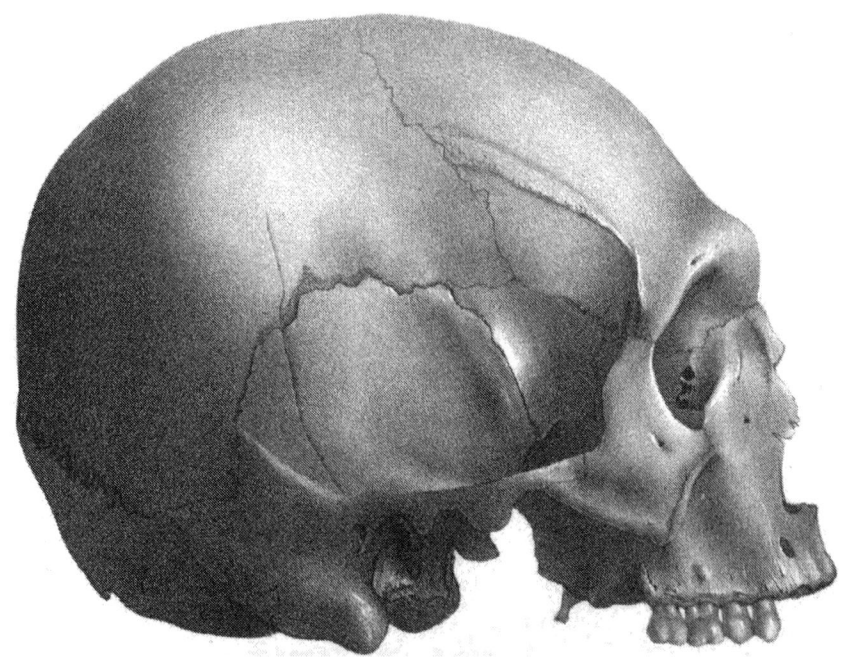

FROM AN ANCIENT TOMB
AT OTUMBA IN MEXICO.

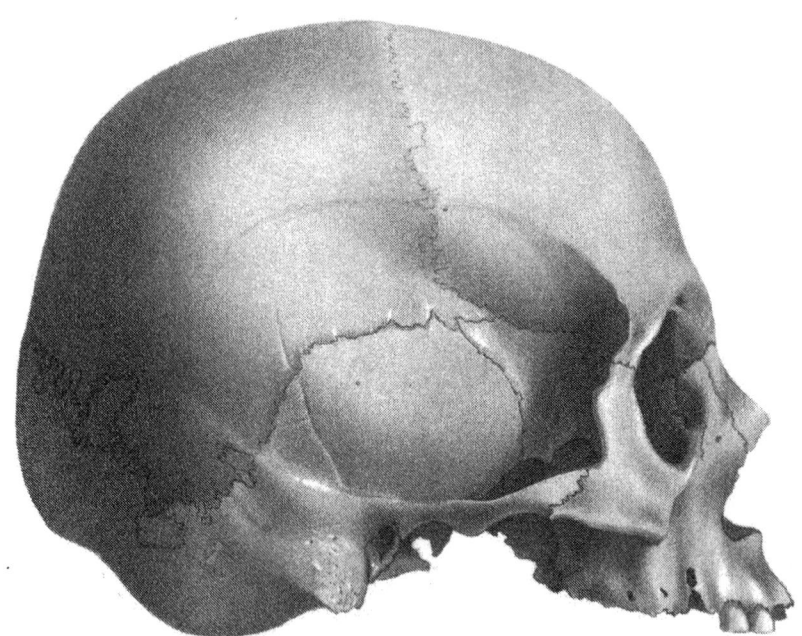

FROM A CAVE AT GOLCONDA,
IN ILLINOIS.

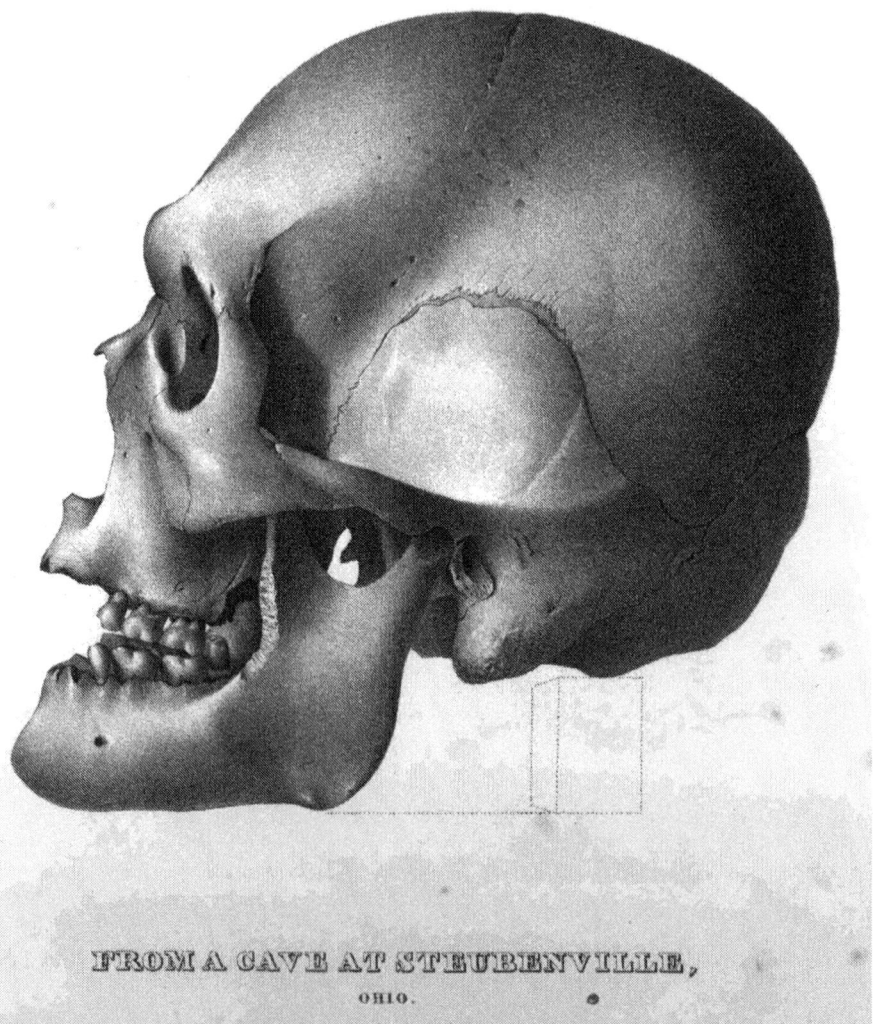

FROM A CAVE AT STEUBENVILLE, OHIO.

Morton's Crania Americana. Pl. 64.

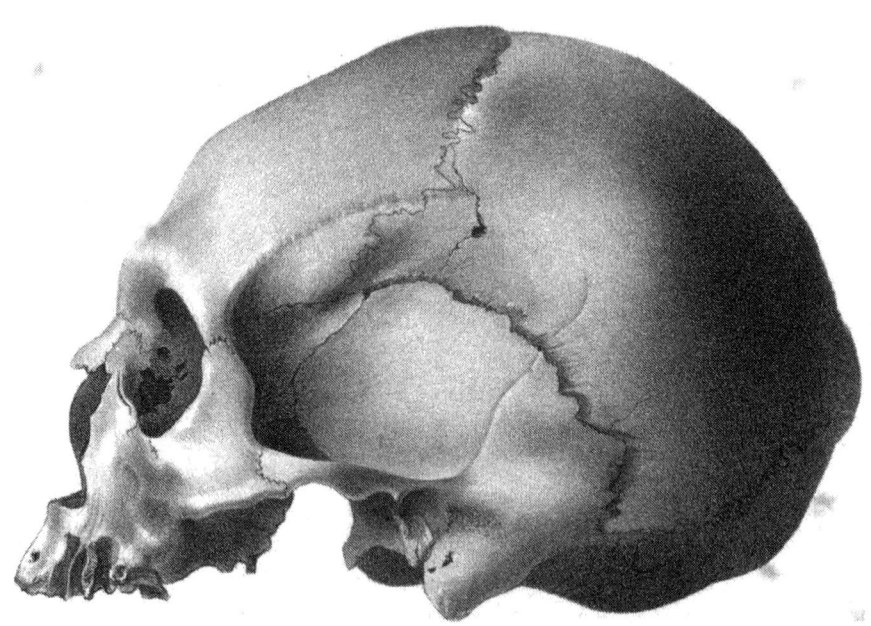

CHARIB OF VENEZUELA.

Lith of John Collins, N° 79 S. Third St. Phil^a

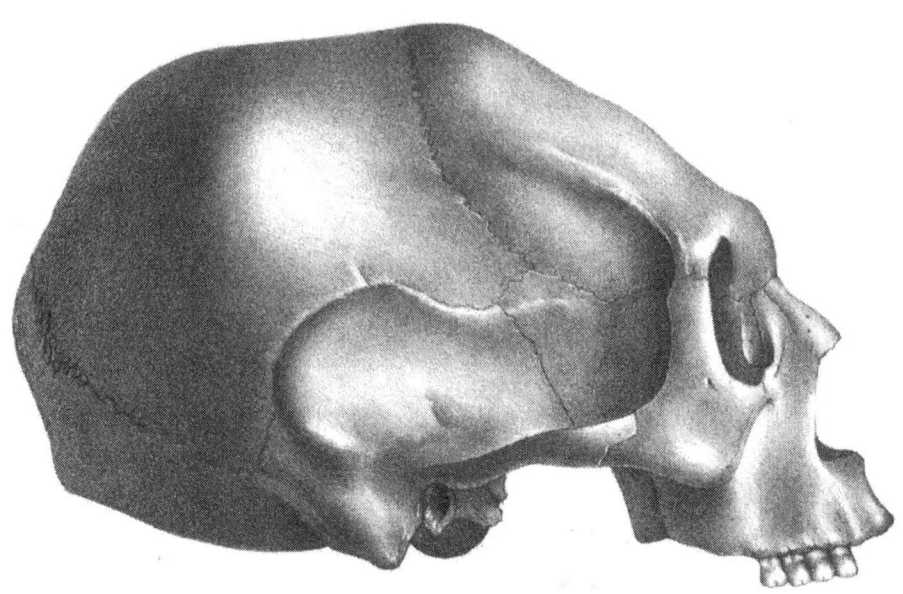

CHARIB OF ST. VINCENT.

Lith of John Collins, N° 79 S. Third St. Phil^a

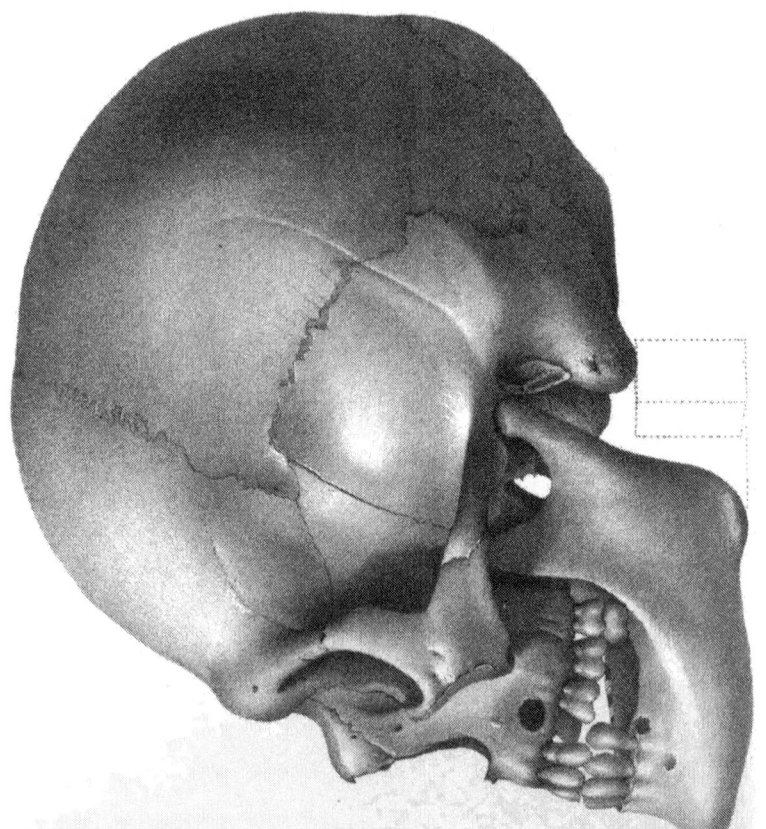

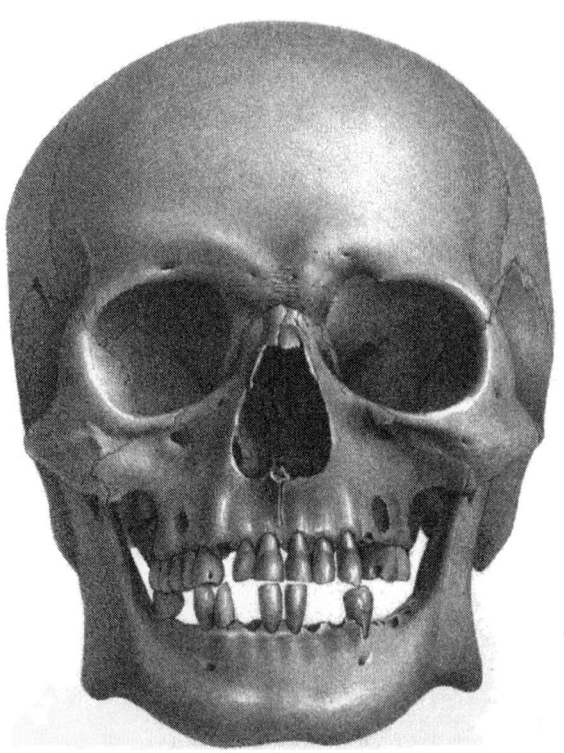

A RAUCANIAN.
N° 2

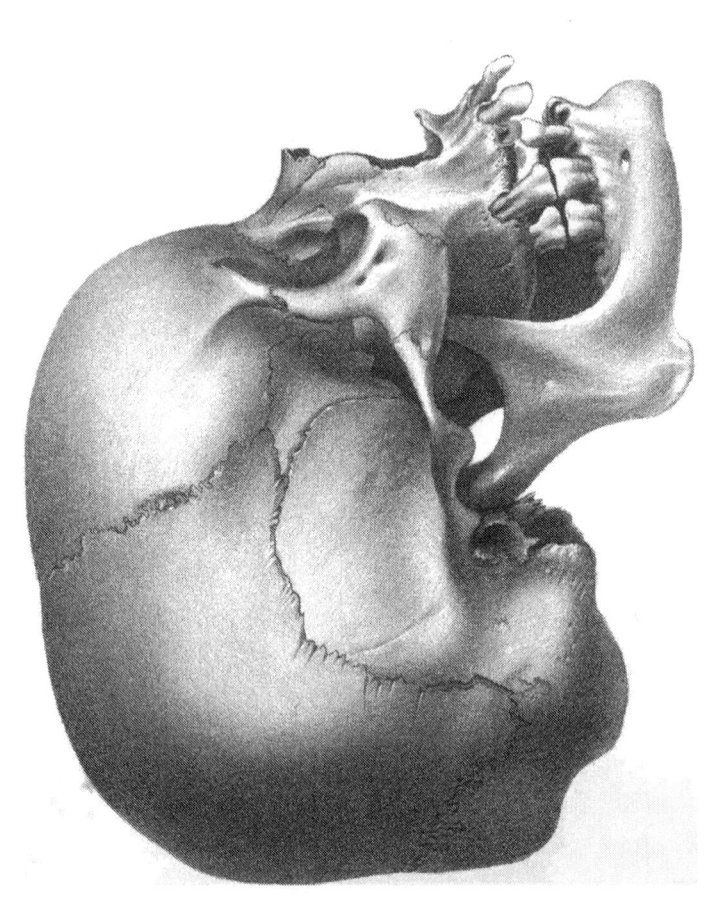

Crania Americana

Pl. 69.

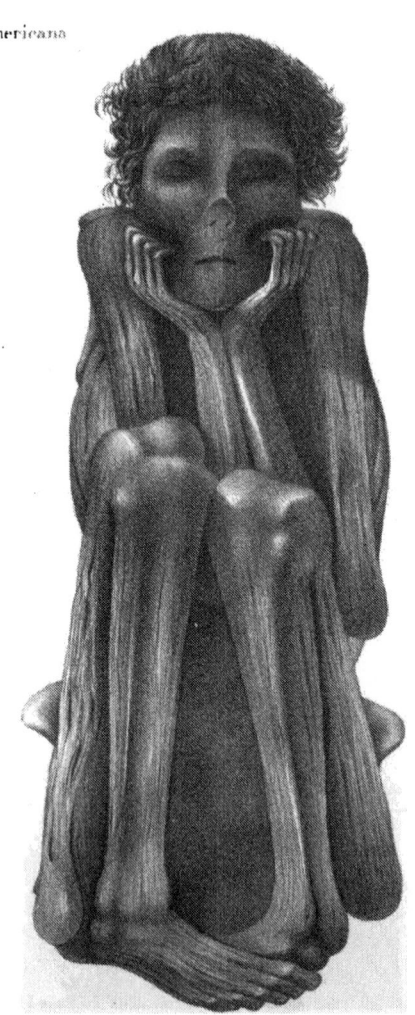

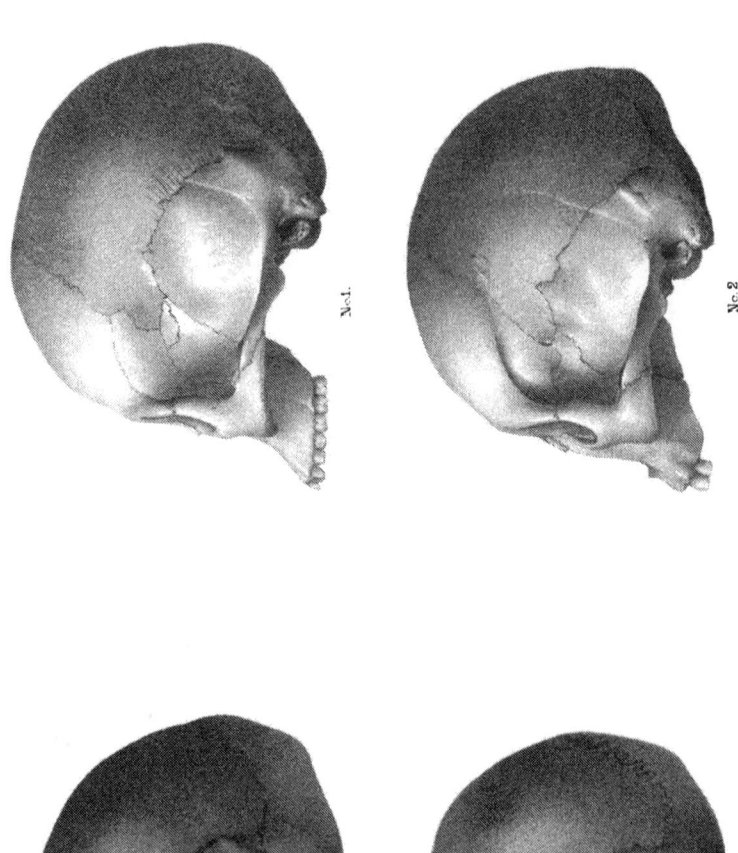

Pl. 70.

Morton's Crania Americana.

No. 1.

No. 2.

No. 3.

No. 4.

MONGOL-AMERICANS.

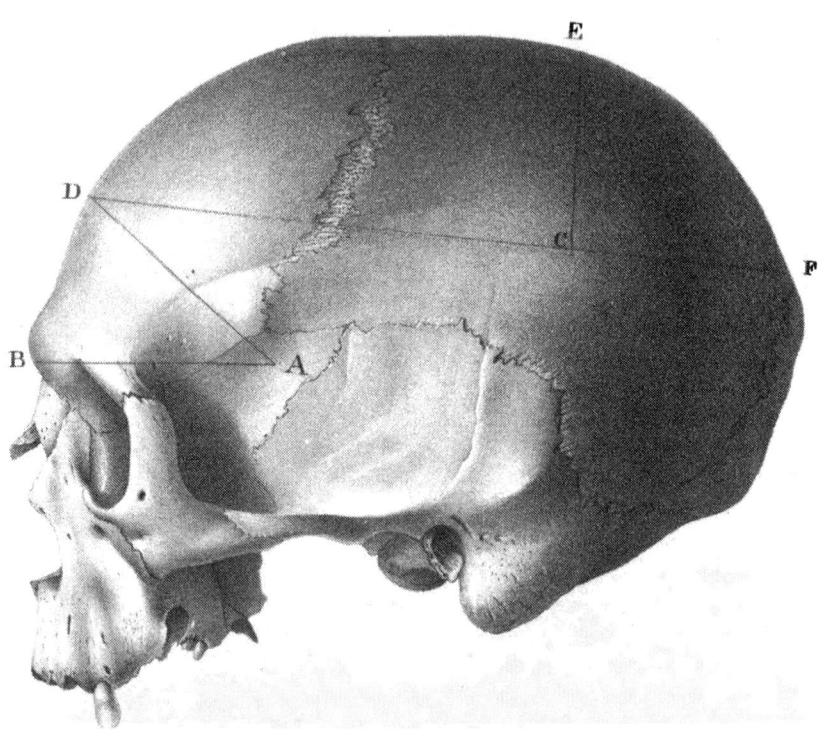

SWISS.

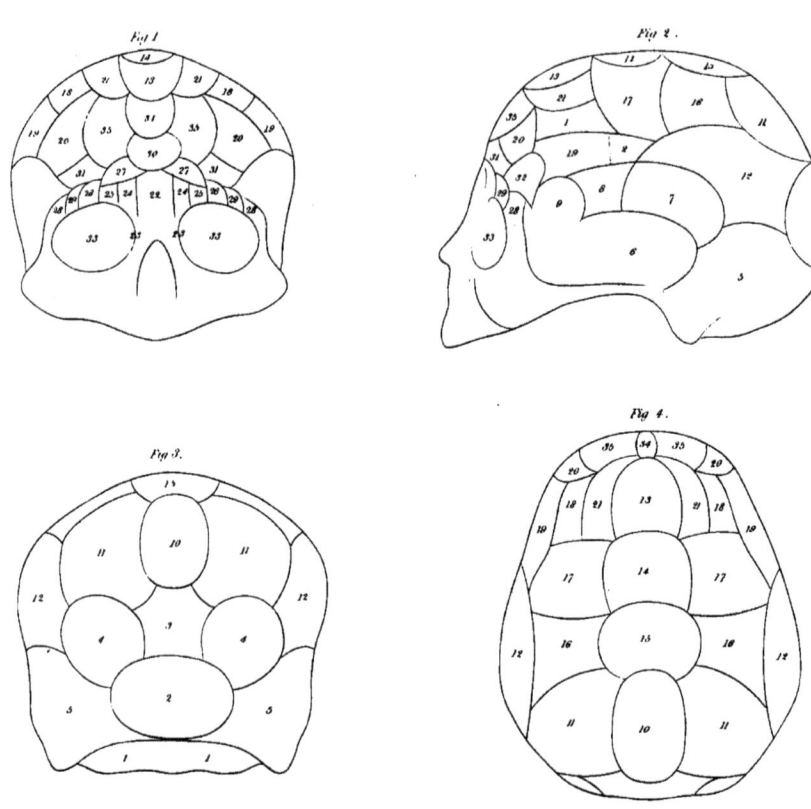

PHRENOLOGICAL CHART.

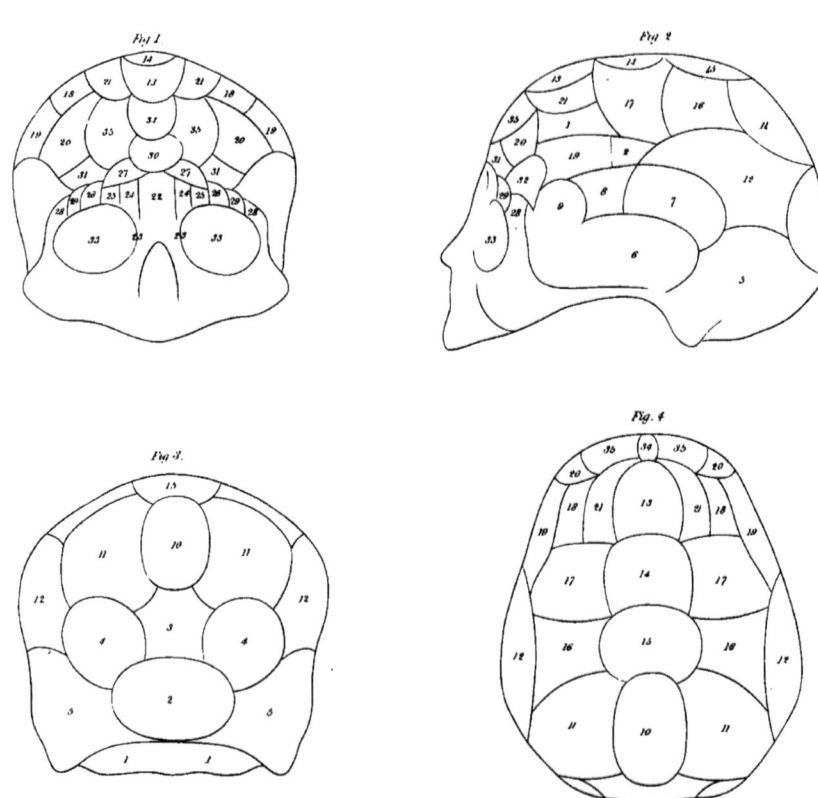

PHRENOLOGICAL CHART.

ERRATA.

Page 95, in the *Note*, for Atlas Mountains, read "Mountains of the Moon."
" 109, ninth line of *Measurements*, for 8.2 inches, read "8.7 inches."
" 180, for Plate XXXIV, read "Plate XXXII."
" 204, tenth line from the bottom, *dele* the words "the purpose of."
" 283, for Plate LXXI, read "Plate LXXII."

I have inadvertently omitted to mention my obligations to Dr. Paul Swift, of Nantucket, for the series of Natick Skulls measured in the Anatomical Table.

Corrections of the Phrenological Table.

	No. in Catalogue.		for	read	destructiveness. for	destructiveness. read
Peruvian.	91.	Causality to same,	3.85	1.85	3.7	2.6
Peruvian.	450.				3.2	2.9
Peruvian.	95.	Secretiveness,	4.	3.3		
Peruvian.	97.	Cautiousness to same,	4.4	4.8		
Peruvian.	402.				3.	2.7
Peruvian.	85.				3.	2.7
Peruvian.	90.				2.7	2.5
Peruvian.	446.	Self-esteem,	5.45	4.45		
Peruvian.	406.				2.7	2.5
Peruvian.	77.				3.8	2.7
Peruvian.	86.				2.85	2.75
Peruvian.	400.				2.9	2.7
Peruvian.	449.	Marvellousness to same,	3.3	4.3		
Peruvian.	76.	Constructiveness to same,	3.8	4.		
Peruvian.	73.	Meatus to caution.	2.25	3.25	2.55	2.9
Mexican.	559.				2.7	2.4
Pames.	681.	Meato-temporal line.	3.6	2.6	2.9	2.7
Lenapi.	40.					
Miami.	562.				2.8	2.5
Sauk.	561.				3.	2.8
Menominee.	78.	Constructiveness to same,	5.45	4.45		
Menominee.	563.	Secretiveness to same,	6.85	5.85		
Muskogee.	441.	Secretiveness,	4.85	3.85		
Cherokee.	634.	Causality,	3.35	4.35		
Golconda Cave.	A.N.S.	Secretiveness to same,	4.25	5.25		
Peruvian.	449.	Ideality to same,	5.25	4.25		

☞ The list of subscribers' names will be furnished without delay.

Lightning Source UK Ltd.
Milton Keynes UK
UKHW021628071121
393541UK00014BA/370